# BLUES
## KEEPING THE FAITH

**AUTHOR:** KEITH SHADWICK

# BLUES
## KEEPING THE FAITH

Eagle
Editions

A QUANTUM BOOK

Published by Eagle Editions Ltd
11 Heathfield
Royston
Hertfordshire SG8 5BW

Copyright ©MCMXCVIII
Quintet Publishing Ltd

This edition printed 2001

ISBN 1-86160-352-5

QUMBLH

This book is produced by
Quantum Publishing
6 Blundell Street
London N7 9BH

Printed in Singapore by
Star Standard Industries Pte Ltd

# contents

# BLUES | Keeping the Faith

aat the age of fourteen, during my young days growing up in England, I was lucky enough to fall in with a group of music enthusiasts who were mostly a year or so above me in school. Being that little bit older, they usually had more pocket money that I did to pursue their musical interest, but by pulling together the resources I had I was able, under their guidance, to start a record collection: at first Nat "King" Cole and Sammy Davis Jr. and then King Oliver and Louis Armstrong, Sidney Bechet, Red McKenzie's Mound City Blue Blowers, Count Basie and Jimmy Rushing. By the time I had enough confidence in my own judgement and taste to buy records without a helping hand, I found that things like Armstrong's "Black and Blue," Jelly Roll Morton's "Winning Boy," and Basie/Rushing's "Goin' To Chicago" had created in me a love for vocal jazz – and blues.

That was also the year Lonnie Donegan, Chris Barber, and Beryl Bryden put skiffle at the top of the charts in the UK with "Rock Island Line," and I heard Lonnie say that the song came from a guy called Leadbelly – whose real name was the scarcely less exotic Huddie Ledbetter. Off I went to the record store where my Saturday allowance could be transformed into shiny 78rpm records, and bought my first Leadbelly. Not that he was by any means exclusively a blues singer – in fact his extraordinary eclectic mix of blues, gospel, pop, folk, and worksong had a great influence on my own catholicity of taste – but whatever style he was performing, he would do so with a depth of involvement, a complete commitment, that all great singers share but which great blues singers often seem to have in abundance. I was hooked.

My exploration of the blues took off in all directions – from Leadbelly to Big Bill Broonzy, Lightnin' Hopkins, Sonny Terry and Brownie McGhee, from Jimmy Rushing to Helen Humes, Jimmy Witherspoon, Wynonie Harris, Big Joe Turner and Pete Johnson, from Louis Armstrong to Bessie Smith, Lonnie Johnson, Victoria Spivey, Willie Dixon, Memphis Slim, T-Bone Walker – and Junior Wells. The sound of Junior's harmonica on T-Bone's "Play On, Little Girl" was (and I can still feel what it felt like, even as I write this) the thing that made me want to play the blues myself.

All of these artists, from Leadbelly onwards, can be found in this book, together with scores more whose music I discovered in my teens and never lost its grip on me: Muddy Waters, John Lee Hooker, both Sonny Boy Williamsons, Howlin' Wolf, Jimmy Reed, Ray Charles, Elmore James, Robert Johnson, Little Walter, Big Walter, Otis Rush, Buddy Guy, Lightnin' Slim – there is, I'm happy to say, no way to end this list.

Except that you do have to stop, somewhere. So if you insist on playing 'How could they leave out X but include Y?' – as all blues fans will inevitably do – remember these rules: don't add to the total number of blues performers, songwriters,

composers, and musicians included in this book (there are approximately 300), do send me your list when it's finished, but don't ask me to contribute anything to your therapy sessions. There's nobody here I haven't played on my radio show over the years, and if there are those I have played who are absent, put it down to the fact that I've clocked up thousands of hours on the blues.

In addition to the biographical entries included with each blues artist in the book, there are many wonderful photographs – some of them famous, some I have never seen before. I have found myself studying them, looking for clues to give me an extra understanding of records I've had for years but never quite come to grips with.

It's forty years after my first adolescent wonder at the blues, and having "gone round the houses" on a few detours since then, I count myself fortunate all over again to be still involved in this superficially simple, deeply complex music. If you're standing at a similar crossroad, start walking.

By **Paul Jones**, perhaps best known as the voice of Manfred Mann on such 1960s hits as "Do Wah Diddy." He has also starred on film and television, at the Royal National Theatre (England) and on Broadway. Most of his current work maintains a strong focus on the blues: broadcasting, compiling, and annotating blues and gospel CDs, interviewing blues artists and theorists, as well as singing and playing with top British rhythm & blues group, The Blues Band.

# Johnny Adams

**fact file**

**BORN** 1932

**MUSICAL SELECTION**
Room With A View of
The Blues
Walking On A Tightrope

Johnny Adams,
king of cool
blues, with his
ever-present
shades

**a**dams has an unusually wide stylistic ambit upon which to draw, his own natural musical inquisitiveness and his love of the many genres of music that make up the patchwork quilt of his native New Orleans being major influences on his approach to the music. Adams's urbane baritone voice, like Joe Williams's, sits easily in jazz/blues and R&B settings, and these are the latter-day styles that have earned him belated success.

Adams grew up in New Orleans and began his singing career with gospel groups like Spirit of New Orleans. In 1959 he decided, as his twenties were coming to an end, to switch to secular music, signing a record deal and cutting a string of New Orleans-style R&B singles, none of which had an impact outside of the South. During the 1960s and 1970s he persevered with different mixes of R&B, soul, and New Orleans-type country: he landed a hit in 1962 with "A Losing Battle," which made the R&B top 30. After that he went progressively more "pop," culminating in 1968–69, when he made the pop charts with "Release Me," "Reconsider Me," and "I Can't Be All That Bad." That was the high-water mark of his pop career, and he spent most of the following 15 years appearing live in and around his home town, holding down a long residency at Dorothy's Medallion Lounge. In the mid-1980s Adams took a change of direction, on the album *Room With A View of The Blues* heading into the blues territory as defined by such Crescent City musicians as Red Tyler, Foots Samuel, and Dr John. The repertoire ranged from Lowell Fulson to Dr John and Percy Mayfield: the album was warmly received and sold well, Adams repeated his success on later Rounder albums, including *Walking On A Tightrope* (1989). He continues to run a successfully revived career, as cosmopolitan in his approach as ever, but always with the gospel singing of his youth evident in his voice.

**SEE ALSO:** Lowell Fulson, Dr John

# Alger "Texas" Alexander

**fact file**

**BORN** 1900

**DIED** 1954

**MUSICAL SELECTION**
"Penitentiary Moan
Blues"
"Justice Blues"

Texas Alexander
sang with some
of the greatest
performers of
his day

a lexander, a native of Leona, Texas, was probably born around 1900, although some would place him more than a decade older. He began as a farm hand and cotton picker before moving into Dallas, where he took a variety of menial jobs, including working as a store hand. It is generally thought that he spent at least some time in jail, possibly for murder, possibly for robbery, and that he learned some of his repertoire there. Certainly some of his best songs, such as "Penitentiary Moan Blues," "Justice Blues," and "Section Gang Blues" suggest a close acquaintance, if not familiarity, with the due process of the law.

Alexander was a true musical primitive, never learning to play any musical instrument and singing basic blues melodies that are close to field hollers and work songs, using his tough, low voice, sometimes simply humming, to superb, stark effect. "Levee Camp Moan," from 1927, demonstrates many of these techniques. He was judicious in his choice of partners and accompanists, recording with people such as Lonnie Johnson, Eddie Lang, Clarence Williams, and the Mississippi Sheiks. Dropped by Vocalion in 1934, Alexander kept singing the blues through World War II but found it increasingly difficult to hold an audience. In 1947 his cousin Lightnin' Hopkins used him on a session for Aladdin, but this failed to give new impetus to a stalled career. He dropped from the fringes of the Texas blues scene and died in 1954, just a few years too early to be rediscovered by the white folk-blues enthusiasts and given a second blues career.

**SEE ALSO:** Lonnie Johnson, Mississippi Sheiks, Sam "Lightnin'" Hopkins

# Bernard Allison

## fact file

**BORN** 1965

**MUSICAL SELECTION**
Born With The Blues

Bernard Allison
performing in
Cornwall
(England) to
enthusiastic
crowds

**a**llison, son of the France-based Chicago blues legend Luther Allison, has emerged in recent years as a fine bluesman in his own right, combining the classic forceful but gamboling Westside Chicago blues style with a friendly but streetwise sensibility which is very much of today's generation.

Allison was born in Chicago and moved with his family to Peoria, Illinois, where he grew up surrounded by music. Learning the guitar from his father, he quickly became proficient enough to begin sitting in around town, eventually reaching the level where he successfully appeared with his father at the 1983 Chicago Blues Festival. After that he spent his formative bluesman years in the bands of Koko Taylor and Willie Dixon, incorporating their feel for blues into his younger sensibility and taste, a taste that embraces Jimi Hendrix as much as Buddy Guy or Albert Collins. Spending time with his father in Paris, Allison finally decided to move to France and pursue his career from a base in his father's adopted city. A persuasive singer and an exciting guitar stylist at any tempo, Allison cut his first album as leader, *Born With The Blues*, in 1997 for Ruf records. He continues to enjoy an expanding career.

**SEE ALSO:** Luther Allison, Koko Taylor, Willie Dixon

# Mose Allison

**fact file**

**BORN** 1927

**MUSICAL SELECTION**
Gewgaws &
Gimcracks

Mose Allison
incorporates
elements of jazz
in the blues,
having per-
formed in the
New York jazz
scene in the
1950s

ianist/singer Allison has enjoyed a sustained and inventive career through an astute but entirely natural-sounding combination of the formative influences of his youth in Tupelo, Mississippi, where he heard as much zydeco and jazz as he did straight blues, country, or otherwise. A talent for lyrics and a penchant for mordant witticisms have also helped his profile both as a club performer (and model for Georgie Fame) and a recording artist.

Allison learned piano while a student at grammar school, then had a try at trumpet during high school. World War II interrupted his musical and educational progress, but after the war ended he completed an English degree at Louisiana State University, graduating in 1950. While there he also completed informal studies of many records of jazz and blues musicians, especially Nat Cole and the Delta singers he'd heard when younger. Allison began playing clubs and bars around his part of the country. Encouraged by the gradual growth in appreciation of his soft, small voice and his clear, light but emphatic piano style, he moved to NYC in 1956, making his debut on record in 1957 for Prestige with *Back Country Suite*, a trio date that reflected typical Allison

interests, mostly containing Allison originals of wit and taste, but also taking a new look at songs like "Blueberry Hill." The relative success of that album, plus his warm reception in the New York watering holes such as the Village Vanguard and Village Gate, often in the company of people such as Zoot Sims and Stan Getz, led to a string of follow-up records, including the late 1957 classic, *Local Color*, which included his famous version of "Parchman Farm." The following year he was runner-up in Down Beat's International Critics' Poll, New Pianist category. Allison swapped to Columbia/Epic in 1960 and established a firm, unwavering international audience. This fan base stayed with him during his long stint at Atlantic (1962–78), during which he refined his style and took in such technology as electric piano and other wizardry, but remained a cult favorite on both sides of the Atlantic and in Japan. This was enough to keep his career moving, and he has since recorded for a number of labels, including the revived Blue Note in the 1980s (*Ever Since The World Ended*, 1987). Allison, now a revered figure in American music, continues to perform the regular club circuits in various countries and make new recordings.

**SEE ALSO:** Jimmy Dawkins, Magic Sam

# Luther Allison

guitarist/singer Allison has had a varied and at times checkered career, early on being one of the coming men in Chicago blues, then moving into rock- and soul-based music before, more recently, returning to the blues with which he first made his reputation. Allison has never had an easy time from critics in his home country, but he has built a large and loyal following overseas, especially in France, where he is viewed as a major postwar bluesman. Recent albums for Verve/Gitanes tend to bear out the truth of this assessment.

Allison was born in Mayflower, Arkansas, into a musical and religious family: he gained his first experiences of singing in public through the family gospel group. His parents took him when they relocated to Chicago in 1951, and Allison joined the local gospel group, the Southern Travelers, but by his later teens he had become fascinated by the blues he was hearing all over Westside Chicago and eventually formed his own band when he was 18, after sitting in with various bands and playing in his brother Ollie Lee's group between 1954 and 1957. Influenced by the slashing guitar of Magic Sam, Allison fit into the Westside scene capably, often playing in bands led by Jimmy Dawkins and Magic Sam himself. He had to wait until 1967 to make his recording debut as a leader, on an album that finally saw the light of day on Delmark. But his introduction to a wider audience was the 1969 Ann Arbor Blues Festival in Michigan, a move that saw him invited into the Fillmore East and West venues and introduced to the rock audience. Allison's personal fusion of Westside blues and rock began to gel around this time, and, although he experienced commercial failure when signed to Berry Gordy's label in the early 1970s, his appearance on the blues packages touring France from the mid-1970s onward gave him eager live audiences and opportunities to record in his older style for Black & Blue records. These albums have him operating at a peak.

Since then Allison has spent much of his time in France and other parts east of the Atlantic, and as a result his reputation has not grown in the US as it has elsewhere. He recorded for a plethora of small labels before signing to Verve/Gitanes in the early 1990s, since when he has been consistently providing high-quality Chicago blues-type albums which have reached a wider audience than ever before. He now lives in France.

## fact file

**BORN** 1939

**MUSICAL SELECTION**
Life is a Bitch
Hand Me Down My
Moonshine

Luther Allison has moved freely between blues, funk and rock-influenced guitar styles during his career.

SEE ALSO: Eric Clapton, Willie Mabon

# Pinkney "Pink" Anderson

fact file

**BORN** 1900

**DIED** 1974

**MUSICAL SELECTION**
Carolina Blues Man
Ballad and Folksinger

Pinkney "Pink" Anderson was known for his medicine show performances

anderson was a country-blues man whose style echoed some of the traits of the Carolinas where he was born, though his guitar style was less complex than that of many of his contemporaries. Born in Laurens, South Carolina, not far from Spartanburg, Anderson spent most of his working life playing with the traveling medicine shows, going out with Dr Kerr of the Indian Remedy Company at the age of 14 and staying with him until 1945, when Kerr retired.

Anderson himself was unwilling to see his main role as that of a blues singer, more correctly seeing himself as an entertainer playing a whole range of popular tunes, rags, and sprightly songs for the benefit of the medicine-show audiences. Indeed, he'd been out with Kerr for two years by the time he met the bluesman Simmie Dooley, who began teaching him the standard blues repertoire in the time shortly before America entered World War I.

He and Dooley spent long hours practicing the blues, and outside of medicine-show hours Anderson would play at parties and other functions, playing blues and other types of "entertainment" music with Dooley. Four sides, with Dooley, for Columbia in 1928, constituted his entire recorded output until 1950, when Riverside recorded him in Virginia playing his medicine-show repertoire. Anderson suffered from heart trouble during the 1950s and after Dooley died in 1960, he withdrew from any public performing. Brought back by Sam Charters, Anderson made three albums for Bluesville in 1961: these albums were instrumental in bringing him to the attention of the young folk audience, and Anderson enjoyed a widespread interest in his music unprecedented in his experience. He even appeared in a film documentary, *The Blues*, in 1963. Always somewhat frail, Anderson finally succumbed to his weak heart in 1974.

**SEE ALSO:** Rev Gary Davis

# Billy Boy Arnold

fact file

BORN 1935

MUSICAL SELECTION
Ten Million Dollars

Billy Boy Arnold's talent brought him to the attention of blues legends Sonny Boy Williamson, Bo Diddley, Johnny Shines and Otis Rush.

a well-respected harmonica player on the Chicago scene in the 1950s and 1960s, Arnold created his style from the obvious sources, including Sonny Boy Williamson and, later, Junior Wells. Arnold is one of those rare Chicago bluesmen actually born in that city, and was drawn to the music of John Lee Williamson while still a boy. After studying his 78s for years, at the age of 12 Arnold sought out Sonny Boy and benefited from a number of lessons from the great man before his untimely death in 1948.

Arnold got work in the early 1950s with the pianist Blind John Davis, and also worked on street corners with Bo Diddley, before making his first single, for Cool Records, in 1953. Bo Diddley, Otis Spann, and Clifton James were in the backing group. This and a number of sessions in the 1955–57 period failed to sell, even though Arnold was sent on a tour of Southern states on the strength of his Vee Jay work. He also appeared on some of Bo Diddley's sessions. For a while after this, Arnold ran his own group in Chicago, playing harp and singing lead with his light, pleasant voice. But the lack of long-term opportunities led him to relegate music to a part-time occupation. In 1963 he recorded twice, once in a duo with Johnny Jones, the other with his own tight-knit band featuring Mighty Joe Young on guitar. This latter was for the Bluesville label. Arnold made a 1970 album in Chicago for the French Vogue label and enjoyed some European recognition during that difficult decade for blues. This led to a 1984 Blue Phoenix album, *Ten Million Dollars*, but Arnold has not to date managed a full-time blues career. He still lives and performs in Chicago.

SEE ALSO: Sonny Boy Williamson, Otis Spann, Mighty Joe Young

# James "Kokomo" Arnold

fact file

**BORN** 1901

**DIED** 1968

**MUSICAL SELECTION**
Master of the
Bottleneck Guitar

Playing slide guitar left-handed, James "Kokomo" Arnold made it look easy and sound rough

One of the archetypal early country blues performers, Arnold was a noted exponent of the slide guitar, using a bottleneck or glass flask on a steel guitar laid on his lap. Arnold records reveal a high-pitched, keening voice which often doubles the line of the wailing guitar, and his eccentric efforts are often seen as an influence on later slide experts such as Robert Johnson and even Elmore James.

Arnold was a Georgian, born in the small town of Lovejoy. He concentrated most of his efforts on different types of manual work, including that of farmhand and, later, steelworker, once he'd moved up North. His guitar playing and singing were used more as an entertainment than a livelihood, as is evidenced by the fact that, when he made it to Chicago in 1929, he spent most of his time attempting to set up a bootleg liquor scam. Retiring unscathed to Memphis, he cut two sides in 1930 for Victor under the name of Gitfiddle Jim. Both demonstrate his urgent approach to performing. Back in Chicago, he waited until 1934 before another recording opportunity came his way, this time for American Decca: his first session for them produced classics such as "Milk Cow Blues" and "Old Original Kokomo Blues," the latter a reworking of a Scrapper Blackwell tune which was again later adapted by Robert Johnson to become "Sweet Home Chicago." Arnold recorded intensely for the next four years, making over 70 titles, and by 1936 was appearing on the prolific Peetie Wheatstraw's sessions as well. Yet his career petered out as the 1930s came to a close. Tiring of the changeable nature of the business, he concentrated once more on a day job he believed reliable: work in a Chicago steel mill. Rediscovered during the 1960s folk and country blues boom, Arnold chose to keep his retirement permanent. He died in 1968 of a heart attack.

# Marcia Ball

fact file

**BORN** 1949

**MUSICAL SELECTION**
Circuit Queen
Play With Your
Poodle

Marcia Ball with Angela Strehli (middle) and Lou Ann Barton (bottom), all powerful performers of the blues

b all was born in Orange, Texas, but spent her formative years in Louisiana, a central fact in the overall development of her musical style. She graduated from Louisiana State University and in the early 1970s became part of the music scene in Austin, Texas, first as a member of Freda and the Firedogs, a young country outfit.

That band split up in 1974, and Ball began changing direction, combining the R&B and Cajun influences of her earlier Louisiana days with the blues and white music she found around her in Texas. Ball is a two-fisted piano player and persuasive vocalist, with deep roots in music as played by people like Professor Longhair, Fats Domino and Etta James. Her talents were first picked up by Capitol, who made her album, *Circuit Queen*, in 1978; but during the 1980s she moved on to Rounder, where she has made a string of records, starting with *Soulful Dress* (1983). Her latest, *Let Me Play With Your Poodle*, was released in 1997.

Marcia Ball combines the blues with Louisiana-derived R&B, and this mixture has proved potent with audiences worldwide; she continues to tour and record today, a popular favorite whenever she performs.

# Barbecue Bob

Barbecue Bob had no trouble accepting his given nickname, as shown in this now-infamous photograph

## fact file

**BORN** 1902

**DIED** 1931

**MUSICAL SELECTION**
"Blind Pig Blues"
"Cold Wave Blues"
"Yo Yo Blues"

orn in Walnut Grove, Georgia, Barbecue Bob was an important stylist on the 12-string guitar, bringing a ringing, luminous quality to his playing, something he often echoed in his voice through the occasional use of falsetto. He and his brother Charlie worked in Atlanta and became the hub of a group of Atlanta blues performers, including Curley Weaver and Buddy Moss.

Bob Hicks was raised on a farm and worked the land before moving to Atlanta with his brother, who also taught him the rudiments of guitar (and who recorded under the name Charlie Lincoln). Working all kinds of jobs to sustain himself, Hicks was discovered by a Columbia scout performing at a barbecue joint: hence his professional name. His short recording career got under way in 1927 with the appropriately titled "Barbecue Blues," a bestseller which was also typical of his 12-string style. Recording mostly only with his own guitar accompaniment, Hicks was a regular visitor to the Atlanta studio, clocking up a fair number of classics, including "Blind Pig Blues," "Cold Wave Blues," "Goin' Up The Country," "Yo Yo Blues," and "It Just Won't Hay." He was an able performer, often willing to try new twists in the construction of his songs and melodies in the pursuit of his own "signature" on a performance. His last recording was in December 1930, and he died the following October after a long illness. His brother, broken by the early death, dropped from the music scene soon after.

SEE ALSO: Curley Weaver, Buddy Moss

# Lou Ann Barton

Lou Ann Barton jumped in with both feet when it came to singing her blues-based style

**b**arton was born in Fort Worth, Texas, into a truck driver s family, and became interested in music while still at school. She began singing when she moved to Austin in the early 1970s, moving into a vibrant young blues scene which included Stevie Ray Vaughan and his brother, Jimmie. Barton's hell-for-leather voice and aggressive stage act brought her fans and respect from musicians, and she became a member of Jimmie Vaughan's Fabulous Thunderbirds while that band had a long residency at Antone's. She also did a stint with Roomful of Blues, going out on tour with them across America.

After this, she formed and led a variety of groups in and around Austin. This led to her first album as a leader, *Old Enough* (1982, Asylum); the LP managed to register strong sales in the locality where Barton was well-known.

More albums followed in 1986 and 1989; the latter, *Read My Lips*, appeared on the Antone's label and featured top Austin bluesmen and saxophonist David "Fathead" Newman. This further established her in critical circles, and gave her an audience beyond Austin. Lou Ann has continued to make records for Antone's and give her scorched-earth vocals a workout to live audiences up to the present day.

Working with Angela Strehli and Marcia Ball on the album *Dreams Come True*, Barton demonstrated that hers is definitely a blues talent to be reckoned with.

## fact file

**BORN** 1954

**MUSICAL SELECTION**
Old Enough
Read My Lips

**SEE ALSO:** Stevie Ray Vaughan, Roomful of Blues

# Carey Bell

fact file

BORN 1936

MUSICAL SELECTION
Carey Bell's Blues Harp
Harp Attack!

Carey Bell has touched on virtually all musical aspects of the blues, including singing, guitar, bass guitar, and the blues harp

though there has been a plethora of outstanding blues harpists in postwar Chicago, Carey Bell has proven one of the most distinctive. Born Carey Bell Harrington in Macon, Mississippi, Bell embraced music in his boyhood and taught himself harmonica when very young. Indeed, he made an unusually thorough job of it, learning chromatic harmonica rather than the usual type, which is pitched in a particular key.

Bell's first paying job was in the early 1950s with a white Country band in the Mississippi area – a highly unusual position for a black musician at that time. A parallel gig with Lovie Lee led to Bell's move to Chicago, when Lee took his band there in 1956. After struggling for a time, Bell began meeting the Chicago blues set, learning much from Little Walter, Honeyboy Edwards (who showed him how to play bass and slide guitar,) and Walter Horton. Working with a number of people on Maxwell Street during the 1960s, Bell was in the Robert Nighthawk band that was recorded "live" on the street in 1964. Bell remained a

sideman during that decade, but appeared with Earl Hooker on the latter's *Love Ain't No Plaything* (Delmark) in 1968, and toured Europe the following year with John Lee Hooker. He also recorded his debut album as a leader, *Carey Bell's Blues Harp*, for Delmark that same year. Working his way up the Chicago echelon, Bell joined Muddy Waters in the 1970s, played and recorded with a wide range of leaders, and produced and played on Walter Horton's 1973 album for Alligator, *Big Walter Horton with Carey Bell*. Bell spent most of the 1970s and 1980s as a sideman with various outfits – in particular that of Willie Dixon – but was getting progressively more exposure, making his own albums and occasionally running his own gigs. The 1990s have seen him mostly with his own bands and recording regularly under his own name; his appearance on the 1992 album *Harp Attack!* (Alligator) with James Cotton, Junior Wells, and Billy Branch greatly enhanced his international stature. Carey Bell continues to pursue his career in the US and abroad today.

SEE ALSO: Little Walter, Honeyboy Edwards, Walter Horton, Robert Nighthawk, Earl Hooker, John Lee Hooker

# Lurrie Bell

**fact file**

**BORN** 1958

**MUSICAL SELECTION**
Everybody Wants
To Win
Mercurial Son

Lurrie Bell has been exposed to the blues all of his life, playing on stage with his father as a child and with Koko Taylor in his teens

Lurrie Bell, son of Chicago blues harpist Carey Bell, was naturally born into a blues family and grew up with blues legends as daily guests in the household. A talented boy, Lurrie quickly developed a desire to play music (his four brothers would also become blues musicians) and taught himself guitar. In between his schooling and the usual boyhood pursuits, Lurrie spent his time with older bluesmen, learning their secrets and absorbing their craft. He also became an avid listener to other styles of music, from Ray Charles to Jose Feliciano. Before he was twenty he joined Eddie Campbell's band and started gigging seriously around Chicago.

An introduction from his father in 1977 began his friendship with harp player Billy Branch. Once the two of them had teamed up with Willie Dixon's son Freddie, the idea for the "Sons of Blues" was born. This dynamic band quickly established itself as a top crowd drawer, their name soon being affectionately shortened by fans to the S.O.B.s. – and for over half a decade they played headlining concerts all around the world wherever blues was popular. Their recorded legacy, however, was unfortunately not extensive. The best occurred on an Alligator anthology, *Living Chicago Blues*, where four tracks convey the vivid urgency and character of the band to perfection. Bell left the group in 1982, gigging around Chicago and then landing a job in Koko Taylor's backing band. For the rest of the decade he stayed with Taylor, touring widely, and appearing on records with his father Carey. Lurrie's first album as leader was *Everybody Wants To Win*, on JSP, made in 1989. Soon after, Bell ran into a rough patch in his life, and his career went on the back burner for the first half of the 1990s. In the last few years, however, Lurrie has begun performing regularly once again, making a much-lauded appearance at the 1996 Chicago Blues Festival and making two excellent comeback albums for Delmark, *Mercurial Son* and *700 Blues*.

**SEE ALSO:** Carey Bell, Billy Branch, Koko Taylor

# Big Maceo

m ajor "Big Maceo" Merriweather was both a persuasive vocal stylist and a key figure in the development of piano blues between the older players of the classic period, such as Eddie Boyd and Leroy Carr, and the later Chicago giants, Otis Spann and Johnnie Jones. He was the contemporary of men like Sunnyland Slim and Roosevelt Sykes and an older contemporary to Memphis Slim, a man ten years younger but on the Chicago scene a number of years before Maceo.

Born and raised in farming country outside Atlanta, Georgia, Merriweather lived first on his family's farm, and then in their home in College Park until his mid-teens – when he felt he'd taught himself sufficient piano to make it on his own in the city. He played in low-life Atlanta tonks and restaurants until 1924, when he moved to Detroit, near one of his married brothers. It was in the Motor City that his performing name was coined; standing well over 6 feet and a solid-set man, the "Big" was understandable, while Maceo was a jive corruption of his unusual first name, Major. He stayed in Detroit until 1941, keeping busy and learning his craft, but as with most other bluesmen in that town, he went unrecorded. A marriage to Hattie Spruel – one of the women whose houses he often played at, and a shrewd, organized character – put Merriweather on the road to Chicago and a recording contract. She set up a meeting, through Tampa Red and Big Bill, with RCA's Lester Melrose. Maceo arrived in June, 1941 and was recording within days. His first release, "Worried Life Blues," was a major hit and has since become a blues standard, with hundreds of cover versions recorded right up to the present day.

Maceo and Tampa Red struck up a profitable and creative partnership, recording 16 sides before the 1942 recording ban. During the ban Merriweather stayed in Detroit, making a steady "live" living off the back of his successful singles, and occasionally performing with groups including horns and guitar. Although there were some lean times when Maceo was reduced to working as a porter, he and Tampa Red resumed recording together in 1945, and he also played as an accompanist on dates led by his friend Big Bill Broonzy. The hits kept coming, and the piano solo "Chicago Breakdown" has since been recognized as a classic. But Maceo's time was running out: a stroke in 1946 severely hampered his piano playing, and with it his capacity to earn. His wife Hattie, still a working woman, supported him and got the best medical attention she could afford. But his last session for Victor, in 1947, found him only singing, accompanied by pianist Eddie Boyd; worse, times had changed and the record didn't sell. Big Maceo was to record just once again, for a small Detroit label in 1950, but by then he was a shadow of his former self; the stroke and a lifetime of heavy drinking had worn him down. He died from heart failure early in 1953.

**fact file**

**BORN** 1905

**DIED** 1953

**MUSICAL SELECTION**
"Worried Life Blues"
"Chicago Breakdown"

Big Maceo, so called because of his size, was perhaps at his best when performing with his guitarist Tampa Red

**SEE ALSO:** Tampa Red, Big Bill Broonzy, Eddie Boyd

# Big Maybelle

**fact file**

**BORN** 1924

**DIED** 1972

**MUSICAL SELECTION**
"Gabbin' Blues"
"Whole Lotta Shakin'
Goin' On"
"Candy"

Big Maybelle blues shouting style earned her a number of hits (as well as penning the classic "Whole Lotta Shakin' Goin' On")

**b**ig Maybelle had a vast, incredible voice, a large girth, and considerable stage presence. Born in Jackson, Tennessee, young Mabel Smith first came into contact with music through gospel, and sang in her local Sanctified Church. Her voice and her girth were already impressive, and when impresario Dave Clark approached the teenager to switch to rhythm and blues, she gladly accepted. Starting out in Memphis, she spent a number of years graduating through a series of bands of increasingly national stature, moving into the more jazz-based outfits of the International Sweethearts of Rhythm and Tiny Bradshaw, with whom she made a series of excellent singles between 1947 and 1950.

Maybelle became a headliner in her own right after signing her first solo contract, with Okeh records, in 1952. The company's faith in her was quickly rewarded when, in 1953, her "Gabbin' Blues" went to No.3 on the R&B charts. She made the charts twice more that year, but her years at Okeh were crowned by her fire-eating original version of Roy Hall's "Whole Lotta Shakin' Goin'

On," recorded in 1954. A similarly blistering piece of vinyl, "One Monkey Don't Stop The Show," was cut the same year. But although Maybelle was among Okeh's top three money-earners, an addiction to heroin – one she would never be able to shake – was causing her career problems. She left Okeh and signed with the smaller Savoy label in 1956, registering a hit with "Candy" in her first year. Savoy attempted to move Maybelle in the direction Dinah Washington was taking at the time, and her talents certainly were broad enough to become a more sophisticated all-round entertainer. However, anyone who has seen her performance in the film of the 1958 Newport Jazz Festival (in which Washington was also featured) will recognize her temperamental difficulties with maintaining this approach.

Maybelle moved to Brunswick in 1959 and recorded into the 1960s, moving closer to the soul style which was fashionable at the time. Unable to maintain discipline in either her personal or her professional life, Big Maybelle slipped from view, dying from complications due to the onset of diabetes in 1972.

**SEE ALSO:** Big Joe Turner

# Elvin Bishop

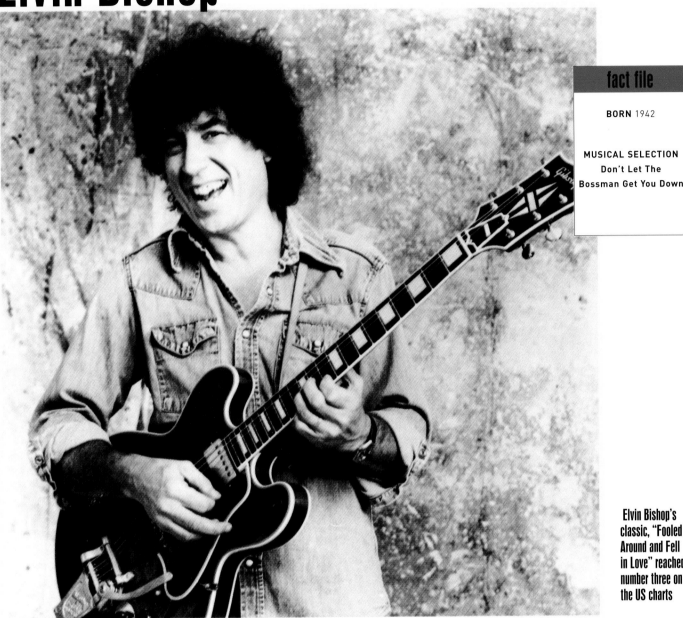

**fact file**

**BORN** 1942

**MUSICAL SELECTION**
Don't Let The
Bossman Get You Down

Elvin Bishop's classic, "Fooled Around and Fell in Love" reached number three on the US charts

bishop made his reputation initially as one of two outstanding guitarists (the other being Mike Bloomfield) in the original Paul Butterfield Blues Band. After pulling off a top five chart hit in 1975 with the Capricorn single "Fooled Around and Fell in Love," Bishop failed to sustain a wider audience, and in the past decade or more has returned to his blues-rock roots.

Bishop was born in Tulsa, Oklahoma, discovering the blues and other vernacular musics from the radio and records. He moved to Chicago to study at the university, but spent a fair amount of his time with his university pal Paul Butterfield hanging around the black blues clubs instead, sitting in with a number of local legends in the early 1960s, including Magic Sam. The two blues addicts formed their own band, using Butterfield's name, in 1963. Bishop was a basic ingredient of that band's sound and success, staying with it for three albums and five years, leaving in 1968

to move to San Francisco and run his own group there. After a fruitless time with Bill Graham's Fillmore label and a marginally more successful four years (1970–73), with Epic, during which he moved his music ever closer to the new R&B/pop mainstream, Bishop signed his band to the new Capricorn label. Between 1974 and 1978 Bishop made six albums for the label and scored with his major hit single listed above, a single that featured the iron lungs of the singer Mickey Thomas, later of Jefferson Starship fame. By the late 1970s Capricorn was bankrupt, Thomas gone, and Bishop battling with drug and alcohol problems, as well as a general move of the pop scene away from blues and guitar-based repertoire. Bishop moved back toward the power-blues he loved, reconstructed a career that still flourishes today, mostly on the West Coast when playing live, and on Alligator when in the studio. His album, *Don't Let The Bossman Get You Down* (1993), shows his guitar playing to be unaffected by the passage of time.

# Black Ace

Black Ace withdrew more or less from performance after WWII, only to be "re-discovered" during the 1960s

## fact file

**BORN** 1907

**DIED** 1972

**MUSICAL SELECTION**
Black Ace
"Whiskey and Women"

black Ace, also known as The Black Ace, spent most of his life away from the spotlight of publicity and success but managed to pursue a career of sorts in music for a number of decades before poverty and musical fashion changes forced him into manual-labor jobs in the 1940s and 1950s. A fine singer with a deep, resonant voice, he also developed a complex and technically accomplished slide guitar style by playing a steel guitar Hawaiian style across his lap.

Born Babe Kyro Lemon Turner in Hughes Springs, Texas, Ace was a self-taught guitarist who was an adept from early childhood. He began his professional career by appearing at house parties, dances, and picnics. With the onset of the Depression, Ace moved to Shreveport, Louisiana, and there met the guitarist Buddy Woods. The two teamed up and played all over the Shreveport area. It was from Woods that Ace learned his slide guitar style. Ace

moved again, back to Texas in Fort Worth, in the mid-1930s, and managed to get regular appearances on the local radio station KFJZ. This in turn led in time to his first recording sessions, as Buck Turner (the Black Ace), made for ARC in 1936. Both tracks from this date were left unissued, but the following year there was a session for American Decca where Ace appeared on the label as Black Ace. The records did little in terms of sales, and Decca dropped him. He made a fleeting appearance in a 1941 film, *Blood of Jesus*, and kept up his broadcasting on radio, he remained a little-known figure outside of Fort Worth. After serving in WWII, Ace withdrew from music. His blues career went on hold until he was rediscovered by Chris Strachwitz of Arhoolie records, with whom he recorded two sessions in Fort Worth, in August and September 1960. However, he did not join the circuit, preferring retirement instead. He died in 1972, of cancer.

**SEE ALSO:** Andrew "Smokey" Hogg

# Francis "Scrapper" Blackwell

Though Scrapper Blackwell dropped out of sight during the 1940s, his return in the 1950s revealed his music to be more intense and personal than ever

born in North Carolina, Blackwell was one of the first generation of blues guitarists to develop a truly urban style for an instrument still a decade or so away from amplification. Like the similarly gifted Lonnie Johnson, Indiana-based Blackwell took significant steps past the country picking and strumming which the vast majority of bluesmen of his era used, developing in particular a strong and independent single-line style which he could use to devastating effect either in brief breaks or solos, or in accompaniment, usually in the vicinity of his partner Leroy Carr's piano playing. Carr and Blackwell enjoyed wide popularity in the blues world as a recording duo between 1928 and Carr's death in 1935. Among the classics these two waxed were "How Long How Long Blues," "Kokomo Blues," and "Good Woman Blues," where Blackwell displays abundant discipline, sophistication, and good taste in his guitar lines.

By all reports Blackwell was a taciturn man, not given to selling his greatest asset – his musical ability – particularly well. It was only with the more outgoing Carr that he successfully reached a wide audience, and indeed when Carr died, Blackwell decided not to continue his career in music, working instead in a series of low-paid positions in and around Indianapolis. Blackwell disappeared from the music scene, thereby missing the rise of the new postwar urban-blues styles. It was only during the revival of interest in early blues that he was rediscovered, still living in Indianapolis, and brought once again in front of a microphone. His latter-day recordings were all made in Indianapolis, between 1958 and 1961, the last one being for Prestige's blues subsidiary, Bluesville. Seeming set for a new stage of his musical career, in October 1962 Blackwell was shot dead for no known reason by an unknown assailant.

**fact file**

**BORN** 1903

**DIED** 1962

**MUSICAL SELECTION**
"How Long How Long Blues"
"Kokomo Blues"
"Good Woman Blues"

SEE ALSO: Leroy Carr

27

# Arthur "Blind" Blake

**fact file**

**BORN** 1890

**DIED** C.1933

**MUSICAL SELECTION**
"Diddy Wa Diddy"
"West Coast Blues"
"Georgia Blues"

Much of Blind Blake's history is unknown, though his clean guitar style demonstrates considerable talent.

espite his contemporary fame and posthumous influence, little is known of Blind Blake's life. A publicity flyer from his record company, Paramount, states that he was a native of Jacksonville, Florida. His contemporaries put Blake in his thirties when he first began making a name for himself among Chicago's blues-playing community in the early 1920s, and remember him as a hard-living bluesman who was constantly in fights over card games.

In a profession awash with guitarists with only the most basic technical skills and the ability to play in only one style, Blake quickly stood out as a virtuoso capable of playing across a gamut of styles and roles, from solos to small group work. Blake's technique was precise yet fluid, his melodic embellishments across the steady bottom-string rhythm echoing the ragtime idiom, while his sense of form was highly developed. His light baritone voice was warm and persuasive, but he placed no great emphasis upon

it, clearly preferring to make his musical points with his intricate guitar – whether playing strict blues or other genres such as stomps or rags. Blake continued to record throughout the early years of the Depression, remaining one of the few popular blues figures on record alongside such men as Blind Lemon Jefferson and Big Bill. He recorded close to 80 sides and his hits included "Diddy Wa Diddy" (later covered by performer and musicologist Ry Cooder), "West Coast Blues" (an instrumental and his first success). and "Georgia Blues."

When Paramount ran into financial difficulties and closed down in 1932, Blind Blake was not picked up by any other company. He died in such obscurity that neither the precise date nor the place of his death is known. Now, more than 60 years after his passing, it's unlikely anything more will ever be discovered about early blues' greatest picker, to the dismay of blues fans everywhere.

**SEE ALSO:** Blind Lemon Jefferson, Big Bill Broonzy

# Rory Block

**fact file**

**BORN** 1949

**MUSICAL SELECTION**
Rory Block
High Heeled Blues

Rory Block
came to the
blues through
the best,
including the
Rev. Gary Davis
and Mississippi
John Hurt

lock, born in New York, grew up in the Greenwich Village area of the city and was the daughter of a sandal-shop proprietor who used his premises for informal meetings of the older black blues players then being rediscovered and the young and earnest white musicians who were intent on learning the mysteries of the old-style folk music and country blues. Rory herself became one of the most accomplished acolytes in this group, being attracted to the Delta style of singing and picking personified by such players as Mississippi John Hurt, Son House, Skip James, and Robert Johnson.

A musician with a considerable emotional punch of her own, she became a fluent and accomplished guitarist in the Delta style and a vocalist capable of raising the hairs on the listener's neck. This early promise was only partially realized before she retired from

the business to start a family at the start of the 1970s. By the end of that decade she was back in the recording studio, but this time she spread her talents across many musical genres, including disco and pop music. This approach proved only partially successful and she parted company with the major international labels who had encouraged these things. Her return to folk and blues roots began in earnest with her signing in 1981 to Rounder Records, a label involved in the roots of music rather than pop output. With Rounder's encouragement Block made a string of outstanding records, sometimes acoustic, sometimes electric, covering her formative influences in the folk and blues area. These have remained the cornerstone of her blues reputation, and although she has continued to diversify her musical interests, a core of blues songs is always part of her repertoire.

# Bobby "Blue" Bland

b land is one of the unsung heroes of the post-war blues scene. Not especially blessed with good looks or onstage charisma, Bobby Bland is a first-rate singer who early on could bring the church into the blues as well as his contemporary, Ray Charles, could. Although he had his fair share of hits on the Memphis-based Duke records and a popularity that endured for two decades, Bland rarely crossed over to the burgeoning white blues audience, and his particular brand of soulful blues has remained something of a well-kept Memphis secret.

Robert Calvin Bland was born near Memphis, Tennessee, and was attracted early on to singing gospel. A family move to Memphis in 1947 quickly introduced him to the fast life of Beale Street as well as the gospel singing of the Memphis church community. His soulful style of singing made contacts for him in the local music business, and he became part of a blues community which included such future stars as Junior Parker, Roscoe Gordon, and Johnny Ace. By 1951 Bland was sufficiently well-known for a number of record labels to cut some sides with him, including Sun, Modern and, the following year, Duke. A stint in the Army kept Bobby out of the scene for close to three years, but on his return to civvies he took up again with Duke records. By 1957 he was enjoying his first R&B hit, "Farther On Up The Road," which reached the top spot in the R&B charts; it featured a style which Bland had evolved as his own, with his light, melodic vocals riding over an ebullient shuffle. His other staple was the soul ballad, as much a product of the Charles Brown approach of the 1940s (often using large horn sections) as of his gospel background or his addiction to melodic sophistication.

At this point in his career Bland was still not sufficiently confident to go out as a headliner, and for six years (from 1955-61) he worked as Junior Parker's warm-up act and personal valet. This period saw him struggle for a follow-up hit, and it wasn't until the double 1961 success of "I Pity The Fool" and "Turn On Your Love Light" that Bland split from Parker and went out on his own. Yet wider popularity always eluded Bland, and although every single he put out in the next few years did well in the R&B charts, he rarely penetrated pop consciousness. He moved to ABC-Dunhill in 1972, releasing a string of more squarely blues-based albums which won critical acclaim. But the white blues audience still proved elusive for Bobby, even as his old friend B.B. King made the transition and established himself as a virtual blues and pop legend by the end of that decade. Bland continues to play and record right up to the present, but remains a cult performer unable to get his artistry across to the larger audience – in some ways, an artist trapped by his success in the genre of his choice.

## fact file

**BORN** 1930

**MUSICAL SELECTION**
"Farther On Up The Road"
"I Pity The Fool"
"Turn On Your Love Light"

Bobby "Blue" Bland went from gospel to the blues via the infamous Beale Streete musicians in Memphis

# Mike Bloomfield

## fact file

**BORN** 1943

**DIED** 1981

**MUSICAL SELECTION**
If You Love These
Blues, Plays 'Em
As You Please

Mike Bloomfield,
part of the Paul
Butterfield Blues
Band and a real
force on the
blues scene, had
a career that
wandered far
and wide

**b**loomfield was one of the first of the young white guitarists of the 1960s to prove that it was possible for a man with such a background to play authentic blues guitar, both in the country-blues and the then-contemporary urban-blues traditions of Chicago, the city in which he was born. Bloomfield took up the guitar as a teenager and became aware of the music being generated on Chicago's South and West sides at the outset of the 1960s. Within a couple of years he was sitting in with some of the players he'd been so assiduously watching. This experience was fundamental to his being involved in the founding of the Group (along with Charlie Musselwhite and Nick Gravenites), a band that landed a deal with Columbia in 1964. Bloomfield, however, left to become a member of the Paul Butterfield Blues Band in 1965, and was a member for the first two years, including the infamous 1965 Newport Folk Festival appearance of Bob Dylan, where the folk bard went electric. Bloomfield subsequently appeared on a number of Dylan albums before relocating to San Francisco and combining blues with the emerging rock sounds of the late 1960s, through the near-legendary Electric Flag. He proved impatient again, leaving while the band's first album was still in the charts. By this time his reputation was worldwide, his every recorded note studied by budding blues guitarists the world over.

This interest was intensified by his playing on the famous Super Session of 1968, pitting Bloomfield with Stephen Stills and Al Kooper. A bestseller in its day, the album has subsequently been subject to savage revisionism by the critical fraternity. Around this time Bloomfield acquired the heroin habit which was to be with him for much of the rest of his life. For a while he dropped out of sight, making a return in 1973 with an album featuring Dr John and John Hammond, but, in a pattern that was to prove unbreakable, Bloomfield returned to his reclusive lifestyle, making a living for the rest of the decade by teaching music in San Francisco and writing soundtracks for pornographic movies. Another comeback in 1975 with the so-called "supergroup" KGB, which featured, among others, Carmine Appice of Vanilla Fudge and Beck-Bogert-Appice fame, was little short of a disaster, but by 1977, though plagued by drug addiction and insomnia, Bloomfield made a series of fine albums, including the Grammy-nominated *If You Love These Blues, Plays 'Em As You Please*, his clean, singing blues guitar lines coming through strong as ever. Yet he could not sustain this level of creativity or output, and although he managed other recordings – some in the country style of his youth – he died in 1981 of a drug overdose, another case of early promise unfulfilled.

**SEE ALSO:** Charlie Musselwhite, Paul Butterfield, Dr John, John Hammond

# Lucille Bogan

## fact file

**BORN** 1897

**DIED** 1948

**MUSICAL SELECTION**
"Tricks Ain't Walkin'
No More"
"Drinkin' Blues"
"Shave 'Em Dry"

Lucille Bogan's somewhat raw lyrics and singing style earned her as much notoriety as fame

b ogan was one of the toughest characters among the female blues singers of the 1920s and 1930s. Blessed with a big, expressive voice and a delivery bursting with personality and nuance – often of a blatantly risqué nature – Bogan was one of the few classic singers from the 1920s who managed to continue recording well into the 1930s, albeit under the pseudonym Bessie Jackson. She also had every right to the claim of being a blues singer, having total control of her idiom and transcending any vaudeville or traveling-show overtones in her work.

Bogan was born Lucille Anderson in Amory, Mississippi, but moved to Birmingham, Alabama, at an early age with her family and reached her majority there. Little is known of her life prior to her 1923 recording debut in Atlanta, Georgia, but she must have married (and perhaps left) Nazareth Bogan by that date. At some point she also produced a family of her own. The subject matter of many of her songs – poverty, prostitution, and the search for sexual satisfaction, from both men and women – tends to suggest a harsh life prior to this date: her "Tricks Ain't Walkin' No More," one of many references to prostitution in her work, later became something of a blues anthem to the world's oldest profession,

while the songs of alcohol consumption ("Cravin' Whiskey Blues," "Drinkin' Blues") and sexual gymnastics (the notorious "Shave 'Em Dry," "Bed Rollin' Blues," and "My Georgia Grind") give the listener a picture of someone who lived life hard and enjoyed her own sensual nature.

Bogan for the most part used a pianist as accompaniment, with other musicians such as Tampa Red and Papa Charlie Jackson appearing on a casual basis. She recorded in New York and Chicago during the 1920s, making sides for Paramount, Brunswick, and Okeh. After a three-year hiatus in recording, 1930–33, she made a score or so of sides for the New York label, Banner, 1933–34. All of these recordings featured Walter Roland on piano (who probably introduced her to the label he was recording for), as did her last series of sides, for ARC, made in 1935, the year she made her two "Shave 'Em Dry" recordings, the uncensored version of which remained unissued until the days of the LP. Bogan retired to Birmingham, Alabama, after her recording contract was not renewed in 1935. Sometime later she managed her son's band, Bogan's Birmingham Busters, but in 1941 she moved to the West Coast, finally settling in Los Angeles. She died there of heart failure in 1948.

**SEE ALSO:** Tampa Red, Papa Charlie Jackson

# Weldon "Juke Boy" Bonner

## fact file

**BORN** 1932

**DIED** 1978

**MUSICAL SELECTION**
They Call Me Juke Boy
1960-1967

"Juke Boy" Bonner, billed as the "One Man Trio" at one point, was known for his strong guitar, powerful bursts of harp and persuasive vocals

One-man-band Bonner was born in Bellville, Texas, and his first experience of music came via the church his parents attended. Interested in most types of music that came to his attention, Bonner learned guitar while an adolescent and listened avidly to what he heard on the radio and on jukeboxes, thus picking up his nickname. By his late teens Bonner had moved to Houston to facilitate his career in music, eventually winning a talent show in 1948 and making occasional radio broadcasts in the city. He became well known on the house-party and club circuit in Houston, but unknown elsewhere. Stalled in his career by the mid-1950s, he made the move to California and was picked up in 1957 by the Irma label, singing and playing guitar and harp. After this he made little headway in California, moving back east to cut a session in Lake Charles, Louisiana, in 1960 for the Goldband label. He was to return to Lake Charles twice more for singles sessions, but eventually resettled in Houston, where he was based for the rest of his life. Bonner by this time was billing himself as a one-man band (with occasional accompaniment), and this is how he appeared on a long series of private recordings in Houston between June and December 1967, part of which have been issued on Flyright. However, he remained little known until his inclusion on the American Folk Blues tour of England in 1969, after which he slowly became part of the burgeoning blues festival and tour circuit of the 1970s. In addition to some Arhoolie sides, Bonner made albums in Europe, but by the middle of the decade he was ailing. Progressive liver deterioration (due to incipient alcoholism) curtailed his activity and eventually killed him in 1978.

**SEE ALSO:** Katie Webster

# Roy Book Binder

## fact file

**BORN** 1943

**MUSICAL SELECTION**
The Hillbilly
Blues Cats
Travelin' Man

Though Roy Book Binder began playing guitar later in his life, his 'teacher' the Rev. Gary Davis, thought him one of the best

ook Binder has taken a path to the blues similar to that of John Hammond, whose intense and detailed studies of old masters presented him with a route to discovering his own mature blues style, one that was steeped in classic country styles and attitudes but accurately reflects his musical personality (as well as his own).

Book Binder was born in NYC and discovered music through the first and second waves of rock 'n' roll as it poured through the radio in the late 1950s and early 1960s. He also discovered its antecedent and fellow traveler, R&B, and his quest had begun. Interrupted by a stint in the armed forces (1962–65), he at least was able to use the time there to begin playing blues guitar and finding out about country blues. By the time he became Rev. Gary Davis's chauffeur in the late 1960s, Book Binder had abandoned the thought of a conventional career and opted instead for the life of an itinerant bluesman. He made his first album in 1968 and recorded prolifically up to around 1979, when he moved into a traveling home and stayed on the road for close to 10 years, establishing a worldwide reputation as a talented and authentic modern-day representative of many of the old country blues traditions, his gentle voice and intricate guitar-picking appealing to many types of audience. In the 1980s Book Binder resumed recording, occasionally varying his solo routines with albums featuring other players – 1992's *The Hillbilly Blues Cats* featured harmonica and string bass. Book Binder continues to actively pursue his career.

**SEE ALSO:** John Hammond, Rev Gary Davis

# James Booker

James Booker was born and died in New Orleans, a talented child and one of the few blues musicians to have studied classical piano

## fact file

**BORN** 1939

**DIED** 1983

**MUSICAL SELECTION**
"Gonzo"

**b**ooker was a highly talented New Orleans pianist who was taught by all the right people and seemed destined for a prominent place in the New Orleans musical firmament before afflictions bore down on him and his involvement in the music became somewhat peripheral. A partially successful comeback put him before the public again prior to his death, but his recorded legacy remains meager for the size of talent.

Booker was born in New Orleans and took to the piano while still very young, having formal classical training alongside lessons from the Big Easy's very own professor, Prof. Longhair. After some time away from the city he returned there in his teens and played piano on a local radio station. In 1953 he cut his first session, supervised by Dave Bartholomew, under the name Booker Boy and the Rhythmaires. The tracks failed to sell, but Bartholomew used him as accompanist to many New Orleans artists, including Fats Domino, for whom Booker would often record the piano parts while Fats was out on tour, leaving

the star free to come back and just drop in the vocal. Booker also accompanied Joe Tex, Earl King, and Lloyd Price, among others, becoming a much-in-demand pianist on the R&B scene as the 1950s went on. Booker seemed on the brink of big things, especially when his single, the organ instrumental "Gonzo," charted in 1960, but by then he was wrestling with heroin, becoming a serious addict all through the 1960s. He supported himself through accompanying work, but a jail term at Angola in 1970 took him out of the picture. On his return he did rock session work in New York, but drifted back to New Orleans, appearing at the city's Jazz & Heritage Festival in 1975 and finally making it to Europe in 1977, where he was given a rapturous welcome and recorded a number of interesting albums.

However, his addiction was at its peak and his health was severely compromised: rarely leaving New Orleans, he deteriorated on every level until his death in 1983 from general heart and lung collapse.

**SEE ALSO:** Professor Longhair, Earl King

# Eddie Boyd

Eddie Boyd was a true wandering musician, born in Mississippi, working throughout the Southern US, settling in Chicago before moving to England and then Finland

**b**oyd, from the same plantation as Muddy Waters and a cousin of the great man, is a pianist and singer who made his presence felt in postwar Chicago and had a major R&B hit in 1952 with "Five Long Years." Like his half-brother Memphis Slim, Boyd was comfortable working as a single or as a leader of a small group, though his recording bands usually featured guitars and a saxophone (and in the 1960s guest stars such as Buddy Guy, John Mayall, and Fleetwood Mac). In later years, also like Slim, he found a more equable lifestyle and musical appreciation through living in Europe.

Boyd grew up working on Stovall's Plantation in Mississippi, teaching himself guitar and piano while there. By 1936 he had long quit the plantation, working around the South and eventually settling in Memphis, where he played the local scene, including the Beale Street blues clubs. In 1941 he moved on to Chicago, working in a steel mill there to keep his night-time activities financed and playing with stars like John Lee "Sonny Boy" Williamson

and Big Maceo (he played piano on one 1947 Maceo session after the star's incapacitating stroke). He also played with the young Muddy Waters.

In 1947, he recorded with J.T. Hogan's Boogie Band for Victor, and the combination of boogie and jazz-tinged blues and R&B gave him a formula that, in 1952, landed him his hit for JOB records, "Five Long Years." He had two more top 10 R&B hits the following year, then switched to Chess, where he made quality music but failed to recapture his earlier success. Seemingly on a slow slide in Chicago, Boyd became part of the Chicago blues invasion of Europe in the early and mid-1960s, making an impact on the 1965 American Folk Blues Festival tour. He found audiences receptive to his kind of blues and opted to stay in Europe, basing himself in Paris and traveling extensively. He recorded in just about every country in what is now the European Union and beyond, his vocals and lyrics consistently amusing his audiences. His career has continued on a steady basis in Europe up to the present day.

## fact file

**BORN** 1914

**MUSICAL SELECTION**
"Five Long Years"

**SEE ALSO:** Muddy Waters, Memphis Slim, Buddy Guy, John Mayall, Sonny Boy Williamson, Big Maceo

# Ishman Bracey

**fact file**

**BORN** 1901

**DIED** 1970

**MUSICAL SELECTION**
**Ishman Bracey**
"Suitcase Full of Blues"
"Run To Me At Night"

The direct style adopted by Ishman Bracey complemented his direct personality perfectly

Ishman Bracey was, like Tommy Johnson, born in Hinds County, Mississippi, and his style was very much of the Delta variety. His guitar playing used drones and bent notes, constant rhythms and melodies echoing his vocal lines, and he claimed to have learned much of his guitar style from his Delta contemporary, Rubin Lacy.

His voice was raw and powerful, using a fast vibrato. Bracey was one of the many players who claimed to have acted as a guide for Blind Lemon Jefferson over the years, and is said to have aided him when he was traveling through the Delta area. Ishman made fourteen sides between 1928-29 in Jackson, Mississippi – one more than his colleague Tommy Johnson, who also split them between the Victor and Paramount companies. Bracey's intense singing style and his concentration on themes of loneliness and loss makes him one of the more memorable bluesmen of his generation. His career was truncated, however, by the pervasive economic downturn of the early 1930s, and after that he played music only occasionally.

In 1950 he turned to the church, adopting gospel music as his chosen form of musical expression wholeheartedly. Ordained as a minister in the 1950s, Ishman Bracey died in 1970 after collapsing at his home.

**SEE ALSO:** Blind Lemon Jefferson, Tommy Johnson

# Billy Branch

**fact file**

BORN 1953

MUSICAL SELECTION
Harp Attack!
Where's The Money

Billy Branch
continues the
long-standing
tradition of
passing on the
story and style
of the blues to
younger
generations

branch has been widely recognized as one of the most promising of the younger generation of blues harp players and has been publicly accorded such status by his elders in a number of ways, such as his inclusion on the blistering four-harmonica line-up of 1990's *Harp Attack!* on Alligator records, where he held his own with stalwarts Carey Bell, Junior Wells, and James Cotton, among others.

Branch was born in Great Lakes, Illinois, not far from Chicago, but moved to California with his family when quite young. Returning to Chicago in 1969 to study, Branch began playing with a local musician, Jimmy Walker, but made a major impact in 1973 when he played at the "Battle of the Harmonica" and emerged as the popular favorite (although he failed to win the

actual contest). Appearances and work as a session musician followed, and Branch put in valuable work experience with Johnny Winter, Willie Dixon, Lou Rawls, and others. He also formed Sons Of Blues with Lurrie Bell and Freddie Dixon, and that band's recordings (including *Where's The Money* on Red Beans) helped him establish an international reputation. Since then he has been a regular guest on top-flight Chicago musicians' sessions and a regular crowd-pleaser in clubs and at concerts and festivals. He travels extensively, impressing with his harp style, which takes the best from a number of Chicago blues harpists but most surely shows the imprint of people such as Carey Bell, Walter Horton, and Little Walter. Branch continues to perform and record.

**SEE ALSO:** Jimmy Walker, Johnny Winter, Willie Dixon, Lurrie Bell, Freddie Dixon

# Big Leon Brooks

**fact file**

**BORN** 1933

**DIED** 1982

**MUSICAL SELECTION**
Let's Go To Town

Big Leon Brooks owes much of his style to Little Walter Jacobs, but that can never take away from Brooks's natural talent

**b**rooks, born and raised in Sunflower, Mississippi, was one of the postwar Chicago harmonica players who helped make the scene such a rich one, but never quite broke through to the front line. Originally basing his style on Sonny Boy Williamson II (Rice Miller) and later on Little Walter, he ran his own groups and played with other leaders through the 1950s and into the 1960s, before leaving the business for over a decade.

Brooks arrived in Chicago in the early 1940s and hung out with his peer group on the streets, learning his trade. As a teenager he started frequenting in clubs on the South Side, even managing at one point to sit in with Muddy Waters at the Zanzibar. But his first regular work was with Freddie King as the 1950s

commenced. After a short stint leading his own unit he joined up with Jimmy Rogers, the first of a series of jobs as sideman in the groups of leaders like Willie Johnson, Otis Rush, and Robert Nighthawk. As the Chicago scene changed in the early 1960s, Brooks lost heart and changed careers, driving trucks for a living instead. He only came back on the scene in 1976, playing in North Side establishments and carving out a new audience for himself. In 1980 he appeared on the Alligator Records *Living Chicago Blues* compilation and also cut his first full album as a leader, *Let's Go To Town* – but by then his health had begun to give way, and in 1982 he succumbed to grave long-term heart and lung illnesses at the age of 49.

**SEE ALSO:** Muddy Waters, Freddie King, Jimmy Rogers, Otis Rush, Robert Nighthawk

# Lonnie Brooks

**fact file**

**BORN** 1933

**MUSICAL SELECTION**
Broke and Hungry
Bayou Lightning

Lonnie Brooks, occassionally known as "Guitar Junior," has only enjoyed real success in the later years of his career

rooks, a native of Dubuisson, Louisiana, has long used his Louisianan musical heritage to play a cross-genre patois of musical styles, including blues, Louisiana R&B, soul, and rock. His guitar style is able to go through a couple of these modes in the course of a single solo. After putting in the time to learn the guitar in his teens, Brooks spent his early career in the backing bands of the zydeco headliners Clifton Chenier and Lonesome Sundown, after which his talents were represented by a short-lived deal with the local Goldband label, from which emerged three singles in 1958 under the name "Guitar Junior," none of which made a dent outside the immediate locality. The same was the case with a single from 1959 for Mercury on which Katie Webster played the organ.

By 1960 Brooks had moved to Chicago and followed up on his contact with the Mercury label, going for a more Chicago-blues sound on subsequent singles (which bore the name Lonnie Brooks for the first time) for a variety of labels, including Mercury itself. He remained something of a local hero, even making a good blues album, in 1969, *Broke and Hungry*, for Capitol under his old name of Guitar Junior, which disappeared without trace, and it was not until the mid-1970s that Brooks began to establish a broader reputation. He was part of a tour package led by Willie Mabon which went to Europe in 1975, and made the obligatory album for Black & Blue while there, in the process making a start on a European career. Brooks finally began to make a noise in the US in 1979, when his debut album for Alligator, *Bayou Lightning*, was released to good notices. Centering himself between the Louisiana and Chicago blues styles, adding Southern melody to the drive of the Northern style, Brooks built himself a large live and record audience in the clubs and campuses of America and sustained his career growth in Europe. He remains a popular if largely unoriginal figure in the music today.

**SEE ALSO:** Lonesome Sundown, Katie Webster, Willie Mabon

# Big Bill Broonzy

broonzy, known to all and sundry before 1943 simply as "Big Bill," was one of Chicago's pre-eminent bluesmen of the 1920s and 1930s, as well as one of the most prolifically recorded artists of the period. Born in Mississippi but raised in Little Rock, Arkansas, Broonzy started out as a sharecropper and came into music playing the fiddle at country dances before serving in the armed forces during World War I. At war's end he returned to Arkansas and resumed his old existence – this time playing guitar instead of fiddle – and singing when the occasion demanded. As the 1920s progressed and the blues boom spread across America, Broonzy decided that the only way to succeed was to pull up stakes and move his family to Chicago. Once there he found a town teeming with talent and opportunity. He quickly established himself on the house-rent and general entertainment scene on Chicago's South Side. By 1926 he was making records, and began recording regularly two years later. Over the rest of the pre-WWII period Broonzy – under the name Big Bill, various other pseudonyms and the leadership of other bluesmen – became one of the most-recorded musicians of his time. A natural songwriter, he amassed a portfolio of over 300 tunes and became widely popular within the black community.

Broonzy's guitar style was driving, intricate and rhythmically precise – traits he probably culled from virtuosos like Lonnie Johnson and Blind Blake – while his creative disposition was usually good-spirited and happy. Big Bill preferred celebrating the good things in life rather than mourning the usual domestic and personal tragedies. An exception is the tense "Worrying You Off My Mind" from 1932, an early model for Howlin' Wolf's "Sittin' On Top of the World." Big Bill's mixture of hard-driving blues and hokum – liberally splashed at times with sexual double entendre – made him an important and formative figure around Chicago, helping mould the early city blues style. His fame was sufficiently wide for him to be used by music-loving philanthropist John Hammond during his 1939 Carnegie Hall Concert, "Spirituals to Swing."

Big Bill kept working in the greater Chicago area right through the 1940s, switching like many others at this time to electric guitar, although he continued to alternate between electric and acoustic. When peace and relative prosperity returned to postwar Europe, Broonzy began making trips overseas, becoming especially popular in France, and for many Europeans of the period he became the personification of the authentic blues. By this time, however, his urbane and entertaining style – now expanded to emphasize the type of folk and spiritual material favored by the Europeans – had been eclipsed in Chicago itself by a new generation of players. But Big Bill Broonzy remained very active up until his death, from throat cancer, in 1958. His autobiography, *Big Bill's Blues* (written with the aid of the Belgian Yannick Bruynogne), was published on both sides of the Atlantic – in both English and French – in 1957, making him the first blues performer to be so honored in his own lifetime.

## fact file

**BORN** 1893

**DIED** 1958

**MUSICAL SELECTION**
Remembering Big
Bill Broonzy
Good Times Tonight

Big Bill Broonzy worked as a soloist, accompanyist and talent scout, with hundreds of sides recorded during his career

**SEE ALSO:** Lonnie Johnson, Blind Blake, John Hammond

# Andrew Brown

Andrew Brown moved to Chicago from Mississippi with his mother in the 1950s but never forgot his blues roots, performing with such luminaries as Magic Sam

## fact file

**BORN** 1937

**DIED** 1985

**MUSICAL SELECTION**
Big Brown's Chicago
Blues
On The Case

born in Jackson, Mississippi, Brown was a blues guitarist who was also perfectly happy playing in other musical contexts – including jazz, gospel and soul, these last two genres being very evident in his "witness"-style singing. His guitar playing shows signs of a number of Chicago influences, but also the mark of B.B. King in its crisp tone and economical phrasing.

Brown met most of the top bluesmen working through his part of Mississippi when he was still very young, but also had experiences in other genres, including sitting in with Charlie Parker. He arrived in Chicago in 1946 and immediately gravitated to the music being produced on the West Side, especially by the likes of Magic Sam and Freddie King. Brown eventually played with these musicians as well as with jazz combos, including that of organist Baby Face Willette. By the end of the 1950s, Andrew Brown was one of the most respected guitarists on the scene. But a two-year stint in the Army took him away

from the blues scene at a time of great change – and when he returned in 1962, he found the newer sounds not to his taste. He settled into a day-job outside the music world, and only very occasionally became involved in performing. A trickle of singles appeared up to the early 1970s, but nothing much happened to bring Brown any real attention, and he resigned himself to a more or less permanent life in the steel mills.

However, after a heart attack and a serious back injury prevented him from working in the late 1970s, Brown was looking to take up his music career again to earn some money. Ironically, tracks on the *Living Chicago Blues* series and two albums in the early 1980s – *Big Brown's Chicago Blues* (1982) and *On The Case* (1985), both made for the European audience – brought him back into the spotlight to the delight of blues fans everywhere, but by then it was too late; before 1985 was out, Andrew Brown was dead, a victim of cancer.

**SEE ALSO:** B.B. King, Magic Sam, Freddie King

# Clarence "Gatemouth" Brown

Taught by his musician father, Brown has been a prolific performer and recording artist throughout his career, concentrating on guitar and fiddle

**b**rown was born in Louisiana but in infancy he was taken to Texas. Raised in a musical family, he was playing fiddle before the age of 10, subsequently going on to concentrate on the guitar, although he was accomplished on the drums and harmonica as well. While still in his teens he became a familiar figure around Orange County playing in a variety of bands, none of which made sufficient impact to become more widely known. World War II interrupted his musical career, but on his return Brown got the break he needed when playing one night in Houston for T-Bone Walker, a fellow Texan and star of stage and records. The owner of the club, Don Robey, quickly became Brown's manager and, by 1947, owner of Peacock, the record company Brown exclusively recorded for until 1960. Gatemouth's many singles for the Peacock label were mostly modest sellers (only 1949's "Mary Is Fine" penetrated the national R&B top ten). But as he formed his own musical imprint from a number of typically Texan sources, Brown became a respected and influential blues stylist in his own right.

Brown himself always cites T-Bone Walker as his mentor and prime source of inspiration, but is also quick to insist that he is not content to play within just one genre, intead using a rich mix of Texan-based styles to produce his own sound. Brown has taken elements of Western Swing, blues, zydeco, jazz and country music and woven them into both his guitar playing and his overall blues concept. Although his career suffered a temporary eclipse during the 1960s, he was discovered by European audiences in the 1970s and made regular trips, often as part of the blues tour packages which were beginning to garner great popularity in France and Germany. His career renewed, Brown started making records again in the US, earning recognition as one of the few authentic blues voices of the immediate post-war period who could still deliver the goods. Gatemouth Brown continues to tour and record to this day.

## fact file

**BORN** 1924

**MUSICAL SELECTION**
"Mary Is Fine"

**SEE ALSO:** Ruth Brown

# Charles Brown

Charles Brown is an exception to so many blues "rules" that it might be better simply to write a new rule book just for him. For a start, he has rarely "raised his voice in anger," relying instead on a soft-voiced expression of emotion which owed as much to Nat Cole and T-Bone Walker as to anyone operating on the blues circuit in the early 1940s. In that sense, he is a link between the urbane Cole and the more sophisticated blues of Jimmy Witherspoon. Brown is exceptional in other ways as well, not least in that he was born into a middle-class black family in Texas – one which demanded that its offspring go out into the world with a good education.

And Brown certainly did this, completing college equipped to teach high school math and chemistry. During his education he was also soaking up the musical message laid down in the early 1940s by a series of fine musicians: Nat Cole and his popular trio, the boogie pianists Meade Lux Lewis and Pete Johnson, the urbane blues of Jay McShann and his vocalist Walter Brown, and the well-crafted arrangements of Andy Kirk's Clouds of Joy. Charles Brown taught for a while in Texas before deciding to head out west, arranging for a transfer to the Bay Area and a stint at California University. But by 1944 he was living in L.A., holding down a menial day-job while trying to get gigs as a pianist at night. His break came with Johnny Moore's Three Blazers. This group, modelled on Nat Cole's trio, had a hit in 1945 with Brown's own "Drifting Blues" – a song which he'd written years before – recorded for Aladdin. Brown's soft vocals and easy piano style created an instant hit, and the Blazers enjoyed three straight years of success. They (and Brown) helped launch the new taste for smooth, slow blues to complement the plethora of frenetic R&B sides which were also proving popular juke-box hits, inspired by Lionel Hampton and others.

The Blazers broke up in 1948 and Brown went it alone, consolidating his career with a string of hit singles for Aladdin including "Black Night" (1951) and "Hard Times" (1952). But the bubble burst with the advent of rock 'n' roll, and Brown's contract with Aladdin expired as the hits dried up. His fall from grace was quick, and the man who had been an influential inspiration to a generation of black crooners and soul singers dropped from sight. Brown's style changed little during the next thirty years, and long periods were spent once again holding down day jobs to keep his career on track. But during the 1980s there were signs of renewed interest from the public and the industry, and Brown began appearing at the New York club, Tramps. This led to his appearance in the film documentary, *All That Rhythm and Those Blues*, along with Ruth Brown, another veteran on the way back up again. An album, *One More For The Road*, came out on Alligator in 1986, and as the 1990s opened Brown was hired by long-time fan Bonnie Raitt to open for her on her US tour. Still doing the same basic thing with the same quality and integrity, Brown was introduced to a brand new audience. His comeback album, *All My Life*, followed in 1990, recorded for Bullseye Blues and featuring stars like Clifford Solomon, Keith Copeland and Heywood Henry, with a guest appearance from Ruth Brown. Charles Brown has continued to record new albums and tour since then, keeping his new career buoyant and his public entertained as of old.

**fact file**

**BORN** 1922

**MUSICAL SELECTION**
One More For The Road

Charles Brown, a charismatic and charming performer, began as a chemistry teacher, choosing music as a more lucrative career option

**SEE ALSO:** T-Bone Walker

# Nappy Brown

**fact file**

BORN 1929

MUSICAL SELECTION
Tore Up
"The Right Time"

Nappy Brown's deep gospel-influenced vocals kept him popular with blues fans throughout his career

brown was born in Charlotte, North Carolina, and, as with so many others, his first experience of music was in the church. An inquisitive teenager, he learned about the low life and the music often accompanying it by hanging around the Charlotte jukes and chicken shacks, but his first experience as a performer was as a member of the Golden Bells gospel quartet. This experience and others like it left a deep mark on his music and his vocal style when he switched to the blues.

He came to the attention of Savoy Records' Herman Lubinsky as a member of the Heavenly Lights gospel quartet, recording with them for that label in 1955. Lubinsky also saw that Brown could handle the blues and signed him to a solo contract. His third single for the company, cut in 195, "Don't Be Angry," was a major R&B hit, and Brown concentrated for the next four years on perfecting his R&B formula of roaring rockers and soulful,

gospel-drenched ballads. His label, Savoy, constantly sold the cover rights to more established artists (often white groups), and Brown slowly realized that he was not making progress. This was crystallized by his 1957 version of "(The Night Time Is) The Right Time," a classic blues song and a popular number world-wide. It was immediately covered by Ray Charles in a similar arrangement and was a massive hit. Brown's version disappeared. By the early 1960s Brown had also disappeared, going back to Charlotte and taking up the threads of his gospel career.

Screamin' Jay Hawkins encouraged him to return to the blues in the early 1980s, and a European tour confirmed what he had heard. Brown made the Alligator album, *Tore Up*, in 1984, and has since then been recording and performing regularly on both sides of the Atlantic. Today his blues pedigree is more evident than at any previous time in his career.

**SEE ALSO:** Ray Charles, Tinsley Ellis

# Roy Brown

**fact file**

**BORN** 1925

**DIED** 1981

**MUSICAL SELECTION**
"Good Rockin' Tonight"
**Complete Imperial Recordings**

"Roy Brown and His Mighty Mighty Men," from a publicity shot celebrating his golden voice

**b**rown, born in New Orleans, was exposed at the earliest age to black church music, singing in church groups while still a young boy. As he grew he became aware of the multitude of musics in the air in prewar New Orleans, and during his early teenage years he became known for his powerful vocal style as a member of a string of gospel groups. On the death of his mother in 1942 Brown decided to move to Los Angeles. This decision coincided with a desire to take up professional boxing, and for a while Brown made his living in the ring. Yet music remained his first love and in 1945 he entered a string of singing contests, eventually winning one at the Million Dollar Theater. Buoyed by this, in 1946 he moved to Galveston, Texas, in an effort to kick-start a musical career, but within a year he was back in New Orleans, touting a song he'd written called "Good Rockin' Tonight." After the usual tribulations, he convinced Cecil Gant of its worth and made a recording of the song in July 1947 which made it into the R&B top 20, although Wynonie Harris, the star of the moment, made a cover version which outsold Brown's.

Yet this did not discourage the singer, whose unique and earthy combination of solid rhythm and gospel-inspired vocals anticipated Ray Charles by nearly 10 years and helped reinvent the rhythm-and-blues genre in a way that ultimately pointed to the formation of rock 'n' roll. Brown enjoyed a sequence of hit singles for the rest of the 1940s and remained an R&B star well into the 1950s, but although his most famous song was one of the first to be covered by a young man named Elvis Presley, he failed to make the transition himself to the new style and by the close of the 1950s was largely forgotten. Brown was a man possessed of considerable onstage charisma and was not above the most blatant crowd-pleasing antics, but his time had passed: although he attempted comebacks in the 1970s, his records failed to sell and his personal appearances ignited no great popular demand. He died in 1981 from a heart attack: had he lived another decade he would no doubt have experienced a rediscovery of his talents.

**SEE ALSO:** Ray Charles

# Ruth Brown

**fact file**

**BORN** 1928

**MUSICAL SELECTION**
"Teardrops From My
Eyes"
"Lucky Lips"

Like many of
her peers, Ruth
Brown's blues
singing career
touched on
gospel, R&B and
even rock 'n' roll

uth Brown was initially a big-voiced and enthusiastic urban-blues belter in the Dinah Washington mode who progressed from blues to R&B and thence to the rock 'n' roll charts before a temporary retirement in the 1960s. Since her return to a musical career in the late 1970s she has cast her net wide, even appearing on Broadway, but most often performing in a jazz setting.

Brown was born in Portsmouth, Virginia, and began her singing in her father's church. The influence of this early experience is evident in her work right up to her first retirement. She followed Sister Rosetta Tharpe into the Lucky Millinder Band in the mid-1940s and made an immediate impression. After marrying Jimmy Brown and taking on Blanche Calloway as her manager, Brown appeared in New York and drew a lot of attention. However, immediately after signing for Atlantic

records in 1948, she was involved in a car crash, and it was close to a year before she was ready to resume her career. Her first record, "So Long," sold well and was the beginning of a run of 23 chart successes for her with Atlantic. Her biggest hit, "Teardrops From My Eyes," was one of 1950's major R&B hits, while 1953's "Wild Wild Young Men" suggests the type of hybrid that Ray Charles was about to make famous. Brown spent much of 1953 and 1954 out touring with bands such as Count Basie and Billy Eckstine, and was one of the hottest acts in the country. With the advent of rock 'n' roll, Brown shifted her style, landing a hit with a Lieber–Stoller song, "Lucky Lips," in 1957, and by the time she left Atlantic in 1961 she was moving toward the supper-club approach. Her comeback in the 1970s and up to the current day has been an immensely successful one, but falls outside the scope of this book.

**SEE ALSO:** Ray Charles

# George "Mojo" Buford

**fact file**

BORN 1929

MUSICAL SELECTION
State of the
Blues Harp
Harpslinger

George "Mojo" Buford received his nickname for fulfilling requests to play "Got My Mojo Workin'"

harmonica ace Buford gained most from his long off-and-on association with Muddy Waters, which began in 1955 when Buford's band, the Savage Boys, was used by Waters as his substitute band in Chicago while Waters himself was out of town. This association didn't end until Waters' death in 1983.

Buford is one of that seemingly endless stream of bluesmen to have been born in Mississippi (Buford comes from Hernando) and has been equal in his young enthusiasm for both gospel and blues music, which he heard all around him and participated in as well. Buford moved to Memphis at the age of 15, where he quickly heard all the top local musicians and, after being bowled over by Little Walter's "Juke" single, decided that harp blues was going to be his meal ticket as well. A move to Chicago in 1952 after several visits there led to his 1955 meeting with Waters. By 1959 Buford was a regular in Waters' own band, staying with him until

1962, when he resettled in Minneapolis and ran his own band, gigging all over town. Buford's first run of singles and an album came during this period, and for the majority of the 1960s he prospered in Minneapolis, a short return to the Muddy Waters band in 1967 aside.

Buford got few opportunities to record whole albums during this period and his national profile remained low: as the blues began to sink in the 1970s he went back to Waters in 1971–72, but his main activities were still with his own Mojo Buford Band in and around Minneapolis. It was not until Waters had died and Buford became involved in some of the many tributes across the United States to the blues great that his own abilities became more widely appreciated. Since then there have been albums on JSP and Rooster Blues as his Little Walter-based style became more properly appreciated.

# Jimmy Burns

**fact file**

**BORN** 1943

**MUSICAL SELECTION**
Leaving Here Walking

His career as strong as ever, Jimmy Burns remains a strong advocate of the true blues tradition

burns is a journeyman blues musician based in Chicago who uses a personal combination of Delta and Chicago blues to create a convincing if understated style and who plays part-time on the current Chicago scene. Born in the Delta, into the same family as the Detroit bluesman Eddie Burns, Jimmy got his first guitar when he was around 10. Listening to jukebox records, he picked up licks and songs from stars such as Muddy Waters and John Lee Hooker, and when he moved on to Chicago (linking up with members of his family who had already made the trip) he spent time playing and singing on street corners for change.

Making a quickly forgotten single in 1959, Burns returned to the studios every few years, but nothing of great moment was made, and he gradually drifted away from his blues style toward the soul that was becoming the dominant force in popular black music in the mid-1960s. He stuck with soul until the early 1970s, when he was in the middle of raising a family and consolidating his day job. At this time he turned once again to the blues he'd loved in earlier times, gigging around Chicago's north side with the guitarist Glen Davis. The steady work and exposure gave him the impetus to join up with a young band, Rockin' Johnny and the Lazy Boys, and this group, with Burns as its singer and co-guitarist, began to make an impact on the north and west sides. This finally led to his making his first album as a leader, *Leaving Here Walking*, for Delmark in 1997, a record that reveals him to be a guitarist with a deft touch and a singer prepared to deliver subtlety as well as punch. His Delta roots are revealed in his often delicate picking, while the drive of the band shows it to be a real Chicago concern. Burns continues to run his career out of Chicago today.

**SEE ALSO:** Muddy Waters, John Lee Hooker

# R L Burnside

fact file

**BORN** 1926

**MUSICAL SELECTION**
Hill Country Blues
Mr Wizard

Burnside, pictured with his nephew Cedric (r.), enjoyed performing with family members in Sound Machine

b urnside is a musician whose career came to fruition in the postwar period but whose musical style is a throwback to the Mississippi bluesmen he heard and admired in his own youth. Born in Coldwater, Mississippi, Burnside took to music at an early age, listening to the musicians around him and learning to play the guitar in the manner of neighboring players such as Bukka White, Son Hibler, and, especially, Mississippi Fred McDowell. In his teens Burnside began playing the local juke joints and getting a reputation for himself, using the same single-chord, highly rhythmic and often open-ended structures his mentors employed. Hearing on the radio R&B and the new blues being made by younger players living up North in the immediate postwar years, Burnside moved to Chicago for a time and attempted to get established on the burgeoning scene there, but music work was scarce and he had to take day jobs to get by. He returned South at the start of the following decade, keeping to the same playing pattern as he'd employed as a youth, singing and performing at parties and jukes. He remained a local Mississippi blues celebrity until August 1967, when the researcher George Mitchell discovered

him while on a trip South: some tracks appeared on an Arhoolie anthology, *Mississippi Delta Blues Vol. 2* (1967).

After this Burnside began receiving regular calls to play at festivals and concerts in America and Europe – his first trip to Europe took place in 1971 – and gradually became a well-known international name energetically playing the older style of music. He made a number of records in Europe while being unable to attract the attention of record labels in the US. The Dutch company Swingmaster made two late-1980s records, *Hill Country Blues* and *Plays and Sings the Mississippi Delta* and Burnside has appeared on a number of other labels.

He finally cracked it back home by recording for the Mississippi label, Fat Possum, in 1991 and 1994, the latter being *Mr Wizard*, a typically abrasive and varied set of slashing, visceral blues. Burnside has also appeared with the band, Sound Machine, composed largely of members of his extended family. Now in his seventies, he continues to actively pursue his musical career, creating excitement wherever he performs his muscular and down-home electric blues.

**SEE ALSO:** Bukka White, Fred McDowell

# George "Wild Child" Butler

A true "Wild Child", George Butler took to the road with his harmonica in hand very early on

## fact file

BORN 1936

MUSICAL SELECTION
These Mean Old Blues

Singer/harmonica stylist Butler has been patching together a career in the blues since the late 1950s when he was in his early twenties in Alabama. Possessed of a style that owes a great deal to the earlier harmonica greats of harp blues like Hammie Nix and John Lee "Sonny Boy" Williamson, Butler traveled widely before settling in Chicago in the mid-1960s and attempting to enjoy a career as a leader. His late arrival on the scene and the abundance of harp virtuosos in Chicago made such a career path difficult, to say the least, but in recent years his persistence has seen its reward in a belated recognition of his talents.

Born in Autaugaville, Alabama, Butler derived his nickname from his mother as a comment on his juvenile behavior. He grew up on a sharecropper's farm and prior to his teen years picked up harmonica from a family friend. By his mid-teens he'd left home and headed for Montgomery, where in 1963 he paid for his own recording sessions – four sides which appeared later on other labels.

He'd also attracted the admiration of Lightnin' Hopkins, who was to use him as a sideman during this decade. By 1966 he'd moved on to Chicago, signing a deal with Jewel Records of Shreveport, which produced some high-quality singles but had little impact outside of a small distribution area. A similar problem with distribution marred the sales of a 1968 album for Mercury, *Keep On Doing What You're Doing*. A mid-1970s effort, *Funky Butt Lover*, disappeared without trace. Butler moved to Ontario in the early 1980s as well as touring regularly with Jimmy Rogers.

His first record in 15 years, *These Mean Old Blues*, was recorded in England in 1991 and released in the US on Bullseye Blues. Its combination of tough Chicago-based Muddy Waters-type group playing and a more traditional harp style, pulled together with a voice like a single-malt whiskey, has given Butler a new lease on his professional career, one that is well deserved. Follow-up albums and live appearances have given him a profile undreamed-of ten years ago.

SEE ALSO: Sonny Boy Williamson, Lightnin' Hopkins, Jimmy Rogers, Muddy Waters

# Butterbeans and Susie

Butterbeans and Susie
formed one of the longest
partnerships in blues history

t he vaudeville-based duo known as Butterbeans and Susie (aka Jody and Susie Edwards) enjoyed popularity in the "race" market of the 1920s and early 1930s, mixing their on-stage patter with some admirable blues singing, most notably from Susie, whose big alto voice had an unmistakable authority and panache.

Little is known of the duo's lives prior to their marriage in 1917, though it is thought that Jody Edwards ("Butterbeans") hailed from Georgia, and Susie Hawthorn was born in Florida. The two made an effective comedy partnership, using stand-up routines and comedy songs to amuse their audiences. The pair toured on the TOBA circuit (short for Theatre Owners Booking Association, although the circuit's black performers joked that the acronym stood for "Tough on Black Asses"), appearing with many other stars in the process and earning wide popularity. Their recording debut was in 1924 for Okeh, and from the start Susie took the lead vocals, leaving Butterbeans for the most part to deliver the one-liners, a satisfactory arrangement

for all. The duo made many records, heading up various recording groups which were often fronted by regular accompanist Eddie Heywood and included such future luminaries as Louis Armstrong, Louis Metcalf, and Joe "King" Oliver. Butterbeans and Susies' recordings – which halted in 1930 but resumed after WWII – are an important illustration of the strong connections between classic blues and the vaudeville of the day. They range from stately rhythms to talking comedy routines to the occasional outburst of powerful singing, all backed invariably by a two-fisted pianist at home in blues, barrelhouse, or jazz.

Butterbeans and Susie kept going through the Depression, staying on the circuit until it expired in the late 1930s. They also enjoyed long-term residencies at the Grand Theater, Chicago and, later, the Apollo in New York, and stayed on the bill well into the 1950s. By that time health problems were beginning to surface for Jody, leading to his retirement several years before Susie's death in 1963; he followed his wife four years later.

## fact file

**AKA** JODY EDWARDS

**BORN** 1895
**DIED** 1967

**AKA** SUSIE EDWARDS
NÉE HAWTHORN

**BORN** 1896
**DIED** 1963

**MUSICAL SELECTION**
**Butterbeans and Susie**

**SEE ALSO:** Trixie Smith

# Paul Butterfield

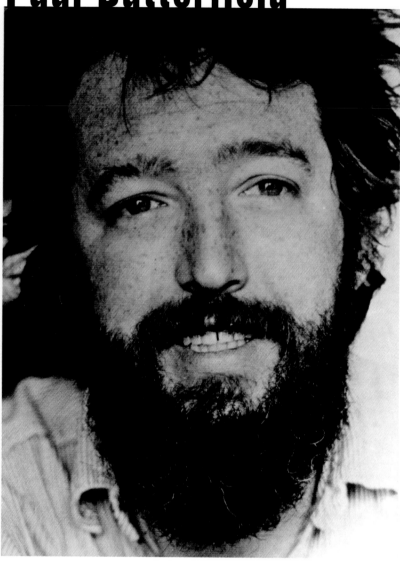

Founding member of the famous Paul Butterfield Blues Band, Paul Butterfield always kept close to the blues tradition he loved

## fact file

**BORN** 1942

**DIED** 1987

**MUSICAL SELECTION**
The Resurrection of
Pigboy Crabshaw

butterfield was an important catalyst for the emergent young white American blues players of the early and mid-1960s who were listening to the powerful electrified blues of people such as Muddy Waters, B.B. King, Little Walter, John Lee Hooker, Howlin' Wolf, and many others, and were wishing to emulate their urban-blues heroes. Butterfield was able to observe and listen to such men in person, having been born and raised in Chicago, the city where the majority of these role models were based.

Butterfield chose the harmonica as his instrument in his early teens, and by the beginning of the 1960s he was producing sounds from his harp and vocal performances that were convincing enough to spur the formation of a band playing the hard-edged music he wanted to be involved in. This band was the Paul Butterfield Blues Band, formed in 1963. By 1965 it had as members Mike Bloomfield and Elvin Bishop and was making its widely imitated and influential self-titled debut album for the Elektra label. It also supported Dylan for his first electric performance, in 1965. Bloomfield was gone within two

years, but Butterfield stuck with the formula in which he believed, creating a second classic album, *East-West*, in 1966, before Bloomfield quit, where the marriage of rock and blues was at its most enticing. After this he began exploring other blues-based areas, as evidenced on 1968's *The Resurrection of Pigboy Crabshaw*, where R&B and soul, in the form of a horn section, was prominent. This diversifying, allied to the increasing fragmentation of the rock scene of the late 1960s, led to a falling in the band's popular standing. It never recovered from this, despite further albums and an appearance at Woodstock in 1969. The band broke up in 1973 and Butterfield went on to form the band Better Days. After a couple of not wholly convincing records this band, too, broke up, and by the mid-1970s Butterfield was adrift. His decline aided by alcohol and drugs, Butterfield struggled to pull his career together again, and, though he managed a couple more albums and sporadic touring, his best days were well gone by the time of his death, from a drug- and alcohol-induced heart attack, in 1987.

**SEE ALSO:** Mike Bloomfield, Elvin Bishop

# Gus Cannon

Gus Cannon, the son of slaves, built his first banjo using an old pan and an abandoned guitar neck

One of the most popular offshoots of the classic country-blues style was the jug band, popular during the 1920s owing to its lively sounds and endless humor and hokum. One of the most famous of the jug bands, certainly from the Memphis area, was the band led by Gus Cannon, Cannon's Jug Stompers, which enjoyed a three-year recording stint from 1927 to 1930.

Cannon came from Red Banks, Mississippi, and was taught banjo by the Alabaman Bud Jackson. He made his own first instrument on the plantation by adapting a frying pan. Around 1910 he began playing on traveling medicine shows and the like, joining up regularly with Noah Lewis, a talented harmonica player. He also came into contact with other bluesmen such as Furry Lewis and Will Shade. Cannon opted to stay in Memphis around 1916, playing banjo and singing on the streets and in the usual medicine shows. During the rise to popularity of the slide guitar technique Cannon learned how to adapt the banjo to such slide playing, resulting in a highly unusual sound. By the mid-1920s Cannon had rigged a jug around

his neck to add fashionable rhythmic push to his performances. Soon after, he began forming the first edition of Cannon's Jug Stompers, featuring Cannon, Ashley Thompson, and Noah Lewis. Cannon's Jug Stompers recorded prolifically, mostly for Victor, between 1927 and 1930, and were consistent sellers for the label. But like so many others they were flattened by the onset of the Depression. Cannon returned to his former life, playing on streets and with occasional gatherings of Stompers, but he had to wait until 1956 for an upsurge in fortunes, when he was one of the first to benefit from the nascent folk music movement's interest in the older artists. He recorded in that year for Folkways, accompanied by Will Shade and Milton Ruby, and also as an honorary member of Shades's reconvened Memphis Jug Band. He also began appearing at the Folk Festivals, which older blues artists frequented. One of his songs, "Walk Right In," became a folk hit in 1962. He remained popular until his death, appearing in the occasional documentary about early black music and on a couple of vinyl compilations.

## fact file

**BORN** 1883

**DIED** 1979

**MUSICAL SELECTION**
"Walk Right In"
**Complete Cannon's Jug Stompers, 1927-30**

**SEE ALSO:** Walter "Furry" Lewis

# Cliff Carlisle

**fact file**

**BORN** 1904

**DIED** 1983

**MUSICAL SELECTION**
Blues Yodler and Steel
Guitar Wizard

Cliff Carlisle (l.) pictured with his brother Bill, created a sound that crossed over many genres

C arlisle is one of a handful of white artists operating in the 1920s and 1930s who crossed easily and with conviction between country and blues genres. Writing mostly his own material and regularly using the harmonic framework of the blues and related music, Carlisle was able to blend the yodels of "the singing brakeman" Jimmie Rodgers into the lonesome sounds of the blues within a single song. For this alone his significance should not be dismissed.

Debates as to who introduced the yodel into American folk musics still rage today, but, even if Rodgers heard people like Tommy Johnson do it before them, their twin inspiration seems to have been the traveling groups of Swiss and Austrian folk singers whose paths across the US in the 1920s have now been well documented, and Rodgers's huge hits undoubtedly inspired many more people to imitate him than vice versa. Certainly, Carlisle started with Rodgers as a model, taking an even more carefree and risqué approach than Rodgers: his lyrics often sail much closer to the wind in sexual imagery and other earthy topics than Rodgers and his other acolytes dreamed. Carlisle's vocals were clean, clear,

and full of personality, his guitar playing a strange amalgam of Hawaiian and Delta slide steel guitar (or dobro), while an accompanist would keep the rhythm chugging along in a way at times not far removed from Leadbelly. Carlisle himself saw his music as a cross between hillbilly and blues. Born in Spencer County, Kentucky, he teamed up with a Louisville construction worker, Wilbur Ball, in 1924, and the two of them toured constantly as a duo, playing hillbilly and Hawaiian style. By 1930 Carlisle was debuting as a solo recording artist for Gennett, the start of a successful career in which he would cut more than 300 sides, either solo or in duets. His "blue yodeling" was very popular in the Depression years, but as the decade progressed its popularity waned, and Carlisle moved further from the blues toward the hillbilly and country element, earning him long runs on radio in Memphis and even an appearance in a film "short" in 1937. By the 1950s Carlisle had retired from music, playing only for his own amusement and taking up painting in his retirement. A brief return to performing in the 1960s only reconfirmed his determination to keep music to a part-time hobby in his life.

**SEE ALSO:** Tommy Johnson, Leadbelly

# Leroy Carr

**fact file**

**BORN** 1905

**DIED** 1935

**MUSICAL SELECTION**
Leroy Carr
Hurry Down Sunshine

Leroy Carr, pictured here in the year he died, brought an urbane style to blues piano

Carr's career was relatively brief, but his was a key contribution to the burgeoning urban blues style which was largely formulated in Chicago in the second half of the 1920s. His light but emotion-soaked vocals, along with his deft piano-playing and tight working relationship with guitarist Scrapper Blackwell, gave others a winning formula which would be embellished but remain largely unchanged until after WWII.

Carr came from Nashville, Tennessee, but in early youth his family moved to Indianapolis, at the time a significant urban center for blacks and for blues. Self-taught, Carr went out on the road early, playing any number of gigs, from circuses to bars and parties. Along the way he acquired a wife and a demonstrated liking for liquor (later celebrated in "Sloppy Drunk Blues"). During the 1920s, still using Indianapolis as his base, he became friendly with another Indianapolis bluesman, Scrapper Blackwell. In 1928 this team made a single for Vocalion, "How Long-How Long Blues," which became an instant best-seller (claimed to be over a million copies); Carr's keening vocals were perfectly matched by his piano and by Blackwell's intricate but driving guitar. The duo enjoyed an unbroken string of successes across a range of material – most of it written by Carr and embracing many moods and subjects drawn from everyday life – including "Carried Water for the Elephant," a tongue-in-cheek, uptempo number verging on children's rhyme. Carr and Blackwell recorded prolifically between 1928 and February 1935, cutting more than 160 sides. But during this period Leroy Carr's love of the bottle became uncontrolled alcoholism; in April 1935, at the age of 30, he died of alcohol poisoning, still at the height of his career.

SEE ALSO: Scrapper Blackwell

# Bo Carter

**fact file**

**BORN** 1893

**DIED** 1964

**MUSICAL SELECTION**
"Corrina Corrina"
"Banana In Your Fruit Basket"

A part of the Mississippi Sheiks, Bo Carter, seen here in the 1930s, was not appreciated in his lifetime but recorded prolifically

C arter aka Armentier Chatmon was the leading light of the talented Chatmon family, which was influential in the Mississippi blues in the 1920s and 1930s and formed the kernel of the Mississippi Sheiks string band. Although he performed and recorded with the Sheiks, on guitar and violin and occasionally singing, he also recorded prolifically during the 1930s under his pseudonym of Bo Carter, mostly restricting the accompaniment to his own guitar playing. His songs were often ribald and upbeat, as befits an ex-member of a string band.

Carter came to maturity in a highly talented and musical family, and performed with the Sheiks for over 10 years. He suffered from deteriorating eyesight. Too poor to have corrective surgery, he was effectively blind by the end of the 1920s. By then he had made his debut on record as a leader (two years before the debut of the Sheiks), on Brunswick with a group featuring Charlie McCoy which bore a strong resemblance to the family band. The songs recorded included a very early version of the traditional

blues, "Corrina Corrina." By 1930 his own recordings were pared down to himself with Walter Jacobs accompanying on a second guitar; by 1931 his repertoire was becoming bawdy, with tracks like "Banana In Your Fruit Basket," "Pin In Your Cushion," and "Ramrod Daddy" leaving little to the imagination. Carter was capable of more than just ribald material and country dance music, as he displayed from time to time during his recordings in the 1930s for Okeh and Bluebird such as "To Her Burying Ground" and "Trouble In Blues," but the emphasis was rarely on such subject matter for long. Carter traveled extensively during this period, often playing on street corners, and his recordings come from New York, Memphis, Atlanta, and New Orleans, to name a few centers. By the early 1940s his personal extension of string-band hokum had begun to pall in his audience's ears, and he disappeared from the blues scene by the end of World War II. Living in penury in his later years, Carter died poverty-stricken and largely forgotten in Memphis in 1964.

**SEE ALSO:** Mississippi Sheiks, Charlie McCoy

# John Cephas

**fact file**

**BORN** 1930

**MUSICAL SELECTION**
Dog Days of August

Though often treating music as a sideline, John Cephas came into his own during the 1970s alongside Chief Ellis and Phil Wiggins

uitarist/singer Cephas, although treating his blues career as a part-time affair (his day job is in civil engineering), has made an impact as a latter-day interpreter of the older country-blues styles, both as a solo performer and as one half of the duo Cephas and Wiggins, with Phil Wiggins supplying harmonica. The obvious parallel is with Sonny Terry and Brownie McGhee, and while Cephas is similarly influenced by the Piedmont stylist Blind Boy Fuller, thus emphasizing the affinity, his own guitar style contains more ragtime elements than McGhee's, while his voice is of a different, much deeper timbre.

Cephas was born in Bowling Green, Kentucky, the son of a Baptist preacher, and he was a boy with a lot of natural musical talent. Picking up guitar skills from the records of players such as Fuller, Buddy Moss, and Blind Blake, Cephas developed his own

twist on the Piedmont style, augmenting this in the early 1970s when he began appearing with the barrelhouse pianist, Chief Ellis. Cephas and Ellis performed and recorded together before meeting, in 1976, harp player Wiggins, after which the duo became a threesome performing under the name Barrelhouse Rockers. Ellis's death in 1977 reduced the trio to a duo, with Cephas and Wiggins deciding to make a go of it in the new format. Tours with various packages have spread the duo's reputation far beyond the USA, and their first recordings together were made in Germany. An American album was finally produced in 1987, *Dog Days of August*, which garnered domestic praise and awards. Cephas and Wiggins continue to perform as a duo while Cephas also nurtures solo projects, both live and in the studio. Both men are still active on the blues scene.

**SEE ALSO:** Sonny Terry, Brownie McGhee, Buddy Moss, Blind Blake

# Ray Charles

C harles has not inhabited the middle ground of blues, but the blues, along with gospel and the jumping jazz of such luminaries as Nat King Cole and Louis Jordan, are at the very root of his early and greatest musical achievements, when he produced a new mixture of musical styles to pioneer modern R&B and soul with a string of massive hits through the 1950s. A change of direction in the 1960s took him to superstar status but took him largely out of the blues firmament. However, his impact has been so deep that traces of his style can be found in the majority of soul- and blues-based performers today.

Brother Ray was born in Albany, Georgia, but moved to Greenville, Florida, with his mother when still in nappies. Desperately poor, she was unable to find treatment for Ray's youthful glaucoma, and he was blind by the age of seven, but not before he'd seen his only brother drown in a washtub. By then, he was already interested in music, swapping his concentration between church and boogie music and learning a number of instruments at the St Augustine School for the Blind. Listening to records in local juke joints, he heard a massive range of black music, from big-band swing to older blues masters. On the radio he developed a passion for Grand Ole Opry broadcasts – a significant passion, considering his 1960s music. Ray was now an only child, and his mother and father were both dead before he was out of his teens. A move to Seattle in 1948 led to his forming a trio in imitation of Nat Cole and Charles Brown, and his performing style at this time hewed closely to their urbane West Coast models. Moving to LA in 1950 at the behest of Downbeat/Swingtime Records, for whom he'd signed in 1949, Charles went out on the road with many blues acts, including Lowell Fulson, attracting attention as he went. In 1952 Atlantic Records bought out Charles's Swingtime contract and assigned Jesse Stone to produce Charles. They made good records but nothing mold-breaking until Charles went to New Orleans in 1953 and experimented for a while before moving on to Dallas and putting together his own band. In late 1954 he recorded "I Got A Woman" in his new style and had instant success. From then until he left Atlantic in 1960 he had an unbroken string of R&B/soul hits, including "Drown In My Own Tears," "Hallelujah I Love Her So," "What'd I Say," "Tell The Truth," and "I Believe To My Soul," the last being one of his deepest blues-groove songs of all. Along with all this Charles made a series of outstanding albums in other genres, from the Quincy Jones-arranged big-band sessions to the two small-group jazz albums with Milt Jackson where, on piano or sax, Charles digs deep into his primal blues experience.

With his switch to ABC-Paramount in 1961, Charles at first stuck to old habits, enjoying worldwide success with songs like "Hit The Road Jack" and "One Mint Julep," but a sea-change in 1962 saw him covering country songs backed by orchestras and female choirs. It was in this period that he enjoyed his greatest commercial success, going number one worldwide with "Crying Time" and "I Can't Stop Loving You." After that Charles settled into his role as all-around music legend and entertainer, his live shows often unstoppable explosions of music, his records often disappointing, utilizing poor material. He has had many TV specials dedicated to him and appeared in movies, including *The Blues Brothers* in 1988. He continues to lead an active career outside the blues genre.

## fact file

**BORN** 1930

**MUSICAL SELECTION**
What'd I Say
The Genius of Ray
Charles

Ray Charles' genius lay in his ability to bring together many influences and create a sound uniquely his own.

SEE ALSO: Louis Jordan, Charles Brown, Lowell Fulson

# Eric Clapton

**fact file**

**BORN** 1945

**MUSICAL SELECTION**
Layla
From The Cradle

Eric Clapton began with the blues at the age of 14 and returned to these roots more than 35 years later

C lapton has long been recognized as the outstanding blues guitar talent to have emerged from the British beat-and-blues boom of the 1960s. Born in the Home Counties of England, Clapton came to the guitar late, picking up a determined interest in the instrument while at Art School.

After searching out for a group to play in and a style to adopt, Clapton found the Yardbirds and modern blues in short succession, becoming uncommonly fluent at approximating such different styles as B.B. and Albert King, Robert Johnson, and Muddy Waters by the mid-1960s. Clapton brought his natural affinity with like souls in the blues movement to the fore when he left the Yardbirds in 1965 and joined John Mayall's Bluesbreakers. Although with Mayall for around a year, Clapton cut the classic BritBlues album, *Blues Breakers with Eric Clapton* (with John McVie on bass). Clapton's own tastes can be seen from the repertoire including songs from Otis Rush, Ray Charles, Freddie King, Mose Allison, Robert Johnson, and Little Walter.

As the album was released, Clapton left to form Cream with Jack Bruce and Ginger Baker, combining the blues sensibilities of Clapton with the jazz and pop approaches of Bruce and Baker. They enjoyed massive success but their live work was almost exclusively blues-based jams, using vehicles like Willie Dixon's "Spoonful" and Howlin' Wolf's "Sittin' On Top Of The World" for extended improvisation. After the break-up of Cream in 1968 and the failure of Blind Faith with Steve Winwood to last further than the initial tour and album, Clapton went through a period of self-doubt and drugs problems. From this emerged his greatest single recorded musical statement, the album *Layla*, which found him articulating his angst with passionate vocals and scorching blues-drenched guitar against a rock background, often entwined with the electrifying guitar of Dwayne Allman. After dropping out of the scene for some time, Clapton returned in the mid-1970s to rebuild a career, mostly with rock and pop pastiches with little blues content.

In the late 1980s and early 1990s, however, he began turning his attention once again to his first love, often playing blues sets live with guest artists and using young blues guitarists such as Stevie Ray Vaughan and Robert Cray. This continued apace as the 1990s developed so that, by 1994, he was back in the studio recording a straight blues album, *From The Cradle*. Clapton's own playing and singing was wholly within his first tradition. Clapton's career continues apace.

**SEE ALSO:** Jimi Hendrix, B. B. King, Albert King, Robert Johnson, Muddy Waters, John Mayall, Otis Rush, Ray Charles

# William Clarke

**fact file**

**BORN** 1951

**MUSICAL SELECTION**
Blues From Los
Angeles
Rockin' The Boat

Inglewood,
California is a
long way from
the Delta, but
William Clarke's
harp playing
stems from the
best of the old
school

**a** n energetic and talented singer/harmonica player, Clarke has spent most of his career on the West Coast, building a following which finally went nationwide and then international after beginning a series of award-winning albums for the Alligator label in 1990.

Clarke has roots in blues, R&B, and jazz, and his remarkable dexterity on chromatic harp echoes the sound of one of his teachers, George "Harmonica" Smith. Clarke was born in Los Angeles and discovered his passion for music in his early teens, when the British beat invasion of the early 1960s brought the sounds of America's black minority into the homes of the affluent and not-so-affluent whites. Clarke took up the blues harp and began singing the blues, playing with a disparate collection of local LA musicians, and by the end of the 1970s was ready to

begin recording as a leader. He made a batch of albums for small LA companies, including *Blues From Los Angeles* (1980) and *Rockin' The Boat* (1988), all of which established his musical turf and proved popular with local fans, but failed to travel much beyond California. With the switch to Alligator in 1990 Clarke landed a winner first time out with "Blowin' Like Hell" which enabled him to break out and tour across the United States.

Since then he has been an energetic performer and recording artist, his latest album, *The Hard Way* (1996), being a typical mix between tough Chicago blues repertoire ("Evil"), Kansas City-style jazz ("Moten Swing") and updates on older numbers ("Five Card Hand" by Mercy Dee Walton). Clarke's personal amalgam of jazz, R&B, and blues makes him an unusually attractive and interesting latter-day bluesman.

**SEE ALSO:** George "Harmonica" Smith, Mercy Dee Walton

# Doctor Clayton

**fact file**

**BORN** 1898

**DIED** 1947

**MUSICAL SELECTION**
"Pearl Harbor Blues"
"'41 Blues"

Don't let the glasses fool you – the "Doctor" was one in name only, though he taught many a lesson to the blues musicians who followed

biographical detail on Clayton is scant, much of it garnered from spoken reminiscences by Big Bill Broonzy in his autobiography, as recorded by Yannick Bruynoghe. Clayton was born in Georgia, but moved to St. Louis in his early twenties. There he worked in various menial industrial jobs, and claimed to have had a wife and four children. He also worked occasionally as a singer in the popular style of the day, entertaining friends and the odd gin-joint audience. Tragically, the turning point in his life appears to have been the complete annihilation of his family in a domestic fire, which left Clayton devastated. Soon thereafter he left St Louis for good and headed for Chicago, where he gained an unwanted reputation as one of the hardest drinkers and most compulsive gamblers in a city full of such people. But Clayton also slowly became known as an acute and expressive blues singer with a rich tenor voice.

Clayton appeared on record for the first time in 1935, as "Doctor Clayton," accompanied by Beatrice "Toots" Willis, but only two sides from this session were ever released. Six years later he was recorded again, this time by Okeh, with old friends like pianist Blind John Davis and guitarist Robert Junior Lockwood along for the ride. Ten sides were cut; though not all were issued, the sales were encouraging enough for Victor to try twice more with Clayton, in November 1941 and again in March 1942. This latter session proved Clayton to have larger concerns than the average bluesman, with his "Pearl Harbor Blues" denouncing Imperial Japanese "treachery" in no uncertain terms. The same session is unusual for another reason – the presence of Ransom Knowling, playing a remarkably dextrous tuba.

Never the most reliable of performers, Clayton disappeared from the studios once more until 1946, when two more sessions were cut. The results proved successful, but decades of hard drinking and chaotic living (it is said that he never had a bed of his own, often sleeping on pool tables or in alleys) caught up with Doctor Clayton; he died in the depths of the winter of 1947.

**SEE ALSO:** Big Bill Broonzy, Blind John Davis, Robert Junior Lockwood

# Eddy Clearwater

**fact file**

**BORN** 1935

**MUSICAL SELECTION**
Help Yourself

Eddie
Clearwater
aka the "Chief"
in Toronto, 1996
– he was
influenced by a
wide variety of
music, including
Country &
Western

Clearwater has often been referred to as a disciple of Chuck Berry's, and indeed he has often played in situations giving open tribute to the great rock 'n' roller. But his music has more breadth to it than simply being that of being a mere imitator. His early and sincere attraction to rockabilly and country music is equally discernible in his mature style.

Born in Macon, Mississippi, the young Edward Harrington moved to Birmingham, Alabama in 1948, where he was a regular churchgoer, sang in church vocal groups and played guitar. A left-hander, like many others he learned the guitar by playing a right-handed instrument upside-down. After about five years in Alabama, he moved on to Chicago, hoping for a slice of the action there as Eddy Clearwater. His Chicago work quickly exhibited signs of his fondness for Chuck Berry, country and other genres, as well as some of the emergent West Side blues

players such as Otis Rush. By the mid-1950s Clearwater was making singles for Atomic-H, all of them featuring a driving beat shared at the time by rockabilly and rock 'n' roll. He was also garnering some success with his wild live act of the day, which included throwing himself around onstage, amazing guitar dexterity and outlandish stage outfits. Clearwater enjoyed a devoted if small following, and stuck with his rock 'n' roll-based formula for most of the 1960s and 1970s.

As blues came back into favor in the 1980s, Clearwater began shifting his musical base back toward where he started out – retaining his rockabilly beat and wild vocalizations, but going for a more disciplined, stark blues sound on his instrument. He made a series of blues albums for Rooster and Blind Pig, including the outstanding *Help Yourself* in 1992. Eddie Clearwater continues to play the blues circuit in the US and abroad.

**SEE ALSO:** Otis Rush

# Albert Collins

texas bluesman Albert Collins has been an inspiration to generations of blues musicians on both sides of the Atlantic, but his actual style of guitar playing is regarded by most as inimitable. It is also one of the few instantly recognizable sounds in blues. Collins comes from the great Texas tradition of hard-edged guitar, being a relative of Sam "Lightnin'" Hopkins and a keen observer of the many blues players in post-war Houston. Initially a fan of the jump-blues style popularized by such artists as Pete Brown and Louis Jordan, Collins played both piano and guitar. He built his own first instrument and learned to play (through a cousin) in the open tunings of E-minor and D-minor. Collins eventually found his inspiration in the work of T-Bone Walker, Lightnin' and others, including the biting attack of Clarence "Gatemouth" Brown. He made the open tuning a trademark of his approach, and this old-time technique, grafted onto electric guitar, helped give him a distinctive sound.

Collins continued to develop his technique along unusual avenues, soon abandoning the use of picks in favor of the attack, and employing different picking patterns he found for himself when plucking the strings with his fingers or thumb. Collins toured extensively in the 1950s with Piney Brown and began recording, for the Kangaroo label, in 1958. These and other sides of the early 1960s featured titles like "The Freeze," "Thaw Out," "De-Frost" and "Icy Blues," but Collins remained a local phenomenon. He followed Jimi Hendrix into Little Richard's touring band, maintaining a contact with the younger guitarist that lasted until Hendrix's death in 1970. Collins, meanwhile, moved into a soul-blues phase in line with the contemporary blues style of the late 1960s, but his career sputtered to a near-halt in the following decade. Only his alliance with Alligator records in 1977 brought him back into the recording studio, and his first record for that label, *Ice Pickin'*, brought him an international audience bigger than any he'd previously enjoyed. Having finally made it through the lean years, Collins consolidated his position in the 1980s as one of the modern blues living legends, constantly touring and recording as well as helping younger men such as Robert Cray find success. His career continues successfully today, and his live act remains one of the most watchable and listenable in the blues firmament.

## fact file

**BORN** 1932

**MUSICAL SELECTION**
Ice Pickin'

Texan bluesman through and through, Albert Collins always electrified audiences with his bigger than life performance

# Johnny Copeland

Johnny Copeland, aka Clyde, was happiest playing the blues but revealed an interest in traditional African music with his later recordings

**fact file**

**BORN** 1937

**MUSICAL SELECTION**
Showdown!
Bringing It All
Back Home

johnny Copeland has actually had more than one career. His early years, spent first in Houston and later in New York, established him as a red-hot performer capable of great intensity, whether through his full-tilt vocals or his taut, powerful guitar playing. He was also a dynamic stage performer. After a trip to Africa in 1984, however, Copeland began a re-evaluation of his music and his career, and has since broadened and deepened his wellspring of inspiration – often recording with African musicians and people from related disciplines, including Marrakesh-based jazzman Randy Weston. In doing so, he has become a key blues player of the last two decades.

Copeland may have been born in Louisiana and spent his boyhood in Arkansas, but Texas formed his mature blues style. He arrived in Houston in the early 1950s and began performing in the city's clubs not long after. His guitar playing followed in the T-Bone Walker tradition, and while he was a member of the band the Dukes of Rhythm, they backed solo artists such as Big Mama Thornton and Freddie King. He made a string of singles for small Texas labels starting in 1958 and continuing into the next decade, but was never more than a local success. As with many other long-term Texan bluesmen, Copeland finally tired of the limited opportunities he was offered and decided to head for greener pastures, making the unusual decision to head for New York rather than the mid-West or the West Coast. Copeland's big personality and liveliness, as well as his Texas guitar and energetic vocals, quickly established him as a favorite in that city. As the 1980s opened he began making records on a regular basis, mostly for Rounder (*Make My Home Where I Hang My Hat*, *Bringing It All Back Home*, and *Boom Boom*) but also for Alligator (*Showdown!* with Albert Collins and Robert Cray).

*Bringing It All Back Home* (1984) was important as Copeland's first album demonstrating his fascination with Africa and African music. This is an area he has continued to explore from within his secure blues base, using African musicians and writing music which embraces both cultures, especially in the rhythm department. His album, *Jungle Swing* (Verve Gitanes, 1995), continues this highly unusual and intriguing work, confirming Johnny Copeland as a major presence in the world of blues music today.

**SEE ALSO:** T-Bone Walker, Big Mama Thornton, Freddie King, Albert Collins, Robert Cray

# James Cotton

James Cotton picked up his harp and hit the road at the tender age of nine

**C**otton followed a similar career path in postwar Chicago as Little Walter, Walter Horton, and Junior Wells, coming through the Muddy Waters band of the 1950s to find worldwide fame and adulation through his outstanding playing and stage presence.

Cotton was another of the Delta bluesmen who eventually made the trip north, starting life in Tunica, Mississippi, in a family dominated by a Baptist minister father with stern views on the blues. His mother gave him a harmonica while the boy was still small, and James decided to push out on his own at the age of nine to find Sonny Boy Williamson II (Rice Miller), whose *King Biscuit* show he heard on his radio. Finding Williamson in Molina, Arkansas, he somehow convinced the worldly Williamson that he was an orphan: for the next half-decade or more, the older man became Cotton's mentor, teaching him the rules of life and music. By the early 1950s Cotton was spending a lot of time in Memphis; while there he recorded with Howlin' Wolf on the latter's sessions for Sam Phillips's Sun Records as well as playing with Little Junior Parker. In 1954 Cotton was spotted in Memphis by Muddy Waters during a Southern tour, and Waters persuaded him to join

his band, replacing George "Harmonica" Smith. Cotton subsequently moved to Chicago with Waters and stayed in the band until 1966, in the meantime creating a sizable legend for the grace, verve, and power of his harp playing in every situation Waters placed him in, electric or acoustic. When he went out on his own, only Williamson and Little Walter were more widely known blues harp contemporaries. His harp licks, many adapted from things he'd learned from Williamson, had by then become some of the most imitated in the world.

Cotton took the same path as many other bluesmen in the late 1960s, playing to the recently emerged young rock audience with an interest in the blues, playing the Fillmore and various festivals. Cotton kept his own group going during the lean 1970s, although he also occasionally played with Muddy Waters and the young white blues rocker Johnny Winter. During the 1980s he made a string of records for Alligator, showing no diminution of his powers, while a new contract with Verve in the 1990s has seen him in a variety of blues contexts, 1996's *Deep In The Blues*, with Charlie Haden, Dave Maxwell, and Joe Louis Walker being a fine example.

## fact file

**BORN** 1935

**MUSICAL SELECTION**
Deep In The Blues

# Ida Cox

**fact file**

**BORN** 1896

**DIED** 1967

**MUSICAL SELECTION**
"Wild Women Don't
Have The Blues"
"Last Mile Blues"

Ida Cox is one of many performers to come out of the Theatre Owners Booking Agency's productions

It's often forgotten that the first great wave of popular success the blues enjoyed came from recordings made for the most part by female singers. Many of these singers came to the attention of record executives through their years on the vaudeville circuits, especially that organized and run by the Theatre Owners Booking Agency – a company which focused on black entertainers, but had a reputation for low pay and poor working conditions. Georgia-born Ida Cox was no exception to this general career path; she and her husband, Jesse Crump, joined the TOBA circuit in 1919 and stayed until the darkest years of the Depression.

During that time she developed her singing style, using her characteristically accomplished delivery to move easily between blues, vaudeville and jazz, varying her approach to different tunes and different audiences. By 1923 she'd made her first records, accompanied by Lovie Austin on the piano (one of the pieces was Austin's own "Any Woman's Blues"). Cox continued to record regularly under contract for Paramount right through until October 1929, the month of the Wall Street Crash; she also did moonlighting sessions for other labels under such names as Jane Smith and Kate Lewis. By this time Cox was running her own touring company, Raisin' Cain, and was seen by many as a performer particularly in tune with the desires and aspirations of women. A fine songwriter, many of her best pieces have entered into the general blues repertoire, including "Wild Women Don't Have The Blues," "Death Letter Blues," and "Last Mile Blues."

In the Depression years between 1929 and 1939, Cox made no recordings, and in the early 1930s actually withdrew from the TOBA circuit. As with many others, her career was revived by John Hammond's 1939 "Spirituals to Swing" concert, and that year she resumed recording, this time with a swing-based jazz band including Hot Lips Page and Charlie Christian. She made no more records until 1961 – by which time her voice was all but gone. Ida Cox succumbed to cancer in 1967.

**SEE ALSO:** John Hammond

# Robert Cray

**fact file**

BORN 1953

MUSICAL SELECTION
Bad Influence
Strong Persuader
Some Rainy Morning

Robert Cray, feeling the power of the blues at the Shepherd's Bush Empire theatre (England), 1997

more than any other artist, Robert Cray was at the center of the general revival of interest in the blues during the 1980s. Cray was prepared to take the blues closer to the pop mainstream than many older artists, and has reaped the career rewards as a consequence. He was born in Columbus, Georgia, to a career military father, and the family moved with every reposting, giving young Robert an unusually broad look around the USA (and even a peek at Germany) during his boyhood and youth. The family finally settled in Tacoma, Washington, where Robert, originally trained on the piano, switched to guitar with the advent of British beat bands in the 1960s. Cray's first band played rock, but he gradually discovered a strong response to the contemporary Chicago blues musicians, especially Budy Guy, and soon after this he persuaded his own high school to book Albert Collins for the graduation ball.

By 1974 Cray was leading the Robert Cray Band, over the next three years building a good local following and earning notoriety in the film *Animal House* as a member of the so-called Otis Day and the Knights. John Belushi even used Cray's own band as a loose model for the idea of the Blues Brothers. Cray's career continued to develop, hitting problems only when his first album, the 1978 *Who's Been Talkin'?*, spent two years in the can before being released just prior to the record company going under. The next album, *Bad Influence* (Hightone/Mercury), was delivered in 1983 and was instrumental in breaking Cray internationally to blues and soul fans, his covers of songs like "Phone Booth" and "Got To Make A Comeback" and his soul-drenched vocals on, for example, "Where Do I Go From Here?" defining Cray's appeal.

Cray's career continued on an upward graph, *Showdown* (Alligator) with Albert Collins and Johnny Copeland making an impact in 1985 and winning a Grammy, while the next Cray album, *Strong Persuader* (1986), his first under his new Mercury contract, hit the charts and spawned a hit single. By this time Cray was top of the new blues wave, a position he has yet to relinquish, although he has appeared in films like *Hail! Hail! Rock 'n' Roll* with rock stars like Keith Richards and Eric Clapton, and his more recent albums have reflected his original broad base of musical interests. Cray has also regularly appeared as support band for Clapton during the latter's prestigious concerts in Europe and the USA.

**SEE ALSO:** Ray Charles, Buddy Guy, Albert Collins, Johnny Copeland, Eric Clapton

# Connie "Pee Wee" Crayton

**fact file**

**BORN** 1914

**DIED** 1985

**MUSICAL SELECTION**
Things I Used To Do

Born in Texas, Connie Crayton aka Pee Wee was established only when he moved to the West Coast

C rayton was another Texan bluesman who, once influenced by the massive talent of T-Bone Walker, found his direction in the music and, once established on the West Coast, helped define what the modern West Coast blues sound would be.

Born in Rockdale, Texas, Crayton moved to Austin at an early age and learned his instrument (his first stringed instrument was a ukulele) while based in the Austin area. Tired of the harsh realities and lack of job prospects in the area, Crayton took off to California in 1935 before his 21st birthday, but took a number of years to establish himself there, finally gaining a position in Ivory Joe Hunter's band and recording with him in 1946. This led to his own first sessions, in 1947, and a deal in 1948 with Modern, by which his style was settled. In the meantime he had met and become a friend of T-Bone Walker, coming deeply under the

influence of the more famous man, especially in his adopting of more jazz-based techniques, more sophisticated chords and rhythm, and his choice of session men – one Modern session from 1950 features the swing stars Ernie Royal, Harry Edison, and Ben Webster. He enjoyed a number of R&B hits in the early 1950s, though nothing topped his No. 1 from 1948, "Blues After Hours." A swap to Vee Jay in the second half of the decade saw his career slowing down, although he enjoyed a hit with "Peace of Mind" and continued touring. As the next decade approached, he was supporting himself with session work in other people's bands, and from 1962–69 his own recording career came to a halt. Something of a comeback was staged with a sprightly album for Vanguard in 1970, *Things I Used To Do*, but Crayton's career never again reached its early heights. He toured and recorded for minor labels, making a living but not much more, until his death in 1985.

# Debbie Davies

**fact file**

BORN 1951

MUSICAL SELECTION
Live!
Picture This

Debbie Davis has been immersed in the blues her entire career, sharing the stage with the best in the field

**d**avies is a California-based blues artist who has gradually built a reputation as one of the most consistent performers on the blues circuit today and certainly one of the toughest female blues musicians playing and recording, her guitar style containing touches of 1960s rock as well as classic electric blues such as Freddie King and Buddy Guy. Her initial contact with the blues came by way of a copy of the ground-breaking *John Mayall's Bluesbreakers Featuring Eric Clapton*, and Clapton's imprint is still discernible on her mature style. Born and raised in LA, Davies went to college further north in California and there witnessed many of the modern blues greats on stage as they came through on campus tours. She also began gigging herself before completing her college studies and returning to LA, where she quickly became a member of the

support band for John Mayall, led by Mayall's wife Maggie. After this she gigged around LA with a number of bands, often at the same time, and came to the attention of Albert Collins, who at the beginning of the 1980s asked her to play at the San Francisco Blues Festival and, subsequently, join his backing band. Her role with Collins's band for three years was to be the guitarist and singer for the Icebreakers, opening the show every evening and warming the audience up. This she did to great success, and after three years, followed by a number of other supporting roles, she formed her own band and made her first album, *Live!* (1992). This was followed by the rather better-distributed album on Blind Pig, *Picture This* (1993), which featured her old boss Albert Collins on one track. Davies continues with her career, her songwriting proving her a front-rank contemporary female blues artist.

SEE ALSO: Eddie Taylor

# Arthur "Big Boy" Crudup

**a**rthur Crudup, born in the Delta in Forest, Mississippi, made his move relatively late in life, arriving in Chicago not far short of his fortieth birthday. But he was to unknowingly provide a vital link between the old-style country blues and the rock 'n' roll music which would sweep the world in the following decade.

Even the briefest acquaintance with Crudup's highly colored vocals reveals his early involvement with the searing emotions of gospel music. Scratching out a living on farms, Crudup kept up his contacts with church music and, after settling in the Clarkstown area of Mississippi while in his thirties, decided to learn an instrument. Completely self-taught, he learned on instruments so crude or damaged that it was only with difficulty that he managed to hold the strings down on the fretboard. This led Crudup to stop well short of a complete technique, even for the blues – but it didn't prevent him from developing a driving rhythm on the instrument, or from writing a series of memorable songs. He established a reputation in the local area at parties and gatherings, but knew he had no future as a performer if he stayed in Mississippi. He made the move to Chicago in 1939, but found himself in the position of so many other migrant musicians – penniless and homeless, sleeping on the streets, playing for small change. Crudup finally got his break when the RCA talent scout and publisher Lester Melrose happened upon him playing in the street one day. Melrose introduced him to the blues community in Chicago and signed him up for publishing and recording. After a false start between 1942 and 1945 when work for the war effort intervened, Crudup made a string of postwar blues sides for RCA, registering a number of hits including "My Baby Left Me," "Rock Me Mama" and – most importantly, in September 1946 – the driving "That's All Right," spurred along by his crude but propulsive electric guitar.

Perennially cheated out of his royalties by Melrose and others, and disgusted with the music business in general, Crudup ceased recording in 1954 and returned to farming in Virginia. When Elvis Presley made his "That's All Right" into a massive worldwide hit, Crudup saw little or nothing in terms of money. He remained distant from the music world until the 1960s blues revival, when blues enthusiasts rediscovered him and persuaded him to perform again. This led to many folk festival appearances across America and a resumption of recording activities, and for a decade Crudup finally made a decent living at his art. Still, "Big Boy" Crudup never saw any proper royalties for his songs covered by Presley, and died from a stroke suffered at home in Frankstown, Virginia, in March 1974.

## fact file

**BORN** 1905

**DIED** 1974

**MUSICAL SELECTION**
"My Baby Left Me"
"That's All Right"

Arthur "Big Boy" Crudup at a recording session for RCA Victor in Chicago, c. 1946

**SEE ALSO:** Albert Collins

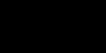

# James 'Thunderbird' Davis

**fact file**

**BORN** 1938

**DIED** 1991

**MUSICAL SELECTION**
Check Out Time

James Davis was nicknamed "Thunderbird" after a solid drinking bout with Guitar Slim

davis in effect had two careers – one which culminated in the mid-1960s with a small number of highly-treasured sides for the Houston-based Duke label, and another stemming from a short but welcome comeback in the 1980s, which gave him a larger blues following than ever before.

Davis was born in Mobile, Alabama, and it is hardly surprising to find that this fine baritone sang gospel and spirituals as a young boy. He'd just finished high school when he sat in with Magic Slim one night in 1957 in Pritchard, Alabama. Slim was so impressed that he hired Davis as an icebreaker for his touring show. After Slim's early death in 1959, Davis settled for a while in Thibodaux, where he was put in touch with Duke Records in 1961. Duke used him mainly as a demo maker for their hit artist Bobby Bland, but in 1963 Davis managed two regional hits, "Blue

Monday" and "Your Turn To Cry." Little more happened after this, and Davis once again became the warm-up act for a string of touring soul and blues acts, keeping him busy into the 1970s. But he eventually tired of the road and settled in Louisiana, working day jobs and playing by night, unable to make a change even when his earlier single, "Blue Monday," became a hit for other artists, including Z.Z. Hill in 1981.

But Davis was exhumed from his ill-deserved obscurity in 1988 by researchers for the Black Top label, who signed him that same year and cut the album *Check Out Time* with a studio band which included Anson Funderburgh and Earl King. Ironically, just when it seemed that the favorable response garnered by this album would re-launch him worldwide, "Thunderbird" Davis succumbed to a heart attack in 1991.

**SEE ALSO:** Magic Slim, Bobby Bland, Anson Funderburgh, Earl King

# Larry Davis

## fact file

**BORN** 1936

**DIED** 1994

**MUSICAL SELECTION**
Funny Stuff
Sooner or Later
I Ain't Beggin' Nobody

Though "Texas Flood" was a hit for Larry Davis — and later for Stevie Ray Vaughan — Davis was often underrated

davis was a superior blues vocalist and guitarist with a large dose of soul in his vocal delivery and a solid musical background covering a number of genres, including the bluesy side of jazz and soulful side of the early postwar blues and R&B scene, people such as Bobby "Blue" Bland, with whom Davis worked at one stage.

Davis was born in Kansas City, Missouri, but at the age of eight he moved with his father to Little Rock, Arkansas. Interested in music while still at school, Davis first learned the drums, and during his early career played with Little Rock bluesmen such as Sammy Lawhorn and Sunny Blair, as well as playing in a band with Fenton Robinson and Charles McGowan in the early 1950s. This band, with Davis as leader, moved on to St Louis and then California, where Bobby Bland heard them and recommended that Duke records sign them up. Duke signed Davis to a deal, and in 1958 his first single, "Texas Flood" (showing the Bland influence), was recorded in Houston, making something of a local splash (Stevie Ray Vaughan was to cover it some decades later). After two more singles for Duke in 1958–59, Davis joined Albert King's band and stayed with the great guitarist until 1968, when he cut the single "The Years Go Passing By" for Virgo, B.B. King's label. A series of singles followed as Davis's career developed, but a near-fatal motorcycle accident in 1972 left him paralyzed down one side for a year. Soon after, he suffered a stroke, and kept away from performing for most of the decade. Encouraged to pick up his career by Rooser Blues owner Jim O'Neal, he recorded *Funny Stuff* for the label in 1981, and it won a whole raft of awards the following year. Somehow, Davis failed to capitalize on its success, and his career remained a relatively low-key affair, a notable release in 1992, *Sooner or Later* on Bullseye Blues, being one of his best and most integrated efforts. He died in Los Angeles while still pursuing his proper status in the music.

**SEE ALSO:** Bobby "Blue" Bland, Fenton Robinson, Stevie Ray Vaughan, Albert King

# Reverend Gary Davis

## fact file

**BORN** 1896

**DIED** 1972

**MUSICAL SELECTION**
Blues and Ragtime

The very Reverend Gary Davis, self-taught guitarist, ordained Baptist minister and preacher of the blues, in New York, 1962

davis, blind for the full extent of his long professional career (and possibly blind from birth, although he never divulged this secret to any interviewer), was born in Lawrence County, South Carolina, and from an early age showed interest in music. Like most early blues musicians an autodidact, he eventually became adept at guitar, harmonica, and banjo and enjoyed a local reputation in South Carolina, often appearing both as a solo act and as a member of a string band. By the end of the 1920s, however, he had relocated to North Carolina, plying his trade on street corners. His guitar playing had by this time gained the expertise and intricacy associated with the Piedmont style of the East Coast, as is revealed by the records he made in 1935, his first sessions.

By this time, however, major changes had taken place in his life: he had met another fine picker, Blind Boy Fuller, and they often traveled and performed together. More importantly, however, Davis had found religion, and by 1933 had completed his studies to the level required to be ordained a Baptist minister. From this point on his powerful, blues-drenched vocals and

mesmeric guitar playing would be used almost exclusively in the service of his religious beliefs. His first record session, made as Blind Gary in New York for American Record Company was exclusively religious in content.

Davis moved permanently to New York at the start of the next decade, but apart from a 78rpm single in 1949 made no studio recordings until the mid-1950s, when within two years both Stinson and Riverside made two fine religious albums. During the intervening years Davis had made a living from being a Harlem street-corner singer, and his reputation had grown to the point where he was a well-known performer to many of the city's folk music lovers. This stood him in good stead when the folk revival of the late 1950s began, and his passionate delivery of his material, accompanied by his bewitching guitar and rich harmonica, left a deep impression on young musicians as diverse as Bob Dylan and Taj Mahal. During the 1960s he became a regular part of the folk-festival circuit and enjoyed true international fame. Davis succumbed to a heart attack in 1972 just prior to a festival he was due to appear at in New Jersey.

**SEE ALSO:** Blind Boy Fuller, Taj Mahal

# Walter Davis

fact file

**BORN** 1912

**DIED** 1963

**MUSICAL SELECTION**
"Let Me In Your Saddle"
"That Stuff You Sell Ain't
No Good"

Walter Davis,
impeccably
dressed, had to
work hard to get
away from his
rough St Louis
upbringing

**W**alter Davis was part of a St Louis blues scene which is often overlooked presently in favor of the guitar-based Texas and Mississippi Delta players who made such an impact on subsequent generations. Davis was a pianist and singer born in Granada, Mississippi, and spent his early years subjected to harsh treatment from his family. He decamped to St Louis at the tender age of 13, where he learned blues piano and began scraping a living as a musician. His style naturally mirrored that of established St Louis pianists such as Henry Brown, especially the staccato walking bass, and he also picked up on the St Louis fashion for piano/guitar duos, pairing up with Henry Townsend, an associate of Roosevelt Sykes. Indeed, it was Sykes, an East St Louis resident, who noted Davis's progress and eventually recommended him to Victor, who signed him up and brought him into the studio in 1930 for his first session. Big Bill Broonzy was the guitarist, Sykes the pianist.

Davis didn't begin accompanying himself on records until 1935, his highly eccentric playing, oblivious of fellow musicians in a manner typical of self-taught players, often losing his accompanists completely. Yet he maintained his popularity well into the 1940s, suffering a dip in sales only as the jump and R&B bands began to electrify their instruments and their audience. Remaining based in St Louis, he stayed with RCA, either on Victor or Bluebird, until 1946, but by then his career had nosedived: a 1950 session in Nashville for Bullet produced six singles, but none were hits. A 1953 session for Victor in St Louis with Henry Townsend resulted in two last singles, but they provoked little interest from the public. Davis turned from the music business to religion, taking up as a preacher, but within a few months suffered a debilitating stroke. Unable to play piano, he worked as a night porter in hotels around St Louis and continued his religious work. A heart attack stilled him in 1964.

**SEE ALSO:** Henry Townsend, Roosevelt Sykes, Big Bill Broonzy

# Jimmy Dawkins

## fact file

**BORN** 1936

**MUSICAL SELECTION**
Fast Fingers

Jimmy Dawkins at the Gloucester Blues Festival, 1995 – he was as interested in promoting the careers of new artists as much as his own

guitarist Dawkins has gone largely unnoticed in the US during a long career in Chicago which stretches back to the mid-1950s, but his playing has adorned the records of many more famous men, including Willie Dixon, Luther Allison, Walter Horton, and Johnny Young. His intense, fleet, and often surprisingly inventive guitar playing shows a man with a wide knowledge of blues and jazz and an equal desire to communicate what's on his mind. His own albums as a leader don't make the lists of essential purchases for most blues fans, but they are held in very high regard by blues musicians themselves.

Dawkins was born in Tchula, Mississippi, and taught himself to play guitar. Arriving in Chicago around 1955, he started out playing on street corners, working his way into the groups of the men listed above and getting to the stage toward the end of the decade where he could run his own band for occasional gigs in between work for Magic Sam and the Chicago session king Sonny Thompson. This pattern remained fixed until 1969, when Chicago's Delmark records signed him for an album: the resultant *Fast Fingers*. Although it failed to change Dawkins's material circumstances in the US, it had a considerable impact in Europe, even winning an award in France.

This allowed Dawkins to address the burgeoning European blues audience, touring and recording in both France and England in the 1970s and 1980s. He made two more fine albums for Delmark in 1975–76, and in more recent years has been recording for the Earwig label. He has also shown a talent for writing about music, his articles appearing in *Blues Unlimited* magazine, while his organizational abilities were demonstrated in the 1980s when he ran his own label, Leric. Dawkins continues to perform on both sides of the Atlantic.

**SEE ALSO:** Willie Dixon, Luther Allison, Walter Horton, Johnny Young, Magic Sam

# Detroit Junior

## fact file

BORN 1931

MUSICAL SELECTION
Chicago Urban Blues

Emery H. Williams Jr, aka Detroit Junior, came to music in his teens, coming to fame through stints with Howlin' Wolf

etroit Junior (AKA Emery Williams, Jr) has come to international attention mainly due to his stints as pianist with Howlin' Wolf and saxophonist Eddie Shaw. Born in Arkansas, Emery Williams moved to Detroit and became a hardy perennial on the Motor City's early-1950s blues scene – running his own band (Blues Chaps), playing Detroit clubs and backing visitors like Eddie Boyd and John Lee Hooker.

It was Boyd who, convinced that "Junior" (as Williams had come to be known) would make an impact in Chicago, brought him to the Windy City in 1956 with the idea that Chess records would sign him up. Although the Chess deal didn't pan out, Junior did get solid work with Eddie Taylor, J.T. Brown and others, and his songwriting talents also came to be appreciated by the Chicago blues community. Junior struck up a partnership with harp man Little Mack Simmons and the pair ran a gig on the South Side for a few years. In early 1960 Bea & Baby records had the duo make a single of "Money Tree," one of Junior's compositions. This led to a session with Chess later that year and subsequent singles with other small Chicago labels, but none sold particularly well.

In 1968 Junior joined Howlin' Wolf's regular band and stayed with that great bluesman until his death in 1976. During his time with Wolf's band Junior participated in Antilles's *Chicago Urban Blues* series. Later, his role in the *Living Chicago Blues* series from Alligator consolidated both his colorful performing and his solid songwriting credentials. Detroit Junior continues to play the Chicago clubs and bars, mostly in partnership with his longtime collaborator, Little Mack Simmons.

**SEE ALSO:** Howlin' Wolf, Eddie Shaw, Eddie Boyd, John Lee Hooker, Eddie Taylor

# Floyd Dixon

Floyd Dixon, pictured here 1950, brought tremendous heart and soul to his music

## fact file

BORN 1929

MUSICAL SELECTION
Wake Up and Live

**a** fine pianist and a rough-hewn vocalist, Dixon was born in Marshall, Texas, and specialized in a big-hearted approach to blues and R&B which brought him considerable attention in the 1940s and 1950s. He moved progressively closer to rock 'n' roll as the 1950s wore on, although his roots in various areas – including his smooth blues crooning patterned after Charles Brown – kept him from closing his options down completely.

Dixon left Texas for the West Coast in the mid-1940s, arriving in LA with his family as they searched for secure work. Determined to make it in music, young Floyd started appearing in amateur talent contests; he met a number of stars, including Charles Brown and Amos Milburn (both of them originally from Texas, too), and finally came into contact with the influential musician and entrepreneur Johnny Otis. Through Otis, Dixon obtained a contract with Modern Records, and his first single, "Dallas Blues," appeared in 1949. He joined up for a while with Johnny

Moore's Three Blazers, replacing Charles Brown in the group, and with them had one of his most substantial hits, "Telephone Blues" (1951). This and a follow-up, "Call Operator 210," topped the R&B charts. But Dixon's most memorable song – and one which has been covered countless times by others, including the Blues Brothers, Belushi and Ackroyd's band, in the late 1970s – was his 1954 hit, "Hey Bartender."

Dixon's career went into a slow eclipse as rock took over from R&B and he slid down the entertainment ladder until he subsisted on one-nighters, appearing in all-star bills on package tours specializing in old-time rhythm and blues. Always a committed player, Dixon has found favor in recent years. A 1996 record for Alligator, *Wake Up and Live*, helped return him to the spotlight. The album, features many Dixon originals, from "Hey Bartender" to the Ray Charles tribute, "A Long Time Ago," and has introduced Floyd Dixon to a new generation of blues fans.

**SEE ALSO:** Charles Brown, Amos Milburn, Johnny Otis

# Thomas A. Dorsey

Thomas A. Dorsey aka
Georgia Tom, pictured here in
1928, is sometimes named
the father of gospel music

P ianist Dorsey effectively experienced two careers: his early musical career revolved around the blues as it was played in Georgia and Chicago in the first three decades of this century; his second career was in the gospel field, both running and performing in groups and writing material for them to sing and record. This career continued from the early 1930s until his death in 1993. Thomas was born in Villa Rica, Georgia, at the end of the last century, to a family steeped in the Baptist tradition of worship, his father being a minister in the local Baptist church. Dorsey was trained to sing and read music as well as play piano, and when he left to live in Chicago as a teenager it was to study composition and orchestration. While he did this he began playing in bars and clubs to supplement his small income. By the end of the teens, Dorsey was well enough known to land a job on Ma Rainey's traveling show. Based once again in Chicago, Dorsey finally came in front of a microphone in 1928,

making a series of sides for Vocalion under the name of Georgia Tom, accompanied by Tampa Red. Now a performing duo, within a couple of months the pair had recorded (under the name Tampa Red's Hokum Jug Band) "It's Tight Like That," a bestseller and an oft-imitated blues classic. For the next two years Dorsey worked at a dizzy pace, recording by himself and with Tampa Red as well as other musicians, arranging dates for a variety of performers and playing once again with Ma Rainey, among other things. By 1930 he was recording with Scrapper Blackwell, moving to New York in the spring of that year to cut some sides with Big Bill Broonzy.

By the fall of the same year he was back in Chicago making his last sides as a blues musician, "Don't Leave Me Blues/Been Mistreated Blues." His subsequent career as one of the greatest and most successful gospel composers and musicians of modern times lies, unfortunately, outside the scope of this book.

## fact file

**BORN** 1899

**DIED** 1993

**MUSICAL SELECTION**
"It's Tight Like That"

**SEE ALSO:** Ma Rainey, Tampa Red, Scrapper Blackwell, Big Bill BroonzY

# Willie Dixon

**i**t is possible to ascribe the general course of postwar blues to Willie Dixon; it is impossible to imagine that same period without his presence and influence. His abilities as a sideman, songwriter, talent scout, and organizer during the heyday of Chicago blues – the 1950s and 1960s – led to his creating countless hits for acts as diverse and significant as Muddy Waters, Howlin' Wolf, The Rolling Stones, Led Zeppelin, and Cream, just to mention a bare minimum.

Dixon was born in the Delta, coming originally from Vicksburg, Mississippi. He first came to music through gospel, reaching the level of singer in the Union Jubilee Singers, a local Vicksburg group. Dixon spent part of his youth plying his trade as a professional boxer, but gradually realized that a career in music held more long-term promise. In 1936 he cut his ties with Mississippi and moved up to Chicago, mixing laboring work with further forays into prizefighting. The boxing ended first, when Dixon became aware of the amounts being skimmed off by his manager. By the end of the 1930s Dixon was proficient enough as a bassist (a fairly rare breed in the blues circles of the day) to join a Chicago group called the Five Breezes. When the war interrupted normal life the band was broken up and Dixon, as a conscientious objector, spent most of the war years in prison. On his release he joined up with Leonard Caston of the Five Breezes and started a trio, the Big Three, which signed with Columbia and had a string of local Chicago hits. The trio was an acoustic outfit with a strong blues angle, its unique selling point its three-part harmonies on many of its pieces – another echo of Dixon's gospel roots.

The group continued until the early 1950s, touring extensively in the South as well as pumping out new records and playing around Chicago. Dixon, possessed with plenty of restless energy, spent his spare time jamming with other Chicago blues musicians and gradually came into the orbit of Chess Records. In 1948 he became a full-time member of staff, appearing on many sessions, scouting for talent and writing songs. Yet he stayed well in the background until 1954, when three Chess artists hit it big with three Dixon classics – "Hoochie Coochie Man" (Muddy Waters), "Evil" (Howlin' Wolf), and "Mellow Down Easy" (Little Walter). Dixon quickly became a mainstay of Chicago blues sessions, switching to Cobra Records in 1957, where he advanced the careers of Buddy Guy and Magic Sam, among others, ushering in a new generation of Chicago bluesmen. After this he began recording under his own name for a variety of labels, making a particularly fine pair of albums (for two different companies) with the pianist Memphis Slim at the close of the 1950s. Dixon's combination of simple but effective rhythms and melodies with punchy, cliché-free lyrics continued to appeal widely, and his songs featured strongly in the recording itineraries of many of the best rock groups of the 1960s, including Cream and the Yardbirds.

Dixon managed to avoid most of the pitfalls that bedeviled many of his peers. He controlled the copyright on most of his classic songs and worked as producer on many sessions, as well as touring and recording under his own name. By the early 1980s he was sufficiently secure to set up a nonprofit group, the Blue Heaven Foundation, to aid and finance charitable blues projects, scholarships, and hardship funds from the royalties accruing to his publishing company. Dixon continued to work sporadically up to the close of the 1980s, and collaborated on a biography, *I Am The Blues* (1989), but ill health began to take its toll. He died in 1992.

Willie Dixon, the man who once claimed, without an ounce of hyperbole, "I am the blues"

**SEE ALSO:** MuddY Waters, Howlin' Wolf, Little Walter, Buddy Guy, Magic Sam

# K C Douglas

**fact file**

**BORN** 1913

**DIED** 1975

**MUSICAL SELECTION**
K.C. Blues
The Country Boy

K.C. Douglas,
son of a baptist,
was baptized
with initials only
– no-one knows
what they stand
for, if anything

douglas is another bluesman who first saw daylight in Mississippi, born and raised on a farm near Canaan, within 50 miles of Memphis. He knew and loved music from an early age but worked as a farm hand for his own family until young adulthood. After that he took up the guitar and, in between a variety of laboring jobs, began to build up a technique good enough to gain himself some casual musical employment. He heard most of the great Delta musicians operating in his area, including Blind Blake and Blind Lemon Jefferson; but it was Tommy Johnson, a rough, powerful singer and guitarist, who impressed him most deeply. Douglas took Johnson as a model and at times even got to work with him at picnics and outings. At other times he would perform as a street singer, but it was mostly non-musical work with which Douglas kept body and soul together.

In search of a better life for himself, Douglas moved to the West Coast in 1945. There, again, he worked as a migrant laborer, doing largely the same agricultural jobs he'd done in Mississippi; blues gigs proved as hard to come by in California as they had back home. Gradually, however, Douglas's reputation spread, and he even made a couple of singles – the first in 1948 for Down Town, the second for Rhythm in 1954, billed as "K.C. Douglas & His Lumberjacks." But only with the advent of the folk-blues revival did Douglas find his musical star briefly on the rise; at the dawn of the 1960s he made around three or four albums's worth of material, mostly for the Bluesville label, courtesy of Chris Strachwitz's advocacy. These records show Douglas to have stuck to his Delta traditions, with a brutal, emotional guitar style and keening voice, and a reliance on direct communication rather than subtlety.

Douglas's career continued to sputter along and he became a fixture at local San Francisco folk and blues events. Although he made just one more single after the Bluesville recordings, in 1967, K.C. Douglas managed to sustain himself through gigs in Berkeley coffee bars and at festivals until his death in 1975.

**SEE ALSO:** Blind Blake, Blind Lemon Jefferson, Tommy Johnson

# Dr Ross

**fact file**

**BORN** 1925

**DIED** 1993

**MUSICAL SELECTION**
"Dr Ross Boogie"
"Texas Hop"
"Industrial Boogie"

Isiah "Doctor" Ross and his "up to the minute blues" was popular on the club scene in the Detroit area

d r Ross (aka Charles Isiah Ross) was one of the small number of one-man blues bands who managed to connect with an audience larger than just their home town. His performance included guitar, harmonica, singing, and percussion effects, and his emphasis on entertainment in good down-home style meant that he was a perennial "live" favorite.

Born in Tunica, Mississippi, and one of eleven children, Ross was raised in fertile Delta blues country, learning blues harp before he was 10 years old. As a young teenager he was deemed good enough to appear with Willie Love in clubs and on radio shows in Mississippi and Arkansas, but his career was interrupted by service in the armed forces during World War II. Back in Mississippi in 1947, Ross returned also to performing, finding his brand of blues still palatable to radio audiences both in Clarksdale and Memphis. After a stint back in the armed forces as the Korean War loomed, Ross returned once more to radio work: some of these broadcasts were heard by the discerning owner of Sun records, Sam Phillips, who brought Ross into his Memphis studio in November 1951 to cut his first records. By this time Ross had evolved his one-man-band approach, and although he often

had a backup guitarist on his sessions, there was no mistaking whose show was being recorded. His work revolved around stomping riffs and show-stopping routines such as "Dr Ross Boogie," "Texas Hop," "Industrial Boogie," and "Boogie Disease," and he stayed with Sun until late 1954, when Phillips began his Elvis Presley sessions. Ross moved to Detroit, Michigan, but failed to make much of an impression on the local scene, working in the auto industry and performing part-time. In the late 1950s he released a single on his own label, DIR, making another version of "Industrial Boogie," but went unnoticed outside of Detroit until the advent of the country blues revival of the 1960s. Ross was taken up by the younger audience and recorded more during the 1960s than at any other time in his career. He also became a feature of the touring circuit, making an impression in the 1965 Folk Blues package which came to Britain and other European blues-loving centers. His profile dropped in the 1970s after a promising start, playing in London and appearing at the Montreux Festival on the same bill as the Muddy Waters Band. It was only in his last half-decade that he once again played live to international audiences. He died in 1993.

**SEE ALSO:** Muddy Waters

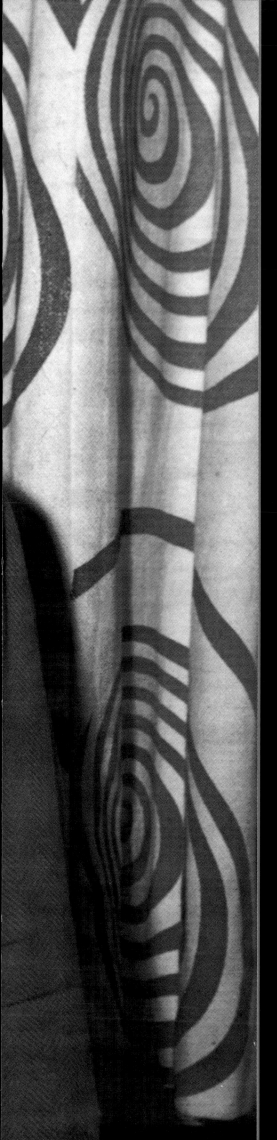

# Champion Jack Dupree

O ne of the most colorful characters in the blues fraternity, Champion Jack Dupree (aka William Thomas Dupree) was born in New Orleans, probably in 1909 (no one knew for sure, least of all Dupree himself). While still in infancy, Dupree was orphaned when the general store his parents ran burned down, and was taken to the same Colored Waif's Home which had raised Louis Armstrong. Fascinated by the piano from an early age, Dupree taught himself the rudiments of keyboard technique. Soon after moving out of the Waif's Home as a teenager, he was playing at parties and bars as well as washing dishes and doing menial, unskilled work. He stayed in New Orleans during the Prohibition era, playing in speakeasies and eking out a living along with other self-taught players by sticking to basic barrelhouse style and playing requests.

Around 1930, Dupree decided to quit New Orleans and moved up to Chicago, where he had a brother, but stayed no more than a year. Times were hard, and a part-time piano player earned barely a pittance. Continuing to move around in search of any type of work, Dupree visited Detroit and met boxer Joe Louis, who convinced him he could make a few bucks in the ring. Dupree took an interest in the sport and during the 1930s a good deal of his income came from professional fights throughout the US. The moniker "Champion Jack" was bestowed upon Dupree around this time, although he'd been known as plain "Jack" since early infancy. He got through the 1930s dividing his time between boxing, music and other work – including emceeing at a theater in Indianapolis, where he settled for a few years and married. Finally, in 1940, Dupree made a trip to Chicago to record for Lester Melrose and Okeh. His self-penned sides, many painting a bleak picture of low life, drugs and prison, made a quick impact. So did his rough-hewn piano style, and Dupree quickly dropped his other pursuits to become a full-time musician for the first time.

Confusion surrounds Dupree's departure from Indianapolis, but it is probable that he left the city after the death of his first wife, just prior to America's entry into World War II. He was soon drafted, seeing non-combat Navy duty in the Pacific, then spending two years as a Japanese POW. After the war Dupree settled in New York, where he looked up an old buddy, Brownie McGhee; for a time the pair lived in the same redbrick near the Apollo theater. Both were struggling, making singles for a host of record companies as leaders and session men. But Dupree finally ended up in a more or less solid relationship with King Records between 1953-55, where he had a minor hit with "Walkin' The Blues." In 1958 he made a blues classic for Atlantic – "Blues From The Gutter," featuring jump-band saxophonist Pete Brown – but by 1959 he'd grown tired of the US. Hearing of the new interest in blues in Europe, Dupree accepted an invitation to travel to England in 1959, and spent the next three decades – virtually the rest of his life – living in various countries across Europe. His popularity was buoyed by his charismatic and witty stage shows, as well as by a long string of records for various European labels. Renewed US interest in the blues led to an invitation in 1990 for Dupree to appear in New Orleans, which he did with great success. In 1991, however, Champion Jack Dupree was hospitalized with prostate cancer, and he died the following year in his adopted city of Hanover, Germany.

## fact file

**BORN** 1909

**DIED** 1992

**MUSICAL SELECTION**
"Walkin' The Blues"
"Blues From The Gutter"

"Champion Jack" Dupree earned his nickname the hard way – as a boxer

**SEE ALSO:** Brownie McGhee

# Big Joe Duskin

**fact file**

**BORN** 1921

**MUSICAL SELECTION**
Cincinnati Stomp
Don't Mess With The
Boogie Man

The aptly named "Big Joe" Duskin met key blues contacts during WWII, on USO tours

d uskin is a rollicking, modern-day barrelhouse pianist and vocalist in the Roosevelt Sykes/Champion Jack Dupree tradition – able to lay on a fine mess of rocking blues, or slow it down and get the crowd on his side with suitably heartfelt, low-down slow drags.

Born in Birmingham, Alabama, Duskin moved as an adolescent to Cincinnati, Ohio with his family. He learned piano there, favoring the sounds of the boogie pianists who were making headlines in the late 1930s, including Sykes and Pete Johnson. Before his own career got underway, however, Duskin was drafted into World War II service, which gave him an opportunity to rub elbows with many fine musicians in the same situation. After the war Duskin had hoped to begin a full-time blues and boogie career, but his Reverend father made Joe swear he would never do such a thing while Duskin senior lived. Joe agreed – only to endure two decades of day jobs well removed from music as his father lived past the 100 mark – and began his musical career at a very late age. As with so many other musicians who had been previously buried in obscurity, he found Arhoolie's Chris Strachwitz to be supportive enough to make an album of his playing, *Cincinnati Stomp*, released in 1979.

This record gave Duskin the impetus to begin touring beyond his local area, and during the 1980s and 1990s he became known in Europe, making it to Britain in 1995 for a few gigs and an appearance on television. This led to another album, *Don't Mess With The Boogie Man*, for Indigo in 1997, which has added further impetus to Big Joe Duskin's late-blooming but viable blues career.

**SEE ALSO:** Roosevelt Sykes, Champion Jack Dupree

# Fird "Snooks" Eaglin

### fact file

**BORN** 1936

**MUSICAL SELECTION**
That's All Right
Snooks Eaglin
"Lucille"

Snooks Eaglin —
live on stage in
New Orleans in
December 1995.

eaglin, from New Orleans, suffered the misfortune to be blinded by complications which set in after major surgery performed on him before he was two years old. From early childhood Eaglin showed immense interest in all the music he heard around him, whether on the radio or in the street, and when he received a guitar as a present for his sixth birthday he set about teaching himself songs on it with great industry. With the indiscriminate enthusiasm of youth he embraced all the styles he heard, and this stood him in good stead when he progressed to attempting to support himself as a street singer: Snooks would be as adept at Jimmie Rodgers-type country as he was boogie, old-fashioned country style blues, or typically Bayou-based highly rhythmic music. He was also attracted to jazz and ragtime, and the patterns of these musics can also be found in his. In the early 1950s Eaglin was caught up in the New Orleans R&B style, which was proving popular nationally, and he was a member of Allen Toussaint's band as well as penning a number of R&B-type songs, one of which, "Lucille," would eventually prove to be a major hit for Little Richard.

Eaglin did not record under his own name until 1958, when he made a series of solo sessions for Folkways. The relative success of these led to Folklyric releasing a 1959 date, quickly followed by two for Bluesville. The folk/blues boom had many companies looking for authentic blues talent at this time, and Eaglin was signed by Imperial, making records with them between 1960 and 1963. The rest of the blues boom passed him by, and Eaglin, essentially an old-style entertainer, went back to plying his trade on the streets of New Orleans. In 1987 he was signed to a new deal by Black Top records and has been cutting albums with them ever since, bringing his name once more in front of the blues audience.

**SEE ALSO:** Jimmie Rodgers

# Ronnie Earl

## fact file

**BORN** 1953

**MUSICAL SELECTION**
Deep Blues
Surrounded By Love

Ronnie Earl's popularity brought him all the way from New York to the Royal Festival Hall in London (England), in the summer of 1997

**e**arl came to the blues late, being in his twenties before he even began playing guitar, but his quick progress since then has established him as one of the outstanding guitarists in the music today. No vocalist, he has concentrated on honing to perfection the guitarist's art, from solos to accompaniment, proving himself an adept at virtually every type of blues, acoustic and electric, and more besides, as some of his recent albums, emphasizing jazz and swing-type tunes, have demonstrated.

Earl was born in New York and spent his childhood in the city, absorbing the huge range of musics that cosmopolitan center had to offer. A move to Boston in the early 1970s led to his witnessing a Muddy Waters gig in 1975 which so entranced him that he took up guitar studies, homing in on the blues. By the late 1970s Earl was ready to look for paying gigs and in 1980 he took the place of Duke Robillard in Roomful of Blues, one of the most successful

white blues bands of the past 25 years. Earl's clean technique, his range and his imagination, as well as his sheer good taste, quickly led to his signing a deal with Black Top and producing a string of highly acclaimed and versatile guitar-based blues albums for the label, including the often raunchy *Deep Blues* (1982–84), featuring Sugar Ray Norcia and Kim Wilson on vocals and his own band, The Broadcasters. He also appeared on a spate of Roomful of Blues albums, including *Hot Little Mama* (1985) and *Dressed Up To Get Messed Up* (1986), both on Varrick records.

Earl has continually looked for new challenges, and the eclectic *Surrounded By Love* (1991) includes T-Bone Walker-inspired swing-type instrumentals, acoustic numbers with Robert Jr. Lockwood and soul-drenched blues ballads. Earl now has a truly international following and the respect of the entire blues community, achieved not by flash but by subtly brilliant uses of incredibly varied traditional techniques.

**SEE ALSO:** Muddy Waters, Duke Robillard, Roomful of Blues, T-Bone Walker, Robert Jr Lockwood

# David "Honeyboy" Edwards

**fact file**

**BORN** 1915

**MUSICAL SELECTION**
Ragtime Selection

David "Honeyboy" Edwards, before a show in Oxford (England), 1995

Guitarist/singer Edwards is one of the last surviving Delta bluesmen from the generation of Son House, Robert Johnson, and Skip James. In time-honored style, Edwards, born in Shaw, Mississippi, taught himself guitar and took lessons from the players he saw around him on the plantations in the area, graduating eventually to appearing at the same picnics and jukes. During the 1930s he crossed the path of most of the practicing Delta bluesmen, including Big Joe Williams and Charley Patton, and finally came to the attention of the field recordist Alan Lomax for the Library of Congress in midsummer 1942, who had him play more than a dozen titles for him in Coahoma County Agricultural School, Clarksdale, following that two days later with four more at Delta Tourist Camp, up the road apiece from Clarksdale. These recordings show Edwards to be typical of the Delta musicians of his time, capable of intricate blendings between voice and guitar and consistently delivering a tense, passionate vocal line in such songs as "Worried Life Blues"

while also having an ear for the lighter side of life in "I Love My Jelly Roll" and "Tear It Down." His connections with non-blues forms can be heard in the *Ragtime Selection*.

Edwards made no more recordings until 1951, when he made his first commercial session for ARC under the name Mr Honey. By 1953 he was using the professional name of Honeyboy Edwards and making records in Chicago for Chess, though most of these sessions were left unreleased. In a familiar pattern, Edwards worked the streets in Chicago to make his meager living. He benefited from rediscovery in the 1960s, and although a number of companies recorded him and left the material unreleased, he managed a good date for Adelphi in 1969, accompanied by Mike Stewart. During the next couple of decades he became a regular if infrequent part of the European package tours and made solid Delta-style records for various small companies, often substituting electric guitar for his old acoustic. He continues to play and record in a variety of venues.

**SEE ALSO:** Big Joe Williams, Charley Patton

# Robert "Big Mojo" Elem

Big Mojo Elem kept the strong, driving style for which he was always known throughout his career

**fact file**

**BORN** 1931

**MUSICAL SELECTION**
Mojo Boogie!

Elem is a journeyman bass player/guitarist who has played with many of the top Chicago bluesmen of the 1950s and 1960s. Born in Itta Bena, Mississippi, he left his hometown in his late teens, finally arriving in Chicago in 1951 after having caught up with and witnessing the talents of major stars like Robert Nighthawk and Sonny Boy Williamson (II) out on the road. Once in Chicago, he was lucky enough to be spotted playing his guitar on a house porch by a friend of Arthur "Big Boy" Spires, who was in need of a second guitarist. After a year with Spires, Elem moved on to Otis Rush's band, staying about a year before striking out on his own. This band used Freddie King as a second guitarist, but in time-honored fashion King gradually took over the band.

By the time it first recorded in 1956 for El-Bee it had become King's own, with Elem gradually assuming the position of electric bass in the band. Elem stayed with King until the early 1960s, doing the occasional gig with other Chicago giants like Magic Sam and Junior Wells, just to keep his hand in elsewhere. During the 1960s Elem stuck to West Side bands like Jimmy Dawkins and Luther Allison. He continued as a bandmember through the subsequent decades, finally cutting his first album as a leader, *Mojo Boogie!*, in 1994.

"Big Mojo" has stuck to bass guitar and has carved a special niche for himself playing the hard-driving West Side 1950s style with which he first made his name known four decades ago.

**SEE ALSO:** Robert Nighthawk, Sonny Boy Williamson II, Otis Rush, Freddie King, Magic Sam, Junior Wells, Jimmy Dawkins

# Tinsley Ellis

Tinsley Ellis, feeling the moment at the Brewhouse in Oxford (England), 1995

e llis is a blues guitarist and singer who has brought the intensity of rock and hard-driving modern guitar styles to a contemporary blues feel, using the influences of Chicago greats like Albert and Freddie King and many others to deliver a disciplined but driving, exciting modern blues. Brought up with rock and converted to blues, he is a natural for today's US blues scene, where the two styles often merge and mix in single players such as Stevie Ray Vaughan and Robert Cray.

Ellis was born in Atlanta, Georgia, and began his musical career by playing in Atlanta bar bands doing cover versions of R&B material recorded by British beat bands. Coming into contact with classic Chicago blues in the form of Howlin' Wolf, Muddy Waters, and the rest,

Ellis began heading toward the blues in his own playing, and in 1979 joined such a band, the Alley Cats, which at the time had Preston Hubbard as a member. In 1981 Ellis moved on to the Heartfixers, co-led with the singer Bob ("Chicago Bob") Nelson, and the albums this band made in the next six years established them both in the US and abroad. After *Cool On It* (1986), a classic mid-1980s blues set, Ellis began preparing for a solo career, and in the following year formed the Tinsley Ellis Band. Signed to Alligator, this unit has made a consistent run of high-octane blues records, unashamedly searching for the same market identified and sold to by Stevie Ray Vaughan and doing the job convincingly. In 1997 the band released its latest effort. Ellis continues to promote his career.

**SEE ALSO:** Albert King, Freddie King, Stevie Ray Vaughan, Robert Cray, Howlin' Wolf, Muddy Waters

# Sleepy John Estes

John Adams Estes was born in Ripley, Tennessee (some claim the year of birth as 1904), and was an influential singer and songwriter at an early stage of the blues' progress to national prominence in the US. Some of his songs have not only long been recognized as classics, but pieces such as "Milk Cow Blues," "The Girl I Love She's Got Long Curly Hair," "Divin' Duck Blues," "Someday Baby," and "Special Agent" have been performed by noted musicians right up to the present day.

Estes moved with his family as an adolescent to Brownsville, working on the family farm and learning guitar on his father's instrument. An accident at a local baseball game impaired the sight in one eye, but it was the death of his father in 1920 that gave John the impetus to take up music as a full-time occupation. He teamed up with the harp player Hammie Nixon and Yank Rachell (the latter on mandolin) and the trio slowly built a reputation in Brownsvlle and nearby Memphis during the 1920s. The trio was noticed by a Victor scout, and Estes, along with Rachell and a drafted-in pianist, made four classic sides in Memphis in 1929. His keening, high voice, his unusual subject matter (often dealing with everyday concerns rather than just affairs of the heart), and the distinctive edge of Rachell's mandolin made the records strong sellers, and Estes made further sides in 1930. Caught up in the Depression, Estes and his group ceased recording and soon after made the move to Chicago, hoping for more regular work, but it was not until 1935 that he recorded again, this time with Hammie Nixon only. A more sustained recording career emerged this time, ending only in 1942 with the recording ban which killed off many music careers. Estes returned to Tennessee and attempted to sustain himself there, even making a session for Sam Phillips's Sun Records in 1952, though nothing was issued at the time. In 1950 his precarious eyesight failed altogether when he lost the sight in his previously "good" eye. He was now back in Brownsville, married and leading a quiet family life until his rediscovery by a photographer/researcher in 1962.

This led to an album for Delmark, *The Legend Of Sleepy John Estes*, which quickly received rave notices worldwide, fortuitously timed as it was to coincide with the renaissance of interest in early blues. He and his old pal Hammie Nixon were tempted back out onto the road, playing festivals and on packages (he was one of the major hits of the 1964 Newport Folk Festival), recording a string of albums for Delmark and Vanguard over the next three years. Estes also traveled to Europe, where he was lionized and appeared on many festival bills as well as making more records, often live. He even made it as far afield as Japan in the 1970s before his death, at the age of 78, in 1977.

## fact file

**BORN** 1899

**DIED** 1977

**MUSICAL SELECTION**
The Legend Of Sleepy
John Estes

**Sleepy John Estes was among the earliest , most successful recorded blues artists**

**SEE ALSO:** Yank Rachell

# Sue Foley

**fact file**

**BORN** 1968

**MUSICAL SELECTION**
Young Girl Blues
Big City Blues

Sue Foley, one of a handful of Canadian blues artists

oley, though born in Ottawa, Canada, has become a respected part of the blues scene that began emerging from Austin, Texas, in the early 1970s in the form of talents like Lou Ann Barton and Angela Strehli and continues to produce tough new sounds. A fan of many of the rock groups that first emerged with the beat boom of the 1960s, Foley was attracted to the guitar while in her pre-teens and began learning the instrument at the age of 13. After mastering the basics, she experienced a conversion to the blues at the age of 15 after seeing James Cotton live in concert. From then on her aim was to play in blues bands and after much jamming and sitting in around Ottawa, she formed a band at the age of 18 when she moved to Vancouver. Deeply influenced by such Chicago stalwarts as

Freddie King and Magic Sam, she ran a tight band with a powerful blues punch and quickly built up a following on the West Coast, in both Canada and the USA. Determined to expand heR career and audience, she sent a cassette tape to Antone's in Austin, Texas, a move that resulted in her signing with the label and eventually moving to Austin. Her first record after this, *Young Girl Blues*, was released in 1992, and was followed in 1993 by *Without A Warning*, a record more geared to reveal her own songwriting. Foley has a light, somewhat fragile young voice, which is in direct contrast to the confident and sometimes slashing guitar work she produces: this contrast is perhaps part of her appeal. She continues to develop her career in the blues with recordings (*Big City Blues* was released in 1995) and live work.

**SEE ALSO:** Lou Ann Barton, Angela Strehli, James Cotton, Freddie King, Magic Sam

# Robben Ford

**fact file**

**BORN** 1951

**MUSICAL SELECTION**
Talk To Your
Daughters
Love's A Heartache

Robben Ford,
seen here in
February 1996,
has enjoyed
success in a
wide range of
genres and with
a variety
of musicians

ord is a competent and fluent guitarist at home in a number of styles, including fusion, mainstream-modern jazz, R&B, rock, and blues. A native of Woodlake, California, he became a constant presence on the West Coast rock and blues scene of the 1970s before spending most of the 1980s involved in various jazz and fusion projects. The 1990s have seen him return to his blues roots.

Ford, born into a musical family (his father was the country musician Charles Ford), was first inspired to play by the records of people such as Eric Clapton, John Mayall, and James Cotton. Learning guitar and sax while still at high school, he played in bands imitating the Hendrix-inspired guitar rock of the late 1960s and also came to appreciate the jazz being forged by John Coltrane and Miles Davis before, in 1970, joining Charlie Musselwhite's blues outfit. A year later he joined his brother Patrick's family group, the Charles Ford Band (named after their father), and played around San Francisco in 1972 (making an album for Arhoolie) before he struck out on his own. Backing

Jimmy Witherspoon at a gig, he and the band were offered the chance to become Spoon's permanent backing unit, an offer that was accepted. Ford and the band moved to LA and played with the singer for around three years before he went off with Tom Scott's LA Express on a tour with Joni Mitchell. This led to Ford's long involvement with rock, fusion, and jazz, a time when he made countless sessions and was a founder member of Yellowjackets as well as being part of the latter-day Miles Davis setup for a year in the early 1980s. By the end of the 1980s Ford was playing the blues for kicks with his family members and old friends, and he decided late in the decade to head back toward that area, marking his blues comeback with the fine *Talk To Your Daughters* of 1988. This and other projects, all centered on his outstanding guitar playing, led finally to the formation in 1992 of the Blue Line, a group that gave Ford the room to flex his blues muscles. Their self-titled debut disc of 1993 is a good indication of the group's talents. Ford continues to play music on a number of fronts today.

**SEE ALSO:** Eric Clampton, John Mayall, James Cotton, Charlie Musselwhite, Jimmy Witherspoon

# Blind Boy Fuller

Blind Boy Fuller, like many other blind blues musicians, turned to music to support himself

### fact file

**BORN** 1907

**DIED** 1941

**MUSICAL SELECTION**
"Rag, Mama, Rag"
"Ain't It A Cryin'
Shame?"

Self-taught like most prewar bluesmen, "Blind Boy" Fuller was born Fulton Allen and raised in the southwestern corner of North Carolina. The only member of his family with an aptitude for music, he became proficient as a guitarist while still a teenager, adopting the Piedmont style of guitar playing and using the intricacies of rag and dance as well as more Delta-inspired bottleneck technique, the latter to vary his musical output. Allen, who was not born blind, initially had no intention of becoming a professional musician. He held down a regular job and played only for his own and his friends' amusement. But the onset of his affliction caused him to take up the blues as a means of making a living.

In 1925, at the age of 18, he met a girl named Cora Mae Martin, who was just 13 at the time; they married within a year and settled down to enjoying a life where they both worked day jobs. However, before the end of the decade, Allen was totally blind – the causes were never established – and he resorted to becoming a street musician to supplement Cora Mae's income. Fuller would probably have remained Fulton Allen, street singer of Durham, North Carolina, had not a local shopkeeper, James Long, begun scouting talent for the American Record Company. Through his efforts Allen was sent to New York with several other bluesmen in 1935 and recorded by ARC, who changed his performing name to Blind Boy Fuller. His first records sold well, with some, such as "Rag, Mama, Rag" and "Ain't It A Cryin' Shame?" becoming blues classics in their own right.

Fuller's success was sustained through the 1930s. He used a number of people as backing musicians, including Blind Gary Davis and Sonny Terry, and due to Long's efforts, he actually received royalties on his ARC record sales. Later hits included "I'm A Stranger Here" and the classic "Step It Up And Go" in 1940. Fuller's health was failing quickly, apparently the result of kidney disease. In February 1941, "Blind Boy" Fuller died at home, tended by Cora Mae, at the age of 34.

**SEE ALSO:** Sonny Terry

# Jesse Fuller

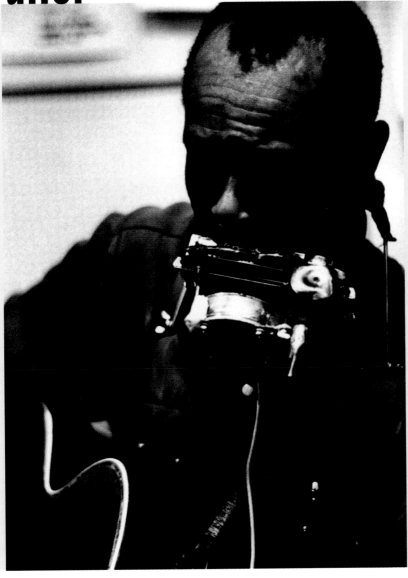

The "Lone Cat" himself, Jesse Fuller, included the kazoo in his repetoire of instruments

f ame came late to Jesse Fuller; Georgia-born and raised and an exponent of the Piedmont-style finger-picking guitar technique, he was in his mid-fifties before he took to full-time music-making. His childhood had been brutal and he escaped into the life of a hobo and odd-job man as soon as possible. By the early 1920s his train riding had taken him west, where his energetic hustling even saw him earning money as an extra on the set of the silent film, *The Thief of Baghdad*. He eventually settled in Oakland, on San Francisco Bay, where work was plentiful on the railroad and, during the War, in the shipyards. But by the end of the 1940s regular work was hard to find, and Fuller finally began to think seriously about a full-time musical career.

Jesse Fuller's novelty was that he made himself a one-man-band, playing a self-created string-bass contraption and a hi-hat, as well as guitar, harmonica and singing. Specializing in his own arrangements of folk tunes and old blues – as well as penning a few of his own numbers –

Fuller very slowly began building a musical following, though he continued doing manual labor up until the end of the 1950s.

As his reputation spread among younger folk musicians, he finally came to the attention of record companies and his song, "San Francisco Bay Blues," was recorded for the first time in 1955. Good Time Records made his second album in 1958, with a new version of his calling-card song. This was followed by an appearance at the 1959 Monterey Jazz Festival, with Fuller providing the intermission entertainment with such success that he became one of the most talked-about acts at the festival. Appearances at the Newport Folk Festival and in England furthered his impact, and when people such as Bob Dylan, Barabara Dane and Country Joe & The Fish performed and recorded his "San Francisco Bay Blues," his success was worldwide. Jesse Fuller's high-spirited music was a regular presence on the folk and traditional circuit up to his death in 1976.

## fact file

**BORN** 1896

**DIED** 1976

**MUSICAL SELECTION**
"San Francisco Bay Blues"

**SEE ALSO:** No one - he was a one-man band!

# Lowell Fulson

**fact file**

**BORN** 1921

**MUSICAL SELECTION**
It's A Good Day
Hold On!

Lowell Fulson's "Every Day I Have the Blues" was recorded with a young Ray Charles in the orchestra

ulson was the son of an American Indian father and black mother, and was born on an Indian reservation near Tulsa, Oklahoma. Like so many other bluesmen, he first enthused about music through the gospel singers and spirituals he heard as a boy, only in his teens developing both a taste for the blues and a sturdy competence on the guitar. Leaving home before he was 18, Fulson first gained experience in a string band, then in 1940 teamed up with Texas Alexander, from whom he learned not only the rules of the road for a blues artist, but much of his performing repertoire. Fulson ventured out on his own, only to be drafted in 1943, spending part of his WWII service time on Guam as well as finding himself based in Oakland. After VJ Day Fulson decided to stay in the Bay area, by chance coming into contact with Big Town Records owner Bob Geddins. Their first records together started Fulson on his successful recording career, and in 1950 he had a hit for Swingtime Records with his version of Memphis Slim's "Everyday I Have The Blues." Fulson's

sophisticated style and high-energy performances of blues pieces built him a large and loyal following. His switch to the Chess subsidiary Checker in 1954 brought immediate dividends when his single "Reconsider Baby" became a substantial hit. It was later covered by Elvis Presley, among others, and has now become a blues perennial. Fulson stayed with Checker for the rest of the 1950s, and after a period of change went to Kent Records in 1964. He also toured prolifically throughout this period, establishing himself as a solid live attraction on both sides of the Atlantic. Kent encouraged him to move closer to the type of blues young whites were listening to, but the waning interest in the blues affected Fulson as much as all the others, and it wasn't until the early 1980s that things picked up once more. Since then, albums like *It's A Good Day* (1984, Rounder) and *Hold On!* (1991, Bullseye) have re-established Lowell Fulson in the eyes and ears of today's blues audience, and he continues to enjoy interest in both his live and recorded performances.

**SEE ALSO:** Texas Alexander, Memphis Slim

# Anson Funderburgh

## fact file

**BORN** 1954

**MUSICAL SELECTION**
Talk To You By Hand

A festival favorite around the world, Anson Funderburgh has worked with everyone from the Fabulous Thunderbirds to Snooks Eaglin

f underburgh, born in Plano, Texas, is one of a generation of white blues guitarists who came to prominence through combining gritty blues feel with the technical and emotional expansiveness of rock and related musics. Thus he is of the same wave as Duke Robillard and Stevie Ray Vaughan. Running his own band for over a decade, Funderburgh is constantly renewing his blues inspiration through a reinvestigation of the roots of the music.

Born and raised in Texas, Funderburgh taught himself guitar by playing along with records of seminal 1950s and 1960s Chicago players such as Magic Sam and Freddie King. Beginning his professional career in the 1970s, Funderburgh tried a number of local bands before forming his own, The Rockets, in 1978, using the talents of the singer/harpist Darrell Nulisch to give the outfit a spearhead. After time spent on the live circuit, the band had a sufficient buzz about them to land a contract with Black Top records in 1981, releasing their first album, *Talk To You By Hand*, that same year. The group became one of the most popular touring units of the 1980s and Funderburgh kept their records interesting with a string of guests (including Snooks Eaglin in 1990). In 1986 the older-generation bluesman Sam Myers (b. 1936) replaced Nulisch as front man, giving the band a broader appeal than hitherto. Funderburgh continues to use the Rockets as his blues base.

**SEE ALSO:** Duke Robillard, Stevie Ray Vaughan, Magic Sam, Freddie King, Snooks Eaglin

# Burton Gaar

**fact file**

**BORN** 1943

**MUSICAL SELECTION**
Still Singing The Blues
One Hundred Pounds
of Trouble

Burton Gaar, the
one and only

aar was born in Baton Rouge, Louisiana, and has become part of the contemporary Louisiana blues scene which includes people like Kenny Neal and Sherman Robertson. A belting singer and accomplished bass player, Gaar has played in blues and zydeco bands for the best part of thirty years, though for much of that time he has stayed in the background, playing for other artists.

Gaar originally learned guitar in his pre-teen years, gradually deciding he preferred the bass, swapping prior to becoming a professional with Slim Harpo's band in 1959. But he continued his education at McNeese State University in Lake Charles; his courses there, plus his pursuits during leisure time, led him to strike up a friendship with members of a band called the Boogie Kings. This association kept Gaar wedded to the blues and committed to playing it until the lean years of the 1970s, when for a time he withdrew from music altogether. As the 1980s arrived Gaar began supplying zydeco star Rockin' Sidney with his regular backing band, the group appearing on Sidney's big hit, "My Toot Toot." Gaar himself, however, hindered by various contractual difficulties, failed to benefit directly from this experience. In fact, he did not record as a leader until his 1995 album, *Still Singing The Blues* – an appropriate title considering that he was 51 years old and making his debut recording. This driving, Louisiana-style blues album garnered much praise, and Gaar toured in both the US and Europe to good notices. Burton Gaar followed up his first effort with another excellent swamp-blues style album, *One Hundred Pounds of Trouble*, in 1997, and continues to pursue his renewed blues career.

**SEE ALSO:** Kenny Neal, Sherman Robertson, Slim Harpo

# Cecil Gant

**fact file**

**BORN** 1913

**DIED** 1951

**MUSICAL SELECTION**
"I Wonder"
"We're Gonna Rock"
"Rock Little Baby"

Cecil Gant,
known as "The GI
Sing-sation" for
a while due to
his time in the
military

ant was a major vocal star of the period immediately after World War II whose legato, crooning vocal style fit neatly into the prevailing fashion for sophisticated and somewhat silky R&B and jazz-trio approaches, exemplified elsewhere by Charles Brown, Nat King Cole, Billy Eckstine, and Joe Williams. Gant was born in Nashville, Tennessee, and listened to most of the music being played in his area as he grew past adolescence. He came to a musical career relatively late, playing piano and singing in Nashville clubs at the end of the 1930s before going into the army at the beginning of World War II. While in the army he experienced a career makeover when, unbilled, he made a spontaneous appearance at a War Bond concert in Los Angeles in 1944. The audience reaction to his self-accompanied singing was so great that he was invited to sing at other rallies. This led to the inevitable recording contract (for Gilt-Edge records) and a massive 1945 hit, the ballad "I Wonder." At the time Gant was still in the forces and the resultant publicity made much of this connection. After discharge, Gant quickly followed up on his success with a series of records with a plethora of labels, including King and Decca, using the ballad, R&B, and boogie styles in an effort to sustain public interest. His latter-day boogie-type discs are now judged to have presaged rock 'n' roll both in the piano style used (copied by rock musicians like Little Richard and Jerry Lee Lewis) and the lyrics penned (on such 1950 sides as "We're Gonna Rock" and "Rock Little Baby"), although he covered the field by cutting at the same sessions such songs as "God Bless My Daddy," "Goodnight Irene," and "Hello Santa Claus," among others. Unable to repeat his 1945 success, Gant turned to drink, an alcoholic by the time he died, of pneumonia, in February 1951.

**SEE ALSO:** Charles Brown, Joe Williams

# Terry Garland

Terry Garland's performance sometimes verges on the possessed, but his style is a unique mix

**fact file**

**BORN** 1953

**MUSICAL SELECTION**
Trouble In Mind
The One To Blame

arland is one of a young wave of blues performers reinvestigating the country-blues tradition and bringing new vitality to it. Rather than respectfully making careful and tepid versions of old classics, Garland brings to the older repertoire the energy (bordering occasionally on a state of possession) with which it was invested when it was first minted by the pioneers some 80 or 90 years ago.

Garland was born in Johnson City, Tennessee, and spent his formative years in and around the same location. His first enthusiasms in music came from the white rock 'n' rollers of the 1950s – people like Carl Perkins, Jerry Lee Lewis, and Elvis Presley, and the bands he first played in reflected these enthusiasms; but by the mid-1980s Garland had thoroughly researched the roots of the music he'd picked up and played in various bands and decided the

time had come for a commitment to those earlier forms. He began gigging as a solo artist, drawing heavily on the older bluesmasters for his performing repertoire, as was made clear on the first album he made under his own name, for First Warning Records, *Trouble In Mind* (1991). Composers such as Willie Dixon, Skip James, Willie McTell, Bukka White, and Lightnin' Hopkins were represented alongside his own songs and those of Johnny Winter and Jimmy Reed. His second album, *The Edge Of the Valley*, came out in 1992, while his latest, *The One To Blame*, appeared in 1996 and represented the same judicious mix, showing on Champion Jack Dupree's "Nasty Boogie Woogie" his original fascination with Jerry Lee Lewis's way of delivering a lyric. Garland continues to record and perform in the US and has now established himself worldwide as a serious blues contender.

**SEE ALSO:** Willie Dixon, Skip James, Willie McTell, Bukka White, Sam "Lightnin'" Hopkins, Johnny Winter, Jimmy Reed

# Larry Garner

At the age of 11, Larry Garner was already appearing in a local gospel group in Louisiana, performing on the radio

**g**arner came to prominence relatively late, being in his late thirties when he began to create an international audience for his individualistic approach to the blues. A fine vocalist with a rich, smooth baritone voice and an inborn ability to deliver lyrics with unusual depth of meaning, Garner spent a number of years out of the music before winning awards in the 1980s and making a quick impact in Europe in particular.

Garner was born and raised in Baton Rouge and learned his guitar style from a relative while still a pre-adolescent. Playing in a gospel group before he was 12 years old, Garner gradually gravitated toward Crescent City R&B as his teen years arrived. He and a cousin ran a local Baton Rouge R&B band for a number of years before the draft delivered him to the army at the close of the 1960s. He stayed 10 years, playing music all the while and traveling far beyond the US. After he left the army, he married and raised a family, staying away from the itinerant lifestyle of music while he was doing this. By the early 1980s he felt ready to return to music, writing and performing his own music. In 1988 he won a B.B. King Lucille Award for his song "Dog House Blues," and the recognition helped move him on apace: two years later his first album, *Catch The Feeling*, was recorded under his own direction and released on cassette, to be sold at gigs. At the dawn of the 1990s he was able to tour more widely, making it to Europe as well as other parts of the USA: albums were cut on both sides of the Atlantic, and a deal with Verve/Gitanes resulted in his most accomplished disc to date, *You Need To Live a Little* (1994), a record that, while rooted deep in the Louisiana blues, is not deaf to other musical currents pulsing through the Crescent City and beyond.

## fact file

**BORN** 1952

**MUSICAL SELECTION**
Catch The Feeling
You Need To Live
a Little

# Clifford Gibson

**fact file**

**BORN** 1901

**DIED** 1963

**MUSICAL SELECTION**
"Brooklyn Blues"
"Society Blues"

Clifford Gibson, in one of his only existing photos, had already finished the majority of his recordings when he was 28 years old

**g**uitarist/singer Gibson was one of the most respected bluesmen in St Louis during the golden era of country blues. Born in Louisville, Kentucky, Gibson was a friend and colleague of Roosevelt Sykes and fell under the musical influence of the St Louis-based guitarist Lonnie Johnson, whose jazzy single-line picking he emulated and embellished. A sure technician with a fertile musical imagination, Gibson, once established in St Louis, quickly came to the attention of the town's musicians and eventually made it onto records in June 1929. His sides for QRS, recorded in New York, show him to be a lyricist with an eye for the inequities in life and a guitarist of surpassing quality. "Tired of Being Mistreated," parts 1 and 2, are examples of this. Gibson swapped to the Victor label in November 1929, making another excursion to New York, and his keen

observations of NYC life are preserved on "Brooklyn Blues" and "Society Blues." Gibson suffered like most country blues players in the Depression, and he returned to the studios just once more for Victor, in June 1931, when he made two sides accompanied by Roosevelt Sykes, "She Rolls It Slow" and "Railroad Man Blues." He continued to ply his trade in and around St Louis, gaining little recognition, for the next three decades, often supplementing his income with day jobs. In 1960 he made two singles for the tiny Bobbie label in St Louis, under the name Grandpappy Gibson, and also reportedly worked regularly at St Louis's Gaslight Square.

Missed by the keen young researchers looking for surviving bluesmen from the 1920s, he died in 1963, his latter-day music virtually entirely unrecorded.

**SEE ALSO:** Roosevelt Sykes, Lonnie Johnson

# Jazz Gillum

**fact file**

**BORN** 1904

**DIED** 1966

**MUSICAL SELECTION**
Jazz Gillum

Like many Southern blues performers of his day, Jazz Gillum used music to supplement his income, performing on the street for change

illum was born in Indianola, Mississippi, and suffered hardship early on. His parents died soon after his birth and he was raised by other relatives. He was attracted to the harmonica practically in infancy, getting tones out of the instrument when as young as three years old. By the time he was 19 he was ready to leave Mississippi and, not surprisingly, opted for Chicago, which in 1923 was a rapidly-expanding industrial center and a Mecca for blues and street musicians of all kinds. He met and teamed up with Big Bill Broonzy there in the mid-1920s, and was often heard on the latter's 78s. He also cut sides with other Chicago-based notables, including Tampa Red, Lil Green and Black Bob. Gillum became one of the most widely-heard and influential blues harmonica players of the 1920s and 1930s, his dextrous and enthusiastic harp commentaries providing perfect accompaniment to many other players.

Gillum began recording under his own name in 1934, signed to the Bluebird label by Chicago blues 'fixer' Lester Melrose. His band, "His Jazz Boys," often included Big Bill and Washboard Sam, and would continue recording for Bluebird/Victor until 1950, though his peak period for the label was the decade between 1937-47. Gillum operated in the city blues arena, using the strong beat and optimism typical of the genre to entertain his public. This formula was very successful until the shift in public taste following World War II, after which Gillum's star would be on the wane. Sides he recorded in March 1950 went unissued, and his next appearance in a recording studio was 1961, on a Memphis Slim session for Candid. At that time he admitted, "I'm still tryin' to make it, but I hardly play nowhere no more." His career still in eclipse, Jazz Gillum suffered a violent death, in Chicago, in 1966.

**SEE ALSO:** Big Bill Broonzy, TampA Red, Lil Green, Washboard Sam, Memphis Slim

# Otis Grand

**fact file**

**BORN** 1950

**MUSICAL SELECTION**
Always Hot
Nothing Else
Matters

Born in Beirut, Lebanon, Otis Grand was voted UK Blues Guitarist of the Year, 1990

guitarist Grand, although born in Lebanon to American parents and making his first big impact on the blues scene through barnstorming tours of England, has spent the majority of his life in America. Learning guitar at the start of his teen years, Grand quickly gravitated toward the electric blues, finding inspiration in the work of T-Bone Walker, B.B. King, and Otis Rush in particular. Grand has spent time in both San Francisco and the New England area, meeting many of the best artists from both areas, working with musicians associated with the Boston blues boom of the 1980s, including Ronnie Earl and Curtis Salgado.

Grand started touring England in the late 1980s with his band the Dance Kings. He created something of a sensation, being named as the UK Blues Guitarist of the Year four years in a row, 1989–93, while his band also won in its own category. Three W.C. Handy nominations also came his way during this time. He began making records in 1988 – the first was *Always Hot. He Knows The Blues* was an important album for him, being UK Blues Album of the Year in 1992 and being the breakthrough set for him in the US. In 1994 his album *Nothing Else Matters* featured old friends Kim Wilson, Sugar Ray Norcia, and Curtis Salgado. He continues to record and tour extensively.

**SEE ALSO:** T-Bone Walker, B. B. King, Otis Rush, Ronnie Earl

# Lil Green

**fact file**

**BORN** 1919

**DIED** 1954

**MUSICAL SELECTION**
"I Won't Sell My Love"
"Why Don't You
Do Right?"

Li'l Green was yet another powerful blues performer overshadowed by a contemporary's rendition of her work

reen was one of the leading female R&B vocalists of the 1940s, able to give a shot of spice and adrenaline to the most ordinary of material put in front of her and also capable of penning superior material of her own: she was responsible for the hit tune, "Romance In The Dark." She was an astute employer of talent for her own purposes, using such accompanists on her wartime Bluebird records as Champion Jack Dupree and Big Bill Broonzy.

Green was born in Mississippi but moved to Chicago in 1929 and came to consider herself a native Chicagoan. By her late teens she was singing in some of the lesser Chicago clubs, eventually coming via Big Bill Broonzy to the attention of Victor's Lester Melrose, who signed her to Bluebird. She and Broonzy were already appearing at clubs together, so it was natural for him to play on her dates and for her to appear on

some of his for the label. As her reputation spread she went on the road with a number of big bands, including Luis Russell and Tiny Bradshaw (she recorded with a big band just once, Howard Callender's band, in July 1946), and proved popular with black audiences, but never managed to land a crossover hit in the way Nellie Lutcher was to do just a year later. In 1941 she had recorded a fine version of "Why Don't You Do Right?" with Big Bill on guitar, but Peggy Lee, who covered it with Benny Goodman's band, had the million-seller.

Green swapped labels and bands toward the end of the 1940s, trying a new angle with Aladdin ("My Be Bop Daddy") in 1949 but with little progress, and making just one date for Atlantic in 1951. But by then her health was on the wane, and she died in 1954, catching pneumonia while in a rundown condition. Her legacy remains an influence on the blues today.

**SEE ALSO:** Champion Jack Dupree, Big Bill Broonzy

# Buddy Guy

I n George "Buddy" Guy, most blues fans recognize a performer who represents a major watershed in blues guitar style. Through the force of his playing and the audacity of his invention, Guy carved out a new role in which the guitarist could claim a solo or lead spotlight during the course of a song, along with (or instead of) the vocalist or the sax players.

Guy hailed originally from Louisiana and taught himself the rudiments of guitar playing, often copying guitar styles from what he heard on the radio, on juke boxes and in juke joints around Baton Rouge. Music was strictly a part-time pursuit, however, until he left Louisiana in 1957 and headed for Chicago. After a few months of struggling he wound up, through a contest, an accidental participant in a recording session with Otis Rush. As a result, Guy was befriended by Rush and Muddy Waters, and hired for live work by the owner of the club where the recording contest had taken place. Waters drew him into the wider Chicago blues world, and before long he was making records for the small Cobra label's subsidiary, Artistic. There, Guy was overseen by Muddy's colleague Willie Dixon, then Cobra's leading blues talent handler. Guy's singles, along with those of Magic Sam and Otis Rush, exposed the wider world to the updated sound of what was quickly termed West Side Chicago blues, as distinct from the Chicago blues of Chess stalwarts Waters and Howlin' Wolf.

Chess signed Guy up after Cobra's demise in 1960, and the sides he made there as both leader and sideman are a graphic illustration of his virtuoso talents and versatility: Guy could move from country blues (he was the backing guitarist on Muddy Waters' "Folk Singer" album of 1963) to Wes Montgomery-inflected, jazzy blues instrumentals, as well as soul-based vocal scorchers replete with tight brass section arrangements. His records became widely influential, with younger players from both sides of the Atlantic enthusiastic in their praise, from Jimi Hendrix to Eric Clapton. European tours in the mid-1960s widened his appeal, with his wild live act appealing to a younger audience than Chess was aiming for. Not long after Guy cut the famous "Hoodoo Man Blues" session under a pseudonym for Junior Wells over at Delmark, he and Wells teamed up for a long-running live partnership, their double-act especially appealing to the audiences on the gradually expanding European festival circuit. Always able to pick up on the music around him, Guy felt at ease borrowing from the blues legacy of a man he'd deeply influenced earlier – Jimi Hendrix – and building elements of the Hendrix style into his own formidable musical persona. Such adaptations kept Guy at the cutting edge of blues playing through the 1970s and 1980s, but reduced interest in the blues during those decades somewhat limited his activities.

Guy was always resourceful enough to get himself through hard times, and by 1991 – when Eric Clapton featured him in his Albert Hall concert series and delivered him to a new blues audience – he had already been the proprietor of his own Chicago blues club, Buddy Guy's Legends, for three years. He took the opportunity of his renewed popularity to record a couple of his best-ever albums in the early 1990s, *Damn Right, I've Got The Blues* (1991) and *Feels Like Rain* (1993). Today Buddy Guy continues to perform, record and run his Legends club, featuring the best of contemporary blues talent.

**fact file**

**BORN** 1936

**MUSICAL SELECTION**
Damn Right, I've Got
The Blues
Feels Like Rain

Buddy Guy's prolific career was encouraged largely by an appreciative young crowd turned on to the blues by rock musicians such as The Rolling Stones and Eric Clapton

**SEE ALSO:** Otis Rush, Muddy Waters, Willie Dixon, Magic Sam, Jimi Hendrix

# Guitar Slim

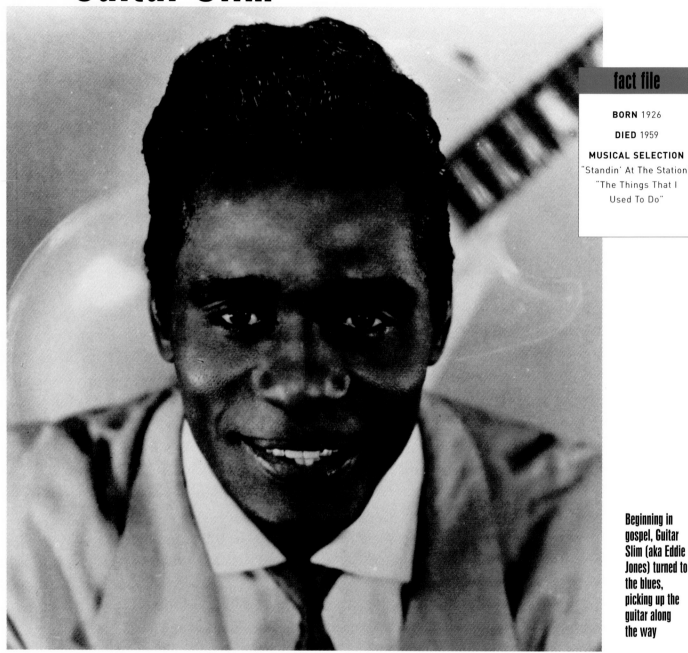

## fact file

**BORN** 1926

**DIED** 1959

**MUSICAL SELECTION**
"Standin' At The Station"
"The Things That I
Used To Do"

Beginning in gospel, Guitar Slim (aka Eddie Jones) turned to the blues, picking up the guitar along the way

**t**he Louisiana "swamp" sound was never far away from Slim's music, and his driving combination of characteristic sounds from both the rural and urban Louisiana traditions made him a pivotal figure in the gradual development of the rock 'n' roll sound of the 1950s. Slim was also a hard-living, flamboyant showman who thought nothing of throwing himself to the floor while playing, or of trailing his guitar lead off the stage and across the room to play his instrument and sing in the men's room – anything to amaze the fans.

Eddie Jones (aka Guitar Slim) started out as a gospel singer, later switching to the blues. But it was after army service in WWII that he began striking out as a guitarist as well as a singer, leaving the Delta area for the richer economic pastures of New Orleans and playing regularly at the Dew Drop Inn, among other

places, as Guitar Slim. He signed for Imperial in 1951 and made half a dozen sides where his strikingly powerful, gospel-inflected vocals and tough-sounding guitar were beginning to form a strong identity. But it was with the Speciality label in 1954 that he got it spectacularly right, cutting "The Things That I Used to Do," a No.1 on the R&B charts and an influential number in terms of the sound and rhythm created. Unable to repeat the vast success of "Things," Slim was dropped from Speciality in 1956, signing instead for the Atlantic subsidiary, Atco.

There he continued to make good records without enjoying significant chart action. But by the end of the decade his wild lifestyle caught up with him; in the depths of the winter of 1959, Guitar Slim contracted pneumonia, dying shortly after a concert in Buffalo, New York, not yet 35.

**SEE ALSO:** Earl King

# John Hammond

**fact file**

**BORN** 1943

**MUSICAL SELECTION**
I'm Satisfied
Got Love If You
Want It

Carrying on the torch his father sparked with the Spirituals To Swing concerts, John Hammond III is a strong blues performer in his own right

S on of the famous A&R man, civil rights activist and record producer John Hammond, John Hammond III shares his father's dedicated commitment. It has been blues – mostly but not exclusively of the prewar country variety – which has been his endless well of inspiration, and he has stuck at being a blues singer and acoustic guitarist for over 30 years.

Hammond grew up with a background more financially secure than most of his fellow bluesmen and also benefited from a thorough education not available to the average Southern black in the immediate postwar period. Hammond's own instincts and integrity have ensured that he has never used these privileges to be a mere dilettante in the music. Discovering the blues when in his late teens, Hammond began learning guitar and harmonica, appearing at New York coffee houses and folk hangouts in the early 1960s and eventually making his eponymous recording debut for Vanguard records in 1963. His vitality and commitment was evident from the first, as was his ability to precisely match the subtleties and inflections of the Delta blues, which was his first inspiration. His appearance at the 1963 Newport Folk

Festival confirmed his attractions to the burgeoning folk/blues audience. During the rest of the 1960s he traveled widely, including most of Europe, playing in a variety of contexts, including backing from folk-rock and beat musicians such as the Hawks (later to become The Band, who also appeared on *So Many Roads*, 1967) and Bill Wyman. He also jammed with guitarists such as Duane Allman and Jimi Hendrix. Hammond's career continued to prosper in the 1970s, with a move to Columbia at the beginning of the decade seeing him embark on some of his most ambitious recording projects, including a more Chicago-type and R&B-inspired couple of sets, *I'm Satisfied* (1972) and *Triumvirate*, with Dr John and Mike Bloomfield.

Later decades have seen Hammond mostly returning to his original conceptions, especially with a long series of quality albums for Rounder such as *Fattening Frogs For Snakes* (1982), while the 1990s have seen his return to a larger record company (Virgin/Pointblank). *Got Love If You Want It* (produced in 1992 by J.J. Cale) and 1993's *Trouble No More* succinctly tell Hammond's always intriguing blues story.

**SEE ALSO:** Jimi Hendrix, Dr John, Mike Bloomfield

# W C Handy

handy's role in the propagation of blues is not without controversy: his early status as "Father of the Blues" – a title he himself endorsed by using it for his autobiography – has been under constant scrutiny in the decades since his death, and the picture that has begun to emerge is one of an astute and sharp-eared musician/publisher who was sufficiently on the ball to incorporate blues elements into the music of his bands, collect blues material on his travels, and publish some of the earliest blues songs. Whether these were his own compositions or 'realized' and codified from the melodies and samples he came across in his professional life is often a moot point, but in this respect he is not alone, for copyrighting the work of others was a widespread practice in the first four decades of this century.

Handy was born in Florence, Alabama, and was trained in music while still a young man, learning not only to play a variety of instruments to a decent level of proficiency (specializing in the cornet) but to read and notate music. He also learned the basics of arranging. All these skills were put to use when he chose to earn a living by traveling with minstrel shows and other· such variety groups, which were the principal means of entertainment for the common folk of the day. He was a fixture in Mahara's Minstrels from 1896 to the mid-1900s, when he began running his own troupes. A song written in 1908 as "Mr Crump" was in 1912 published as "Memphis Blues" and became a runaway success, even though its blues roots are very shallow. Two years later came the classic "St Louis Blues," utilizing a rhumba section echoing the "Spanish tinge" mentioned by Jelly Roll Morton as an essential ingredient in jazz. It is possible that Handy took the two simple melodies in "St Louis Blues" from folk sources and wove them into his own composition. Whatever the roots of the music, the song became immensely popular and helped launch what was within half a decade a blues craze. During the 1920s and 1930s Handy ran his own businesses for a while and used a variety of orchestras, working with Jelly Roll Morton and, later, swing players such as J.C. Higginbotham and Big Sid Catlett. By this time quite out of step with performing practice and fashion, Handy concentrated on publishing and songwriting. This withdrawal from performance was confirmed by an accident which left him blind in 1943. He spent the rest of his life involved in writing his autobiography, arranging publishing matters, and being an elder statesman for his race and his musical peers, often busying himself with events on and off Broadway and in vaudeville.

## fact file

**BORN** 1873

**DIED** 1958

**MUSICAL SELECTION**
"Memphis Blues"
"St Louis Blues"

W.C. Handy, pictured here with the jazz great Duke Ellington (r.)

SEE ALSO: Walter "Furry" Lewis, Otis Grand

# James Harman

From his slick hairstyle to his 1950s-inspired shows, James Harman celebrates the blues with a touch of theater

**fact file**

**BORN** 1946

**MUSICAL SELECTION**
This Band Won't Behave
Do Not Disturb

harman was born in Alabama and spent his youth in that state before leaving home and traveling extensively around the American South. He acquired a taste for the blues early in life, and taught himself harmonica as a double for his persuasive vocals. This led to work for him in bars and clubs through Florida, Missouri, and Louisiana, but in 1972 he decided to relocate to California. Over the next decade, first with the Icehouse Blues Band and then with the James Harman Band, the singer became a fixture on the local Californian scene, his up-to-date lyrics and sense of humor winning him a loyal following as well as the respect of headline acts his band often played support for.

With little happening on the recording front for young blues artists of any persuasion in the late 1970s, Harman eventually formed his own record label to release his first album, *This Band Won't Behave* (Icepick, 1981). Sold both in stores and at the band's gigs, the album helped spread the word sufficiently for other companies to check the band out, and Harman made records for three labels in the next half-dozen years. The band also began to expand their touring schedule, moving overseas as well as ranging across the States as the new blues boom arrived. Their driving, cheeky, power-packed blues appealed to audiences looking for a good time, and the discipline of the band always impressed on records. The album *Do Not Disturb* (Black Top, 1991) begins with a typical lowlife scene in which a sleeping man is woken by a chambermaid knocking on the door of his hotel room at the same time as the phone ringing – it's the proprietor wanting to know when he's going to check out; such a scenario is part of the blues tradition, but also a clever updating of it. James Harman continues to record and perform, ever a popular favorite with blues fans.

**SEE ALSO:** Hollywood Fats

# Slim Harpo

Born James Moore, Slim Harpo was known as "Harmonica Slim" before receiving his more familiar moniker

arpo, born in Baton Rouge, Louisiana, was commercially one of the most consistently successful blues artists of the late 1950s and the 1960s, his easy-grooving blues shuffles, soft nasal voice, and punchy harp playing being overlaid with Louisiana "soul" from a relaxed, Louisiana R&B-influenced backing strongly reminiscent of his erstwhile employer, Lightnin' Slim.

Harpo was born and raised in Baton Rouge and saw no reason to depart from that neighborhood. By his late teens he was gigging around his home town, playing the usual assortment of juke joints and parties. By the mid-1950s he was often in Lightnin' Slim's band, recording with the older man in 1955 on J.D. Miller's Excello label. This contact led him to signing for Excello: his very first recording session in 1957 yielded the hit "I'm A King Bee." A string of minor hits and a steady career in music was given a rocket boost by "Raining In My Heart," recorded in November 1960 and a major hit in 1961. Harpo and Excello fell out over royalties before the end of the year, and he recorded for Imperial, though J.D. Miller took out an injunction and no Imperial sides were released. A two-year hiatus lost Harpo much of his commercial momentum, but on his return in 1963 he and Excello proved adept at packaging his simple songs with slinky, contemporary beats. His huge 1966 hit, "Baby Scratch My Back," is dominated by such a rhythm, all else being incidental to its insinuating movement. Harpo was one of the small number of blues artists to make an impression on the rock scene in the late 1960s, performing at Fillmore East and Whisky A-Go-Go as well as opening for James Brown, among others. His death from a heart attack came at a time when he was still one of blues'S most commercially viable figures.

## fact file

**BORN** 1924

**DIED** 1970

**MUSICAL SELECTION**
"I'm A King Bee"
"Baby Scratch
My Back"

**SEE ALSO:** Lightnin' Slim

121

# Wynonie Harris

fact file

**BORN** 1915

**DIED** 1969

**MUSICAL SELECTION**
"I Like My Baby's Pudding"
"I Want My Fanny Brown"

Don't let the innocent looks fool you, Wynonie Harris could be as raunchy as the best of 'em

arris, known as "Mr Blues" at his late-1940s popular peak, was a graduate of the Lucky Millinder Band and used his powerful blues voice, his sharp dress sense, and his smolderingly sensual good looks to become for a while the top R&B performer in America, racking up hit after hit before subsiding under the initial waves of rock 'n' roll, a hybrid he'd helped inspire and define.

Harris was born in Omaha, Nebraska, and in his teens learned to play the drums before deciding that it was easier and more glamorous to be a singer. Learning from such boogie singing greats as Joe Turner during his early travels, Harris arrived in Los Angeles in the immediate prewar period and honed his entertaining skills in a variety of ways, even appearing briefly in a Hollywood film in 1943. After that he joined up with Millinder in the Midwest, where he was the vocalist on a late Millinder hit for Decca, "Who Threw The Whiskey In The Well?" Convinced

that this was the time for a solo career, Harris went solo in 1945, making LA his operational base and using jazz personnel on his records, but the hits started racking up only after his signing to King records in 1947. No songwriter, he was a fine interpreter, and he made "Good Rockin' Tonight" a seminal pre-rock hit in 1947 for King. Rock became a key word in Harris's (and many other King) recordings, being an obvious double entendre for sexual activity, a pastime of which Harris was clearly fond, judging by the weight of anecdotes. Other songs of the late 1940s by Harris include "Sittin' On It All The Time," "I Like My Baby's Pudding," and "I Want My Fanny Brown." Harris stayed with King through to the late 1950s but his recording activity rapidly tailed off with the advent of Bill Haley and Elvis Presley, both of whom took wholesale parts of Harris's style and recycled them. Harris never regained the public's attention and died, in 1969, from lung cancer.

**SEE ALSO:** Joe Turner

# Rosa Henderson

## fact file

**BORN** 1896

**DIED** 1968

**MUSICAL SELECTION**
"Strut Yo' Puddy"

Recording under different names, Rosa Henderson did not receive the praise she may have deserved, but she left a lengthy recorded legacy

osa Henderson (aka Rosa Deschamps) was an important early jazz and blues vocalist who came from the same vaudeville tradition as Ma Rainey and Bessie Smith. Possessed of a lighter, sweeter voice than either of the above, Henderson recorded frequently in the 1920s with a large variety of musicians and labels, starting with Fletcher Henderson (no relation) in New York City in 1923 and finishing with James P. Johnson in the same city in 1931 (an isolated single: her last year of continuous recording was 1927). Her accompanists were invariably musicians based in or passing through New York, although her own roots were in Kentucky. She was born Rosa Deschamps, and her early life is sketchy. She is first documented in vaudeville in the second decade of the century, touring mainly in Texas up to the end of World War I with a troupe led by her uncle. She met Douglas "Slim" Henderson around this time and they later married, working as a duo before settling in New York, where Rosa began picking up recording work.

Henderson recorded virtually without a break for a great variety of labels and under a similar number of pseudonyms to avoid contractual stipulations, thus depriving herself of steady exposure under any one name and killing any chance of building a lasting popularity. She managed a notable hit only with the impressive "Strut Yo' Puddy" in 1924 (released under her own name). Her career on the wane prior even to the Wall Street Crash of 1929, Henderson quietly slipped from sight during the Depression, staying in New York but eventually landing a day job as a shop assistant in a department store and withdrawing altogether from her former career.

**SEE ALSO:** Ma Rainey, Bessie Smith

# Jimi Hendrix

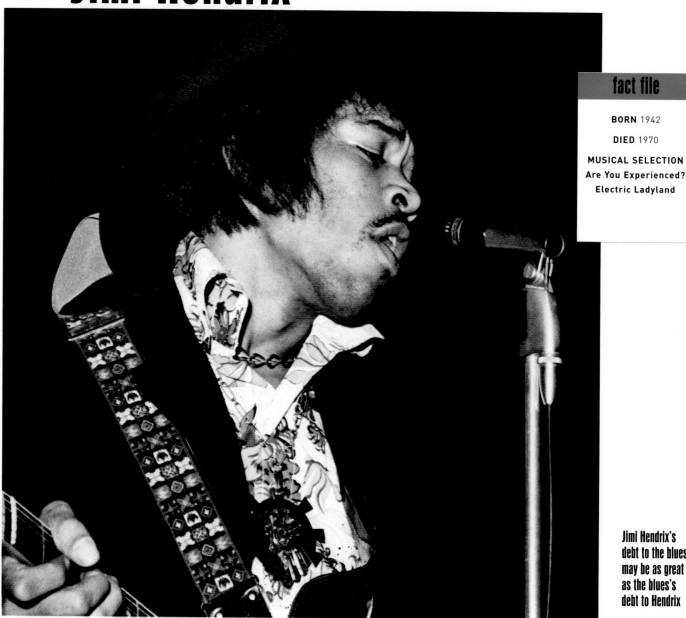

**fact file**

**BORN** 1942

**DIED** 1970

**MUSICAL SELECTION**
Are You Experienced?
Electric Ladyland

Jimi Hendrix's
debt to the blues
may be as great
as the blues's
debt to Hendrix

a lthough the legendary Hendrix is most often thought of in terms of rock psychedelia and guitar heroics, anything more than the most casual listen to his music will reveal a performer steeped in the blues tradition. Any musician who could pick up a 12-string guitar in a studio and improvise the moving, down-home acoustic blues "Hear My Train A-Comin'," as Hendrix did in London in 1967, has nothing to prove on that score.

Hendrix was born in Seattle, Washington, and by the time he hit his teenage years he was obsessed with learning guitar, listening to a range of blues records from John Lee Hooker to Muddy Waters to Elmore James and Buddy Guy. Sidetracked by military service between 1959 and 1961, Hendrix hit the road after his discharge and joined up with a string of rock 'n' roll and R&B units, including the Isley Brothers and Little Richard. Determined to make it as a leader, he suffered neglect in the mid-1960s in New York as he tried to pull together a working group and an identifiable sound.

Ironically, Hendrix only found success after he was invited to London by his manager-to-be Chas Chandler, after Chandler had heard him at the tiny Cafe Wha? in Greenwich Village. Hendrix's first album, *Are You Experienced?* contained much which stretched the existing boundaries of rock and of the electric guitar, but it also included the classic blues "Red House," a song Hendrix would play in concert for the rest of his career. Each subsequent Hendrix album would always include blues and R&B numbers. His version of Earl King's "Come On Pt. 1," on *Electric Ladyland*, for example, is one of the most electrifying guitar tours-de-force on a 12-bar theme in blues history; while "Voodoo Chile," a jam featuring Stevie Winwood, showed Jimi's John Lee Hooker roots. His concerts, too, would feature long guitar extravaganzas on blues themes. Jimi Hendrix was a musician with unusually wide interests and influence, but the blues remained at his core up to his untimely death in London in 1970.

**SEE ALSO:** John Lee Hooker, Muddy Waters, Elmore James, Buddy Guy, Earl King

# Bertha "Chippie" Hill

**fact file**

**BORN** 1905

**DIED** 1950

**MUSICAL SELECTION**
"Low Land Blues"
"Kid Man Blues"

Bertha Hill (aka "Chippie"), pictured at Jimmy Ryan's in 1948, worked with both jazz and blues artists of the 1920s

h ill was an important presence on the classic blues scene of the 1920s, her strong, emphatic vocals and authentic Southern inflection proving as popular with record buyers as her tent-show act had proved with the paying public. Not as extensively recorded as many others – especially the various blues-singing Smiths – Hill moved in similar musical circles, recording with such jazz talent as Louis Armstrong, Preston Jackson, Lonnie Johnson, and King Oliver. She also recorded using Georgia Tom Dorsey and Tampa Red as accompanists, and was the singer on a 1929 date nominally led by the guitarist Scrapper Blackwell.

Hill was born in Charleston, South Carolina, into a large family (there were 16 children). Small and slight of build (hence the nickname), Hill left home as a teenager and started appearing as a dancer and entertainer at the age of 14 on the TOBA circuit, appearing in New York at one stage and, according to her reminiscences, upstaging Ethel Waters at the nightclub Leroy's. This triumph notwithstanding, she decided to settle in Chicago in the early 1920s and made her recording debut there in November

1925, still just 20 years old. Her first sides, "Low Land Blues" and "Kid Man Blues," were made for Okeh and featured Louis Armstrong. She followed this up with a big-seller in "Trouble In Mind," featuring the same musicians and recorded in February 1926. She stayed with Okeh until December 1927: the label released just two of the last eight tracks she recorded for them. Swapping to Vocalion, she went for a more down-home sound, using Tampa Red and Georgia Tom through 1928–29, and cut her second version of "Trouble In Mind" with unknown accompanists including a cornet player and clarinetist. The tailing off of her recording career (it finished midsummer 1929) coincided with her marriage, and she withdrew from the music business for nearly 20 years. After World War II she came out of retirement to sing with Lovie Austin's group and record for Circle records, re-creating the jazz-blues styles of two decades before for a new audience. She also caused quite a stir at the Paris International Jazz Festival in November 1948. Seemingly set for a return to favor as part of the revivalist scene, Hill was tragically killed in New York by a hit-and-run automobile driver.

**SEE ALSO:** Lonnie Johnson, Georgia Tom Dorsey, Tampa Red

# Michael Hill

Michael Hill, pictured here with his Blues Mob (center) came to the blues via Hendrix and Clapton

**fact file**

**BORN** 1952

**MUSICAL SELECTION**
**Bloodlines**
**Have Mercy**

hill is a blues musician very much of the present generation, his red-hot guitar style showing unmistakable traces of rock guitar influences in the shape of Gary Moore, Jimi Hendrix, and Johnny Winter as well as signs of the men who influenced those people, such as Buddy Guy and Freddie and Albert King. His powerful tenor voice, allied to the punchy sound of his band, the Blues Mob, makes Hill's blues very much a sound for today rather than an attempt at re-creation.

Hill was born in New York's Bronx district and exposed to the large pool of different musical cultures New York has to offer. Discovering Buddy Guy around the time he was delving into rock and related guitar styles for his own

ends, Hill decided on a blues career, albeit one with overtones of soul and rock. His first band was his own, Brown Sugar, in which his brother Kevin also appeared. After a series of bands, he joined Black Rock Coalition in 1985 with Vernon Reid, but left to found the Blues Mob in 1987. Gigs around the New York area and the continuation of a career playing with various other bands kept Hill's local profile high, and in 1994 he signed a deal with Alligator records which resulted in the Blues Mob's inaugural disc, *Bloodlines*. This CD brought contemporary and traditional modern blues sounds together. Its follow-up, *Have Mercy* (1996), continues the good work of the first set. His career continues to grow.

**SEE ALSO:** Jimi Hendrix, Johnny Winter, Buddy Guy, Freddie King, Albert King

# Andrew "Smokey" Hogg

As one of seven children, Smokey Hogg used music to get out of the fields

**a** Texan born and bred, Smokey Hogg came to music early, learning guitar through his own endeavors along with a little guidance from his own father. A cousin of Lightnin' Hopkins, he began playing at parties around his home town of Westconnie, often accompanying Black Ace. He recorded in 1937 as accompanist to Peetie Wheatstraw, and his playing fits neatly into the Texas tradition of Wheatstraw, Blind Lemon Jefferson, and Lightnin' Hopkins himself. Hogg worked intermittently up to World War II, served his time in the Army, then came out and settled in California, only to find that blues had been modernized by the advent of R&B. His records for Modern, Speciality, and Sittin' In

With reflected this change, his guitar now amplified and his backing musicians often containing sax and drums. His hits at the turn of the decade included a cover version of "Little School Girl."

Hogg never had a very strong grasp on musical form, and he had the country musician's tendency to dispense with common time: it must have been tricky to accompany him at times, especially when, as was often the case, Hogg had imbibed more than the odd drop of whiskey. This didn't bother him, his record companies, or his fans, and he continued to pursue a full-time blues career with his strong, simple approach, up to the time of his death, in 1960, from stomach cancer.

**fact file**

**BORN** 1914

**DIED** 1960

**MUSICAL SELECTION**
"Little School Girl"

**SEE ALSO:** Sam "Lightnin'" Hopkins, Black Ace, Peetie Wheatstraw, Blind Lemon Jefferson

# Dave Hole

**fact file**

**BORN** 1948

**MUSICAL SELECTION**
Working Overtime

Dave Hole, pictured playing in his unique slide style, the result of a childhood accident

ole, although a Lancastrian born in Heswall, Cheshire, England, migrated to Australia with his family when he was just four years old, settling in Perth, Western Australia. Like many young whites, he was inspired by the British beat boom of the early 1960s to explore R&B and the blues, and began learning guitar. After conquering the basics and following up on information found on records and in magazines, he traced the provenance of songs being recorded by bands such as the Pretty Things and the Rolling Stones as well as Howlin' Wolf, Muddy Waters, and Willie Dixon.

Having found the source, he began to form his own style from what he heard, eventually progressing to slide guitar in the early 1970s. This he played by utilizing a broken finger in his left hand to play slide work from over the top of the guitar's neck: an unusual but effective technique. Dedicated to the blues, he led his band at hundreds of gigs in the cities, towns, and outback of Western Australia, finally making a studio-quality cassette recording of his band which was sent to various movers and shakers in Europe and America.

The tape eventually brought Hole a deal with Alligator records and a spot on Gary Moore's European tour of 1992. Since then Hole has proved a formidable live act, touring Europe and playing in America as well as widening his fan base back in Australia as far as the Eastern Seaboard and cities like Sydney and Melbourne. Hole is still recording for Alligator (*Working Overtime*, 1993, for instance) and running his own band.

**SEE ALSO:** Howlin' Wolf, Muddy Waters, Willie Dixon

# Hollywood Fats

**fact file**

**BORN** 1955

**DIED** 1987

**MUSICAL SELECTION**
Rock This House

Hollywood Fats:
West Coast blues
guitar at its
finest, learned
from the legends
of the blues

f ats was one of the very few white blues guitarists to have been both acknowledged by and welcomed into the black blues-playing community during his lifetime. His driving guitar owed much to his heroes Magic Sam, Buddy Guy, and Freddie King, but he had a free-flowing single-note approach to his solos which was instantly recognizable and very exciting.

Starting out in his hometown of Los Angeles as plain Michael Mann, at the age of 10 he began learning guitar, and within two years he had zeroed in on the blues as his music of choice. By his mid-teens he was playing gigs as an accompanist to blues performers, arranged for him by all-round man Shakey Jake. Before the end of the 1960s his serious intent to play the best blues guitar he was capable of led him to introductions to people like Freddie King and Magic Sam, both of whom showed him many of the tricks of the trade and introduced him around. One of the men he met, Buddy Guy, gave Fats his nickname just prior to his going out on the road with J.B. Hutto and the Hawks. This

was the first in a line of gigs with top-line artists, including Albert King, Muddy Waters and John Lee Hooker, where Fats fit seamlessly into the group format and kept things cooking. Back in LA in 1975, he started up his own band, a group which was influential – along with Roomful of Blues, Stevie Ray Vaughan, and others – in establishing a modern LA blues sound. Fats' group made an album in 1979 called *Rock This House*, which has subsequently been reissued on Black Top; it is a fine summation of all that was authentic and vital in the band's approach. Fats continued to cast a large shadow on the West Coast scene during the 1980s by playing and recording with other groups, including James Harman and Rod Piazza, but his career was prematurely terminated by a fatal heart attack in 1987.

**SEE ALSO:** Magic Sam, Buddy Guy, Freddie King, Shakey Jake, J. B. Hutto, Albert King, Muddy Waters, John Lee Hooker

# Homesick James

## fact file

**BORN** 1905

**MUSICAL SELECTION**
Homesick James
Homesick

Smiling all the while, Homesick James has always been pleased to perform and spread the blues to audiences worldwide

ames Williamson was from Somerville, Tennessee, and his style was formed at a time when much of what would later be the classic Delta blues tradition was still in the process of crystallization. In his voice and playing, it is possible to trace many different streams of folk and blues music, even including work songs and field hollers. Coming from a musical family, it was not surprising that Williamson should turn to the guitar (he was self-taught) and decide to support himself through his playing. Out on the road he met many other players, including Big Joe Williams, and this experience helped form his performing style. By the late 1930s Homesick James was able to briefly run his own band in and around Memphis; this group was recorded by Bluebird in 1937. Moving to Chicago in the early 1950s he began playing with his cousin, Elmore James, learning much about the bottleneck (slide) approach while playing bass for him.

Homesick stayed with Elmore until the latter's death in 1963. Soon after, however, Homesick's career began to tail off; although still a well-known figure around Chicago clubs and bars, he had to take day jobs to make ends meet.

Frequently recorded in the 1960s by a range of labels including Delmark, Vanguard, and Bluesville, Homesick again gradually reached the stage where he was able to tour abroad, traveling with the American Blues Festival to Europe in 1970 and rebuilding a fan base there. Since then, Homesick James has remained a reliable second-string performer, a player building on the legacy of those gone before. But his authentic slide and singing have been a genuine blues experience for anyone coming across him, live or on records (he's made many recordings over the past two decades), in the closing years of a long and distinguished career.

**SEE ALSO:** Big Joe Williams, Elmore James

# Earl Hooker

Cousin to John Lee Hooker, Earl was a standout performer on stage or in the studio

h ooker was born in Clarksdale, Mississippi, a cousin of John Lee Hooker, and like many bluesmen taught himself guitar at an early age by watching and listening to the music being made around him. Listening to and learning from players of the caliber of Robert Nighthawk, he developed into one of the greatest postwar slide players once he became ensconced in the Chicago scene.

Hooker's Delta upbringing was typical for the time, and his parents made the decision so many other poverty-stricken black families did in the prewar period: they upped and moved to Chicago, when Earl was just pre-teens. Once there, Earl had the good fortune to attend a music school and learn piano, among other instruments, but it was during his teenage performances on street corners that he met Robert Nighthawk and discovered the direction he wanted to pursue. This led him for a while to Memphis, where he played with, among others, Ike Turner, but his first recordings were made in Florida in 1952–53. A Memphis session with Pinetop Perkins didn't see the light of day until many years later on LPs, and Hooker was back in Chicago in the late 1950s before things began to go his way. Plowing through some undistinguished sessions for little labels which slowly made him more widely known around Chicago, Hooker came into his own during the 1960s, when he became a staple of the Chicago blues clubs (often in tandem with Junior Wells) and his records were reaching fans on both sides of the Atlantic, his mature slide style exciting admiration and imitation.

The late 1960s were a time of intense gigging and recording for Hooker (he even cut an album with Steve Miller), and it is this period that stands as testimony to his talent. He died tragically in 1970 from tuberculosis.

**SEE ALSO:** John Lee Hooker, Robert Nighthawk, Ike Turner, Pinetop Perkins, Junior Wells

# John Lee Hooker

**h**ooker is, along with B.B. King, probably the most famous and successful bluesman in history, managing million-selling hits at both ends of his distinguished career. His raw, compelling style combines both modern and prewar elements, and his music can quite safely be described as that of a modern primitive, using up-to-date sound and technology to deliver a simple and often overpowering message.

Hooker was born into a large family in Clarksdale, Mississippi, learning guitar from the age of nine onwards from his stepfather William Moore, who was steeped in the Delta tradition exemplified by Charlie Patton. Moore showed John Lee many of the special boogie guitar rhythm patterns which would become his trademark in adult life. Hooker left home at 14, traveling around the South doing day jobs and playing clubs at night; he finally settled in Detroit in 1943, where he was a car assembly worker by day and a jobbing musician after hours. John Lee became a local attraction on the blues circuit, but had to wait until 1948 before Bernard Besman, owner of the Detroit-based Sensation Records, hired him for a session. Besman specialized in licensing product to larger companies. From Hooker's first session, he licensed "Boogie Chillen" to Modern Records; it was John Lee's first million-seller. Besman continued to license or sell material to Modern, King and Speciality until he quit the business in 1952. That year Hooker signed with Modern, but continued to moonlight for many other companies, in time becoming one of the most-recorded bluesmen ever. An exclusive deal with VeeJay of Chicago kept him more or less on one label between 1955 and 1964, and produced a fair number of hits, including "Dimples," "Boom Boom," "Big Legs, Tight Skirt" and "Crawlin' Kingsnake." His incredible baritone voice and expressive guitar, whether electric or acoustic, guaranteed a powerful experience for any listener, and Hooker was one of a handful of blues artists to reach the 1960s with a large audience intact. He quickly became a key icon for the 1960s beat and blues revival, and many of his better compositions were covered by British and US acts, especially The Animals.

Hooker recorded in a variety of settings, from voice and acoustic guitar to sessions with large backing groups; at one time VeeJay even matched him with an all-girl trio of soul singers – not his greatest moment on record! However, his credibility was never called into question and he survived the 1970s with his reputation unscathed. By this stage he was a relatively wealthy man and had become a role model for virtually every blues performer younger than him, even if his style was inimitable; his influence on, say, Jimi Hendrix, is noticeable in the latter's "Voodoo Chile," a typical slow Hooker-type boogie.

John Lee was happy to associate with young white blues players and made successful collaborations with many, including *Hooker 'n' Heat* from 1970, with Canned Heat. This idea was revived when he made *The Healer* (Silvertone/Chameleon) in 1988. Here he had guests such as Bonnie Raitt, Carlos Santana and Robert Cray help him out, and the subsequent TV appearances and publicity made the record a world-wide best-seller. Hooker had by this time long departed Detroit, moving out to Oakland on the West Coast, but his sudden return to the spotlight in the 1980s has kept him on the road ever since. *Mr Lucky* (1991) repeated the "Healer" formula to great success, and Hooker even appeared in TV commercials. Now in his eighties, John Lee continues to record and perform, and is rightly seen as a blues living legend.

## fact file

**BORN** 1917

**MUSICAL SELECTION**
The Healer
Mr Lucky

John Lee Hooker is very likely one of the most recognized and celebrated blues artists in the world

**SEE ALSO:** B.B. King, Charlie Patton, Jimi Hendrix, Robert Cray

# Sam "Lightnin'" Hopkins

### fact file

**BORN** 1912

**DIED** 1982

**MUSICAL SELECTION**
The Roots of
Lightnin' Hopkins
Coffee House Blues

A true country-blues singer, Sam "Lightnin'" Hopkins reached greater public acclaim following an autobiographical documentary

One of the blues' greatest talents, Lightnin' Hopkins was born in Piney Woods territory, East Texas, in a little town called Centerville. His spare, expressive playing, taciturn vocals and crisp versification all place him squarely in the tradition of Texas blues; in fact, he claims to have accompanied Blind Lemon Jefferson when the great bluesman visited his area during Lightnin's adolescence. He also picked up blues lessons watching his older brother Joel and their cousin, Texas Alexander.

Lightnin' often accompanied Texas Alexander on his wanderings, along with playing on the streets of Houston. A period in jail during the 1930s interrupted Hopkins's career, but on his release he married Antoinette Charles and spent some time sharecropping near Dallas. Later, he and Alexander teamed up once more and concentrated their efforts on Houston; they became a staple on the Houston scene, but had to wait until 1946 – by which time Hopkins was in his mid-thirties – before a record company, Aladdin, was prepared to try them in the studio. Hopkins went to Los Angeles to make the record date, but Alexander never made the trip; he was substituted by blues

pianist and vocalist Wilson Smith, whom Aladdin quickly dubbed "Thunder," while Sam Hopkins became "Lightnin'" – making the name of the duo on records. The pair had an immediate hit with Hopkins's "Katie Mae." They were soon recording for a whole gamut of labels, Hopkins appearing on Gold Star (Houston), Down Town, and later on, Sittin' In With, Mercury, and Herald. By 1954 Hopkins had appeared on over a dozen labels.

Hopkins relied on his spontaneous creativity to keep him ahead of the game, but for the rest of the 1950s his art was seen as something of a musical backwater while rock and R&B took over. Only with the new interest in folk forms shown by young whites as the decade came to a close did Hopkins find a new audience. As the 1960s progressed, Hopkins moved into the most successful phase of his career. He recorded in a number of formats, the most common being his own vocal and acoustic guitar, and made numerous appearances at venues such as New York's Carnegie Hall. He also appeared on TV and in films, and built a substantial European following. He was universally regarded as one of the true blues giants. Lightnin' Hopkins died of cancer in 1982.

**SEE ALSO:** Blind Lemon Jefferson, Texas Alexander

# "Big" Walter Horton

**fact file**

**BORN** 1917

**DIED** 1981

**MUSICAL SELECTION**
Chicago/The
Blues/Today!

A man of many claims and prodigious talent with the harmonica: Big Walter Horton

horton was a harmonica talent able to live with the best of the Chicago blues harp scene, including Junior Wells, James Cotton, and Little Walter. His distinctive style relied greatly on his ability to influence the tone and attack of the harp through control of air-flow and hand manipulation, giving him a mellow, more hazy sound than most of his contemporaries. He was mostly content to work alongside other players or as a sideman, and even his most famous recordings, on the *Chicago/The Blues/Today!* set on Vanguard from the mid-1960s, finds him asking Charlie Musselwhite to sit in on proceedings.

Horton was from Mississippi but moved with his mother to Memphis while still a boy: there he soon found ways of making money through playing music, especially playing for change on the streets as well as the usual picnics, parties, and other hangouts. Early on he became a good friend of Johnny Shines, also then based in Memphis, and they often played together at gigs or on the streets. Both men moved to Chicago, Shines at the beginning of the 1940s and Horton close to the decade's close, his cautious nature showing for a while as he shuffled between Chicago and Memphis to make recording sessions back down South, where he made his record debut as a leader in 1951. Back in Chicago, he joined Eddie Taylor's band in 1953 and from there progressed to playing and recording with virtually every major blues leader of the time, including Muddy Waters, Jimmy Rogers, and Otis Rush. He also ran his own sessions from time to time, a November 1954 session including the sax players Red Holloway and John Cameron, while a 1956 session for Cobra featured the saxophonist Harold Ashby. During the 1960s Horton was heard in a plethora of bands, including Johnny Shines and Howlin' Wolf. During the 1970s he managed to keep afloat while many others in the blues were suffering neglect, and he appeared at many festivals and events in Europe and America. By now a senior citizen, he had for years been an important teacher of his instrument, and in 1972 he made an album of duets with one of his star pupils, Carey Bell, on Alligator Records. He continued to perform and record right up to his death, at the age of 64.

**SEE ALSO:** Junior Wells, James Cotton, Little Walter, Charlie Musselwhite, Johnny Shines, Eddie Taylor, Muddy Waters

# Eddie "Son" House

**S**on House had a long and influential career, but only in the 1960s did he begin to receive some of the credit due to him. Born on a farm a few miles outside Clarksdale, Mississippi, House was one of the great formative influences on the whole Delta blues style. His family moved to New Orleans when he was still a toddler and he stayed in that city until his early twenties. His earliest experiences in music came from the church and at one time in his early twenties he was an ordained minister. However, the blues found his ear, and he made out for Mississippi on his own, taking up playing the guitar around 1927, learning the rudiments from Willie Wilson, then teaming up with a close friend, Willie Brown, to perform at juke joints, dances and "whites-only" picnics. A year was lost in 1928 to the rigors of Parchman Farm penitentiary when House was found guilty of killing a man, but a judge later overturned the conviction and Son was freed. Meeting up occasionally with the formative Delta bluesman Charlie Patton, he was recommended by Patton to Paramount Records. This led to a 1930 Wisconsin session for the label where six songs were recorded, including his powerfully autobiographical "Preachin' The Blues." Sadly, these were the only commercial records Son was to record for over 30 years, and while he and Brown remained a well-known and influential team in the Delta region, with Son's towering vocals and rough-hewn guitar being supported by Brown's more articulate guitar accompaniment, the larger world remained in ignorance of their efforts.

Yet it was Son House who had a direct influence on Robert Johnson in the 1930s, Johnson often sitting in with the older men and learning from their techniques and repertoires. House also had a direct bearing on the type of blues playing and singing Muddy Waters took with him when he left the South and headed for Chicago. He remained in obscurity, recording again only in 1941 and 1942 when Alan Lomax made some field recordings for the Library of Congress. By 1943 House had quit the South for Rochester, New York, where he worked in a great many capacities, many of them not having the remotest connection with music. This did not disturb him too much, as he preferred playing with Willie Brown, and Brown had stayed down in the Delta. The music tapered off, and when Brown died in Mississippi in 1957 Son House had no compunction in giving up music-making altogether. It was only with the blues and folk revival of the 1960s that Son returned to music, coaxed back to it by young white enthusiasts who spent months tracking him down. He brought himself back up to speed on guitar and began appearing in front of white audiences, scoring a notable success at the 1964 Newport Folk Festival, enjoying his own Carnegie Hall Concert, and then making a classic blues album, *Founder Of The Folk Blues*, for Columbia in 1965 under the auspices of John Hammond. He had TV programs and documentaries made about him but in the early 1970s fell into ill health. The rest of his life was spent fighting recurrent attacks of bad health, and he once again retired from active performing. Widely honored in his lifetime, Son House died in 1988 recognized as one of the true Delta blues greats.

## fact file

**BORN** 1902

**DIED** 1988

**MUSICAL SELECTION**
Founder Of The Folk Blues

Son House's strong voice and rough guitar style influenced everyone from Robert Johnson to Muddy Waters

SEE ALSO: Charlie Patton, Robert Johnson, Muddy Waters, John Hammond

# Peg Leg Howell

## fact file

**BORN** 1888

**DIED** 1966

**MUSICAL SELECTION**
"New Prison Blues"
"Jelly Roll Blues"

In a rare photo, Peg Leg Howell was promoted as "one of the few great singers of the blues"

**P**eg Leg Howell (aka Joshua Barnes Howell) was a major exponent of the string-band tradition within the blues genre, concentrating most of his musical efforts on the type of material suited to country dances, specializing in rags and folklike melodies and harmonies.

Born in Eatonton, Georgia, Howell grew up in the country and became a proficient self-taught guitarist, playing across the gamut of folk material. He earned his nickname when, in 1916, a quarrel with an in-law left him with a nasty gunshot wound to the knee: amputation, the popular medical solution to such injuries at the time, followed, and Howell had his trademark physical characteristic and a pointer to how he should earn a living, farm work now being physically beyond his capabilities. Moving to Atlanta in search of new avenues of employment, he hit upon two ideas – bootleg liquor and music. The busking didn't pay much but kept him out of trouble: the bootlegging earned him a year in jail in 1925. On his release he went back to busking

and was heard by a Columbia field scout. His first sides, in 1926, included "New Prison Blues," while his first 1927 session played on his notoriety with "New Jailhouse Blues." Such songs proved sufficiently popular for Howell to continue recording up to August 1929, and some of the sessions for Columbia included his band: these titles were by Peg Leg Howell and His Gang, which included Eddie Anthony on violin. The sort of rowdy material they made included "Peg Leg Stomp" and "Too Tight Blues."

Dropped from Columbia, Howell and the Gang returned to playing on the streets, but no further progress was made before the Gang guitarist Henry Williams was put in jail (later to die there) and Eddie Anthony died in 1934. Howell faded into obscurity. Rediscovered in Atlanta in 1963 by young white enthusiasts, Howell made just one solo album, in 1966, covering traditional material such as "John Henry" and "Jelly Roll Blues" as well as some of his previous sides for Columbia. It came too late however: he died just five months after its completion.

**SEE ALSO:** Mississippi Sheiks

# Helen Humes

**fact file**

**BORN** 1913

**DIED** 1981

**MUSICAL SELECTION**
"Be-baba-leba"
"Million Dollar Secret"

Helen Humes,
pictured here
c. 1948, enjoyed
a varied career,
combining
ballads and blues
with a touch of
jazz and R&B

humes replaced Billie Holiday in the Count Basie Orchestra in 1938, her lithe and sweet voice proving an ideal antidote to the blues power of the male vocalist with Basie at the time, Jimmy Rushing. However, both before and after her stint with Basie, Humes proved herself to be a more than capable blues singer and won a permanent place in blues history with her R&B hits of the 1940s.

Considering her singing pedigree and style, it is no surprise to find her background was different from the average blues musician's of her period. From a middle-class Louisville, Kentucky, family, Humes was trained as a musician when young and discovered to have an exceptional voice while still an adolescent. Taken to St Louis in 1927 while still just 13, she made her recording debut for Okeh in the company of Lonnie Johnson and De Loise Searcy, cutting four blues sides (just one single was released). Two more sessions followed that year, both with her mentor Sylvester Weaver, the second taking place in New York, all of them blues. But they sold poorly and Humes switched to cabaret singing, staying in New York until John Hammond approached her in 1938 about taking over from Billie Holiday with Basie. Humes stayed with the Basie band until 1942, making a succession of sweet-voiced and perfectly phrased recordings, mostly ballads and medium-tempo love songs. After a return to the New York club scene and a jazz session for New York's Savoy records in 1944 she moved in 1945 to LA, where she cut an R&B session for Philo which landed her a major R&B hit, "Be-baba-leba," featuring Wild Bill Moore on tenor sax. However, she returned to swing-type material soon after, making many fine records but skirting wide of the blues, including a minor hit, the slightly risqué "Million Dollar Secret." By the late 1950s she had withdrawn from singing, making a comeback only in 1973, when she appeared at the Newport Jazz Festival. She picked up her career where she'd left off, singing and recording with the same type of mainstream jazz musicians, until her death. Her pure, light and agile voice was well suited to jazz, although her excursions into blues territory found her adopting a very different but equally convincing persona.

**SEE ALSO:** Jimmy Rushing, Lonnie Johnson, Sylvester Weaver, John Hammond

# Howlin' Wolf

O ne of the handful of true giants emanating from the postwar Chicago scene, Howlin' Wolf aka Chester Burnett spent much of his early life in the Delta region and recorded for the first time in 1951. But in the next 10 years he became the only serious rival to Muddy Waters on the Chicago scene, and was a huge influence on countless musicians since. Well over six feet tall, Wolf would throw himself around the stage with reckless abandon, electrifying his audiences as he reacted to the stark, rough-hewn blues he and his group put out.

Wolf was born Chester Burnett in West Point, Mississippi, into a sharecropper family, and early in his life began showing intense interest in the music around him. As a teenager he heard such key Delta musicians as Charlie Patton and Tommy Johnson, both of whom played in the area. As the 1920s came to a close Wolf himself began performing, playing rudimentary guitar and singing as well as wielding his harmonica. A weekend player, he gathered together his influences (including, according to Wolf himself, the "yodeling brakeman," Jimmie Rodgers, from whom he got his falsetto "howl," which in turn led to his nickname), thoroughly re-inventing them into a barely recognizable new form and sound. He was not heard outside of the Delta region until after World War II though, when he began frequenting Memphis joints and whorehouses and appearing on the occasional radio show. By this time his working band had the core personnel of Willie Johnson on guitar and Willie Steele on drums. It was this band Sun records' owner Sam Phillips heard on the radio and which he rushed to record in the summer of 1951. The first single, "Moanin' At Midnight" b/w "How Many More Years," was leased to the Chess label in Chicago and was an immediate hit, as was Wolf's own cover version for RPM, produced by Ike Turner. By the close of 1952 Wolf had been talked into moving to Chicago by Chess, making definitive recordings not only of his own material, but classic songs by the tireless Willie Dixon. His band comprised guitarist Hubert Sumlin and drummer Earl Phillips, giving him that rough, rowdy edge he preferred.

In the next decade Wolf would make such raw blues classics as "Evil (Is Going On)," "Smokestack Lightning," "I Asked For Water," "The Natchez Burning," "Sittin' On Top Of The World," "Moaning For My Baby," "Back Door Man," "Spoonful," "The Red Rooster," "Goin' Down Slow," "Killing Floor," and many others. Wolf's career received a boost from the British beat boom of the mid-1960s, and he appeared on TV on both sides of the Atlantic. Wolf participated in a lackluster Chess session, titled *Super Super Blues Band*, along with Muddy Waters and Bo Diddley in September 1967, and three years later, in 1970, led a London session for Chess featuring Eric Clapton, Stevie Winwood, and the rhythm section of the Rolling Stones, which he candidly described later as "dog shit." In between this he made his only really off-beam album, *Message To The Young*, wrapped in an inappropriate soul coating.

By now Wolf was in his sixties and a life of hard work and high living, aggravated by a car accident in 1970, was catching up with him. He worked intermittently, recording sessions where he felt at ease, and a revisit to the recording studio with Muddy Waters in 1973 proved markedly more successful than the first effort. Wolf died of complications to his long-term kidney and heart conditions.

## fact file

**BORN** 1910

**DIED** 1976

**MUSICAL SELECTION**
"Moanin' For My Baby"
"Spoonful"
"Killing Floor"

Howlin' Wolf's style brought him tremendous long-term popularity and secured his position as an influence on the blues scene

SEE ALSO: Muddy Waters, Charlie Patton, Tommy Johnson, Jimmie Rodgers

# Alberta Hunter

**fact file**

**BORN** 1895

**DIED** 1984

**MUSICAL SELECTION**
Amtrak Blues

Alberta Hunter began her association with the blues in a brothel, singing for prostitutes and customers

**h**unter was an important link between the rough, country-based female blues of the early 1920s and their vaudeville-based counterparts whose appeal was often greater to white than to black audiences. The first so-called 'blues' record, *Crazy Blues* by Mamie Smith, was made in 1920 and launched the blues craze, although it was not until 1923 that such classic blues singers as Bessie Smith, Ida Cox, and Ma Rainey were caught on record. But Alberta Hunter had started two years earlier, eventually creating an audience for herself that she sustained until the onset of the Depression.

Originally from Memphis, Tennessee, Hunter claims to have run off to Chicago at the age of 11, working disreputable dives entertaining prostitutes and their clients, and sending part of her money back home to help support her mother. She gradually worked her way up on Chicago's South Side to the point where she was playing the Dreamland Cafe opposite King Oliver's band. Hunter was a natural target for record companies, and she cut her first sides for Black Swan in 1921. By July 1922 she was recording for Paramount, with whom she would stay for two years, scoring a minor success with her own "Down Hearted Blues" – a song covered the next year by Bessie Smith in her very first recording session. Hunter's sweet-voiced, rather genteel blues appealed to both live and record-buying fans, and she continued to have hits for a number of labels, including Okeh and Victor. As the 1920s came to an end Hunter began broadening her appeal, as Ethel Waters had done and others would do after her, appearing in jazz settings and musicals – including a London production of *Showboat* opposite Paul Robeson. Eventually, between the early 1930s and the end of World War II, Hunter became a major cabaret and theatrical star on both sides of the Atlantic, gradually moving away from the blues altogether.

Ill-health led to Hunter's retiring from performing in 1956, and except for a fine classic blues recording in 1961 for Bluesville with her Serenaders (featuring Darnell Howard and Lovie Austin), she spent the next 21 years as a nurse, a profession she loved. Then, in 1977, a comeback involving a new album, *Amtrak Blues* (Columbia), TV guest shots and an appearance at Jimmy Carter's White House led to a revival of the octogenarian Hunter's career, including worldwide tours. Alberta Hunter continued working until shortly before her death in 1984.

**SEE ALSO:** Bessie Smith, Ida Cox, Ma Rainey

# Mississippi John Hurt

## fact file

**BORN** 1893

**DIED** 1966

**MUSICAL SELECTION**
The Immortal John
Hurt
Monday Morning
Blues

Mississippi John
Hurt's light touch
and simple style
kept him popular
for years

**J**ohn Hurt spent virtually the whole of his life within the environs of the small village of Avalon, Mississippi. His gentle, insistent style of the blues was as natural to him as the hills and fields around him. Hurt claimed to have begun learning the guitar in 1903, when he was just ten years old and jazz was yet to emerge from the black and Creole districts of New Orleans. The music he first learned was mostly pre-blues in style, much of it showing origins on other instruments such as string bands, accordions, and pianos. Hurt made his living mostly from farm work, though he spent a few years around World War I working on railroad construction and maintenance.

In the 1920s Hurt teamed up for a time with a white fiddler from the Avalon area, Willie Narmour, and became adept at playing accompaniment at dances. In time this connection led to his brief brush with recording at this point in his career, Okeh looking him up after a recommendation from Narmour. Two

sessions in 1928 resulted, one in Memphis, the other in New York, but only half the material was ever issued at the time. Hurt quickly sank back into obscurity, seemingly indifferent to the fate of his musical career. He remained lost to the blues world until a particularly resourceful folk researcher, Tom Hoskins, went looking for him in 1963, more than 30 years later. Hoskins convinced him that the world wanted again to hear his soft-voiced, good-natured music and intricate picking, and he appeared at that year's Newport Folk Festival, as well as making his first LP, for Vanguard.

In the three years that were left to him, he completed work on three fine albums for Vanguard, recording all his old repertoire and adding new tunes to his portfolio, appearing at many festivals and folk venues, even making it onto TV in an American documentary. He died, in 1966, one of the most celebrated of the latter-day country-blues rediscoveries.

SEE ALSO: Taj Mahal

# J B Hutto

Joseph Benjamin Hutto
encouraged a party
atmosphere during his live
performances

## fact file

**BORN** 1926

**DIED** 1982

**MUSICAL SELECTION**
Hawk Squat

J.B. Hutto's band and guitar playing never stood on ceremony, producing some of the most down-to-earth, roughneck sounds to come out of 1960s Chicago. Hutto himself, inspired by Elmore James, was not afraid to go for a stinging, swashbuckling sound and rough-edged delivery of his stripped-down blues, and this endeared him to a generation of Chicago blues fans.

Born in South Carolina, Hutto was raised from infancy in Atlanta, Georgia, thus conforming to the postwar archetype for a Chicago bluesman – the Southern black who moved to the mid-west to better his prospects. Hutto came from farming stock, coming to music initially through gospel, having sung in the Golden Crown Gospel Singers while still in early youth. Hutto's family relocated to Chicago in 1941, with his father looking for work in the heavy industry the city was renowned for. There, J.B. took up drums and

piano, even playing with Johnny Ferguson's Twisters in the immediate postwar period. Before the end of the decade he had made the swap to guitar. He ran his own groups in the early 1950s and played all the Chicago blues clubs, but by the middle of the decade his career had run out of steam, and he disbanded and left the business. About a decade later, the breakthrough success of many Chicago blues artists and the death in 1963 of Elmore James led Hutto, deeply influenced by the searing James bottleneck guitar, to return to the blues circuit. He was recorded regularly by small companies like Vanguard and Delmark and held a loyal audience which spread throughout the US clubs and festivals, until his death in 1982. The albums Hutto made in the mid-1960s are generally recognized as his best, with Delmark's *Hawk Squat*, featuring Sunnyland Slim, coming high on the list.

**SEE ALSO:** Elmore James, Sunnyland Slim

# Jim Jackson

**Jim Jackson took his cues from the minstrel shows from which he emerged**

ackson was one of the first bluesmen to settle and prosper in the Memphis area, like many of his colleagues arising from the medicine-and-minstrel background that gave employment to rural musicians not wanting to stay on in sharecropping work. Up to his death Jackson retained a wide variety of songs and tunes in his repertoire, reflecting the vast experience he had gained on his travels in the first decades of the century and the interchangeability of blues with other forms of musical entertainment and commentary.

Jackson was born in Hernando, Mississippi, and was self-taught on guitar, traveling with the medicine shows for a good decade before settling in Memphis in the mid-1920s. Once there he met up with other Memphis-based bluesmen such as Gus Cannon, Will Shade, Furry Lewis, and Robert Wilkins, often working with such men for

change on street corners. His very first record, "Jim Jackson's Kansas City Blues" (Parts 1 and 2 on either side of the old 78rpm disc), was a bestseller in its day and became a standard of sorts once Jackson's name had been shorn from the title. As befits a medicine-show man, Jackson was always ready to inject humor into a performance, as many of his discs show – 1929's "Hey Mama – It's Nice Like That" being a typical example. Jackson recorded steadily and with sustained success until July 1929, when eight sides cut for Vocalion remained unissued. Between then and his last session of February 1930, Jackson had just four sides released, the last two being retreads of old favorites, "St Louis Blues" and "Hesitation Blues." Propelled back onto the road by the Depression, Jackson died in 1937, just as the demand for his type of entertainment was entering a long eclipse.

<table>
<tr><td colspan="2">fact file</td></tr>
<tr><td>BORN 1890</td></tr>
<tr><td>DIED 1937</td></tr>
<tr><td>MUSICAL SELECTION</td></tr>
<tr><td>"Jim Jackson's Kansas City Blues"</td></tr>
<tr><td>"Hey Mama – It's Nice Like That"</td></tr>
</table>

**SEE ALSO:** Gus Cannon, Robert Wilkins

# John Jackson

**fact file**

**BORN** 1924

**MUSICAL SELECTION**
Step It Up & Go

John Jackson brought both Southern and Eastern US influences to his music

**J**ackson, although born in the early 1920s, continued the turn-of-the-century tradition of the songster, supplying his audience with a judiciously chosen repertoire of songs, tunes, dances, rags, blues, and jigs. The sources of these pieces would be as heterogeneous as the genres themselves.

Born in Woodville, Virginia, Jackson was immersed in music from infancy, learning the rudiments of guitar and banjo from the age of five onward through the medium of the family phonograph and from his father. His guitar style gradually evolved into an attractive variant of the Piedmont style in the blues, with echoes of Blind Blake and other pickers in the rags and dance pieces. As a teenager he began to play at parties and picnics but his music remained a strictly part-time affair. In 1950

Jackson moved from Woodville to Fairfax, Virginia, but his pattern of existence altered little, as he held down a day job and entertained the locals on weekends.

Remaining in Fairfax in a settled existence, Jackson was finally recorded, in Fairfax, by Arhoolie's Chris Strachwitz while on a field trip in 1965. Strachwitz returned in 1967 and '69 for further updates, building a considerable cross-section of Jackson's performing repertoire. These albums eventually led to Jackson's being invited to perform in Europe, and he has continued to make occasional but regular trips to France and Germany for live work and recordings since, often on the folk circuit. Jackson in later years made some fine albums for Rounder, including the memorable *Step It Up & Go.*

**SEE ALSO:** Blind Blake

# Li'l Son Jackson

**fact file**

**BORN** 1916

**DIED** 1976

**MUSICAL SELECTION**
Li'l Son Jackson
Rockin' n' Rollin'

Soft voice and a strong guitar gave Li'l Son Jackson a distinctive and memorable style

a quality blues performer who also managed a flirtation with the R&B charts in the 1940s, Jackson was only briefly ever a full-time musician. Like so many other bluesmen, he found the lack of income and recognition too burdensome over so many years, and turned his hand to many other trades during his lifetime.

Li'l Son was born in Tyler, Texas but spent most of his life in and around Dallas. He trained as a garage mechanic, playing guitar and singing the blues as a pastime. During the 1930s he occasionally appeared at house parties and sang with a gospel group, the Blue Eagle Four. In 1948, spurred on by not much more than curiosity, he cut a demonstration disc in a shopping arcade. His friends convinced him that record companies may have been interested in the results, and he forwarded the disc to Bill Quinn's Gold Star label in Houston. Quinn immediately signed him up, and over the next two years Jackson cut a series of acoustic blues sides in the style of Texas Alexander, Blind Lemon Jefferson, and other Texas greats. One cut even managed

to make the blues charts, and Jackson, for the first time in his life, became a full-time professional. By the time Lil' Son came to the attention of Los Angeles-based Imperial Records in 1950, the peak of popular consumption of the country-blues had passed. Jackson opened his recording career in Los Angeles with two sessions dedicated to the older style, combining a soft-voiced approach with simple, strong guitar work; by 1951 he and his record company had moved on, taking stylistic slivers from a broad range of influences, including T-Bone Walker with his jazz affinities. Jackson went for the popular R&B market, making over 40 sides for Imperial in this genre.

In 1954, however, the singer/guitarist sustained serious injuries in a car accident; shaken by the experience and unsure of his future in music, Jackson returned to life as an auto mechanic. Although he was talked into making some sides for Arhoolie as white audiences rediscovered the older blues styles in the 1960s, Lil' Son Jackson never returned to the road as a musician; he died in Dallas, a victim of cancer, in 1976.

**SEE ALSO:** Texas Alexander, Blind Lemon Jefferson, T-Bone Walker

# Papa Charlie Jackson

**fact file**

**BORN** 1885

**DIED** 1938

**MUSICAL SELECTION**
"Salty Dog"
"Messin' Around"

The great Papa Charlie Jackson was often reduced to playing for pennies to make ends meet

J ackson was one of the first country bluesmen to emerge from the minstrel, medicine, and vaudeville shows and forge a career for himself via records. His main instrument was a banjo variant which he played like a guitar, and his emphasis was on entertaining and often humorous pieces, usually taken straight from his vaudeville routines.

Jackson was born in New Orleans and began to travel with his banjo when quite young, hooking up with various traveling shows wending through the Southern states and staying on the road until sometime after World War I, when he seems to have settled in Chicago. It was there that he made his debut recordings, for Paramount, in 1924 – one of the first country blues performers to record. For most of his records he accompanied himself, making many sides which were taken from the so-called "bawdy" tradition of the blues and vaudeville circuit, little of which was ever recorded or noted down in their uncensored versions, although most blues performers of Jackson's generation seem to have had a working knowledge of this repertoire. Jackson twice had the opportunity to record with notable contemporaries, – in July 1926 with Freddie Keppard's Jazz Cardinals, featuring Johnny Dodds, cutting "Salty Dog" and "Messin' Around," the latter of which remained unissued, and in September 1929 with Blind Blake. By the end of that year Jackson was suffering a precipitous decline in income like most other blues artists. Just three more sessions (for Okeh and ARC) followed between 1930 and 1934, the last with Big Bill Broonzy, a man who, it is sometimes claimed, was something of a Jackson acolyte in his early years. Jackson died in Chicago four years later.

**SEE ALSO:** Big Bill Broonzy

# Nehemiah "Skip" James

fact file

**BORN** 1902

**DIED** 1969

**MUSICAL SELECTION**
"I'm So Glad"

Skip James, live at the 1966 Newport Folk Festival in Newport, Rhode Island

S kip James came from the Delta, being born in Bentonia, Mississippi, and his music is formed from the typical Delta elements of intricate guitar commentary on the vocal line and unembarrassed emotionalism in the voice. The way he forged these elements into a personal style, however, is unique: no one sounds like Skip James except Skip James. James's own personality was withdrawn and generally misanthropic, his viewpoint on life unremittingly bleak. His haunting, keening falsetto is one of the most chilling, unearthly sounds in blues.

James was raised on a plantation near Bentonia; his mother was the cook there and his father, initially at least, was the plantation bootlegger, a position James assumed some years later, long after his father had fled the family nest. In his mid-teens he was sufficiently inspired by the music he heard at buck dances and parties that he took guitar lessons from an old friend, Henry Stuckey. It was this guitarist who was later to show James the uses of the open E-minor guitar tuning, which Skip would feature heavily in his mature playing. James led a peripatetic life, taking jobs in sawmills, in labor camps, and in whorehouses, these as the house pianist. He also tried his hand at gambling. In late 1930, spurred by a friend, he approached the Paramount Records scout H.C. Speir in Jackson, Mississippi, for an audition: this was passed successfully and James was signed to a two-year contract by the ailing company. He made the trip to Wisconsin to record

his songs in February 1931 (26 sides were cut, according to James, but only 18 have ever been found, with three matrix numbers untraced), but Paramount had little money to promote and distribute his singles before itself going bankrupt. The embittered James left the music business within a year. It was to be another 30 years before he was to record again.

James knew little or nothing of the blues and folk revival of the early 1960s, but in fact he had become a sought-after artist. The incredible guitar picking to be found on his "I'm So Glad" (later re-recorded by Cream to become a million-selling single) was revered as a high-water mark of Delta blues playing, while his influence on Robert Johnson had been noted. Rediscovered in a Mississippi hospital, he made an immediate impact at the 1964 Newport Folk Festival and over the next couple of years re-recorded most of his 1930s repertoire. He was unconvinced by this latter-day fame, feeling that he no longer met his own high standards of performance. It is sometimes claimed that his later recordings are in every way inferior to his youthful efforts, not least because James himself disparaged them, but this is to confuse artistic intentions with the actual end product of his artistry. The unrelieved gloom of his later records reaches a tragic intensity rarely found anywhere else in blues, while the richness of the musical tapestry remains intact. James died in 1969 of the cancer he had suffered from at the time of his 1964 rediscovery.

**SEE ALSO:** Robert Johnson

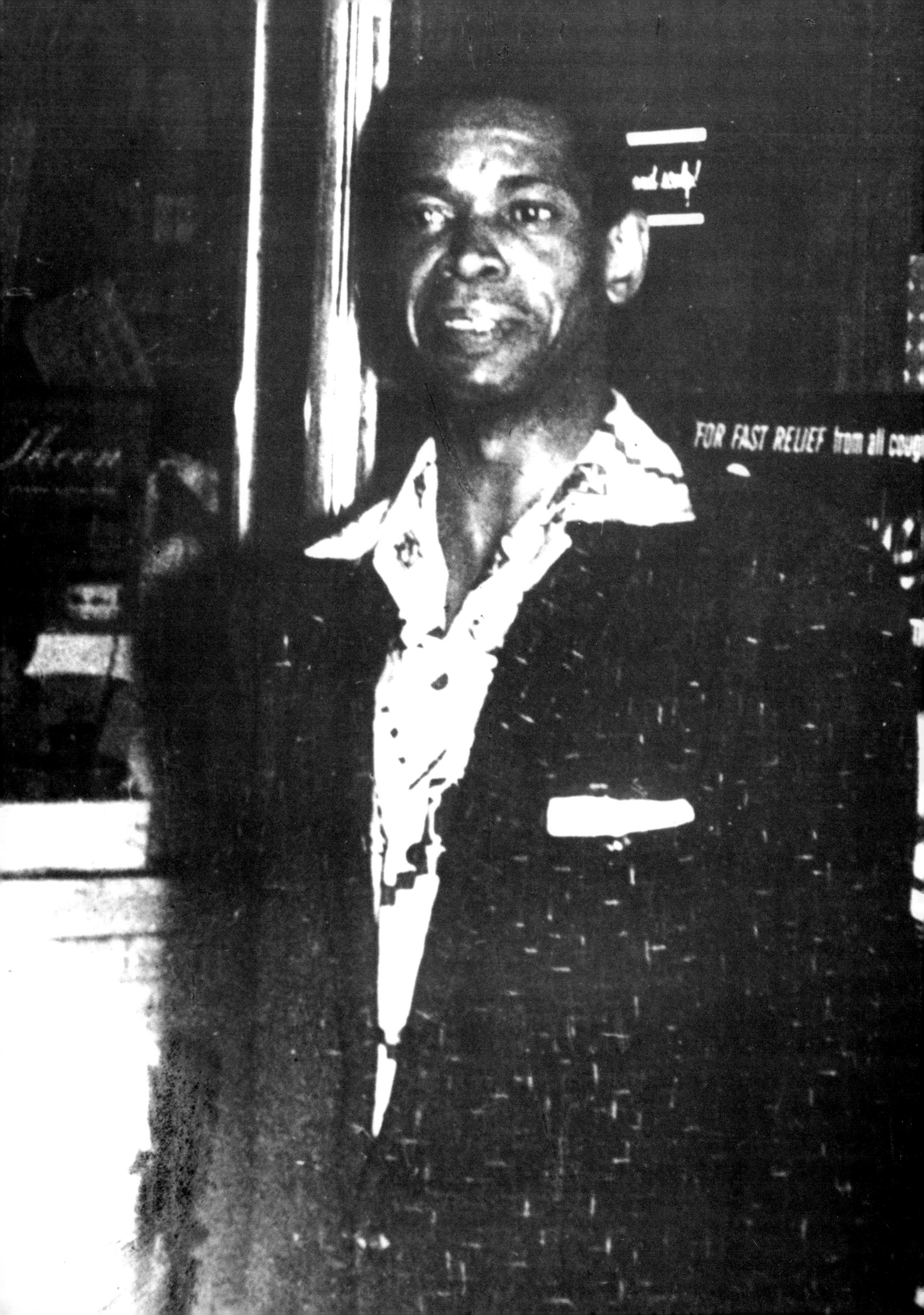
FOR FAST RELIEF from all coug

# Elmore James

One of the most powerful singers and guitarists in blues history, James has certainly been one of the most influential as well, both as performer and as songwriter. Born in Richmond, Mississippi, the product of an underage, out-of-wedlock union, James spent his youth paying his sharecropping dues like so many others. He taught himself the rudiments of guitar playing on a self-made three-string guitar, occasionally appearing at local dances. His family moved to the Belzoni district in the mid-1930s, where Elmore teamed up with his adopted cousin, Robert Earl Houston, and started appearing at more regular gigs. By 1937 James had married Josephine Harris and had met the king of the Delta blues, Robert Johnson. But neither relationship was to last long – by the end of 1938 Elmore and Josephine were separated and Johnson had been murdered (although his influence on James would linger on for the rest of his career). James, however, continued to play with other colleagues such as Sonny Boy Williamson II (a.k.a. Rice Miller), forming his own band featuring his cousin Robert. He also occasionally accompanied Sonny Boy on his King Biscuit Time radio broadcasts.

The Second World War interrupted James's career between 1943 and 1945, but on his return he took up a similar pattern of existence, even trying marriage again. A loose professional relationship with Sonny Boy continued to keep him employed and led directly to his first session under his own name, in August 1951, as a tag-on to a Sonny Boy session for the Trumpet label. Just one song was recorded, but it was enough: "Dust My Broom," a Robert Johnson tune James had performed for years in his own special arrangement, quickly became a substantial R&B hit in early 1952. James was to re-work this same basic song many times for various record companies over the next decade, as his career really took off. Persuaded by Modern Records' Joe Bihari to relocate himself and his band, the Broomdusters, in Chicago, James quickly became a major Chicago blues attraction, his stinging bottleneck and raucous vocals forging a new sound in the blues. James took the raw passion of country blues at its finest in Robert Johnson, and married it to the pent-up electric sounds of the modern era. His guitar sound and phrasing, in particular, was to be of enormous influence both on the early rock 'n' roll movement of the 1950s and the white R&B renaissance of the1960s. James's occasional use of piano and sax also helped form the basic early rock 'n' roll sound. But for such future guitar giants as Eric Clapton, Johnny Winter and Peter Green, Elmore James – with his guitar licks snaking through his whiplash vocals – was the foremost single influence in their own early development.

James continued to have hits for the rest of the 1950s, including the Tampa Red song "It Hurts Me Too" (1957) and the slow, heartfelt "The Sky Is Crying" (1959). But he remained curiously uncommitted to recording, making not much more than 20 tracks during the whole of the 1950s. Heart problems in the early part of the decade had kept him to a sensible schedule, but the hits he enjoyed brought on the pressure which resulted in a second heart attack in 1959. This time, however, James didn't slow down, and the last four years of his life saw him recording and appearing at an unprecedented rate – turning out such classics as "Rollin' and Tumblin'," "Crossroads," "Dust My Broom," "Bleeding Heart," and "Shake Your Moneymaker," mostly for the Fire label. Unfortunately, a third and fatal heart attack struck in May 1963, just at the dawn of a renaissance of interest in the driving blues he helped define.

## fact file

**BORN** 1918

**DIED** 1963

**MUSICAL SELECTION**
"Crossroads"
"Bleeding Heart"
"Shake Your
Moneymaker"

Elmore James, though a prolific performer, did not have much interest in recording his work, preferring to get on stage in front of a live audience

# Frankie "Half-Pint" Jaxon

"FAN IT!"

The aptly named "Half Pint" Jaxon was a fireball of energy, on-stage and off

## fact file

**BORN** 1895

**DIED** ?

**MUSICAL SELECTION**
"How Long How Long Blues"

axon divided his musical career between blues and jazz but was also an adept showman and dancer, also able to run a profitable line of comedy on the side, as his frequent recordings bear out. Born in Montgomery, Alabama, he grew up in Kansas City. By his fifteenth birthday he was ready to enter the world of entertainment, playing in KC clubs and cinemas as well as working in amateur street performances.

Through connections he had built up, Jaxon joined up in 1912 with Gallie DeGaston and went on tent-show tours of the Deep South for over two years, building up a formidable performing repertoire of gags, routines, and songs. Settling into a fixed pattern, Jaxon spent until the mid-1920s alternating between the Sunset Café in Chicago and the Paradise Café in Atlantic City, New Jersey. By that time he'd developed a drag act as well to add to his repertoire, replete with feminine vocalizations – a talent put to good use when recording with Tampa Red's Hokum Jug Band in 1928, as can be heard from his vocals on the famous "How Long How Long Blues." By then he had been recording for two years under his own name, mostly comedy and novelty numbers with piano accompaniment, but by late 1928 he was making sides with top-class jazzmen, going on to record with people like Freddie Keppard, Jabbo Smith, Bob Shoffner, George Mitchell, the Harlem Hamfats, King Oliver, and Lil Armstrong.

Jaxon's stock-in-trade female-impersonator voice became his calling card and he enjoyed a considerable popularity, on radio and on records as well as live, up to World War II. In 1941 he joined governmental service and left behind his musical career. The date of his death is presently unknown.

**SEE ALSO:** Tampa Red

# Blind Willie Johnson

Combining a spiritual leaning with a love of music, Blind Willie Johnson's unique approach brought him great notoriety

**fact file**

**BORN** 1902

**DIED** 1947

**MUSICAL SELECTION**
"I Know His Blood Can Make Me Whole"
"It's Nobody's Fault But Mine"

**J**ohnson would have been the last person to describe himself as a blues performer, having been utterly committed to the Christian religion he sang about for his entire career. The music he employed to communicate his spiritual messages was more often than not wholly woven from the fabric of the blues. This fact, plus his remarkable slide guitar playing and his powerful, rough-edged voice, makes his inclusion hard to refute.

Born near Temple, Texas, Willie moved during infancy to Marlin, south of Dallas, where his father remarried after his mother's early death. At around the age of seven, the boy was deliberately blinded by his stepmother, revenge for a beating by her husband for having had an affair. Unable to work, Willie's interest in music was put to use; by his teens he was on the streets playing for change. Deeply religious his whole life, he joined the Baptist community and eventually became a minister. Johnson became such a familiar and popular figure between Dallas and Houston that in 1927 (the year he married Willie B. Harris) he made his first records, for Columbia, in Dallas itself. He sold over 10,000 copies of his first single, "I Know His Blood Can Make Me Whole." Continuing to record for Columbia through its initial failure in 1932, Willie eventually cut nearly forty sides, many featuring a passionate and yet delicate slide guitar accompaniment for his fierce voice. Johnson's unique style made songs like "It's Nobody's Fault But Mine" and "Motherless Children Have a Hard Time" the purest of blues laments. Johnson's recording career ended in 1932, a victim of the Depression. After remarrying and settling in Beaumont, Texas, he continued to sing on the streets and attend church. He succumbed to pneumonia in 1947.

**SEE ALSO:** L. C. Robinson, Josh White

# Blind Lemon Jefferson

j efferson occupies a place in country blues – and therefore the subsequent development of the blues itself – on a par with that of Louis Armstrong's in jazz. He didn't invent the form, but his influence on its basic techniques and characteristic sounds is so immense that traces of his musical personality can be found in most of what went after him, even if specific techniques were, according to his peers, inimitable.

Lemon lived through a time when it was not seen as important to keep biographical details of black entertainers, and most of what is known about him comes from anecdotes told by his companions and fellow bluesmen. He was most probably born in 1897 (although some claim a date a decade earlier) in East Texas, and was apparently blind from birth. Just how or why he learned guitar and began singing for a living is unknown, but by the time he moved to Dallas in 1917 he was well-known and admired by his peers within a wide radius of the city. Stories of his prowess surfaced in towns along the railroad routes in and out of Dallas as Lemon plied his trade in search of new pickings. Jefferson's guitar playing was admired by fellow musicians, but it was his extraordinary voice which gave him his popularity in every town he visited. His repertoire, like that of most of his contemporaries, reached beyond the blues form into rags and dance pieces such as "Hot Dogs" (a song Leadbelly would record many years later as a tribute to "his friend Lemon"). But his major achievement lies in the heartfelt blues of songs like "Corrina Blues," "Jack O'Diamonds Blues," "Matchbox Blues," and "See That My Grave is Kept Clean."

Jefferson travelled extensively and seems to have met a great many bluesmen, from Robert Wilkins to Son House, who recall meeting him not only in Texas but also in the Delta area, Memphis, and beyond. His contemporaries stress the fact that he was a true professional, playing for money only, finishing his songs as soon as the money dried up. The recording industry caught up with Jefferson in late 1925 – five years after the blues explosion had been launched by Mamie Smith – thanks to Sammy Price, a Dallas talent scout who recommended him to Paramount, and Blind Lemon traveled to Chicago to make his first records. He was immensely successful from the outset when his first single, "Long Lonesome Blues," became a hit in May 1926. For the rest of his short life, Jefferson was an immensely popular recording artist and a moderately rich one as well, with his own bank account and a chauffeured car. He recorded prolifically during those years, although not always wisely. But the best of what he did has become the bedrock of the country blues, and many of his songs later became standards recorded many hundreds of times over – often scoring hits for rock 'n' roll performers from Lonnie Donegan to Bob Dylan and The Beatles. Yet his own recordings remain definitive despite the poor recording quality and the mists of time. Having died when he did – in 1929, probably from a heart attack suffered during the depths of a cold Chicago December – Blind Lemon Jefferson became a legend whose career never suffered the hardships of the Depression, or the gradual shift of popular focus away from country blues to other forms of musical entertainment.

## fact file

**BORN** 1897

**DIED** 1929

**MUSICAL SELECTION**
"Corrina Blues"
"Long Lonesome Blues"

He may have been blind but he was no pushover – Blind Lemon Jefferson was known to be armed and sometimes involved in shootings

**SEE ALSO:** Leadbelly, Robert Wilkins, Son House

# Buddy Johnson

## fact file

**BORN** 1915

**DIED** 1977

**MUSICAL SELECTION**
"That's the Stuff You
Gotta Watch"
"Somebody's
Knocking at My Door"

Buddy Johnson
featured his
sister Ella in
many of his
recordings

J ohnson is one of the rare breed of leaders who ran his own very successful blues-based big-band for two decades. A talented musician and songwriter, he covered a great range of musical styles during his long and successful career. But he is best remembered for the series of singles and albums he made featuring his sister Ella and (until 1952) Arthur Prysock as vocalists, between the close of World War II and his conversion to outright rock 'n' roll in the late 1950s.

Johnson was born in Darlington, South Carolina, and in his early twenties became a professional musician, reaching Europe in 1938 with the Cotton Club Revue. By 1939 he was back in America and running his own swing-based small group in New York, but in 1943 formed a big band which landed a long-term engagement at the Savoy Ballroom. Using the Savoy as his base of operations, Johnson began recording for Decca and placing his emphasis squarely on blues and jump music, often with his sister

Ella's and Arthur Prysock's bluesy vocals embellishing the plot. A fine songwriter whose credits include the pop classic "Since I Fell For You," his hits included "That's the Stuff You Gotta Watch" (1944) and "Somebody's Knocking at My Door" (1947). He also recorded catchy novelties like "Did You See Jackie Robinson Hit That Ball?" Johnson's band toured the southern states throughout the 1940s and 1950s, playing to an almost exclusively black audience, his rhythm and blues band replete with roaring tenors capturing perfectly the mood of the times. Prysock left in 1952, and as the decade developed, Johnson moved closer to out-and-out rock 'n' roll, preserving his popularity into the 1960s with a canny musical policy.

Finally disbanding before the middle of the decade, Johnson went into religious and charity work as well as running his own small group, keeping up a similar mix until his death in 1977. His legend lives on.

**SEE ALSO:** Louis Jordan, Amos Milburn, Wynonie Harris

# Herman E Johnson

**fact file**

**BORN** 1908

**DIED** 1975

**MUSICAL SELECTION**
"Motherless Children"
"Leavin' Blues"
"Depression Blues"

Herman E. Johnson found whatever work he could but remains unforgivably under-recorded

Johnson, born into a desperately poor family in the Louisiana countryside, led the typical life of so many bluesmen in the earlier part of this century. After the most cursory brush with school, Johnson started working at manual labor, as he had no education with which to aspire to a better position. Coming from a religious family, he was the one who went "the other way," having no great religious fervor.

He picked up the guitar in his late teens and, finding that he had musical talent, spent much of his early life wandering far and wide in the South – picking up a taste for alcohol and a broad experience of life on the road. Johnson's style crystallized in the Delta variety, his light baritone voice having a dignified but keening quality, his guitar playing using many drones, his precise picking echoing his vocals. His repertoire included many blues dating from the 1920s. Johnson was one of many bluesmen not to have ever entered the recording studio during his active

musical years, and during the following decades he tried a huge variety of jobs to keep body and soul together – including milking cows, working in steelyards, shipyards and cement works, and cutting sugar cane. For fifteen years he worked for Esso in Baton Rouge, but after being laid off he landed a janitorial job at Southern University in Scotlandville, which he held until his retirement in 1970.

He was finally placed in front of a microphone in 1960 by Harry Oster, owner of the Folk-Lyric label and folk field researcher who also discovered Robert Pete Williams. Johnson's recordings for Oster – made between 1960-61 in both Scotlandville and Baton Rouge – revealed him to be a powerful, brooding performer, equally expressive on acoustic and electric guitars, slide or picking, with a rich and disturbing voice. But Herman Johnson never recorded again, dying in 1975 from the effects of a stroke.

**SEE ALSO:** Robert Pete Williams

# Jimmy Johnson

Jimmy Johnson jams in Toronto (Canada) in 1996, one of many blues artists to enjoy popularity worldwide

## fact file

**BORN** 1928

**MUSICAL SELECTION**
Living Chicago Blues
North/South
I'm A Jockey

Jimmy Johnson, although unknown to most of the fans who have long claimed Robert Cray as their own, was instrumental in bringing about a widening of the blues repertoire prior to Cray's emergence in the 1970s. In fact, he helped bring the later variants and updates of soul and beyond into the blues, which would lay the ground for Cray's own individual synthesis of styles and influences being embraced by a worldwide audience.

Johnson was born in Holly Springs, Mississippi, and his first love was gospel. He came to Chicago via Memphis, arriving in the Illinois city in 1950. After some trouble with Uncle Sam (he was drafted but refused to serve and received a dishonorable discharge), he settled down to work as a welder in the Windy City. But in the 1960s Johnson began taking occasional gigs in and around Chicago, playing both soul and R&B. He worked with a number of bands with roots in more than one stylistic camp, including Albert King's and Otis Clay's. As the 1970s progressed he moved closer to the classic Chicago blues approach, finally making the change when he joined Jimmy Dawkins's band in 1974. By the end of the decade he was a regular on the South Side with his own band, and he appeared in Alligator Records' *Living Chicago Blues* series as the decade ended. This in turn led to Delmark making a couple of excellent albums with Johnson, including *North/South*.

The 1980s proved to be a more consistent time of employment for Johnson, who made records for Alligator, including *Bar Room Preacher* in 1985. He also picked up a fair European following, although he has never become a top-of-the-bill attraction. In 1993 he made the first-rate *I'm A Jockey* for Birdology, an album which also features players like Billy Branch and Lucky Peterson, and this garnered good worldwide response. Jimmy Johnson continues to record and perform today.

**SEE ALSO:** Robert Cray, Albert King, Jimmy Dawkins

# Luther "Guitar Jr." Johnson

Luther Johnson, aka "Guitar Jr." purveyor of the Chicago West side sound, was a member of Muddy Waters's band in the 1970s

ohnson came to the attention of blues fans on Chicago's West Side in the early 1960s as a guitarist much indebted to Magic Sam. He later played with Muddy Waters and in recent years has been running his own band, the Magic Rockers, out of Boston, Massechusetts.

Born in Bena, Mississippi, Johnson moved to Chicago with his family in 1955, at the age of sixteen. Already competent as a guitarist, he joined small Chicago groups and began being heard around the West Side in clubs and elsewhere. By the early 1960s he had earned his nickname; by the middle of the same decade he was playing in the band of his mentor, Magic Sam.

This and other solid support work led to him becoming part of the Muddy Waters set-up in 1972, a position he held and it seems enjoyed thoroughly until 1980, when Waters and his band parted company. Johnson toured worldwide with Waters, and while in France in 1976 he made an album for Black & Blue, *Luther's Blues*, which established him for the first time as a solo act. This harbinger was followed up when, by 1982, Johnson had relocated to Boston and began running his own band out of the city. Since then he has made records on a regular basis, the most recent being in 1995 with Telarc Blues, *Slammin' On The West Side*, and has taken the Magic Rockers with him on tours throughout the States and Europe. His style remains unchanged, conjuring the ghost of Magic Sam and the West Side sound whenever he plays and sings.

## fact file

**BORN** 1939

**MUSICAL SELECTION**
Luther's Blues
Slammin' On The West Side

SEE ALSO: Robert Johnson

# Lonnie Johnson

New Orleans-born Lonnie Johnson was the instrumental link between blues and early forms of jazz. Possessing the technique and musical knowledge to expand and elaborate upon the traditional blues harmonies and melodies, the dextrous and versatile Johnson was equally valuable to both genres, fitting neatly into the accompanying group for leaders of either type. Born Alonzo Johnson into a large musical family, Lonnie became a member of the family string band while very young, moving on to playing bars and dances around New Orleans at the very beginning of the jazz era. He often accompanied trumpeter Punch Miller and in 1917 he visited Europe as part of a large revue. Johnson stayed abroad until late 1919; in the meantime, his family had been virtually annihilated by the dreadful New Orleans influenza epidemic of that year. From that time on, though often based around St Louis, Johnson was a constant traveller. He frequently toured on the TOBA circuit, appearing with many bands and groups and, in 1925, winning a recording contract with Okeh Records. From that time on he recorded extensively, sometimes as a leader but even more often as a member of other groups, such as those of Duke Ellington or Louis Armstrong (Johnson appeared on some of the classic Hot Five sides). His duets with jazz guitarist Eddie Lang, such as "Guitar Blues," have rightly been seen as classics of recorded guitar since their first release. But his unaccompanied solo work – "Playing With The Strings," for instance – is equally breathtaking, if not so jazz-influenced.

Beyond his dexterity, Johnson's main gift lay in the area of melodic and thematic improvisation. His creative imagination was a disciplined one and he often worked with a bare minimum of melodic material – re-arranging phrases in endless subtle ways, giving a melody a new twist with a bent or blue note, and always driving everything forward with a powerful rhythmic impulse. He continued to record prolifically up to the Depression years, when he had to resort to day jobs to sustain his career. A renaissance of sort occurred in the 1940s when Johnson, ever willing to cater his style to modern popular taste, tried his hand at the prevalent R&B style. This resulted in hits for the Aladdin and King labels, some of which found him trying out the electric guitar in direct response to the influence of Charlie Christian, a jazz player who had initially been greatly influenced by Johnson himself.

Johnson found himself out of fashion in the 1950s, his style too sophisticated for the new rock audience and too simplistic for the be-bop based jazz fans. It was only with the revival of the 1960s that Johnson once again found willing ears for his style of playing. People eager to hear an authentic great from the 1920s attended his live performances and bought his new records, most of them made on acoustic guitar and featuring the blues-based repertoire of over forty years ago. Lonnie Johnson's career was cruelly terminated in 1969 while he was in Toronto. Then in his seventies, he was hit by a car and never properly recovered, expiring the following year from the long-term effects of the accident.

## fact file

**BORN** 1894

**DIED** 1970

**MUSICAL SELECTION**
"Playing With The Strings"

Lonnie Johnson was a lightning rod for talent during his career, in all genres of music

SEE ALSO: Robert Johnson

# Tommy Johnson

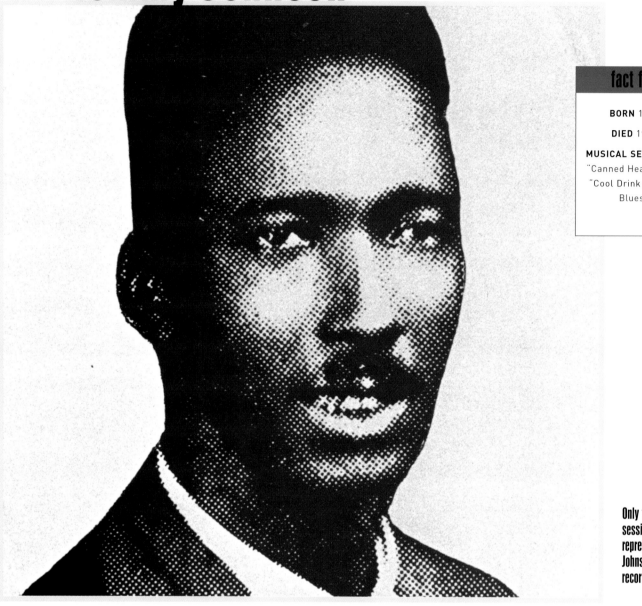

**fact file**

**BORN** 1896

**DIED** 1956

**MUSICAL SELECTION**
"Canned Heat Blues"
"Cool Drink of Water
Blues"

Only four
sessions
represent Tommy
Johnson's entire
recorded career

J ohnson was one of the most colorful of early blues figures, capable of equaling the crowd-pleasing stunts of Charlie Patton and telling stories of selling his soul to the devil in his quest for musical wizardry with which to bewitch his listeners. He was also, along with Son House and Charlie Patton, the best-known and most influential of the early Delta bluesmen, his wild, direct approach and his repertoire being copied by most of the musicians to follow him.

Johnson was born on a plantation near Terry, Mississippi. One of a very large family, he learned guitar from his older brothers. After leaving home around 1911 he met up with Patton and Willie Brown in the Delta area, and the impact of their playing had him abruptly changing his musical course and adopting the blues as his calling card. Johnson traveled extensively plying his trade, and when he came back to his home town he had completed a transformation not everyone saw as a positive one: not only was he now a showman par excellence in the Patton mold, playing his

guitar between his legs and behind his head, but he'd picked up an inordinate love of alcohol in any shape or form, even that used for household purposes. Johnson finally settled in Jackson, Mississippi, around 1926–27, and made his first recordings, for Victor, the following year. He recorded just seven sides for Victor and six the following year for Paramount, but many of those songs have long become classic blues played or adapted by virtually every blues musician to come along since: "Canned Heat Blues," "Cool Drink of Water Blues," "Big Road Blues," and "Black Mare Blues" are good examples, the high, keening howl of "Cool Drink of Water Blues," for example, being a key feature of Howlin' Wolf's mature style.

Johnson's alcoholism, allied to the Depression, limited his potential for a fully successful professional blues career, and he worked mostly as a farm laborer for the rest of his life, playing parties and jukes for spare money and the love of the music. He died in 1956 from a heart attack.

**SEE ALSO:** Charlie Patton, Son House, Willie Brown

# Curtis Jones

**fact file**

**BORN** 1906

**DIED** 1971

**MUSICAL SELECTION**
"Lonesome Bedroom
Blues"

Curtis Jones
settled in and
eventually
passed away in
his adopted home
of Munich,
Germany

ones experienced most of the highs and lows that came the way of bluesmen born in the first decade of the present century. A pianist with a natural sense of accompaniment for his heartfelt and often world-weary vocals, Jones made one of the great blues records of the prewar period in "Lonesome Bedroom Blues" in 1937, a much-imitated piece which made his name; but, although he recorded prolifically in the record's wake, he never again caught the public's imagination in the same way.

Jones was born in Naples, Texas, and made the guitar his first instrument, but once he moved to Dallas as a young man he concentrated on piano. Ending up in Chicago by way of the Midwest, Jones made his recording debut with Vocalion in 1937, cutting the aforementioned single at his first session. In its aftermath he cut a further 50 or more sides for Vocalion before moving to Bluebird in 1940, making one session with Jazz Gillum, but was dropped by the label at the end of 18 months. He virtually disappeared for two decades, cutting a single for Parrot in 1953 and sticking to the clubs and bars around Chicago until recorded in 1960 by Prestige/Bluesville in NYC. That signaled a revival of interest, in the US and in Europe, for his talents, and he played and recorded both sides of the Atlantic, settling in France in 1962. Yet this comeback could not be sustained. He died in Munich in 1971, in abject poverty.

# Robert Johnson

r obert Johnson was abundantly talented in every aspect of blues performance and creation, drawing on a crosscurrent of influences. From the Texan cry of Blind Lemon Jefferson to the strident, passionate delivery of Son House and Charlie Patton, or the guitar-playing dexterity of Lonnie Johnson, Robert Johnson fed upon the very best. Yet he created a fully integrated and compelling personal musical world which, through its sheer brilliance and expressiveness, both musical and verbal, was entirely self-contained. This hypnotic effect was to be felt by every generation of blues artists, right up to the present day.

Johnson was born in Hazlehurst, Mississippi, the result of an affair that made his early life rootless and confused, though much of his boyhood was spent in and around Memphis. He was first known as Robert Spencer, the adopted surname of the man his mother was living with at the time of his birth. Under this name he took what little schooling he was to enjoy and he began developing an interest in music, teaching himself jew's harp and harmonica. Learning his true paternity in mid-teens, he began to use either Spencer or Johnson as the whim took him. By his late teens, living some 40 miles south of Memphis in Robinsonville, Johnson was becoming serious about the guitar, and he heard many of the early greats, being particularly struck by Leroy Carr's music. First-hand tuition and observation came from friend and musician Willie Brown, and blues great Charlie Patton, who often passed though. This was a staging point for Johnson, who jumped into marriage in 1929 (he was 18, she 15). This was a short-lived and tragic turn of events, however, as mother and baby both died in childbirth a year later. During the course of recovering from this blow, Johnson met the bluesman Son House: the effect was to make him determined to take his own music equally seriously.

He went to Hazlehurst, Mississippi, in search of his natural father. What he found was an older woman, Caletta Craft, whom he married in May 1931. She kept him while he learned his craft. When Robert felt ready, he and Callie took to the road. Before long, though, he deserted her, and relations were severed with her and her family. In 1933 he returned to his old haunts, demonstrating his proficiency, and he was accepted by his peers as a truly outstanding talent. Basing himself in Helena, Arkansas, he roamed the Delta area, meeting the great bluesmen of the day and creating his legend. His love of life was almost as well known as his music-making, and his enjoyment of women in particular.

In 1936, Johnson approached H.C. Speir, the well-known Jackson talent scout, who passed his name on to a sales rep for the American Record Company. The rep caught Johnson's act and arranged a recording session in San Antonio. His first and biggest hit, "Terraplane Blues," came from this session. A second date, in Dallas, followed in June 1937. Just 11 records were issued during his lifetime, including "Dead Shrimp Blues," "Cross Road Blues," "Preaching Blues," "Hellhound on My Trail," "Me and the Devil Blues," "Love in Vain," and "Stones in my Passway." These established his increasing popularity as well as his posthumous reputation. As a recording artist, he spent time in Chicago, playing a vast variety of jobs and running a small band. He returned to the South once more in 1938. At a juke joint in Three Forks, Mississippi, Johnson met up with Sonny Boy Williamson II (Rice Miller). Johnson's fondness for women and booze led to his being poisoned that night by a jealous rival: he died a few days later, from pneumonia, just 27 years old. All the rest is legend.

## fact file

**BORN** 1911

**DIED** 1938

**MUSICAL SELECTION**
"Cross Road Blues,"
"Preaching Blues"
"Hellhound on
My Trail"

Robert Johnson may well be the blues's most legendary artist, if only for his supposed "deal with the Devil"

**SEE ALSO:** Blind Lemon Jefferson, Son House, Charlie Patton, Leroy Carr

# Janis Joplin

**fact file**

**BORN** 1943

**DIED** 1970

**MUSICAL SELECTION**
Cheap Thrills
I Got Dem Ol' Kozmic
Blues Again, Mama

Janis Joplin, though earning fame via covers of blues standards, brought the music to a wider audience than ever before

a Texan born into the same generation as Angela Strehli and Marcia Ball, Joplin found a different and quicker route to fame. Born with an earth-shattering, brawling voice which was, however, capable of considerable subtlety, Joplin claimed Bessie Smith as her greatest influence, and although this is difficult to find in her actual singing, certainly the larger-than-life personality projected by her singing coincided with the presence Smith was capable of imposing on the listener.

Joplin was born in Port Arthur and came from a regular Texan middle-class background, showing interest in a number of music and art forms in her early teenage years. Initially trying her luck as a folk singer, then switching for a short time to country, she worked around Austin, Texas, a town with strong blues and country connections, building up live experience and readying herself for something bigger. This came in the form of an audition with the San Francisco band Big Brother and the Holding Company, a group combining basic blues forms with high amplification and a contemporary attitude to soaring guitar solos and drugs. Joplin was accepted as a member and the band played the Monterey Pop Festival of 1967, a performance that landed them a contract with Columbia. Their first album, *Cheap Thrills*, partly recorded at Fillmore West, made Joplin a superstar overnight, her almost scary, tortured vocals touching a deep chord in her mainly young white audience on songs such as "Ball and Chain" and "Piece of My Heart." Leaving Big Brother shortly after, Joplin recorded her first solo album, *I Got Dem Ol' Kozmic Blues Again, Mama*, a rather dissolute and unconvincing album, before forming the short-lived Full Tilt Boogie Band in 1970. It was with this band that she recorded her last album, *Pearl*, which was close to completion at her death, from an overdose, in October of that year. A year previously she had contributed to the fund to put a gravestone on Bessie Smith's unmarked grave. Her biggest hit, "Me & Bobbie McGhee," was a posthumous release, as was *Pearl*.

**SEE ALSO:** Angela Strehli, Marcia Ball, Bessie Smith

# Charley Jordan

**fact file**

**BORN** 1890

**DIED** 1954

**MUSICAL SELECTION**
"Keep Your Yes Yes Clean"
"Cherry Wine Woman"

Charley Jordan's talents lay both in the blues and in talent-spotting (not to mention bootlegging)

uitarist/singer Jordan was a popular and important figure on the 1920s St Louis blues scene, often teaming up with Peetie Wheatstraw in live performances and on record, although the two men recorded together only once using Jordan's name as the principal artist. Jordan had a clear, often high-spirited vocal delivery and a correspondingly light touch on his guitar, making him an ideal accompanist.

Jordan was born in Mabelville, Arkansas, and taught himself guitar. He saw service in the armed forces during World War I, then returned to civilian life by becoming an itinerant bluesman traveling much of the South before eventually settling in St Louis. Combining music with a talent for organizing, Jordan got

on the wrong side of the wrong sort of people in 1928, and was crippled in a punishment shooting which resulted from his meddling in some bootlegging business. Sticking thereafter to music, he began his recording career in 1930 with Vocalion as a solo act, quickly returning to the label a couple of months later as accompanist for Peetie Wheatstraw.

He recorded regularly until 1937, making trips to Chicago and New York to record tracks like "Keep Your Yes Yes Clean" and "Cherry Wine Woman." After that, Jordan mixed music with other business to keep himself going, gradually removing himself from the scene by the time of his death, in St Louis, in 1954. His recorded legacy speaks for itself.

**SEE ALSO:** Peetie Wheatstraw

# Louis Jordan

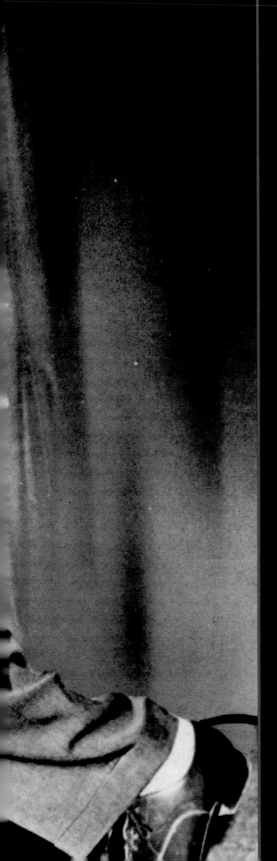

J ordan, more than any other figure, brought the disparate elements of blues, rhythm, jazz, jump, and jive into a coherent song-based genre which clearly anticipated the advent of rock 'n' roll by a good decade. Putting great emphasis on small-group discipline, a shuffle or rocking back beat, and the supremacy of the vocal line, sax-playing singer Jordan became a major star and a seller of millions of records even while rarely straying from a 12-bar-blues format. Virtually every rock and pop musician who came after him owed something to his legacy, and some were generous in their acknowledgment of it, including Chuck Berry, B.B. King, and Van Morrison.

Jordan was born in Brinkley, Arkansas, halfway between Memphis and Little Rock, and learned the saxophone from his father, a musician who was the leader of the Rabbit Foot Minstrels. Jordan became a member of the summer-touring Minstrels as a teenager and later saw time with other touring companies, including that of Ma Rainey and Kaiser Marshall. His travels finally came to an end when he settled in Philadelphia in 1932, joining Charlie Gaines's band. After three years he felt ready to progress and moved to New York, where in 1936 he joined Chick Webb's Savoy Ballroom Orchestra, becoming a section sax player and the male singer opposite Ella Fitzgerald. Quitting the band in 1938, a year before Webb's premature death, Jordan took a residency in Elk's Rendezvous in Harlem and started a small-group which, on its initial Decca sessions in December 1938, was called The Elk's Rendezvous Band, but by the time of his second sessions in March 1939 it had acquired the soon-to-be famous title the Tympany Five (there were always more than five players and the drummer never played any timpani!).

From the first sides Jordan had his "jump" formula in place, his fiery sax melodies serving as perfect intros for his streetwise, often humorous vocals, usually set to a shuffle beat. His band, a normal swing small-group personnel augmented by an electric guitar, did the simple things extremely well and were all excellent musicians. By November 1941 Jordan had recorded his first million-seller, "I'm Gonna Move To The Outskirts of Town," and for the next 10 years he was a major presence in the national charts, appealing equally to black and white audiences. Other massive hits include "Five Guys Named Mo," "Is You Is Or Is You Ain't My Baby?," "Ain't Nobody Here But Us Chickens," "Caldonia," "Saturday Night Fish Fry," "Let The Good Times Roll," and "Choo Choo Ch'Boogie." During this decade he appeared in a string of Hollywood films and also made countless "soundies" for the jukeboxes equipped with visuals. As the 1950s went on Jordan lost his place in the public eye, forming a big band just as the big-band craze had ended and coarsening the material he was recording. He moved record labels to Aladdin (and, later, Mercury and RCA) in an attempt to revive interest, but the bubble had burst and the more aggressive sounds of rock 'n' roll were taking the public's attention elsewhere. Jordan continued to tour and record, but never recaptured his pre-eminence and went through a period of ill health which made him readdress his priorities. During the 1960s and early 1970s he continued to work worldwide at his own pace, even making a record with Chris Barber's Band in England. But two heart attacks landed blows from which he did not recover, succumbing to the second in February 1975.

## fact file

**BORN** 1908

**DIED** 1975

**MUSICAL SELECTION**
"Is You Is Or Is You
Ain't My Baby?"
"Ain't Nobody Here
But Us Chickens"

# Keb' Mo'

**fact file**

**BORN** 1955

**MUSICAL SELECTION**
Rainmaker
**Just Like You**

Kevin Moore aka
Keb' Mo' earned
critical acclaim
portraying
Robert Johnson
in a docu-drama

oore was born in South Central Los Angeles to parents who had come to California from Texas and Louisiana. From the start, his parents instilled in him a love of gospel music, but as he grew into his teens he also began paying due attention to the sounds that were emerging from America during the course of the 1960s and early 1970s, from R&B and soul to rock. Later in the 1970s he was spotted while in a club band doing covers of current top-40 hits by the ex-Jefferson Starship violinist Papa John Creach, who hired him to play in his backing band. Moore stayed with Creach for three years, during which time he was introduced to the thriving Southern California blues scene of the late 1970s. While with the band he continued to pursue his own interests, which included writing his own songs: this led eventually to his leaving Creach and taking a job at A&M's demonstration studios, arranging sessions for Almo-Irving Music. In his spare time he put together his own first album, *Rainmaker* (1980), which

left little trace. Two years later he began playing the blues in Monk Higgins's house band at Marla's Memory Lane in South-Central LA, backing many famous acts while there.

In 1990 Moore was hired to play a blues guitarist in a Los Angeles theater production, *Rabbit Foot*, for which he busied himself with much research into country blues. A subsequent theater production, *Spunk*, again found him portraying a bluesman. Playing after hours with other musicians involved in the play led to his folksy nickname. Moore, now using Keb' Mo' as a professional name, signed a deal with Epic's Okeh subsidiary and released his self-titled debut for them in 1994. It was noticed around the world for its subtle and authentic combining of country and urban blues types. A second album, *Just Like You*, appeared in 1996: this developed the pattern of the first Okeh disc, putting Mo' with many different and imaginative blues combinations. Keb' Mo's career continues apace.

**SEE ALSO:** Robert Johnson

# David "Junior" Kimbrough

**fact file**

**BORN** 1930

**MUSICAL SELECTION**
All Night Long
Sad Days,
Lonely Nights

Junior Kimbrough
has always kept
his playing
simple and
straightforward

Iike R.L. Burnside, Kimbrough has specialized for most of his blues career on the hypnotic repetition of sparse, driving phrases and riffs which constitute a revivification and updating of the so-called "juke" style of blues. Born and raised in Hudsonville, Mississippi, Kimbrough was self-taught as a boy and came under the direct influence of his neighbor, Mississippi Fred McDowell. Becoming an active member of the local blues community and playing the usual joints and parties, Kimbrough gradually became influential in his own right, especially among local rockabilly outfits. He made his first singles in the 1960s, which remained strictly local affairs, and later became the proprietor of his own juke joint, where he and Burnside, among others, continue to perform regularly. Featured in the 1992 film documentary, *Deep Blues*, Kimbrough has kept very active and, like Burnside, has recorded for the Fat Possum label in the 1990s, *All Night Long* and *Sad Days, Lonely Nights* (1994) being two prime examples.

During the 1990s Kimbrough has benefited from the exposure given him by the film and records to the extent that he has been able to travel as far as Europe on occasion to bring his highly unusual and idiosyncratic form of blues to a wider live audience. The popularity of the hard-driven, rough-edged and starkly simple blues his bands play continues to grow around the world, and his style is a strong as ever.

**SEE ALSO:** R. L. Burnside, Mississippi Fred McDowell

# Albert King

## fact file

**BORN** 1923

**DIED** 1992

**MUSICAL SELECTION**
Livewire/Blues Power
I'm In A Phone
Booth, Baby

One of the "three Kings", Albert King remains extraordinarily well-represented on album and on stage

**a**lbert King was self-taught and unconventional in the extreme in terms of technique, he played left-handed with the guitar strung upside down – probably the result of having learned to play on a guitar borrowed from a right-handed player.

King was born Albert Nelson in Indianola, Mississippi. He first sang gospel before discovering the blues via the recordings of Blind Lemon Jefferson and the live performances of a man named Dorothy Daily. The teenaged Albert used to see Daily playing in Forest City, Arkansas, where the family had moved during his boyhood. Albert bought his first guitar in Little Rock, and ended up working in Yancey's Band, a group based in Osceola. At this stage he was inspired by a range of music, from Woody Herman's *Band That Plays The Blues* to T-Bone Walker. The combination of blues with boogie and other elements was to be a lasting fascination for the young musician now playing under the name Albert King. A series of positions in his own and other groups led to sessions for a number of labels, including Sun in Memphis and Parrott in Chicago, the latter in 1953. But even after playing drums for Jimmy Reed for a while, King felt he was getting nowhere and quit the music scene altogether until 1959. That year he moved to East St Louis, where he recorded for Bobbin;

two years later, King finally had a minor hit with "Don't Throw Your Love On Me So Strong." King's career continued to stutter along until he signed with the Memphis-based Stax label in 1965. His long series of singles for Stax – most often made with the Memphis label's house band of Steve Cropper, Booker T. Washington, Duck Dunn and Al Jackson, Jr., plus the Memphis Horns – gave him hit after hit, including "Crosscut Saw," "Laundromat Blues," and "Born Under A Bad Sign."

After nearly two decades of struggling, King became a star and a hero on both sides of the Atlantic, his sound and style pointing the way for many emerging blues guitarists, including Eric Clapton and Mick Taylor. In 1968 he appeared successfully as the warm-up act for Jimi Hendrix, among others, at Bill Graham's Fillmore West; a reissue of two entire nights of this material, from which the best-selling *Livewire/Blues Power* was originally culled, has recently appeared. King continued with Stax until the label's demise in 1974. Shifting between labels for a few years – then staying out of the recording studio altogether – he made a comeback in 1983 with *San Francisco '83* on Fantasy. The next year he released his last album, *I'm In A Phone Booth, Baby*. King continued touring until his death, from a heart attack, in December 1992.

**SEE ALSO:** Freddie King, Blind Lemon Jefferson, T-Bone Walker, Jimmy Reed, Eric Clapton, Jimi Hendrix

# Earl King

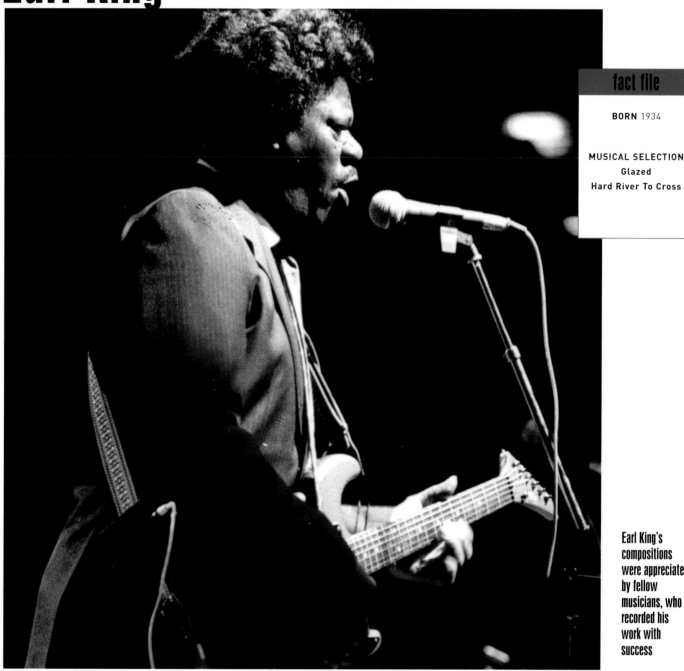

**fact file**

**BORN** 1934

**MUSICAL SELECTION**
Glazed
Hard River To Cross

Earl King's compositions were appreciated by fellow musicians, who recorded his work with success

**K**ing has been a fundamental part of the development of New Orleans rhythm and blues since the 1950s. If Allen Toussaint and Fats Domino enjoyed a higher international profile on the pop charts, King was no less influential in bringing together New Orleans's special musical mix to address a new young audience itching to discover new rhythms and musical colors. Like so many other New Orleans musicians, he has been as important a songwriter as a performer, and his tunes have been covered by a huge range of musicians including Jimi Hendrix, the Neville Brothers, Lee Dorsey, Robert Palmer, and Dr. John.

Born Solomon Johnson, Earl King became a stalwart of many New Orleans bands in the 1950s, starting with Guitar Slim (whose guitar playing was a primary influence on King's) and moving through many others. By 1953 he'd made his debut on record for Savoy, sticking very much to the style he inherited from Guitar Slim. But in 1960 King signed with Imperial and began making a series of hits which would define his own unique style through the rest of the decade. These included "Come On (Let The Good Times Roll)," "Mama and Papa," and "Big Chief." The 1970s, however, were hard for King, as they were for many other blues-based artists. It was not until the 1980s, when his Black Top recording with Roomful of Blues (the Grammy-nominated *Glazed*) caught on, that King's burnished, soulful vocals and polished guitar made a comeback. Since then, two further Black Top albums have appeared – *Sexual Telepathy* and *Hard River To Cross* – and Earl King's career continues unabated.

**SEE ALSO:** Jimi Hendrix, Dr John, Roomful of Blues

# B B King

**P**robably the widest-known and possibly the greatest living blues artist today, B.B. King is a man of erudition, culture, and style, with unusually broad and detailed interests. King has managed, during a long career in the limelight, to retain his music's integrity at every stage of his career while changing some of its external trappings to catch the ever-shifting taste of the public.

King was born in Itta Bena, Mississippi, and first developed a passion for music singing in church. Shown the rudiments of guitar playing by a friendly pastor and using his father's old guitar, King made progress on the instrument while working in stevedore and plantation-worker positions. He heard a lot of music that excited him on the radio, including the young jazz genius, Charlie Christian, a man with very deep roots in the blues.

After an aborted try at living in Memphis and a further year back in Mississippi in 1946–47, King landed in Memphis in late 1947. Through Rice Miller (Sonny Boy Williamson II), he made guest appearances on a few radio shows on WDIA. This led to DJ work for the station in 1949, building a local following, introducing himself to blues personalities living in or passing through Memphis, and availing himself of the radio record library to give himself a broad knowledge of blues and jazz. Operating as the Beale Street Blues Boy, he played many Memphis gigs and finally came to the attention of Sun's Sam Phillips in 1951 (by this time his performing name had been shortened to B.B.), who recorded him for the LA-based Bihari brothers' RPM label. Working with his own band, King had to wait until the following year for a hit, but when it came, "3 O'Clock Blues" established him nationally, hitting the No. 1 R&B spot and staying there for months. His unique interpretative approach to even the most familiar material gave him a long stretch of hits in the 1950s, including Memphis Slim's "Everyday I Have The Blues" and "You Upset Me Baby." Always a hard-working musician, King pushed himself to the limit in the 1950s, playing all year round, touring endlessly, and recording often. With the rise of rock 'n' roll and soul and the return to popularity, through young whites, of the country blues, King experienced a dip in popularity in the 1960s, despite playing perhaps the best, most powerful blues of his career, such as 1965's acclaimed *Live at the Regal* (ABC).

King was popular on the tour circuit but his music remained outside the ken of the new young audience. Only with a change of management and a move into the big rock venues just then opening, especially the Fillmores and the festivals, did King finally connect with young whites and re-establish himself, especially with the album recorded live at Chicago's Cook County Jail in 1970. The album made the pop charts. In the same year King notched a hit with the single "The Thrill Is Gone."

From that point on King was a blues superstar, his live show and repertoire rarely disturbed, his guitar – named Lucille – a major part of the act. At the turn of the 1970s King took a new turn when he made two albums with members of the soul/jazz stars the Crusaders. His vocals and guitar playing unchanged, he slipped into the more funk-oriented blues backgrounds seamlessly, updating his appeal and relaunching himself into the 1980s. This method of popular and musical renewal was repeated with the Irish group U2 in 1988 when King appeared on their *Rattle and Hum*. During the 1990s, though no longer possessed of robust health, King has continued to record and play, a towering presence in the music.

**SEE ALSO:** Sonny Boy Williamson II, T-Bone Walker, Wynonie Harris

## fact file

**BORN** 1925

**MUSICAL SELECTION**
Live at the Regal
"Everyday I Have
The Blues"
"The Thrill Is Gone"

B.B. King, possibly the world's most recognizable blues artist, smiles mid-note at the Royal Albert Hall in London, June 1996

# "Little" Jimmy King

Ever the showman, "Little" Jimmy King's left-handed style and driving sound brought him to the attention of his adopted grandfather Albert King

## fact file

**BORN** 1968

**MUSICAL SELECTION**
Something Inside of Me
Soldier For The Blues

**b**orn into a musical family in South Memphis, Manuel Gales first found himself attracted to pop and rock. When he came to learn the guitar (given a guitar for his sixth birthday, he played it left-handed and upside down, like many left-handers), he took Jimi Hendrix as his first model. Gales discovered the blues in his mid-teens and decided that this was the music he wanted to play. Starting off in parks and on street corners in Memphis, Gales gradually progressed to occasional gigs in clubs that would let him in (he was still well under age), his Hendrix roots tempered by the sounds coming from Stevie Ray Vaughan's band and guitar around the same time. He played in one of these with Mojo Buford's band in the mid-1980s by the blues boss Albert King, who liked what he heard. By 1988 Gales had become a member of

the older man's band. During his four years with Albert King, the two men became close enough for Gales to change his name officially to Jimmy King and become an adopted grandson of Albert King.

Jimmy King made his first album as a leader in 1991, *Little Jimmy King and the Memphis Soul Survivors*, using musicians from the Memphis area. With Albert King's death in 1992, Little Jimmy took over and worked under the name he'd used for his first album. King has continued to build a loyal young following for his very contemporary blues sound: his two follow-up albums have been with the King James Version band; the first, in 1994, was *Something Inside of Me*, the second, from 1997, *Soldier For The Blues*, sporting a cover with King himself in army uniform. King continues to pursue an active career.

**SEE ALSO:** Jimi Hendrix, Stevie Ray Vaughan, Mojo Buford, Albert King

# The Kinsey Report

The Kinsey Report, made up of the sons of Big Daddy Kinsey, performs a mixture of blues-influenced music

t he Kinsey Report is the brainchild of the sons of Lester "Big Daddy" Kinsey, a bluesman who in recent years has returned to the public eye and become an important contemporary blues influence. Kinsey's sons, vocalist/guitarist Donald (born 1953), drummer Ralph (born 1952), and bassist Kenneth (born 1963), first experienced professional music-making as part of their father's backing band, his "Fabulous Sons," before Donald went off to play first with Albert King and later with Bob Marley and Peter Tosh. In 1976 Donald returned to Chicago and began a prototype of the Kinsey Report, called the Chosen Ones, but this project was abandoned when Donald helped Marley out on his final tour in 1981.

By 1984 Donald was ready to have another shot at his earlier family-based project, involving his father as vocalist on their first album, *Bad Situation* (1984), after which Big Daddy went back to his solo career and the three brothers continued alone, producing a typical hybrid of a mass of musical influences, from heavy metal to soul to rock, R&B and blues, with even the occasional echo of reggae. After three albums for Alligator, they switched to the better-distributed Virgin/Pointblank label and made *Powerhouse*, featuring Ronnie Prince, who'd also briefly featured with the Chosen Ones, on rhythm guitar. *Crossing Bridges* (1993) was a full-ahead album containing the statement from the band: "looking forward to a brighter day when the darkness of evil is cast away, no matter what the doubters say the power of love will conquer hate." The Kinsey Report continue to record and tour, their up-to-date blues-rock commanding an international audience.

## fact file

**FORMED** 1984

**MUSICAL SELECTION**
Powerhouse
Crossing Bridges
Bad Situation

SEE ALSO: Lester "Big Daddy" Kinsey

# Freddie King

**K**ing is one of the triumvirate of three great postwar blues Kings (none of whom is related to the others, let alone Earl or Jimmy), the other two being B.B. and Albert. Freddie was a singularly exciting and influential guitarist and singer, his playing in the 1950s and early 1960s more than any other paving the way for the blues-rock boom of the 1960s. He remains a fundamental influence on the young blues guitarists of today who are experiencing once again a blues boom worldwide.

Freddie was the son of John Christian and Ella Mae King of Gilmer, Texas, and became interested in the guitar while still a boy, learning on an acoustic model. During this time he heard a good cross-section of some of the best country blues musicians in Texas. In 1950, when Freddie (still spelling his name "Freddy") was 16, he moved with his family to Chicago and immediately began hearing the music coming out of the South-Side and West-Side clubs. Working by day in a steel mill, King slowly got himself known on the blues scene in Chicago, evolving a guitar style that showed traces of many players, including Magic Sam, Albert King, and even T-Bone Walker. Yet King's razor-edge tone and short, controlled blues melodies stood out from the beginning, and when he started to record in 1956 it was already as a mature stylist. By 1960 King had his own band featuring the pianist Sonny Thompson and he was recording for a King Records subsidiary, Federal. In the next four years for Federal King would record a string of blues classics that have been models for all who have followed him. These include the instrumental "Hideaway," named after the Chicago club King often played in, "I'm Tore Down," "I Love The Woman," "Someday After a While," and the socially conscious "The Welfare (Turns Its Back On You)." King, presumably guided by Federal's Syd Nathan, also recorded a misguided series of bluesed-up twist songs such as "Do The President's Twist" and "The Bossa Nova Watusi Twist," and later attempted to out-hang-five the new surf bands with "Surf Monkey," but his great work transcended such ephemera. King stayed with Federal until late 1966, moving to the Atlantic subsidiary Cotillon in 1968 and, being produced by King Curtis, making music at some remove from his Federal classics. His lionization by the new rock guitar heroes led to his profile being higher than ever as the new decade dawned. His move to Leon Russell's Shelter label in 1970 put him squarely in the then contemporary blues-rock field, using many of the production techniques associated with Russell's other projects, including female backing singers and Crescent City instrumental backings. King's vocals and guitar remained gloriously intact, though, and the years 1970–73 proved a good time in King's career as he found new audiences for his music. With the demise of Shelter, King moved to RSO and a trio of records that saw him unashamedly reaching out for the 1970s soul market, but his live work (as can be heard on the posthumous concert albums) remained gritty and 100 percent blues-led, his guitar and voice up to any standard of the past. Where King would have gone from there will remain unknown: he died, suddenly, of a combination of ailments, including ulcers, heart attack, and hepatitis, after a Christmas concert in Dallas in 1976.

**fact file**

**BORN** 1934

**DIED** 1976

**MUSICAL SELECTION**
"Hideaway"
"I'm Tore Down"

Freddie King aka Billie Myles, the third of the "three Kings" was the king of the blues in the 1960s

**SEE ALSO:** B.B. King, Albert King, Magic Sam, T-Bone Walker, Eric Clapton

# Lester "Big Daddy" Kinsey

fact file

BORN 1927

MUSICAL SELECTION
I Am The Blues

Big Daddy Kinsey made certain to pass on his love of music and the blues to his sons, as well as his debt to Muddy Waters's style

K insey has had a long career in the blues, playing in and around Pleasant Grove, Mississippi as a teenager prior to WWII, as well as spending years as a local bluesman in postwar Gary, Indiana. But it is only since the 1980s that he has expanded his reputation into the international scene, his rich baritone and occasional guitar striking a chord with today's blues audiences.

Kinsey's musical roots lie, as is the case with so many bluesmen of his generation, equally split between church and blues. He grew up involved in both genres, and credits early experiences listening to Muddy Waters at Mississippi fish-fries as influential to his whole approach to playing. Certainly the easy raunch of Muddy Waters's early Chicago years is clearly evidenced in Kinsey's latter-day recordings. After brief service in WWII, Kinsey stuck with Gary, Indiana, as his base, settled and had a family – a fact which is key to his later career. Splitting his working life

between day jobs in Gary (including work in the steel mill) and occasional gigs at night, Kinsey was consistent in his dedication to his music, but remained in obscurity. A change began when his sons, who from an early age exhibited musical talent, were old enough to play with him. As the 1960s gave way to the 1970s, they formed a band – Big Daddy Kinsey and His Fabulous Sons – and Kinsey's reputation began to expand. Although a split with his sons as they decided to play rock and reggae left the elder Kinsey running his own band for a number of years, the family's musical differences had evaporated by the early 1980s. Father and sons then formed The Kinsey Report and made a considerable impact in blues circles, with Big Daddy acting as vocalist and front man. Since the success of the family group, Big Daddy has happily swapped between solo and band projects, his *I Am The Blues* for Verve/Gitanes (1994), dedicated to Muddy Waters, typical of the disciplined, slow-burning blues he prefers.

SEE ALSO: Muddy Waters, The Kinsey Report

# Eddie Kirkland

fact file

**BORN** 1928

**MUSICAL SELECTION**
"It's Time For Lovin' To
Be Done"
"That's All Right"

Born in Jamaica,
Eddie Kirkland's
career spanned
over 40 years

guitarist/singer Kirkland has consistently produced vigorous, down-home blues for many decades without becoming particularly influential or outstanding in any blues genre. An early colleague of John Lee Hooker, Kirkland moved into R&B and soul as tastes changed in subsequent decades, returning to the blues when the European tour circuit once again made it financially viable.

Kirkland was born in Kingston, Jamaica, but left the island during infancy to live with his family in Alabama. By his mid-teens he was working in the car industry in Detroit, biding his time until he could make a living from the blues he was already playing. He met Detroit's leading bluesman, John Lee Hooker, and by April 1951 was accompanying him on record for the Chess label. The following year Hooker returned the favor by appearing as a sideman on Kirkland's first single (for RPM), "It's Time For Lovin' To Be Done"/"That's All Right." Kirkland continued to attempt to run his career from Detroit with a hard-working club band of his own and a spattering of singles for a variety of tiny labels during the 1950s, but by 1961 he was looking further afield. That year he made a jazz/blues record with King Curtis and Oliver Nelson for Tru-Sound/Prestige, and although he continued to play blues on live dates, by the mid-1960s he'd embraced soul as the way forward, only occasionally returning to the blues for sessions with Hooker and other old friends prior to a conversion back to the blues in the mid-1970s. Since then Kirkland has been consistent in his allegiance to the blues, in concert and on record.

# Alexis Korner

## fact file

**BORN** 1928

**DIED** 1984

**MUSICAL SELECTION**
The Alexis Korner
Collection, 1961–72

The king of the UK blues scene, Alexis Korner always sought to promote the music whenever possible

**K**orner has often been called "the father of British R&B," and there is sufficient truth in the idea for it not to be discounted easily. While not outrageously talented himself, Korner had a real fan's passion for the blues and its related musics and was a stickler for proper authenticity in recreating it in a modern context. His nurturing of many young British musicians was one of the major factors in bringing about the abundance of British blues talent during the halcyon years of the 1960s.

Korner was born in Paris and came to England with his family in 1939 as Hitler's armies were poised to invade the rest of Europe. At the end of World War II Korner started out his life in music as a confirmed jazz fan, graduating to blues and its offshoots by the beginning of the 1950s. Drawn into the pool of musicians and enthusiasts embroiled in the thriving trade and skiffle scene of the early and mid-1950s, Korner gradually came to see that much of what was being played was hardly authentic. A spell in the band of Chris Barber – like him a man with real erudition on the subject of jazz and blues – during this time gave

Korner a clear pointer as to the direction he wished to pursue. Along with the blues enthusiast and harp player Cyril Davies he founded the London Blues and Barrelhouse Club, an important meeting place for like-minded souls. By 1961 he had formed Blues Incorporated with Davies (although the latter was to leave within a year), which quickly became a fixture at London's Marquee Club. Over the next six years the band was to employ a galaxy of talent, including half of the Rolling Stones, Long John Baldry, Jack Bruce, Ginger Baker, Paul Jones, and Graham Bond. While his erstwhile employees mostly left to find fame and riches, Korner plied his blues and R&B trail to mediocre success. Blues Inc was discontinued in 1967 and although Korner ran other bands after that, it was under his own name that he mostly performed from then on. Branching out, Korner appeared on television and had a long-running radio show in London during the 1970s and 1980s. He continued to play with varying line-ups up to his death, from cancer, in 1984. Scantily recorded in comparison with his peers, Korner is perhaps best represented on CD by *The Alexis Korner Collection, 1961–72* (Collector Series).

**SEE ALSO:** John Mayall

# Smokin' Joe Kubeck

**fact file**

**BORN** 1956

**MUSICAL SELECTION**
The Axe Man
Cryin' For The Moon

Smokin' Joe Kubeck, sweating up a storm, has enjoyed great success, especially with his stage partner B'Nois King

**K**ubeck has been based around Dallas for most of his career and blues was always his first-choice music. During the early 1970s he was the only white in an otherwise all-black band, Robert Whitfield's Last Band, who played the black clubs in Dallas and augmented their blues playing with some jazz and extended improvisation. Kubeck graduated from this to playing in the bands of Al "TNT" Braggs and Freddie King: he was in King's band up until the great bluesman's death in 1976. Kubeck's typically Texan, slashing guitar style had complemented King's attack perfectly, and it stood him in good stead as a session musician in a number of productions organized by Al Braggs after King's death.

Kubeck eventually formed his own band in the 1980s, using a residency at Dallas's Poor David's Pub in which to develop his own ideas. The trio eventually grew into a quartet when Kubeck invited the black singer and guitarist, Bnois King, to join. This band made a series of records for Bullseye Blues at the beginning of the 1990s that highlight the power-blues, no-frills approach Kubeck favors. King's own more varied, jazz-influenced style gives the band a useful contrast of styles and has led their popularity to grow to the point where the Smokin' Joe Kubeck band tours regularly throughout the States and have built a reputation in Europe, too, as one of the premier contemporary Texas blues bands.

# Lazy Lester

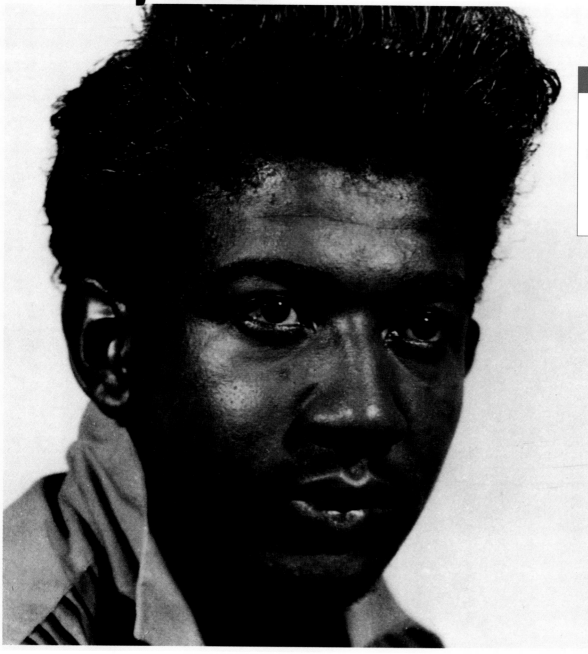

**fact file**

**BORN** 1933

**MUSICAL SELECTION**
Harp and Soul

Lazy Lester
was definitely
laid-back enough
to merit the
nickname that
stayed with him
throughout his
lifetime

the harpist/vocalist Leslie Johnson was born in Torras, Louisiana, and first began gigging professionally around Crowley, Louisiana, where he began recording for Feature records with his longtime friend and associate Lightnin' Slim in 1954 and under his own name for Jay Miller's Excello label in 1956. Johnson around this time acquired his nickname "Lazy Lester" from this insouciance and lack of any ambition to get on in the world. His harmonica style, based on Little Walter, at that time the leading blues harp stylist, was sharp and to the point, rarely wasteful or clumsily phrased, whether he was leading his own band or backing Louisiana Slim. He recorded for the Excello label right through to 1965, using such musicians as Katie Webster, Al Foreman, and Guitar Gable as support, and one of his records, 1957's "I'm A Lover Not a Fighter," was covered by the Kinks, while

"I Hear You Knockin'" has been covered by many British bands.

Lester's solo career never amounted to a great deal, content as he was to cut records occasionally as leader, occasionally as an accompanist, and stay put in Louisiana. By the late 1960s he was drifting out of the music scene altogether, living at first in the country in Louisiana and later, encouraged by Lightnin' Slim, moving to Pontiac, Michigan. Lester returned to recording after touring Europe in 1987, making an album for the British label Blues 'n' Trouble. This led to an album for Alligator, *Harp and Soul*, which showed a wider grasp of the spectrum of Louisiana swamp music than Lester had exhibited on record before, although his vocals were no more interesting or varied than before. Lester has kept up interest in his music since then, enjoying a modest but successful revival.

**SEE ALSO:** Lightnin' Slim, Little Walter

# Julia Lee

**fact file**

**BORN** 1902

**DIED** 1959

**MUSICAL SELECTION**
"Ugly Papa,"
"Do You Want It?"
"King Size Papa"

The queen of the
double entendre,
Julia Lee

Lee was born in Boonville, Missouri, but spent most of her life in Kansas City, where she cultivated a blues-driven, swinging piano and vocal style that was quintessential Kansas City swing. Her vocals were more often than not risqué and her sidemen were usually top-drawer jazzmen, but the very foundation of her insinuating style is the blues.

Sister of bandleader George Lee, Julia married at 16 and soon after joined her brother's band; a test recording she made for Okeh in 1923 has never been found. She played with various bands run by her brother in KC until 1934, when she went solo, becoming a fixture at the city's Milton's Tap Room between 1934 and 1948. Her repertoire was established during this period, and it was liberally laced with songs walking a thin line between double entendre and blatant lewdness – "Ugly Papa," "Do You Want It?," "King Size Papa," and "Don't Come Too Soon" give the general tone of her lyrics. Like her rival Nellie Lutcher, Lee's vocals were always flawlessly presented, her time and intonation perfect, and her piano playing equally delectable. Her group, Julia Lee and Her Boyfriends, enjoyed considerable popular success in the 1940s and early 1950s. As the R&B boom died and the taste for Kansas City blues and swing ebbed, Lee broadened her songbook considerably, from pop to music hall. Lee remained in touch with her Kansas City peers, including Count Basie and Jimmy Rushing, but was content to play out her remaining career in small KC joints. She died tragically from a heart attack in December 1959.

**SEE ALSO:** Jimmy Rushing

# Leadbelly

a true musical legend, Huddie Ledbetter aka Leadbelly was a vitally important link between the older "songster" folk traditions of black America and the more urban-based (and middle-class) folk revival of the 1930s, where political and sociological considerations became evident for the first time. Never seen, even by himself, as exclusively a blues artist (few of his generation were), Leadbelly played blues numbers as part of a wide and rich tapestry of music drawn from many sources. Considering the amount of time he spent in prison during his adult years, it is just possible that his missing the country blues' rise to mass popularity made him the unwitting preserver of an older approach to folk music.

Huddie Ledbetter was born in a low-lying rural part of Louisiana close to the borders of Arkansas and Texas. There he spent his early youth on his parents' farm, working the land and, as his teenage years arrived, attending local dances (the so-called "sukey-jumps"), where he developed a taste not only for fights and pretty girls, but also for the music he heard and danced to. He began learning an array of instruments, including piano and accordion – instruments he could still play in his sixties – but finally settled on guitar as the most versatile and powerful accompaniment to his strong, exciting voice. Leadbelly talked little of his life prior to the World War I years, but it seems he traveled widely over the South after leaving home as a youth, and made a living both at odd-jobs and at performing music. He claims to have had a close relationship with Blind Lemon Jefferson around this time, and while he may have exaggerated, there is no reason to suppose the well-traveled Jefferson didn't occasionally use the services of a junior partner to drum up trade during those years. Whatever the case, by 1917 Ledbetter was behind bars after killing a man in an argument; the sentence was for more than thirty years. Leadbelly, a strong man and no fool, soon learned to be a model prisoner and, in 1925, won himself a pardon by singing a plea for freedom to prison governor Pat Neff. He quickly returned to his former nomadic life.

Just five years later Leadbelly was back inside again, this time at Louisiana's notorious Angola Prison Farm, after an attempted murder. It was here that he was discovered in 1933 by folk historians Alan and John Lomax, on their first field trip to document and record Southern folklore and music. Through their influence he was once again freed, and in 1934 began his bid for fame through the efforts of the Lomaxes themselves. By 1935 he had settled in New York City and married (for a second time), and attempted to impress the locals in the way he had prison governors and folk researchers. This proved a much harder task, and although he recorded frequently, Leadbelly saw little money from these ventures (often made for non-profit organizations) and was often nearly destitute. Yet he was instrumental in bringing the older black folk tradition to the ears of white radicals and intellectuals, who soon came to regard him as something of a living icon. The rest of Leadbelly's life was spent looking for that elusive "hit," and he wrote and adapted many songs to that end, including "Rock Island Line," "Fannin' Street," "New York City," "Black Betty," and "Goodnight Irene." The latter, ironically, was to become a worldwide hit for the folk group The Weavers soon after Leadbelly's death, from a wasting disease, in 1949.

## fact file

**BORN** 1888

**DIED** 1949

**MUSICAL SELECTION**
"Rock Island Line"
"Fannin' Street"
"New York City"
"Black Betty"

The indomitable Leadbelly, master of the 12-string blues guitar, enjoyed great acclaim but made very little money in his long career

SEE ALSO: Blind Lemon Jefferson

# Lefty Dizz

**fact file**

**BORN** 1937

**DIED** 1993

**MUSICAL SELECTION**
Ain't It Nice
to be Loved

Lefty Dizz, so
named for his
left-handed
guitar style and
for his great
impression of
Dizzy Gillespie

a highly talented journeyman guitarist long on the Chicago blues scene, Williams was the bandleader of the Junior Wells band for four years between 1966 and 1970 but rarely had the opportunity to work as a leader until his fifth decade was well under way. Yet his music is pure, undiluted electric Chicago blues and the albums he made before his death are worthy of consideration alongside many others by better-known Chicagoans.

Williams was born in Osceola, Arkansas, but within two years he was resident in Chicago as his parents moved north looking for work. His father was a musician in touch with the Chicago blues community, and his son gained his earliest knowledge of the piano from him, but from early on he had his eye on becoming a guitarist. A natural left-hander, like so many other left-handers he learned a right-handed guitar with upside-down strings. It hardly disturbed his competence. His nickname came from being a left-

handed guitarist in a world unused to such a thing, and from his admiration for Dizzy Gillespie, especially his ability to scat. Williams's frequent attempts to copy Gillespie's vocal ramblings led to his being called "Dizzy," then later, "Dizz." Lefty, as he was now known, made a few singles for different labels, but none of them were noticed, and he first surfaced for the world during his stint with Junior Wells, his slashing guitar and brash onstage presence making something of a mark. During the 1970s he survived the blues doldrums by playing on both sides of the Atlantic, a fact that brought about his first record, for the French Black & Blue label, in 1979. He remained more appreciated in Europe than America during the rest of his life, making two more albums under his own name, but with even the US-recorded date – 1989's *Ain't It Nice to be Loved*, which featured both Carey and Lurrie Bell – being released on England's JSP label. Lefty died of cancer, after a long battle with the disease, in 1993.

**SEE ALSO:** Junior Wells, Carey Bell, Lurrie Bell

# J B Lenoir

**fact file**

**BORN** 1929

**DIED** 1967

**MUSICAL SELECTION**
"Eisenhower Blues"
"Korea Blues"

"Eisenhower Blues" by Lenoir (pictured far left, with Willie Dixon on bass) was a direct political statement, in stark contrast to the fun-filled nature of many of his works

born in Monticello, Mississippi, Lenoir (the initials seem to have been as close to a forename as he ever got) learned the rudiments of music from his parents, both of whom played instruments including the guitar. After playing the usual dances and picnics as an adolescent, J.B. took off for New Orleans, there meeting some of the top bluemen passing through, including Sonny Boy Williamson II, and impressing them with his talent. Finding New Orleans slow as far as the blues went, Lenoir headed north, touching upon many locations before stopping in Chicago in 1949. His fine playing and his unusual, high-pitched voice guaranteed him attention, and when Big Bill Broonzy introduced him around town he soon started working for many of the new generation of Chicago bluesmen and club owners. Inevitably, this led to recordings, and one of the first labels looking for his talents was Chess.

From 1951 onwards Lenoir cut a series of taut, sometimes primitive, often unusual blues songs, many from his own pen. He preferred a band enhanced by piano and saxes, giving his sessions another identifying trait. He also occasionally wrote and recorded topical blues and R&B numbers – a radical departure for the times – with titles such as "Eisenhower Blues" and "Korea Blues." Later, he even updated his topics to include a "Vietnam Blues" in his repertoire. Despite this enterprise, Lenoir never landed a chart hit, and his influence was never that direct – since he was a musician other musicians admired and enjoyed playing with, but something of a connoisseur's choice in terms of audiences. His star, however, was in the ascendant during the 1960s blues boom, and he did two consecutive years of touring in Europe, in 1965 and 1966. Unfortunately, a bad auto accident led to the heart attack which cut short J.B. Lenoir's career, and his life, in 1967.

SEE ALSO: Sonny Boy Williamson II, Big Bill Broonzy

# Walter "Furry" Lewis

ississippi-born Lewis in effect had two careers. The first was a typical 1920s blues-boom affair, in which the young performer was taken from the medicine shows and recorded for a short while before being dropped at the advent of the Depression. But the second, in the 1960s, was a phenomenal rise from cult obscurity to the status of a national and international music figure who was not only invited onto talk shows, but also made cameo appearances in the occasional Hollywood film and became the subject of a Joni Mitchell song, "Furry Sings the Blues."

Walter Lewis moved to turn-of-the-century Memphis as a young boy with his family, but his early interest in music led to him joining the traveling medicine shows as soon as he could get away from home. In 1916 he suffered the loss of a leg through a train accident, using an artificial leg from that time on. This curtailed his wanderings a little and by the early 1920s he was back in Memphis, playing guitar alone on street corners and as a member of jug bands, one of them featuring singer Jim Jackson. Like many others, Lewis supplemented his meager musical income with a day job – in his case, with the Memphis Sanitation Department, as a street-sweeper – which he held off-and-on from 1922 until the early 1960s.

In 1927 Lewis and his friend Jim Jackson struck out for Chicago and the record companies, determined to make some sides; both men did, but not as a team. Lewis's records didn't sell particularly well, but he made sessions for Vocalion and Victor during which he laid down for posterity some seminal Memphis blues style classics, including "I Will Turn Your Money Green," "Kassie Jones," and "Judge Harsh Blues." He also recorded outstanding versions of popular material like "John Henry" and "Stack-o-Lee." Lewis's voice was warm and expressive, but it was his guitar style which was particularly fascinating – a combination of slide and picking techniques performed with an ease and smooth lyricism which made its subtleties all the more delightful.

With the collapse of the blues market in 1929 and the onset of the Depression, Lewis to all intents and purposes disappeared from the blues scene and returned to sweeping the streets of Memphis until his rediscovery by blues historian Samuel Charters in 1959. This led to his second career, which commenced with some fine albums for various labels, the two for Prestige Bluesville in 1961 being consistently excellent. Lewis claimed to have been a friend of W.C. Handy, but it is unlikely he had more than a passing acquaintance with the blues pioneer – although his 1961 version of Handy's "St. Louis Blues" shows just how well Lewis could transform a shopworn piece into a fresh, intense musical experience, however loose his grasp of the song's particulars may have been. Lewis's large personality and showbiz attitude brought him quick and lasting popularity in the 1960s, to the point where he became the most famous of all country bluesmen to have survived the early years. His later recordings are considered rare in the country blues field, since they are generally regarded as having merit, rather than being pale imitations of his earlier triumphs. With this sterling reputation intact, Furry Lewis remained active and revered until his death in 1981, at the age of 88.

## fact file

**BORN** 1893

**DIED** 1981

**MUSICAL SELECTION**
"I Will Turn Your Money Green"
"Kassie Jones"
"Judge Harsh Blues"

Furry Lewis brought the blues with him, appearing at the Fourth Annual University of Chicago Folk Fest in January of 1964

**SEE ALSO:** Jim Jackson, W. C. Handy

# Smiley Lewis

Smiley Lewis's Trio included Herman Scale on drums and Tuts Washington on piano (pictured here in New Orleans, 1949)

### fact file

**BORN** 1913

**DIED** 1966

**MUSICAL SELECTION**
"I Hear You Knocking"
"One Night"

Lewis was a major presence in New Orleans R&B during the 1950s, singing and writing a number of hits which have remained in the repertoire of thousands of bands worldwide, but his own career never took off in the manner for which he must have hoped. His singing and piano playing had that essential New Orleans lilt and amble to it, making him a necessary precursor to the worldwide hit success of Fats Domino, and many of his best songs remain staples in the repertoire of working bands all over the world to this day, as well as hit material for latter-day recording artists.

Lewis was born in DeQuincy, Louisiana, and learned piano while still living at home. In his teens he moved to New Orleans and began playing the clubs and bars in the crescent city, but it took a long time before he was able to make a living out of the music, having to work day jobs for

years prior to this. Lewis finally made his recording debut as late as 1947, appearing for Deluxe records as Smiling Lewis. Nothing happened to those singles and his next foray into the studio was in 1950, for Imperial, with Dave Bartholomew on trumpet. He recorded regularly for Imperial, often using Lee Allen on sax, and had a string of regional hits before landing it big with "I Hear You Knocking" in 1955. There were minor hits with "Blue Monday" and "One Night" but both songs were much bigger hits for Fats Domino and Elvis Presley respectively. Lewis also recorded "Shame, Shame, Shame" in 1956, a song that is now an R&B standard, but his career stubbornly refused to take flight outside the South. He continued to record right through to 1965, changing to the Okeh/Epic labels in 1961, but further success, even of a limited nature, eluded him. He died, from cancer, in 1966.

**SEE ALSO:** Professor Longhair

# Joe Liggins

Joe Liggins (l.) introduces members of his fabulous Honeydrippers

iggins was one of the key rhythm-and-blues performers and recording artists of the postwar period, making two of the biggest hits of the era in "Pink Champagne" and "The Honeydripper," and his legacy is easily detectable in virtually every R&B revival band since then.

Liggins was born in Guthrie, Oklahoma, but moved with his family as a teenager to San Diego. He had become interested in music, beginning with the trumpet but moving on to the piano and then taking on music theory. Once in San Diego the 18-year-old began looking for work in music, quickly finding jobs with a range of jazz bands. Liggins moved on to Los Angeles in 1939 and began performing with bands using the jump style currently being perfected by people like Louis Jordan, Pete Brown, and others. By 1945 he cut his first disc, the one that

would define him: "The Honeydripper." It launched a thousand imitators and Liggins's career. Between 1945 and 1948 he had nine top-10 R&B hits for Exclusive Records, then switched to Speciality, where he hit No. 1 with "Pink Champagne" in 1950. This was the high-water mark of his popularity, however, and within five years he was out of contract. A solitary album for Mercury in 1962 recapping his old hits did little but point up the gap between his early achievements and his later lack of direction.

Liggins stayed in the music business, experiencing every type of musical vagary but sticking to the R&B style that had brought him initial fame. Finally, the strong revival of interest in R&B by a new young audience during the 1980s benefited Liggins, who toured widely and once again began recording his old repertoire with the verve of earlier years. He died in 1987, his reputation restored.

## fact file

**BORN** 1915

**DIED** 1987

**MUSICAL SELECTION**
"The Honeydripper"
"Pink Champagne"

**SEE ALSO:** Louis Jordan, Pete Brown

# Lightnin' Slim

**fact file**

**BORN** 1913

**DIED** 1974

**MUSICAL SELECTION**
"Rock Me Mama"
"Bad Luck Blues"

Working with
Lazy Lester,
Lightnin' Slim
came from a
musical family in
Baton Rouge

S lim came to prominence late in his career, having been playing Louisiana blues for 20 years before reaching his natural audience in the 1950s and making a number of successful recordings. Slim specialized in the easy singing sounds and razor-edged, crude but effective guitar playing of the swamp-blues sound, and was one of the first artists to make a success of this approach in the postwar years. As such, he brought a powerful blues influence to bear on those who followed.

Slim was born Otis Hicks in St Louis, Missouri, and learned the rudiments of guitar from his father. The family moved to Louisiana when Slim was a teenager and Slim gradually moved from playing at home to making his presence felt in the jukes and bars of Baton Rouge. In the postwar period Slim gradually came to be regarded as a paramount exponent of Louisiana swamp blues, but it was not until May 1954 that he cut his first sides, at the age of 41, for Feature records in Crowley, Louisiana. Slim's "Rock Me Mama" and "Bad Luck Blues" were probably the first swamp blues captured on disc and preserved the rough, down-home feeling of the Baton Rouge clubs Slim frequented. Slim stayed in Louisiana, making records for Excello and Ace between 1955 and 1965 where his sound and approach remained essentially unchanged. His partners often included the harpists Lazy Lester and Slim Harpo, and in 1964 Katie Webster also recorded with him. Around 1966 Slim moved to Detroit, joining up with Slim Harpo full-time; he also joined in on the beginnings of the European blues packages, but by the time this seasonal circuit was fully operational, Slim was dying of cancer, passing away in 1974.

**SEE ALSO:** Lazy Lester, Slim Harpo

# Mance Lipscomb

**fact file**

**BORN** 1895

**DIED** 1976

**MUSICAL SELECTION**
You'll Never Find
Another Man Like
Mance
Texas Blues

Mance Lipscombe
played locally in
Texas for years
before making his
first recording at
the age of 65

L ipscomb had elements of both a typical early blues career and an entirely extraordinary one. Born in Navasota, Texas, to sharecropper farming parents (his father was an ex-slave who taught him the rudiments of fiddle-playing), Lipscomb taught himself guitar and singing, racking up an impressive repertoire of turn-of-the-century songster entertainments as well as blues and more diverse genres. He spent all of his youth and early manhood on the same farm, playing his music only on weekends to entertain the locals of the district. This was the pattern of Lipscomb's life until he was recorded by Chris Strachwitz, who was on a field trip through Texas in summer 1960. This previously untapped source of early black Texan musical tradition created a considerable stir among folk and blues fans and musicologists at the time and changed the course of Lipscomb's life. From that time on he was extensively recorded by a number of labels, though Arhoolie made by far the most – well over a hundred tracks. He also appeared at many US festivals and became the subject of a number of film biographies and documentaries: there is little doubt that the quality of his work, from the intricacies of his guitar to the telling expressiveness of his voice, deserved such belated recognition. Lipscomb died in 1976.

# Little Willie Littlefield

fact file

**BORN** 1931

**MUSICAL SELECTION**
Happy Pay Day
House Party

Littlefield's rise to fame was like a rocket initially, only to taper off until a move to Europe later in his life revived his engines

ittlefield was briefly an important R&B presence in the late 1940s, as the Joe Lutcher and Amos Milburn style of R&B was at a popular peak. Littlefield, born in El Campo, Texas, moved with his family to Houston while young and taught himself piano. As a young teenager he was playing in bars and dives in and around Houston, singing and playing a boogie-shuffle type of piano in the manner of Louis Jordan and Amos Milburn, whose music he heard on jukeboxes and on the radio. At the age of 17 he made his recording debut, for the tiny Eddie's records, a derivative set of boogie pieces distinguished by the presence of the saxist Don Wilkerson. A move to Los Angeles in 1949 through a contract with Modern brought Littlefield into the limelight, with his first session yielding a major R&B hit, "It's Midnight (no place to go)." Despite strong accompanists

(including Don Wilkerson, Johnny Moore, and John Handy) and good material, Littlefield found it difficult to land a follow-up hit and Modern dropped him in 1951. Two years at Federal followed, as did the bad luck, even with Wardell Gray on tracks like "Goofy Dust Blues" and "Falling Tears." Littlefield managed a respectable hit with "K.C. Loving," a "Kansas City" prototype, but Leiber & Stoller later cleaned up with that one. Littlefield continued in the business and remained a popular local live act in northern California, whence he moved in the late 1950s, making San José his primary base.

He also began touring Europe and becoming part of the nostalgia scene there. He continued to make albums through the 1970s and 1980s, though his style remained largely unchanged. He continues to play and record today.

**SEE ALSO:** Amos Milburn, Louis Jordan

# John Littlejohn

fact file

BORN 1931

MUSICAL SELECTION
So-Called Friends

Varied style and
a subtle touch
characterize John
Littlejohn's guitar

ohn Littlejohn was one of many Chicago blues players to have been born and raised in Mississippi. He was self-taught on guitar and, in the fashion of so many of his contemporaries, played at juke joints, dances, and other gatherings in between a variety of day jobs, including field work. During this time he continued to practice on a guitar his father had won one night gambling. He and his brother James left Mississippi in 1949, following a string of jobs which took them out of the South and as far north as Rochester, NY.

Further fluctuations in employment finally found Littlejohn in Indiana in 1951, where he turned to the idea of making money from music; over a period of half a year he pulled his guitar-playing and a band together. Within a short time his band was playing gigs in the postwar migrant black communities, pumping electricity into the old Delta-style blues and creating a style in emulation of his new hero Elmore James. Littlejohn's outfit became one of the most respected working bands in America's industrial belt before he settled down in Chicago. He also gained work supporting the well-known bluesman Jimmy Rogers, but somehow his talents were missed by record company owners. It was not until 1968 that Littlejohn finally entered a studio, making a Chicago studio session for the West Coast label, Arhoolie. This album shows him to be an exciting and committed blues performer, with a raking guitar style possessed of a tart, biting edge in the Chicago tradition, and a convincing vocal style. Unfortunately, John Littlejohn has never broadened his reputation much beyond Chicago, where he continues to play to this day, both in the Elmore James slide guitar and the more modern West Side tradition.

**SEE ALSO:** Elmore James, Jimmy Rogers

# Robert Lockwood Jr

## fact file

**BORN** 1915

**MUSICAL SELECTION**
Steady Rollin' Man

Never one to enjoy having his photo taken, Robert Lockwood Jr learned guitar from Robert Johnson

elta bluesman Lockwood was born near Marvell, Arkansas, the stepson of the blues legend Robert Johnson. He developed an interest in music during his teens and around the age of 19 began playing the blues professionally, inspired by his stepfather's example. Leaving Marvell, Lockwood moved to Memphis, but by his own admission he found his own style and orbit only after Johnson's death. In 1939 he moved to St Louis, where he made the acquaintance of Doctor Clayton, among others. This connection led to his appearing on Clayton's 1941 Chicago session for Bluebird, his first time in a studio.

Hooking up with Sonny Boy Williamson II (Rice Miller), Lockwood returned south to appear with him on the occasional *King Biscuit Time* radio broadcast. By the time he moved back to Chicago in 1950 his mature guitar style had evolved, showing considerable sophistication and a liberal application of jazz ideas, especially those of Charlie Christian and T-Bone Walker. During the 1950s in Chicago he worked and recorded with virtually every

top band, including Muddy Waters, Willie Mabon, Little Walter, and Sonny Boy Williamson, and made occasional sessions under his own name, usually in tandem with Sunnyland Slim. Yet he remained a player's player rather than a star: even the duet album on Candid from 1960 with Otis Spann, now regarded as a classic of the genre, did little for his profile at the time. A move to Cleveland with Sonny Boy Williamson in 1961 became permanent after Williamson had decamped to Europe, and Lockwood has spent the rest of his career in that city, occasionally traveling to Chicago for work and record sessions. His first record as a leader was for Delmark in 1970, *Steady Rollin' Man*; he has had sporadic recording sessions since. A remarkable guitarist and a true blues guitar original in his maturity, Lockwood has suffered popular neglect owing to having an unremarkable voice and a personality not given to grandstanding stage antics. He has the respect of his peers and blues fans, however, and continues to record as a leader.

**SEE ALSO:** Robert Johnson, Doctor Clayton, Sonny Boy Williamson II, T-Bone Walker, Muddy Waters, Willie Mabon

# Cripple Clarence Lofton

**fact file**

**BORN** 1887

**DIED** 1957

**MUSICAL SELECTION**
Clarence's Blues

Cripple Clarence
Lofton's driving
piano style made
him a popular
favorite and
strong blues
influence

Lofton was important as one of the pioneering boogie piano players, bringing to his playing and performing a great deal of the old-time tent-show and vaudeville antics, including jumping around, whistling, and stomping up a storm while he was playing. Such behavior made him a favorite at parties and other social functions and eventually brought him to the attention of record company scouts, who began recording him in 1935, some years after the first efforts by other pioneers such as Jimmy Yancey and Cow Cow Davenport.

Lofton was born in Kingsport, Tennessee, and taught himself piano, remaining an "ear" player for his entire career. He also learned to tap-dance. His piano style, although highly rhythmic, is basic and unfussy in the same way Jimmy Yancey's was the outline of boogie and barrelhouse rather than the full-blown version of it as espoused by Meade Lux Lewis and others. Lofton moved to Chicago in 1917 when he was just 20, soon proving his worth on the rent-party circuit. His rise to prominence exactly mirrored the rise to national (and later, international) popularity of the boogie woogie: he was successful enough in Chicago to open his own small club, the Big Apple, and start recording for Vocalion and ARC in 1935. Lofton never actually managed a hit that could have sustained his career past the inevitable bursting of the boogie bubble with the advent of R&B in the early 1940s. He made his last recordings in 1943 and continued to play around Chicago, but by the time of his death in 1957 he was largely forgotten and in retirement.

**SEE ALSO:** Walter Davis, Speckled Red

# Lonesome Sundown

**fact file**

**BORN** 1928

**MUSICAL SELECTION**
Been Gone Too Long

Lonesome Sundown's swamp blues style was a natural, born of his Louisiana roots

guitarist/singer Lonesome Sundown has been a major presence on the Louisiana swamp blues and a decided influence on many of the players to come from the area. He also carries a strong allegiance to the zydeco which is such a feature of the area that he comes from, using its supple rhythms and quicksilver sounds to complement his unusually persuasive voice and the biting, hovering sounds he conjures on his blues guitar.

Born Cornelius Green in Donaldsville, Louisiana, he taught himself first piano and then guitar in his early twenties: by the time he began playing professionally – with the zydeco star Clifton Chenier – it was the early 1950s and he was in his mid-twenties. A record deal with Excello in 1956 was the point at which he acquired his pseudonym, via Excello's owner Jay Miller, who thought his given name rather prosaic. In the next eight years Sundown made more than a dozen singles and an album, producing undiluted, hard-hitting swamp blues in the process, but failed to disturb the charts too much and remained strictly a local happening, although some of the songs Sundown recorded, such as "My Home Is A Prison" (1956) and "I Woke Up Crying" (1961), have since been recognized as classics. In the mid-1960s Sundown quit the music business and turned to religion, staying clear of music until 1977, when he was coaxed out of retirement. An album for Alligator, *Been Gone Too Long* (1979), was artistically sound but a financial failure and led to a second retirement which, to date, has been permanent.

**SEE ALSO:** Lonnie Brooks

# Joe Hill Louis

**fact file**

**BORN** 1921

**DIED** 1957

**MUSICAL SELECTION**
"Boogie In The Park"

One time "Be-Bop Boy," Joe Hill Louis earned some status as a one-man band in Memphis early in his career

Louis was a one-man band of some class but not a great deal of commercial success who worked most of his professional life in the Memphis area. Born in Raines, Tennessee, he started making music as a boy on Jew's harp before picking up hints from Will Shade as to how to tackle a harmonica. After hoboing around Tennessee as a teenager, he started playing for small change on Memphis streets, where he gradually evolved his one-man-band routine, adding guitar and foot-operated drum to his harp and vocals. Dubbed Joe Hill Louis after the former world champion boxer, he carved out a niche for himself with his uneven beat, primitive guitar, and unorthodox singing style. Coming to the attention of Columbia, he traveled to

New York City in late 1949 for a first record session, but his career got going once he took over B.B. King's old Memphis radio program and began recording for Sam Phillips in Memphis in July 1950. Phillips sold his sides to Modern, and Louis landed a hit with "Boogie In The Park." Hill Louis stuck with various boogie types for most of his recorded repertoire and often used excellent backing musicians, including Walter Horton, while he also sat in on sessions by Rufus Thomas.

Louis recorded regularly between 1950 and 1954, but after that public demand began to fall away for his rough-hewn type of boogie. Louis had little opportunity to stage a comeback, dying of tetanus in 1957.

**SEE ALSO:** B. B. King, Walter Horton

# Louisiana Red

**fact file**

**BORN** 1936

**MUSICAL SELECTION**
Midnight Rambler
Live at 55

Louisiana Red,
seen here
playing with
serious intent
in Burnley
(England), 1996

red was born in the Delta town of Vicksburg, Mississippi. He was orphaned young, his mother dying from complications of childbirth and his father being murdered soon afterwards. Red's early life remained hard, and he taught himself guitar and harmonica to make some sort of living on the streets. Abandoning the south in 1945, he moved to Pittsburgh looking for work; although he met B.B. King in that city, there was little improvement in his life. So in 1949 Minter headed for Chicago, and there made his first records, in 1952, for Chess's subsidiary, Checker, under the name Rocky Fuller. But nothing much changed and he ended up in the Air Force, stationed on the West Coast, until his discharge in 1958. Two years later Minter turned up in New York, recording a single for Atlas as L.A. Red, followed by an album in 1962 for Roulette under his current working name, Louisiana Red. This featured Panama Francis on drums and was well received but failed to sell. Similar

efforts in 1965 also failed to register a great deal of interest, although they fostered the beginnings of a good reputation for Red in Europe. His basic style was that of the Delta country blues, whether he was using acoustic or electric guitar. But his music remained for the most part unfashionable throughout this period, since he was not old enough to be a genuine "rediscovery," nor young enough to take part in the tough new urban blues scene.

Red spent a great deal of the next decade working only part-time in the music business, basing himself back in Chicago, and very gradually getting himself better known in Europe. In 1982 he decided to leave the States, making one last session in Chicago the day before catching a plane for Europe. This effort, a solo album of great emotional power, was later issued on the British label JSP. Louisiana Red remained in Europe, managing for the first time in many years to make a living from his music, and still performs on the club and festival circuit today.

 SEE ALSO: B. B. King

# Willie Mabon

## fact file

**BORN** 1925

**DIED** 1985

**MUSICAL SELECTION**
"Poison Ivy"
"Seventh Son"
"Knock On Wood"

Willie Mabon's sophisticated stylings put him in the same blues class as Charles Brown

**m**abon, without being a particularly strong influence on anyone outside Mose Allison, was a considerable vocalist and pianist (and occasional harpist) who had his fair share of hits for Chess during the early 1950s, most of them in an updated R&B style.

Mabon was born in Hollywood, Tennessee, and taught himself the piano, mastering the basics of boogie listening to records by Roosevelt Sykes and Big Maceo. His family moved to Chicago in 1942, taking 18-year-old Willie with them: there he discovered Charles Brown's singing and the template for his own vocal style. He also found a piano teacher who could give him lessons to enable him to play a wider and more sophisticated range of music. Wartime service took him off the scene until after 1945, but on his return Mabon got himself well enough known on the Chicago scene to start making records in 1949 for the Apollo label, which was suited to his cross-genre tastes. By 1952 he was with Parrot, the following year signing with Chess, his band of the time featuring piano, sax, bass, and drums. Chess's very first session resulted in an R&B No. 1, "I'm Mad," which was followed in 1954 by "Poison Ivy" and in 1955 by "Seventh Son" and "Knock On Wood." By the end of the decade Mabon's career had run out of steam as tastes had changed, and he scraped a living in Chicago's bars for the duration of the 1960s. Things changed for the better in the 1970s, when Mabon joined the blues package tours of Europe and became a favorite of French and German audiences in particular. From that point on his interest in his American career waned, and he spent much of each year in Europe, recording and playing. Mabon died in 1985 in Paris.

**SEE ALSO:** Mose Allison, Roosevelt Sykes, Big Maceo, Charles Brown

# "Steady Rollin'" Bob Margolin

The one, the only "Steady Rollin'" Bob Margolin celebrating the old school of blues on record and on stage

## fact file

**BORN** 1949

**MUSICAL SELECTION**
The Old School
Down In The Alley

argolin is a white guitarist who has followed the urban/country blues tradition of the great postwar Chicago bands such as Muddy Waters and Jimmy Rogers. Coming from a first love of the type of music Chuck Berry was creating in the 1950s, Margolin learned the guitar trying to emulate Berry's example.

Margolin was born in Brookline, Massachusetts, and by the early 1970s was sufficiently immersed in the blues guitar to become a member of Luther "Snake" Johnson's working group. Through Johnson, Margolin met Johnson's old boss, Muddy Waters, and by 1973 the new band Margolin had formed, the Boston Blues Band, were the support group of choice for Waters in the Boston area. In that same year Margolin was invited to join the master's band, an invitation he accepted eagerly. Margolin stayed with Waters for seven years and nine albums, spread across the Chess and Blue Sky labels, and accompanied Waters during his performance in The Band's filmed concert, *The Last Waltz*. Toward the end of his stay with the band Margolin was fulfilling a number of backstage responsibilities as well, and in 1980 decided it was time to run his own outfit part-time while gaining further experience on the road with a plethora of stars, including Stevie Ray Vaughan and Johnny Winter. By the time of Waters' death in 1983 Margolin was ready to sustain a solo career, and in 1989 cut his own first album as a leader, *The Old School*, on the Powerhouse label. By 1994 he was with Alligator, with that year's *Down In The Alley* proving a stripped-down, powerful brew of post-Waters Chicago blues. Margolin continues to pursue an active career.

**SEE ALSO:** Muddy Waters, Jimmy Rogers, Stevie Ray Vaughan, Johnny Winter

# Sara Martin

Sara Martin's claims to fame included the first recordings of the blues with guitar and jug band

Martin was one of the classic woman blues singers of the 1920s and one of the first to appear on record in that decade. A hard-voiced, rough-house vocalist, she was brought up in the vaudeville and traveling-show tradition. This legacy is marked in her music, her showmanship, and extravagance of vocal gesture (and her extravagant, showbiz-type costumes for the listener to ogle) making up for the lack of her physical presence. Martin was born in Louisville, Kentucky, and her early experience in music stems from both the church and the thrills of vaudeville and traveling shows.

Once she reached an age when she could look after herself she joined a vaudeville outfit and traveled widely learning her craft. By 1915 she had played Chicago and was beginning to acquire a wide reputation, one that was augmented by her arrival in New York in 1922. While there she was signed up by Okeh – the company she remained with and recorded prolifically for until September 1927. From the start she sang the blues, and was one of the first true blues singers to be caught on wax (a year prior to Bessie Smith, for example).

Her accompanist was often Clarence Williams or Sylvester Weaver, and she proved a consistently popular artist for Okeh until the economic downturn of late 1927. After that she continued to perform in New York and made some sides in 1928 for QRS, but with the onset of the Depression she disappeared from the blues world, moving over in the 1930s to the gospel she had always loved. Retired from the music business, she continued to be involved in gospel until her death in 1955.

**fact file**

BORN 1884

DIED 1955

MUSICAL SELECTION
Sara Martin

**SEE ALSO:** Bessie Smith, Sylvester Weaver

# John Mayall

**fact file**

**BORN** 1933

**MUSICAL SELECTION**
Wake Up Call

Among the pioneers of British R&B, John Mayall recorded and performed with almost everyone on the blues scene

a lthough Alexis Korner is rightly known as Britain's father of the modern blues movement, it is possible that John Mayall – through the vehicle of his various Bluesbreakers line-ups – has been the more influential presence in nurturing young blues talent of international class. Mayall himself was a steady guitarist, singer and harmonica player who could perform blues with an authentic touch.

Born in Manchester, Mayall was drawn to music from an early age, the son of a musician with a considerable collection of 78s. Too young for service in World War II, he was inducted during the Korean War. Only after his service, as a student at Manchester's Art College, did he have the time to pursue his interest in performing the blues. His first band was formed in 1955, calling itself the Powerhouse Four, and became a fixture on the northern scene. By 1963, with the first inklings of the beat explosion coming through in venues all over Britain, Mayall moved to London with a new band, the Blues Syndicate. Within a year he had started from scratch again and formed the first version of his Bluesbreakers, a band which included bassist John

McVie and drummer Hughie Flint. Eric Clapton joined, and the now-classic album, "Bluesbreakers," was recorded. For a while Jack Bruce was the bassist before he and Clapton joined up with Ginger Baker to form the rock band Cream. Mayall's magic touch for recruiting talent remained as he hired replacements with the caliber of Peter Green (later to start Fleetwood Mac with John McVie) and Mick Taylor (later to join the Rolling Stones).

At the beginning of the 1970s Mayall led a version of the Bluesbreakers which featured trumpeter Blue Mitchell and saxophonist Clifford Solomon. As the blues faded from popularity later in the decade, Mayall, by then a Californian resident, managed to keep afloat through the viability of his stage act, which remained a draw.

Later Bluesbreaker units featured guitarists like Carlos Montoya and Walter Trout. Mayall has for decades been accepted by the blues fraternity as an important figure on the scene; his international comeback was launched by 1993's *Wake Up Call*, which featured such talents as Mick Taylor, Buddy Guy and Albert Collins. Mayall's talents have not dimmed.

**SEE ALSO:** Alexis Korner, Eric Clapton, Buddy Guy, Albert Collins

# Tommy McClennan

**fact file**

**BORN** 1908

**DIED** 1962

**MUSICAL SELECTION**
"Cross Cut Saw"
"New Shake 'Em On
Down"

All the way from Yazoo City, Mississippi, Tommy McLennan was a stubborn ol' soul both on stage and on album

Yazoo City-born blues singer and steel guitarist McClennan was a typical product of the Mississippi area from which he came, using a spartan technique in a rough-hewn way (sometimes not bothering to go beyond playing just one string) and projecting the lyrics of his songs with a harsh, occasionally brutal voice which was capable of both humor and pathos. As with many bluesmen of his generation, McClennan had no concern for the form of the music he was creating, content to improvise a line and some verses until he felt like stopping.

McClennan's youth was spent out in the fields picking cotton and playing his guitar in "down time." By his teens he was playing juke joints and dances for money, and also playing on the streets of Yazoo City for nickels and dimes. During this time he struck up a companionship with Robert Petway, a bluesman whose own style is often indistinguishable from McClennan's. McClennan and Petway stayed in the South throughout the Depression and into the late 1930s, but both men were finally tempted into moving north to Chicago by an offer from Lester

Melrose to record for Bluebird, McClennan starting with the label in 1939, Petway in 1941. At his first session in November 1939 McClennan cut what was to be his trademark song, "Bottle Up and Go," a piece expressing his typical lust for life in a way that Southerners found exciting and Northerners occasionally offensive, with its reference to "niggers." McClennan, both live and on record unwilling to pander to any audience, couldn't care less, insisting on singing the way he wanted to. He had other memorable moments on record, 1941's "Cross Cut Saw," "New Shake 'Em On Down," and "Deep Blue Sea Blues" being two examples. He also accompanied Petway on a 1942 session (Petway had earlier recorded his version of the influential "Catfish Blues"). After 1942, when Bluebird dropped their recording option, McClennan decided to stay based in Chicago, picking up live work right into the postwar era when the clubs were no longer looking for exponents of the earlier blues styles. He gradually faded from public view, dying in poverty and alcoholism in 1962.

**SEE ALSO:** David "Honeyboy" Edwards, Sonny Boy Williamson II, Little Walter, Elmore James

# Charlie McCoy

**fact file**

**BORN** 1909

**DIED** 1959

**MUSICAL SELECTION**
"It Ain't No Good"

Charlie McCoy
and his man-
dolin, rare
enough in the
blues but a
tremendous
instrument in his
talented hands

guitarist/mandolinist McCoy, along with his brother Joe, was one of the busiest and most consistent working blues musicians of the 1920s and 1930s in the Jackson and Memphis areas. Unlike his brother Joe, Charlie rarely used pseudonyms to record under. He also preferred accompanying others to leading his own bands and recording sessions, and was accomplished in many styles and contexts, from two guitars to string bands.

McCoy was born in Jackson, Mississippi, and spent his early days there. Self-taught, as were most of his contemporaries, McCoy quickly progressed in his teens to playing with various bands and groups of musicians in and around Jackson, progressing to juke joints and other entertainments and striking up shifting partnerships with people such as Walter Vinson, Ishman Bracey, and Tommy Johnson. He also worked extensively with his brother Joe. Both brothers were based in Memphis, Tennessee, by 1927, and Charlie made his first recordings, accompanying Tommy Johnson, in February 1928, his mandolin

particularly effective on Johnson's "Cool Drink of Water Blues." From then on he was in demand for a steady stream of sessions, making his debut as a leader in 1929 for Brunswick using Chatman's Mississippi Hot Footers as accompaniment on a typical bit of hokum, "It Ain't No Good," parts 1 and 2. He continued to record all through the 1930s, making a particularly fine set of dates along with his brother Joe, starting in 1936 with the Harlem Hamfats, a Chicago-based band with feet in both blues and jazz camps. He also cut Chicago sessions with Big Bill Broonzy (with the jazz player George Barnes as a companion guitarist) in 1936.

McCoy's career began to falter in the years immediately prior to America's entry into World War II as the fashion for his type of music waned. He moved to Chicago where his brother Joe was based, but his work as a sideman became progressively more restricted as later styles of music became popular and he failed to make the transition, dropping out of the music scene by the time of his brother's death in 1950. Charlie died, largely forgotten, in Chicago in 1959.

**SEE ALSO:** Joe McCoy, Tommy Johnson, Big Bill Broonzy

# Wilbur "Joe" McCoy

## fact file

**BORN** 1905

**DIED** 1950

**MUSICAL SELECTION**
Harlem Hamfats

Married to Memphis Minnie, Joe McCoy and his wife were popular on the circuit, enough for McCoy to continue on his own when the couple split up

cCoy, brother of Charlie, was a blues guitarist who recorded prolifically during the 1930s, usually as a sideman, often under a host of pseudonyms, and for a while partnered Memphis Minnie both in marriage and in music. Some of the pseudonyms McCoy employed are Hamfoot Ham, Kansas Joe, Hallelujah Joe, Mud Dauber Joe, and Georgia Pine Boy, among others.

McCoy was born in Raymond, Mississippi, and raised among the sounds of the Delta blues pickers. Self-taught, he worked with his younger brother at local picnics and parties before removing to Memphis in the mid-1920s. Once there, he fell in with Memphis Minnie, with whom he made many records (starting in 1929), under the name of Kansas Joe, and whom he married. This partnership continued until the fall of 1934, when Minnie and Joe separated, their marriage at an end.

By this time McCoy was so well known in Chicago that other session work was not difficult to find, whether as the gospel singer Hallelujah Joe (January 1935) or as Big Joe and his Washboard Band (December 1940). At the tail end of the 1930s, McCoy began performing with the Harlem Hamfats, a jazz-oriented outfit which successfully recorded for Decca and Vocalion between 1936 and 1939. By the end of the war McCoy was beginning to fade from the Chicago scene as its musical character changed. He died in 1950.

**SEE ALSO:** Charlie McCoy, Memphis Minnie

# Jimmy McCracklin

Like a number of his contemporaries, Jimmy McCracklin began as a boxer, turning to the blues as a singer in 1945

**fact file**

**BORN** 1921

**MUSICAL SELECTION**
"The Walk"
"Think"

mcCracklin was born in Arkansas and raised in St Louis, but his main impact was in the area of postwar California R&B. Something of an all-round man, McCracklin was adept at many styles of blues-based music, from country to big-band, and also earned a living as a boxer for a while, based in LA.

Pianist/singer McCracklin first made his presence felt in Californian music circles in 1945, when he cut some sides for the tiny Globe label, including "Sweet Home Chicago" and "Highway 101." This was the start of a lengthy and prolific recording career spanning many musical styles and genres. By 1948 he was running a band called Jimmy McCracklin and his Blues Masters, and this outfit recorded for RPM, among others. The musicians who came through his band in the 1940s and 1950s included Lafayette Thomas,

Johnny Parker, Wild Willie Moore, David "Bubba" Brooks (brother of the saxophonist Tina Brooks), and Jack McDuff. During the 1950s McCracklin recorded for a host of Californian labels, including Modern, Irma, Premium, and Imperial, the last being a single from 1956 which disappeared without trace. In December 1957 he recorded his major hit, "The Walk." It sold throughout the world in the spring of 1958 (the Beatles were to make an affectionate version of it in 1969). This hit, made for Checker, got him a deal with Mercury, but nothing he did subsequently sold as well, although "Think," from 1965 on Imperial, made a serious indentation on the charts. McCracklin never gave up his search for further success, but by the end of the 1960s he was no longer able to keep pace with the rate of change on the music scene, and faded into obscurity.

**SEE ALSO:** Johnny Otis

# Larry McCray

Larry McCray, a powerful
guitarist, seen here
performing at the Gloucester
Blues Festival, 1995

like many of the younger blues generation, Arkansas-born McCray (he hails from Stephens) brings a great number of contemporary influences to bear on his blues style. Larry is the brother of Clara McCray, a blues player who runs her own band, and his brothers Carl and Steve are also musicians. He moved from Arkansas to Detroit when twelve years old, and after leaving school took a job in the production line of one of the Motor City's car manufacturers. In his spare time Larry began writing material for a self-produced first album, recorded initially in his family's basement studio. McCray's first album took shape and received its initial release in 1990 on the Virgin/Point Blank label in England, where its refreshing combination of blues, soul and rock influences made an immediate impact, and it sold heavily. This prompted a US release of the album while McCray was still working a day job in the auto industry. McCray's guitar style, showing influences including Clapton, Hendrix and US-based players, and his big, tough baritone voice have been big factors in his success.

Since his debut, Larry McCray has continued to push ahead with recording projects and put his own band together for touring purposes, entertaining blues fans wherever he performs.

## fact file

**BORN** 1962

**MUSICAL SELECTION**
Ambition
Delta Hurricane

SEE ALSO: Eric Clapton, Jimi Hendrix

# Fred McDowell

## fact file

**BORN** 1904

**DIED** 1972

**MUSICAL SELECTION**
"You Gotta Move"

Mississippi Fred McDowell played private functions in Memphis to earn a living, the first steps in a prolific career

orn in Rossville, Tennessee, out in the country east of Memphis, McDowell lost his parents early, forcing him to move in with an older sister who lived in Mississippi. He became interested in the guitar while in his teens, and began a long apprenticeship with it (although without his own instrument) which continued through his return to Memphis for manual labor in 1926, and a recall to Mississippi three years later to pick cotton. One evening near Cleveland, Miss., McDowell attended a juke-joint session where Charlie Patton was appearing. Patton's lifestyle and persona impressed him as much as his music did. Young McDowell continued learning songs from Patton and other blues musicians such as Eli Green and Sid Hamphill, but for many years he was severely restricted in what he could do through not owning his own guitar. In 1940 he finally acquired an instrument and began regularly playing at dances, juke joints and picnics in addition to his normal farm work.

This remained the pattern of Fred McDowell's life until 1959, when blues documenter Alan Lomax discovered him – at the age of 55 – and enabled his first recordings to be made. McDowell's strong Mississippi Delta style of singing and his inspired bottleneck techniques made an immediate impression on blues audiences, and a few years later Arhoolie boss Chris Strachwitz recorded McDowell at his own home in Como, Mississippi. These recordings, and McDowell's subsequent acceptance on the blues and folk festival circuit, meant that the veteran bluesman could for the first time make a living out of music alone. As the 1960s came to a close one of his lately-recorded songs, "You Gotta Move," was covered by the Rolling Stones on their *Sticky Fingers* album. The royalties made McDowell, now in his mid-sixties, more money than anything else before in his life, and spread his name beyond blues circles. He continued to tour and record up to his death from cancer in 1972.

**SEE ALSO:** Charlie Patton

# Blind Willie McTell

**fact file**

**BORN** 1901

**DIED** 1959

**MUSICAL SELECTION**
"Statesboro Blues"
"Broke-Down
Engine Blues"

Blind Willie
McTell brought a
warmth to his
recordings that
shone through
both his guitar
and his vocals

**b**lind Willie was born William McTear (the "McTell" was a result of a mispelling by a clerk) in Thomson, Georgia, and raised by his mother. He attended a number of schools for the blind and learned to read Braille. He prided himself on his education and continued to read books in Braille for the rest of his life. The self-confident Willie soon began travelling as a musician and entertainer and managed to do a lot more than hold his own. His guitar technique was intricate, smooth and rhythmically invigorating, his voice rarely rose above speaking volume, and his articulation was impeccable.

McTell's repertoire and guitar patterns show some similarities with those of Leadbelly and Furry Lewis, but he can't be called a copyist in any meaningful way; his personal combination of East Coast and Delta blues traditions was unique. He began his recording career for Victor in 1927, making his first records in Atlanta, Georgia, where he'd settled. He was soon recording for a number of labels under a host of pseudonyms, but everybody knew his sides as soon as they heard them. Of his early material, such classics as "Statesboro Blues," "Broke-Down Engine Blues" and "Georgia Rag" were to remain influential in later years, with many artists covering "Statesboro' Blues" including Taj Mahal

and the Allman Brothers. McTell married in 1934. He travelled constantly, often with shows but frequently on his own, and recorded prolifically – cutting scores of sides between 1927 and WWII, sometimes with Kate supplying support vocals.

McTell played often at venues in and around Atlanta, including the Pig 'n' Whistle. Although the commercial recordings had dried up after 1935, he recorded a long session for John Lomax and the Library of Congress in 1940. The following year his marriage began to break down, and after the separation he settled quickly with another woman, Helen Edwards. They adopted a daughter, and this led McTell to stay closer to Atlanta, sticking to regular work at the joints like the Pig 'n' Whistle and the Blue Lantern. Most record companies had shifted away from country-blues after the war but McTell managed a substantial session for Atlantic in 1949. During the 1950s he began suffering from the debilitating effects of diabetes; a session made for the amateur Edward Rhodes in 1956 shows McTell below par in the studio for the first time. In 1958, Helen died; deprived of her company and care, McTell himself quickly declined, dying from a stroke in August 1959.His music remains the legacy of one of the greatest country blues artists ever.

**SEE ALSO:** Leadbelly, Walter "Furry" Lewis, Taj Mahal

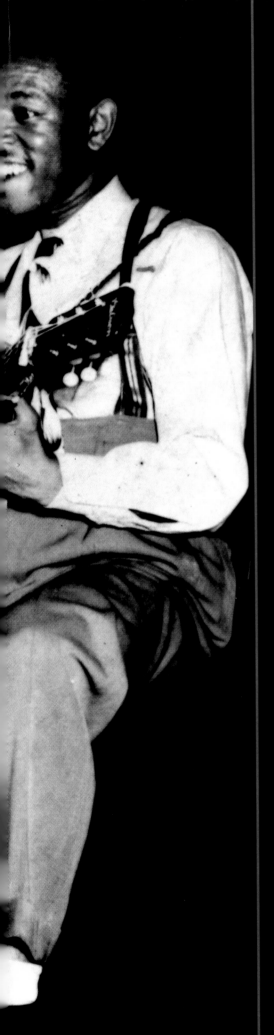

# Walter "Brownie" McGhee

cGhee was born in Knoxville, Tennessee, in 1915, the year and place later to be made famous by James Agee and Samuel Barber's orchestral song. Brownie's father was a guitarist who played in a number of folk and blues ensembles. Attacked in his youth by polio, Brownie was rendered incapable of joining the regular workforce, and his schooling was severely disrupted; he didn't graduate until 1936. But the affliction gave him plenty of time to develop his interest in music and his capacity for playing it. Introduced by his father to the Golden Voices Gospel Quartet, he became a member of that group during the early 1930s. In 1937 McGhee had successful surgery on his polio-affected leg, allowing him to strike out on his own. He subsequently became an itinerant musician and met Blind Boy Fuller, whose guitar technique influenced him greatly. Moving through Virginia, McGhee also befriended washboard player George Washington (aka Oh Red), who in 1940 introduced Brownie to Blind Boy Fuller's manager, J.B. Long. The latter set up a recording session with Okeh in Chicago, and in August of that year McGhee made his recording debut, accompanied by Oh Red on washboard and Jordan Webb on harmonica. A year later Brownie was back in the Windy City, making a string of sides cashing in on the recent passing of Blind Boy Fuller – including the tastefully named "Death of Blind Boy Fuller." He even released a string of sides using the assumed name of "Blind Boy Fuller 2." McGhee experienced modest success and relocated to New York, where in 1942 J.B. Long set up a meeting with harmonica star Sonny Terry in hopes that Brownie might become Terry's accompanist. McGhee's Piedmont style of guitar-picking suited Terry's taste, and the two hit it off. Thus teamed with Sonny Terry, it wasn't long before McGhee was moving in the folk circles of New York, becoming a regular guest at Leadbelly's apartment, among others.

The Terry/McGhee partnership became one of the folk/blues phenomena of the postwar period, garnering almost universal popularity and recording a number of minor hit singles. The pair recorded prolifically, together and separately – and often under assumed names – and eventually reached the point where they were also appearing in plays, films and documentaries. In fact, the duo always remained more popular than the two individuals, and during the 1950s and 1960s became one of the biggest live draws on the international folk and blues festival circuit. This level of success led to complaints that McGhee and Terry no longer played "real" blues; however, their repertoire had actually altered little since the late 1940s in its mix of folk and blues. One of the team's last recordings together was the 1973 album *Sonny & Brownie* for A&M. A rather uneasy mixture of folk and soul/pop material, it featured many prominent Memphis players of the day, but showed little of the old spark that had propelled the team to such heights a quarter-century earlier. Within two years the McGhee/Terry partnership had come to an end; the best years had ended for both men. Brownie McGhee retired from the music business altogether in the mid-1980s.

## fact file

**BORN** 1915

**DIED** 1996

**MUSICAL SELECTION**
Sonny & Brownie

Brownie McGhee (r.) enjoying a session with Granville "Sticks" McGhee during the 1940s

# Memphis Jug Band

The Memphis Jug Band was a somewhat rag-tag operation but changes in personnel kept them fresh

t he Memphis Jug Band was a group led by the guitarist/vocalist Will Shade (1898–1966), a Memphis-born musician, and became one of the most popular of the jug bands that became a craze on "race records" in the late 1920s. The band was something of a movable feast, sporting different line-ups on virtually every one of its considerable number of recording sessions for Victor between 1927 and 1930 (it recorded for Okeh in 1934), but Shade was a common factor to all the sessions, as were Ben Ramey and Charlie Burse up until the last Victor session. Memphis Minnie also appeared on a 1930 session, cutting "Bumble Bee Blues" and "Meningitis Blues" with the band.

The whole approach of the jug bands was different from that of solo artists: the music was lively, often with large dollops of hokum thrown in as extra "entertainment," giving a vivid picture of what street bands must have been like in Memphis and elsewhere at this time. Their natural alliance was with the string bands that appeared at outdoor events and on the streets in the South, which played a different type of repertoire from that of the often melancholic solo artist. The Memphis Jug Band traveled widely in the South prior to World War II and created a number of classic sides for Victor, including "K.C. Moan" (1929) and "Cocaine Habit Blues" (1930). The original band made no more records after 1934, although Shade kept various versions of the name and idea alive until his old age. In 1956 he and Charlie Burse teamed up with Gus Cannon of Cannon's Jug Stompers fame to make an LP for Folkways, using the Memphis Jug Band name, and Shade also made sessions in Memphis as a solo artist during the early 1960s for various European labels, but he was unable to make a deep impression on the new young audience for the old music before his death in 1966.

**SEE ALSO:** Memphis Minnie, Gus Cannon

# Amos Milburn

fact file

**BORN** 1927

**DIED** 1980

**MUSICAL SELECTION**
"After Midnight"
"Down The Road Apiece"

A postwar blues-
man, Amos
Milburn was a
rarity in the blues
scene if only for
his tremendous
success

**m**ilburn was one of a small number of pianists who confidently combined the prewar boogie piano style with the postwar rhythm-and-blues craze. His series of hits for the Aladdin label between 1946 and 1954 (he left the label in 1957) were both enormously popular and instrumental in establishing the rollicking shuffle style which moved the music away from the smoother jump blues of Louis Jordan toward the tougher sounds of the more blues-based artists who became stars at the end of the 1940s.

Milburn was born in Houston, Texas, the fourth child of a very large family, and was picking melodies out by ear on the family piano while still a toddler. An accomplished player before adolescence, he left school when he hit his teens and worked a day job as a delivery boy while playing in clubs and joints at night. Fired up by the advent of World War II, Milburn enlisted in 1942 when still only 15, seeing action both in the Pacific and in nightclubs. He returned to Houston in 1945 and collaborated with Lola Anne Cullum in putting together some songs and an act to sell. In 1946 the pair took their wares to Los Angeles and secured

a contract with Aladdin. Within months the hits were rolling out, including "After Midnight," "Down The Road Apiece" and "Chicken Shack Boogie." By the end of the decade he was a major artist and influence, but his 1950s hits left an even bigger legacy, as "One Scotch, One Bourbon, One Beer," "Bad, Bad Whiskey," and others with a drinking theme became massive hits, covered by many other artists.

Milburn recorded a string of titles using the word *rock* in the name, but his older style of playing, using piano, sax, and blues changes, quickly became passé. Milburn's own private relationship with drink started to dominate his professional life and he slid from view, leaving it to younger blacks like Fats Domino to use elements of his style to conquer the rock audience. A 1963 album for the fledgling Motown label, with Stevie Wonder on harp, did nothing sales-wise, and Milburn suffered the first of a series of strokes in 1969. He experienced a sort of revival in the late 1970s under the auspices of Johnny Otis, but could play piano with only one hand. Within a year he was dead, a late convert to the Baptist religious movement.

**SEE ALSO:** Louis Jordan, Johnny Otis

# Lizzie Miles

**fact file**

**BORN** 1895

**DIED** 1963

**MUSICAL SELECTION**
"Muscle Shoals Blues"
"You Gotta Come And
See Mama Every Night"

Her work with leading jazz artists early in her career established Lizzie Miles as a solid performer

m iles was another of the cabaret and vaudeville singers who could put in a convincing blues performance during the 1920s as the blues rage swept America for the first time and women singers who could handle the blues were very much in demand. Coming from New Orleans, she had a natural affinity with the classic jazz being formed by the Creole bands of people like Kid Ory and Sidney Bechet, and most of her best latter-day singing came in the presence of such musicians.

Miles was born Elizabeth Landreaux in New Orleans and grew up with music all around her. In early teenage she began singing in public, appearing with Kid Ory and King Oliver, among others, between around 1909 and 1911, but then took to the road, singing and performing in a variety of traveling shows (including a circus) before arriving in Chicago after the conclusion of World War I. There she appeared with most of the New Orleans jazzmen who had made good in Chicago, including King Oliver and Freddie Keppard. Having moved to New York in 1921, she made her recording debut the following year, recording "Muscle Shoals Blues" for Okeh. Using New York as her base, she traveled extensively, including Europe, and became a star of the cabaret as well as the recording world, her light vocal style as apposite for novelty numbers as for the urban blues that was proving so popular at the time. Miles suffered health problems at the beginning of the 1930s and curtailed her performing, returning to live work only in 1935. She made no more recordings until some sides for Vocalion with the Melrose Stompers in 1939, by which time she lived in Chicago. Out of music with the advent of World War II in the US, Miles made the occasional foray back into the music business during the remainder of her life, appearing live or recording with New Orleans-style ensembles and musicians.

**SEE ALSO:** Bessie Smith

# Little Milton

**fact file**

**BORN** 1934

**MUSICAL SELECTION**
"We're Gonna Make It"

By incorporating R&B inflections into his works, Little Milton was able to find greater success than most blues performers of his day

ilton has long been recognized by his peers as a first-rate soul and bluesman originally in the tradition of the postwar singers such as Charles Brown and Bobby "Blues" Bland, but his popularity among blues musicians has never translated properly to the wider audience.

Milton was born in Inverness, Mississippi, and taught himself the guitar through copying things he heard around him and on the radio. Like many bluesmen, he heard a range of music on the radio, including jazz and country, and some of all of what he heard stayed with him. As a teenager he played in the Greenville bars and clubs and made it onto record for the first time with Willie Love & His Three Aces in 1951, making records for Trumpet in Jackson. This led to sessions with Sun in 1953, with Ike Turner

helping out on the arrangements. Moving to East St Louis in the late 1950s, Milton kept recording,, with little success, until his change to the Chess/Checker label in 1961. His soulful singing style at first failed to ignite interest, but in 1965 he managed a substantial result with "We're Gonna Make It," which got to R&B No. 1. While with Chess, Milton continued to do moderately well, although he failed to hit the top spot again. At the outset of the 1970s Milton moved on to Stax, looking for that soul/blues sound to take him to the top again, but real success continued to elude him, although he amassed a substantial recording legacy. Since then he has swapped labels regularly. He continues to perform and record, but his popularity is confined mostly to the Southern parts of the US soul/blues market.

**SEE ALSO:** Charles Brown, Bobby "Blue" Bland, Ike Turner

# Roy Milton

Roy Milton, performing behind the kit as he did with the Ernie Fields Orchestra in the late 1920s

## fact file

**BORN** 1907

**DIED** 1983

**MUSICAL SELECTION**
"R.M. Blues"
"Best Wishes"

Vocalist Milton was one of the mainstays of the R&B field in the 1940s, combining the swing and excitement of the big bands with the more urgent, raucous sound of the blues. Born in Wynnewood, Oklahoma, Milton grew up on an Indian Chickasaw reservation, finally moving to Tulsa with his family in his teens. Singing with some territory bands in and around Tulsa, Milton along the way became an accomplished drummer before tiring of the road and settling in Los Angeles in 1933. By the mid-1930s Milton had formed his small-group jump band, the Solid Senders, a band that would deliver the hits for him in the following decade as the world caught up with the new styles of swing-blues that were evolving in different parts of the US. Milton's band had been together for 10 years when they debuted on disc, in 1945, for Lionel Hampton's Hamp-Tone label, then started making records on his own Miltone label. A hit with "R.M. Blues" in 1946 led to a deal with Speciality and a succession of hits stretching into the 1950s such as "Milton's Boogie" (1946), "T-Town Twist" (1951), "Hop, Skip And Jump" (1948), and "Best Wishes" (1951), as well as covers such as "I Want a Little Girl" (1947) and "The Hucklebuck" (1949). Into the early and mid-1950s Milton modified his style, going for more sophistication and even recording Cole Porter songs, but his career gradually tailed off. He left Speciality for King and, later, DooTone and Kent, but remained a number of steps away from popular success for the rest of his career, continuing to tour and even popping up at the 1970 Monterey Jazz Festival, but by now it was all nostalgia. He died in retirement in 1983.

**SEE ALSO:** Johnny Otis

# The Mississippi Sheiks

The Mississippi Sheiks, seen here during the 1930s, were a family unit and successful act, though the group would not last

**t**his family string band from the Jackson area of Mississippi took part of its name from the film by Rudolf Valentino, *The Sheik*. Starting out around the time of World War I, the band (made up of up to 11 members and friends of the Chatmon family, two of whom, Sam and Armenter, sustained independent careers as well) became very popular around their home area. The Sheiks managed to sustain their popularity during the 1920s and by 1930 had attracted the attention of Okeh field scouts. Their first records were made in February 1930, the line-up of the group on that occasion including Walter Vincon (a.k.a. Walter Jacobs), Lonnie Chatmon, and Bo Chatmon. The band scored on record where many other string bands failed, their special combination of tanked-up string swing and verbal double entendre, and their general harmless high spirits, as well as their superior level of instrumental ability, appealing to their home market. At a time when the recording industry was turning its back on the blues, the Sheiks recorded consistently, for three separate companies (Okeh, Paramount, and Bluebird), through to 1935. Among their recorded successes were "Sitting On Top Of The World" in 1930 (along with "The New Sittin' On Top Of The World" in 1932), "Shake That Thing" (1930) – "The New Shake That Thing" appeared in 1932 – "She's Got Something Crazy" (1934), and "Ramrod Blues" (1930). Vocals and instrumental duties were shared among the band members: everybody got a chance to shine at various times. The group came to an end when the vogue for string bands began to fade and individual members decided it was time to pursue separate careers.

**fact file**

**FORMED** C. 1914
**DISBANDED** C. 1935
MUSICAL SELECTION
"Sitting On Top Of The World"
"Shake That Thing"

**SEE ALSO:** Texas Alexander, Bo Carter

# Memphis Minnie

emphis Minnie aka Lizzie Douglas, aka Minnie McCoy, was the first female blues performer to achieve a wide popularity after the efforts of the "classic" singers such as Bessie Smith, Ma Rainey and Victoria Spivey, all of whom had come originally from the vaudeville tradition. Arriving on the scene after these women had largely finished their careers, Minnie created her own personal fusion of country and urban blues, in the process becoming a major figure in the idiom as well as one of the most-recorded and popular personalities of the 1930s and 1940s.

Minnie was born Lizzie Douglas in Algiers, Louisiana, the first of thirteen children. While she was an infant the family moved to Mississippi, close to Memphis. As Minnie grew up, she spent increasing amounts of time in Memphis, attracted by the entertainments to be had there and keen to improve her guitar and banjo playing. A strong personality, by her mid-twenties she was already married (to Casey Bill Weldon) and regularly appearing in travelling shows. The marriage didn't last, and in 1929 she met her next husband-to-be, Joe McCoy. The new husband-and-wife team of Memphis Minnie and Kansas Joe were signed to Columbia records, and Minnie made her first sides. Minnie and Joe moved out of the South to Chicago in 1930, and – along with such popular stars as Tampa Red, Big Bill Broonzy and Leroy Carr – were instrumental in helping the country blues expand its instrumental and rhythmic horizons into the urban blues at which all three were, by the mid-1930s, complete masters. Minnie divested herself of Joe McCoy by 1935 and continued her career, teaming up in 1939 with Little Son Joe; her recordings, on a number of labels, remained popular up to the 1950s. The author of most of her own songs (and not averse to filing her lyrics with barely concealed sexual allusions), Minnie had a number of hits over the years, including "Down In The Alley," "Black Cat Blues," "Hoodoo Lady" and "If You See My Rooster (Please Run Him Home)." In the 1950s she suffered setbacks in health, by the close of the decade leaving the music business, returning to Memphis. She kept to herself during the blues boom of the 1960s. Overlooked at the time Bessie Smith and Ma Rainey were being rediscovered, at her death in 1973 Minnie was still an obscure figure. Only in recent years has this inequity begun to be redressed, and her true stature revealed.

## fact file

**BORN** 1897

**DIED** 1973

**MUSICAL SELECTION**
"Down In The Alley"
"Black Cat Blues"
"Hoodoo Lady"

The unflappable Memphis Minnie left home at 13 to perform in Memphis, hence the nickname

SEE ALSO: Bessie Smith, Ma Rainey, Victoria Spivey, Joe McCoy, Tampa Red

# Eurreal "Little Brother" Montgomery

**fact file**

**BORN** 1906

**DIED** 1985

**MUSICAL SELECTION**
"No Special Rider Blues"
"Vicksburg Blues"

Little Brother Montgomery picked up his tricks early from some of the best who passed through the family door, including Jelly Roll Morton

pianist/singer Montgomery, a native of Kentwood, Louisiana, came directly from the barrelhouse tradition; his earliest musical experiences took place in flop-houses, barrelhouses and brothels. His playing style shares much with that of older players like Jelly Roll Morton and Art Hodes, with the emphasis more on the blues rather than the ragtime part of their heritage, and a link with boogie pianists like Jimmy Yancey and Meade Lux Lewis and the jazz stylings of Earl Hines.

Montgomery was self-taught, watching pianists entertain in his father's own barrelhouse situated in a lumber camp in Kent, Louisiana. Able to play piano from around the age of six onward, he claims to have run away from home when 11 years old to play piano in Holton, Louisiana. He was soon on the road, traveling from place to place throughout Louisiana and Mississippi during the 1920s. This decade also saw him leading his own group, playing with Clarence Desdoumes, Buddy Petit and Big Joe Williams, enjoying an extended stay in New Orleans and settling in Chicago before beginning his recording career in 1930, a single session for Paramount, producing "No Special Rider Blues" and

"Vicksburg Blues." The latter song he re-cast in New Orleans for Bluebird in 1935 (adding "No. 2" to the title) after a four-year recording hiatus which had seen him return South to eventually settle in Jackson, Mississippi. Montgomery spent the 1930s moving around the South with his own 14-piece band, though his recordings invariably featured him as a piano soloist and vocalist. He also made a number of sides accompanying other singers, especially after returning to Chicago in 1942.

After WWII Montgomery became loosely associated with the Traditional "revival," playing and touring with Kid Ory, Franz Jackson and Lee Collins, among others, but spent the 1950s in Chicago either playing solo or accompanying bluesmen like Magic Sam and Otis Rush. In 1960 and 1961 Montgomery made a spate of recordings, both in the US and in Europe, over 170 songs for a variety of labels. He appeared at events such as the Berliner Jazztag (1974). Marrying for a second time in 1967, he and his wife set up their own record label and during the last two decades of his life many albums were released of his live and studio work. "Little Brother" died in 1982.

**SEE ALSO:** Big Joe Williams, Magic Sam, Otis Rush

# Whistling Alex Moore

**fact file**

**BORN** 1899

**DIED** 1989

**MUSICAL SELECTION**
Alex Moore

A 1987 Lifetime Achievement Award from the NEA confirmed Whistling Alex Moore's status as a vital presence on the Texas blues scene

**m**oore was an early exponent of the Texas piano blues, his style showing clear evidence of boogie, barrelhouse, and ragtime and in the process providing evidence of the rich melting pot from which the various blues and jazz strands emerged in the teens and 1920s. Moore was born in Dallas, Texas, and grew up in a section of town dubbed "Freedman's Town," where freed slaves lived in urban congregation. He taught himself piano while a young teenager, developing an unusually sound and flexible technique which he could turn to any material that came to hand. Moore put in years of playing in the Dallas bordellos and whorehouses, and also earned a solid reputation by playing at house parties and the like. He started recording in 1929, soon after his 30th birthday, and specialized in mildly salacious, often quietly humorous material such as "They May Not Be My Toes" (1929) and "Broadway St Woman Blues" (1929), although he could also be as blue as the

next singer on tracks such as "Have Mercy Blues" (1929) and "Black Evil Blues" (1934). One of his best-known songs was "Blue Bloomer Blues" (1929). Moore recorded consistently but hardly prolifically until 1937. He disappeared from the studios until 1951, when he made some sides for RPM. Moore, however, continued to work the nightclubs around Dallas and became a significant influence on blues pianists and other players emanating from the area. An album recorded in Dallas for Arhoolie in 1960, *Alex Moore*, for the first time gave him an international audience and led to sporadic overseas visits, on one of which he was captured live, the results again being released on Arhoolie (1969). During the 1970s this pattern became more institutionalized and he became a regular face on tour in Europe. His contributions to Texas music were recognized in 1987 when he was awarded a Lifetime Achievement citation from the National Endowment for the Arts. He died two years later.

# Eugene "Buddy" Moss

**fact file**

**BORN** 1914

**DIED** 1984

**MUSICAL SELECTION**
Georgia Blues
Red River Blues

Buddy Moss, pictured here at the Newport Folk Festival, July 1969, was a tireless performer

oss started the 1930s as a prime candidate for blues stardom, being a blues harmonica player, singer and guitarist of considerable skill, imagination and individuality. A spell in prison destroyed such hopes, however. Moss was born in Jewel, Georgia, son of a sharecropper, as were so many bluesmen of the period. An autodidact, he took up the harmonica as his first instrument. By the late 1920s he was based in Atlanta and became well known to the other bluesmen operating out of the area.

By 1930 he was a member, along with Barbecue Bob and Curley Weaver, of the Georgia Cotton Pickers, recording with them that year and then, in 1933, beginning his recording career under his own name for the Banner label, cutting his sides in New York City with a variety of accompanists. Moss's Piedmont-style sides were varied and intelligent, often exhibiting humor as well as pathos, and it was a loss to blues when he was sentenced to prison, apparently for murdering his wife. Released in 1941, he made a handful of sides for Okeh with Brownie McGhee and Sonny Terry in attendance, but his time was gone. He drifted outside of the music business, experiencing a minor comeback in the 1960s on his "rediscovery" when he played, infrequently but regularly, at festivals during the 1960s and 1970s and made a spattering of records, but his latter-day career never gained sufficient momentum for him to be sustained by it.

**SEE ALSO:** Barbecue Bob, Curley Weaver, Brownie McGhee, Sonny Terry

# Charlie Musselwhite

**fact file**

**BORN** 1944

**MUSICAL SELECTION**
Ace of Hearts
Signature
In My Time

A festival favorite, Charlie Musselwhite carved a strong niche for himself on the blues harp scene

usselwhite first came to attention during the 1960s, when the great marriage between rock and blues was being effected. Of mixed white and American Indian parentage, Musselwhite took the sounds of postwar Chicago harmonica blues and added the overcharged sounds of rock.

Born in Kosciusko, Mississippi, Musselwhite soon moved to Memphis, where he grew up with his family and gradually took an interest in the local blues scene. He heard Sonny Terry on the local radio and determined to get himself a harmonica: similarly, he met and befriended old-time Memphis musicians like Furry Lewis and Will Shade and learned privately from their example. He moved to Chicago at the age of 18 in 1962, capable of playing impressive harp and guitar, and within a short time on Maxwell Street was able to work with key Chicagoans such as Johnny Young and J.B. Hutto. He also met Mike Bloomfield prior to that guitarist's establishing a national reputation. Musselwhite was signed up by Vanguard, a label to the fore of the new wave of young folk and blues artists: his debut album with the snappy title of *Stand Back! Here Comes Charlie Musselwhite's Southside Blues Band* (1967) gave him an audience worldwide. From that point on, Musselwhite toured and recorded regularly, keeping the flame of harmonica-based blues burning strongly. Not a noted singer, he nevertheless sings idiomatically and with a warmth not possessed by all.

But it was his harp playing that kept him at the forefront of the blues of the 1970s and 1980s: he recorded and played with a virtual *Who's Who* of blues greats during that time. Musselwhite is currently recording for Alligator: his albums, *Ace of Hearts* and *Signature* (1991), demonstrate his mastery of modern blues idioms and show his harp technique to be in great shape, while *In My Time* (1994) takes a look backward. He continues to pursue a vigorous career.

**SEE ALSO:** Sonny Terry, Walter "Furry" Lewis, Johnny Young, J. B. Hutto, Mike Bloomfield

# Kenny Neal

Still young in blues terms, Kenny Neal has been immersed in the music from his youth

## fact file

**BORN** 1957

**MUSICAL SELECTION**
Bayou Blood
Hoodoo Moon

Neal was born into a highly musical Baton Rouge family, his siblings mostly being professional musicians and his father, Raful Neal, being a late-arrival blues harpist of considerable quality working in the New Orleans area. Guitarist/singer/harpist Neal holds to the Louisiana swamp-blues tradition, updating it to fit streamlined sounds of the 1990s.

Neal was interested in music from early on, picking up tips on harmonica technique from Slim Harpo, a family friend who gave him his first harp when he was just three. By his early teens Neal was sufficiently confident to step into his father's band as bassist in 1970. His progress was confirmed when he became bassist in Buddy Guy's band in 1976, and a few years later he was to be found in the Canadian outfit the Downchild Blues Band as well as in

the Neal Brothers Band, who had relocated to Toronto in the meantime to work with him. Looking to head south, he and his brothers returned to Baton Rouge in 1984 and Kenny set about forming his own band. He signed a deal with King Snake records and released his debut album, *Bio on the Bayou* (later reissued by Alligator as *Big News from Baton Rouge!*), in 1986. Neal consolidated his blues standing with a solid diet of live appearances and strong albums for Alligator, then spread his talents further by appearing, in 1991, in the Broadway production of Langston Hughes's Harlem Renaissance-era play, *Mule Bone*, to much acclaim. Since then Neal has continued his career, appearing overseas as well as across the US blues belt. Recent albums include *Bayou Blood* (1993) and *Hoodoo Moon* (1994).

**SEE ALSO:** Slim Harpo, Buddy Guy

# Tracy Nelson

Tracy Nelson, a strong blues voice in the tradition of Ma Rainey and Bessie Smith

**N**elson was Californian-born but moved early on to Madison, Wisconsin. As a teenager in Madison she would listen to late-night blues and R&B radio, and she graduated to playing guitar herself and singing while studying at the University of Wisconsin in the early 1960s. Forays to Chicago around the same time, often in the company of the harmonica man Charlie Musselwhite, gave her first-hand experience of the Chicago greats, and although she made a solo album for Sam Charters in 1964, her first impact on a wider audience took place soon after her move to California in the late 1960s when she formed the prototypical San Francisco R&B band, Mother Earth. The band built up a loyal audience at venues such as Fillmore West and the Avalon Ballroom, and their first album, *Living With The Animals*, made a decided impact on the blues scene as the decade came to a close.

Nelson moved with Mother Earth to Nashville, Tennessee, and the band continued to record and tour, but as the 1970s wore on the band met with less success. The musical climate had changed and Nelson decided to go out as a solo. Her albums showed an increasing eclecticism as the influence of Nashville and the South began to penetrate. For most of the 1980s Nelson made no new records, but kept up her contacts with the Bay area, returning annually for appearances at her old haunts; her fans remained loyal. Fellow musicians also knew where her roots lay, as the invitation to sing at Memphis Slim's funeral in 1988 attested. The 1993 Rounder album, *In The Here And Now*, showed her to be back on form in her favorite musical environment, the blues.

## fact file

**BORN** 1944

**MUSICAL SELECTION**
In The Here And Now

**SEE ALSO:** Charlie Musselwhite, Memphis Slim

# Robert Nighthawk

ighthawk, also known as Robert Lee McCoy (his mother's maiden name), was a seminal slide guitar player of the pre- and postwar period. Based in St Louis for the second half of the 1930s, Nighthawk brought great intensity to his acoustic guitar playing behind many of the blues stars of the period, and was one of the first to transfer that bottleneck intensity to the nascent electric guitar, thus pointing the way for the great postwar players such as Elmore James and all who followed him.

Nighthawk was born Robert McCollum in Helena, Arkansas, and left home in his mid-teens, determined to support himself on his earnings as a harmonica busker. He moved to guitar after learning the basics of the instrument from a cousin, Houston Stackhouse. He and his cousin then did the rounds of the juke joints and house-rent parties in the district to make a living. Involvement in an affray at one of these events in the mid-1930s led Nighthawk to think St Louis may be a healthier place to live. Within a year Nighthawk was recording, under the name Robert Lee McCoy, with Jack Newman for Vocalion in October 1936. His own recording career commenced the following May for Bluebird – the same month he began recording for Bluebird as accompanist to John Lee "Sonny Boy" Williamson. This session included the impressive "Prowling Night-Hawk," the track that was to give him his later professional name. He continued to play on Williamson's discs until December 1938, when Sonny Boy switched to Big Bill Broonzy as his regular recording mate. McCoy, as he was still then known, also made some sides in December 1938 for the pianist Speckled Red, another Williamson alumnus. His term with Bluebird came to an end the same month with a set of eight tracks, all with Sonny Boy accompanying. McCoy continued to base himself in Arkansas and St Louis, playing radio shows and frequently traveling to Chicago and environs: he cut a brief session for Decca there in 1940, but then stayed clear of a studio until November 1948, by which time his electric guitar work, heard in clubs in Chicago and the South, had already influenced a generation of players. Muddy Waters got him a deal with Chess, but by 1951 he'd jumped to United, the first of a series of small labels that failed to ignite his career. Nighthawk continued to play the same Southern and Chicago circuits as had delivered his paychecks for the past decade, and although he never landed a hit, he remained one of the most electrifying and respected blues musicians on the scene until his death, in his home town of Helena, in 1967.

| fact file |
| --- |

**BORN** 1909

**DIED** 1967

**MUSICAL SELECTION**
"Prowling Night-Hawk"

The Great Robert Nighthawk
during a quiet session
with Little Walter (in the
background)

**SEE ALSO:** Elmore James, Sonny Boy Williamson, Big Bill Broonzy

# The Nighthawks

**THE NIGHTHAWKS**

**fact file**

**FORMED** C. 1967

**MUSICAL SELECTION**
The Nighthawks
Trouble
Open All Night
Rock 'n' Roll

Rock 'n' Roll

The Nighthawks, pictured on their album Rock 'n' Roll (Varrick/ Rounder), are carrying the blues torch to the next generation

t he Nighthawks are a group coming out of Washington, DC, who were formed by the latterly independent guitarist Jimmy Thackery and singer Mark Wenner. While not breaking any new ground they have performed for close on 30 years on the East Coast of the US and maintained their standards and popularity.

The band formed in the late 1960s when blues and rock had come together for a brief but fruitful liaison. They played the clubs around Washington, sticking to the type of modern Chicago sound and repertoire most white bands were listening to at the time. This proved a popular approach both in clubs and on the campuses where they began regularly appearing during the 1970s. They were also often used as a local warm-up group for touring blues heavyweights like Muddy Waters and his peers. By 1980 they'd made the album *The Nighthawks*, issued that year on Mercury. Earlier material was available on the Varrick label. Their

reputation by this time was rapidly becoming both national in the US and international in Europe and Australia. By 1985 Thackery felt it was a long enough stint and went solo, signing with the Blind Pig label. His replacements were Jimmy Nalls and the keyboardist Mike Cowan. The band have retained a steady personnel and now record for Powerhouse: their first for the label was *Trouble* (1991). The band continue to perform and record to critical acclaim.

**SEE ALSO:** Muddy Waters

# St Louis Jimmy Oden

fact file

**BORN** 1903

**DIED** 1977

**MUSICAL SELECTION**
"Goin' Down Slow"

James Burke Oden was also known as St Louis Jimmy, Old Man Oden and even Poor Boy during his blues career

O den's reputation rests mainly on his prowess as a singer and composer, although for many years he played piano in the St Louis area – hence his most familiar nickname. His most sustained period of success was during the postwar years in Chicago, when he was supplying songs to a range of artists, from Little Walter to Otis Spann, although his most famous song, covered by a multitude of performers, was "Going Down Slow," which he himself first recorded in Chicago in 1941.

Oden was born in Nashville, Tennessee, to musical parents, both of whom, however, were dead before he was nine. He made his way to St Louis by early teens, working originally as an assistant in a barber shop and teaching himself rudimentary barrelhouse piano. Always dissatisfied with his own playing, he usually performed professionally with able piano specialists, one being his friend Roosevelt Sykes, with whom he would often play around St Louis in the 1920s and 1930s. It was Sykes who was present on his first recording date in Richmond, Indiana, in 1932, where he recorded "Sitting Down Thinking." His recording career was not prolific, and although he made records between 1932 and

1964, fewer than a hundred sides were released in over 30 years.

In 1932 Oden left St Louis, relocating in Chicago where he had friends and companions, including Roosevelt Sykes. He recorded for Bluebird and Decca, although just four sessions covered his recording activity in the 1930s. Oden stuck to the same style and delivery throughout World War II after landing a minor hit with his first version of "Goin' Down Slow." He ventured into management and in the co-running of the JOB label at the end of the 1940s. He used key emerging Chicago musicians like Sunnyland Slim and Muddy Waters in the 1940s for recordings, although Sykes remained his first choice as accompanist. He had a quiet time of it in the 1950s but activity picked up again as the 1960s dawned, with a session for Bluesville in 1960 and a co-starring role on an Otis Spann session for Candid in the same year, although Oden on this date has considerable tuning problems. Most of his 1960s material remains unreleased, although it features musicians such as Homesick James, Washboard Sam, and, in his last recordings in 1964, Mike Bloomfield. He died in 1977.

**SEE ALSO:** Little Walter, Otis Spann, Roosevelt Sykes, Sunnyland Slim, Muddy Waters, Homesick James, Washboard Sam

# Johnny Otis

**fact file**

**BORN** 1921

**MUSICAL SELECTION**
Cold Shot
Cuttin' Up

Johnny Otis (c.)
is all smiles in
a publicity shot
with Mel Walker
(l.) and Little
Esther (r.) aka
Esther Phillips,
during the 1950s

Otis (aka John Veliotes) has occupied a pivotal role, especially on the West Coast, in the development of R&B and related black music since the late 1940s, his combination of shrewd talent-spotting, production techniques, bandleading, and financial acumen proving at times inspirational in providing a direction for successive generations of R&B, soul, and funk musicians.

Otis was born to immigrant Greek parents in Los Angeles, growing up in a predominantly black neighborhood. This was a decisive fact in his musical development, and he chose to go into music playing the drums for local jazz bands, eventually putting in some time with Harlan Leonard's swing-based jump band toward the end of its successful run. In the latter years of World War II and the immediate postwar period Otis found a lot of work as the draft kept so many musicians away from the jazz bands he then preferred working in. In 1945 he ran his own band for a

time, producing a hit with his version of the sultry "Harlem Nocturne." However, during 1947 Otis changed direction, slimming down to a septet and heading off into R&B territory. Between that time and the advent of rock 'n' roll Otis enjoyed considerable success in the charts and became an important discoverer of talent, giving first breaks to musicians such as Etta James, Big Mama Thornton, and Esther Phillips. Otis's own Rhythm & Blues Caravan took much of the talent at his disposal on long tours across the US, further publicizing his acts.

As musical fashions shifted, Otis changed with them, always keeping abreast, if not in front, of popular tastes, keeping his career, in one aspect or another, on the boil deep into the 1980s. His son, Shuggie Otis, became a hot blues/rock property briefly in the late 1960s, and he and Johnny have continued to collaborate on projects from time to time ever since. Otis continues to record and produce, albeit at a slower tempo these days.

**SEE ALSO:** Big Mama Thornton, Esther Phillips

# Jay Owens

**fact file**

**BORN** 1947

**MUSICAL SELECTION**
The Blues Soul of Jay
Owens
Movin' On

Jay Owens,
feeling it at the
Gloucester Blues
Festival, 1995

O wens came to the attention of blues fans late, having spent almost a full professional life in backing bands or local groups playing funk, soul, and other spin-off music, including at one stage a pop band, and also working as a support act for a whole range of black music legends, including Stevie Wonder, Bill Withers, and Al Green. Only in the late 1980s did Owens decide to turn to the blues, from which time he has had a rapid rise to prominence in blues circles as a fine soul-tinged singer and blues guitarist with subtle technique to burn.

Owens was born in Lake City, Florida, and first experienced music through his family's strong gospel ties. From a musical family (his father played piano, his mother drums), Jay picked up a guitar and started playing it in church. Introduced to the blues by an uncle who played country style and reminisced about Son House and other greats, Owens began learning blues licks as well

as the swing style he heard from a neighbor, Jimmy McLin, who played with the Ink Spots. He also took to the trombone and later occasionally used it professionally. Owens then went into a long apprenticeship, playing in a bewildering number of local bands and back-up outfits in many different styles. In the 1980s he put together a top-40-type band, Soundtrack, in New York, but the project folded and the next band he formed, in 1987, was the Pocket, a band dealing in the blues. Based still in New York, Owens picked up work and made a number of tours in Europe as well as playing support for Etta James back in the US. He also recorded an album for Indigo which won awards in the US, Britain, and France on its eventual release. Since then he switched to Code Blues/East-West records, making two solid-selling modern-sounding albums, *The Blues Soul of Jay Owens* (1993) and *Movin' On* (1995). He continues to perform worldwide.

**SEE ALSO:** Son House

235

# Junior Parker

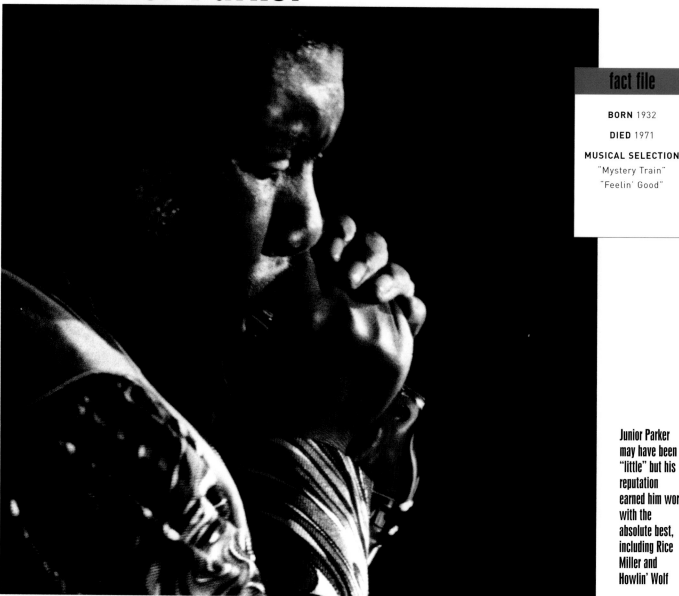

**fact file**

**BORN** 1932

**DIED** 1971

**MUSICAL SELECTION**
"Mystery Train"
"Feelin' Good"

Junior Parker may have been "little" but his reputation earned him work with the absolute best, including Rice Miller and Howlin' Wolf

Parker, the possessor of a burnished light baritone voice of power and subtlety, was an R&B star of influence and magnitude at the beginning of the 1950s who went on to prove himself a remarkably flexible and open-minded musician. Born in West Memphis, Arkansas, Parker came from a farming family and began hanging out in West Memphis music circles during his mid-teens, earning himself the sobriquet "Little Junior." Having learned how to sing while in church, Parker soon found himself capable of delivering the goods in a blues context, and added expertise with the harmonica to his list of credits, learning some of the tricks of the trade from Rice Miller, then a major Memphis presence. Parker played with many of the Memphis stars of the day, including Howlin' Wolf, B.B. King, Bobby "Blue" Bland, and Johnny Ace, some of them in the informal "Beale Streeters" band.

In 1951 he formed the Blue Flames, making his first single for Modern before switching to Sun in 1953. At his second session that year for Sam Phillips Parker cut his "Mystery Train," a song about to be made famous by another Phillips acolyte, while "Feelin' Good," a track from July 1953, made it into the R&B top 5. Parker moved to Houston in 1954 to become part of the Duke Records setup with Bobby Bland, joining the Blues Consolidated tours which took Duke artists around the South and delivered them a faithful audience for their records right into the early 1960s. Parker always had room for outstanding musicians in his bands, especially those with a jazz as well as blues pedigree, so his records are littered with names like Arnett Cobb, Red Holloway, James Booker, and Willie Mitchell. In 1966 Parker appeared on pianist Jaki Byard's *Freedom Together* album of avant-garde jazz, proving his versatility. His career during the last six years of his life provided no more singles hits, either on Mercury or Capitol, but his albums sold to his established audience a newer, more rock-based crowd. Parker died suddenly in 1971 from complications after brain-tumor surgery.

**SEE ALSO:** Sonny Boy Williamson II, Howlin' Wolf, B. B. King, Bobby "Blue" Bland

# Willie "Pinetop" Perkins

**fact file**

**BORN** 1913

**MUSICAL SELECTION**
Born In The Delta

Though a talent in his own right, Pinetop Perkins was often at his best alongside the blues's best frontmen

erkins was a pioneer of the Delta piano style, often playing in groups with major artists such as Rice Miller (Sonny Boy Williamson II), Robert Nighthawk, and (briefly) B.B. King. His boogie-woogie style came from his admiration for the pioneer boogie pianist Clarence "Pinetop" Smith, and his own nickname was bestowed due to Perkins's ability to so precisely imitate his early idol. Born in Belzoni, Mississippi, he took up the guitar as his first instrument, and played regularly at local jukes and parties until he sustained an injury that meant a long rest from guitar playing. Unwilling to be off the scene for so long, Perkins switched to piano and before long made a long-term commitment to the instrument.

During the 1930s and 1940s Perkins spent five years with Rice Miller, often broadcasting with him during the King Biscuit radio slots beamed out of Helena, Arkansas. He also spent a deal of time with Robert Nighthawk, recording with him for Chess, among other companies. Reaching Memphis by 1950, Perkins recorded his version of "Pinetop's Boogie" for Sam Philips's Sun label there, but he remained something of a journeyman player, splitting his time between East St Louis and Chicago for most of the 1950s and settling in as band member of a number of different outfits, including Albert King's. In 1969, he replaced Otis Spann in Muddy Waters' band. He spent 12 years with Waters, touring the world on a number of occasions and recording in many contexts. By the time he left in 1980 to go with the Legendary Blues Band, spurred by the ex-Waters drummer Willie Smith, he was a piano legend. Pinetop left the legends and went out on his own. In his eighties, he considered himself semi-retired, but still made appearances and continued to record, his latest album, *Born In The Delta* (Telarc), appearing in 1997.

**SEE ALSO:** Sonny Boy Williamson II, Robert Nighthawk, B. B. King, Albert King, Otis Spann, Muddy Waters, Willie Smith

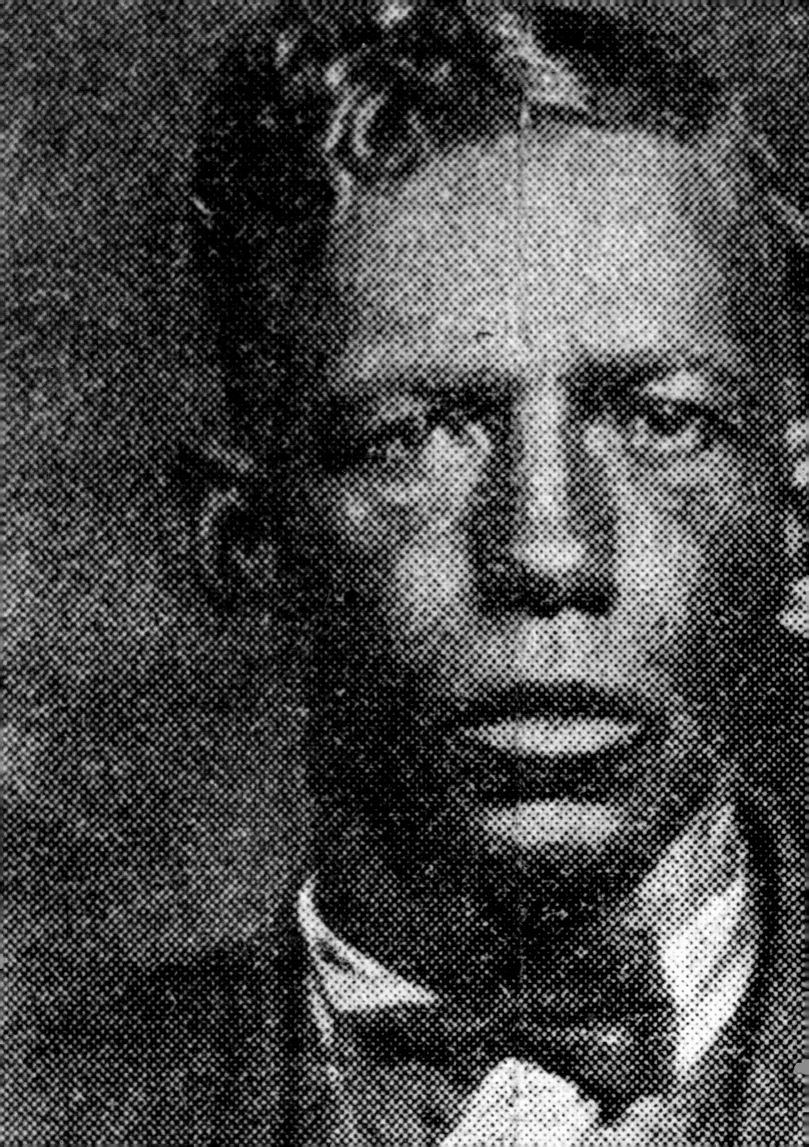

# Charlie Patton

**i**t is difficult to overestimate Patton's position in, and impact on, the development of the Delta blues style. This, in turn, gives him a central position in the overall story of the blues idiom. A compulsive traveler in later years, a gifted entertainer and a man prepared to share his talents with his peers, he came into contact with virtually all of the Delta blues players between the end of World War I and the Depression. He and Son House traveled together, while other performers like Tommy Johnson and Robert Johnson were directly influenced by watching and hearing him play.

Patton was born in Edwards, Mississippi, but while he was young his family moved to the Delta region to work on the giant plantation known as Dockery. Charlie grew up there, working as a tenant farmer and picking up the guitar after witnessing the many dances and parties held regularly all over the farms of the plantation. Learning from bluesmen who lived on the plantation, he created his own tunes early on, and most likely had all the elements of his style and repertoire in place no later than 1915; by that time he was a popular entertainer across the plantation's acres. A wild man, he was liberal with his pleasures, including alcohol and women. But Patton was also recognized as a fantastic entertainer, resorting to all manner of stage tricks – including playing the guitar above his head or between his knees – to get the crowd excited. His songs were tailored to fit into the various stages of dances and picnics, although he invariably altered the traditional forms of the blues to fit his highly individual approach to singing and guitar playing.

Like all the musicians on Dockery, Patton had no opportunity to record on the virtually self-sufficient plantation until 1929, when the talent scout H.C. Speir came there to discover whether the place had any useful performers to record. Speir instantly recognized Patton's outsize ability and set up a deal with Paramount. Patton's first session was in June 1929; his first single, "Pony Blues," sold well, and Charlie cut more than 40 sides that same year. These were the recordings on which his reputation would be based, and included a wide range of topics and titles like "High Water Blues," "Prayer of Death," "A Spoonful of Blues" and "Mississippi Boweavil Blues." Patton's gigantic, rough-house voice and his deceptively intricate musicianship (he played hard, but he had a great deal more technique than normally credited with) made him a charismatic figure at the forefront of blues performers. The first days of the Depression – not to mention a prodigal lifestyle which led him to prison on at least one occasion (refered to in the 1934 recording "High Sheriff Blues") – kept him out of the studios until January/February 1934, when he cut close to 30 sides (many of them unissued) for Vocalion. By this time, however, Patton's voice had begun showing signs of the trauma resulting from having his throat slit in a juke-joint brawl in 1933. He was also suffering severely from heart problems and these performances show all too well his physical frailties. In fact, just a few months after those early 1934 sessions, Charlie Patton died of heart failure at the age of 43.

## fact file

**BORN** 1891

**DIED** 1934

**MUSICAL SELECTION**
"High Water Blues"
"Prayer of Death"
"A Spoonful of Blues"

Charley Patton's overwhelming talent and gregarious lifestyle single him out among the blues performers in the very early years of the century

**SEE ALSO:** Son House, Robert Johnson

# Lucky Peterson

Definitely fortunate, Lucky Peterson grew up surrounded by music and earned great success at a young age

## fact file

**BORN** 1964

**MUSICAL SELECTION**
Triple Play
I'm Ready

Peterson not only learned to play the blues when still very small, but, incredibly, cut his first album when he was just five years old – appearing on *The Tonight Show* in the same year, 1969. His father had run a blues club in Buffalo, New York, where the youngster was born, so Lucky was on first-name terms with blues greats like Junior Wells and Willie Dixon from the time he could speak.

Dixon arranged his first recording session, a record which got plenty of press for the youngster. Two years later, in 1971, Peterson even managed a hit, "1, 2, 3, 4," although the quality of the song itself was less remarkable than his age at the time he recorded it: he was only seven.

After finishing school, the seventeen-year-old Peterson went out on the road with Little Milton for a number of years, then swapped over to Bobby "Blue" Bland, with whom he was featured soloist.

Since that time Peterson has worked as a leader, a session man for various record companies, and as a hired hand for different projects. For Alligator Records he made *Lucky Strikes!* in 1989 and *Triple Play* the following year. But in more recent times Lucky Peterson has been recording with the Verve Gitanes blues line, performing in the US for the French-based venture. *I'm Ready*, from 1993, was the first release from this new partnership and demonstrates more of that Lucky touch.

**SEE ALSO:** Junior Wells, Willie Dixon, LittleMilton, Bobby "Blue" Bland

# Kelly Joe Phelps

Kelly Joe Phelps, a relatively new blues star, seen here performing in November 1997

P helps is one of the latest generation of black musicians who, after hearing and playing a wide range of music, have turned to the classic country blues form for inspiration and creative renewal. Thus he brings his appreciation of jazz, soul, and other genres to his blues playing and singing, creating a music that has a wide resonance.

Phelps was born in Sumner, Washington state, and became fascinated by the music he heard on the radio and from the family. Both gospel and country music were staples in his family home, and these influences have both stayed in him. First instrument was piano, but guitar and drums followed in his teens, and he began playing with local jazz musicians as a guitarist, making the jazz of the 1960s his first preference. After finishing school Phelps worked as a private music teacher, giving courses at Oregon University, among other institutions. In 1989 he discovered the country-blues in a big way, transfixed by the urgent recorded sounds of players such as Robert Pete Williams and Fred McDowell. Following their example, he began performing in the country-blues tradition, cutting his first record, *Lead Me On*, in 1994. Well received, it led to support spots on concerts by major blues acts and a deal with Rykodisc. His second album, *Roll Away The Stone* (1997), was a record that gained international release and announced the arrival of a significant talent.

### fact file

**BORN** 1960

**MUSICAL SELECTION**
Lead Me On
Roll Away The Stone

SEE ALSO: Robert Pete Willliams, Fred McDowell

# Esther Phillips

## fact file

**BORN** 1935

**DIED** 1984

**MUSICAL SELECTION**
"Home Is Where The Hatred Is"

Esther Phillips
aka Little Esther,
was plagued by
both success
and failure,
enduring
substantial
portions of both

P hillips was one of the great female blues shouters; along with her God-given voice, she possessed the talent and soul to rival Dinah Washington as a blues singer of power and grace. She moved easily between musical genres, but her basic grounding in the music of the church and its opposite, the blues, is always identifiable.

Born Esther Mae Jones in Galveston, Texas, Phillips moved with her family to Los Angeles after WWII, winning a Watts talent contest organized by Johnny Otis when she was just 13 years old. This led to appearances with the Otis band and, in 1949, to her first records, cut under the name "Little Esther." In the next year with Otis she had no less than seven top-ten R&B hits, including "Mistrustin' Blues" and "Double Crossing Blues." Still only in her mid-teens, Esther began to crumple from the pressure, leaving Otis and her record company and picking up a heroin habit. By the middle of the decade she was back in Texas

– this time in Houston – trying to straighten herself out. She managed a comeback in 1962, on the strength of a Nashville-recorded country song, "Release Me," which reached the top spot. Atlantic then recorded her in a jazz/blues context in 1966, with Onzy Matthews making big-band arrangements of songs like "In The Evenin'" and "C.C. Rider," in which Phillips showed an undiminished capacity for swinging blues shouting. But more drug problems damaged her capacity to sustain her career as the 1960s came to a close. In 1970, however, she was recorded live in LA with a small group; while the repertoire was mostly standards, her approach was still drenched in the blues as sung by Dinah Washington. A Gil Scott-Heron song, "Home Is Where The Hatred Is," gave her one last hit, in 1972. Although she continued to perform and record – often outside of the blues and R&B genres – she never regained her previous popularity. Esther Phillips died in 1984 of a liver ailment, aged 49.

**SEE ALSO:** Dinah Washington, Johnny Otis

# Piano Red

**fact file**

**BORN** 1911

**DIED** 1985

**MUSICAL SELECTION**
"Mr Moonlight"
"The Right String But
The Wrong Yo-Yo"

Piano Red,
younger brother
of Speckled Red,
influenced artists
in the US and the
UK, including the
Beatles

Piano Red, aka Dr Feelgood, younger brother of Rufus "Speckled Red" Perryman, the famed barrelhouse pianist, was as talented at the ivories as his brother although he played in a somewhat updated style from Rufus. Born in Hampton, Georgia, Red and his family moved to Atlanta when he was still an infant. Although neither their father nor mother showed any musical inclinations (his father was a blacksmith), both boys learned piano, William initially through the encouragement of Rufus. Working a day job as a furniture upholsterer, William used "down time" to practice on a nearby piano. Over the next five or so years Perryman played part-time at various Atlanta watering holes, his reputation growing to the point where in 1936 he made a series of 10 sides in Augusta, Georgia, for Vocalion under the name Piano Red with Blind Willie McTell. All 10 remain unissued.

Red did not record again until 1950, this time for the Victor label and in the R&B and boogie genre he'd adopted in the postwar period. His very first session produced two hits, "Rockin' With Red" and "Red's Boogie," and he recorded prolifically for Victor and its R&B subsidiary Groove right up to 1958, many of his session, including prestige sax players like Budd Johnson. His trademark jumpin' boogie was influential in many quarters, not least the emerging rock 'n' roll scene and, later, the 1960s beat revival coming out of Britain, some of his singles receiving coverage on a number of fronts. Swapping labels and moving to Okeh in 1961, Red used the name Dr Feelgood for a series of Nashville sessions, the first of which produced the famous Dr Feelgood single, "Mr Moonlight" (covered by the Beatles) and "The Right String But The Wrong Yo-Yo," later covered by Gerry and The Pacemakers! Perryman, whether recording under his Piano Red or Dr Feelgood pseudonym, rarely changed his style, and by the end of the 1960s was content to re-record earlier triumphs for whoever wanted them. He continued performing and recording on both sides of the Atlantic until his death in 1985.

**SEE ALSO:** Rufus "Speckled Red" Perryman, Blind Willie McTell

# Rod Piazza

### fact file

**BORN** 1947

**MUSICAL SELECTION**
Harp Burn
Blues In The Dark

Enjoying a good-time approach to the blues, Rod Piazza plays on

P iazza, based throughout his life in California, was born in Riverside and was attracted to the harmonica from the Chicago blues records he heard as a child. His heroes included Little Walter and George "Harmonica" Smith. By the time he was 18 he had formed his own blues group, Dirty Blues Band, which landed a deal with ABC/Bluesway and made three albums in three years.

During his time in this band he met "Harmonica" Smith, who had moved west from Chicago in 1968, and Piazza struck up a close friendship which resulted in the two men often performing together. They even played together in the group Bacon Fat for a time, staying together long enough to make an eponymous album for Blue Horizon in 1969. Sticking to his blues guns, Piazza continued to work from his base in Riverside, recording steadily and working in bars, clubs, and eateries in the larger LA area, slowly becoming known to a wider circle of musicians and fans and building his own loyal following for his impassioned and highly polished harp work. Piazza began appearing on many recording dates run by other musicians, including Michelle Shocked. He spent the 1980s recording either as a solo leader (*Harp Burn*, 1986) or as the leader of his working band, the Mighty Flyers (*From The Start To The Finish*, 1985), but the album that brought him wider attention was *Blues In The Dark*, the first under a new contract with Black Top records. Piazza continues his career today as one of the most complete and colorful harp players in the blues.

**SEE ALSO:** Little Walter, George "Harmonica" Smith

# Snooky Pryor

fact file

BORN 1921

MUSICAL SELECTION
Snooky
Back to the Country

Snooky Pryor
stands as a
significant post-
war blues figure,
despite semi-
retirement during
the 1960s

S nooky Pryor is one of the second wave of Chicago harpists, following on from the impact of the two Sonny Boy Williamsons, and helped consolidate the instrument as an essential part of a postwar Chicago blues band. His 1948 hit, "Telephone Blues," on the Planet label, was a key step in the launching of that new blues style.

Pryor was born in Lambert, Mississippi, listening to records to pick up the elements of blues harp, where he came under the massive influence of the two Williamsons. His prewar years were spent on the road and playing wherever he could find work, marrying in 1941 shortly before entering the services. After a discharge in late 1945 from war duty, which had taken him across the Pacific, Pryor settled in Chicago and began playing the South Side with a number of leaders, including Homesick James and Moody Jones. His novel use of a PA system to give him a raw, distorted, and urgent sound quickly became a Chicago blues staple. Later hits, for Vee Jay and others, included "Judgment Day" (1956). By the 1970s Pryor was virtually off the blues scene and only in the 1980s did he return, his album for Blind Pig, *Snooky*, announcing his return in 1986. By this time he was a grandfather and settled in Ullin, Illinois, and, though he has picked up the threads of his career, he remains based at Ullin. He still records and plays today, one of his most recent records being 1991's *Back to the Country*, with Johnny Shines.

**SEE ALSO:** Sonny Boy Williamson, Sonny Boy Williamson II, Homesick James, Johnny Shines

# Professor Longhair —

O ne of the greats of New Orleans music, Professor Longhair (aka Henry 'Roy' Byrd) enjoyed a long career and was instrumental in establishing the postwar New Orleans piano and jump music style which enjoyed worldwide success later through the auspices of such New Orleans talents as Fats Domino and Allen Toussaint. The Professor himself never attained the levels of fame and popularity these younger artists achieved, but he was equally respected in New Orleans circles for his ability to create a new mixture from the traditional Louisiana musical brew.

Like a number of other musicians from the early days in New Orleans, the Professor combined his musical activities with other more lucrative pursuits, including being a professional gambler, pool shark, and general wheeler-dealer. A streetwise kid, hip on music, he taught himself piano and played at all sorts of venues, including parties and picnics, either with groups or alone, often doubling on other instruments, including guitar. He remained in relative obscurity, however, until after his discharge from the armed services in 1943, after which he began running his own groups and playing the Big Easy club circuit in a more organized manner. This led, finally, to his debut on disc in 1949, "She Ain't Got No Hair" b/w "Bye Bye Baby," for the Talent label. The group was a quartet Byrd called Professor Longhair and his Shuffling Hungarians. Further sides followed in 1949, including a spate for Mercury (as Roy Byrd) and Atlantic (as Roy "Baldhead" Byrd and Professor Longhair), all of which featured the Professor's special mixture of gumbo, R&B, boogie, blues, barrelhouse, the Spanish Tinge, and other things besides. These and other sides to follow were enormously influential in the Crescent City area, and many New Orleans artists claim Byrd to be at the root of most later musical developments in their part of the country.

However, commercial success never really landed at the Professor's door; by the mid-1960s he was off the music scene entirely and working as a janitor. It was only through the determined attempts of young white enthusiasts who went looking for him during preparations for the inaugural 1970 New Orleans Jazz and Heritage Festival that he was eventually run to ground. It took a year, and he was broke and in terrible shape. But he appeared soon after at the 1971 Festival, where he made an immediate and deep impact. From then until his death the Professor enjoyed an Indian Summer of a career which included a number of albums, recorded both live and in the studio, and many concert appearances. His vitality, originality and influence finally acknowledged, Professor Longhair died in 1980 from the ravages of a hard-lived life.

## fact file

**BORN** 1918

**DIED** 1980

**MUSICAL SELECTION**
"She Ain't Got No Hair"
"Bye Bye Baby"

The Professor at work –
Professor Longhair's
stomping piano drove his
powerful blues into the
hearts of many during a long
and healthy career

SEE ALSO: Marcia Ball, James Booker

# Yank Rachell

## fact file

**BORN** 1908

**MUSICAL SELECTION**
Chicago Style
"Stack O' Dollars Blues"

Yank Rachell's talents were rarely enough to get by and he often had to supplement his income with farmwork

mandolinist Yank Rachell's name is undeniably linked to that of Sleepy John Estes, with whom he linked up in the 1920s and often performed and recorded. Rachell is one of a handful of blues musicians to have made names for themselves on the mandolin, and Rachell exhibited a lifelong preference for the smaller stringed instrument.

Rachell was born James Rachel in Brownsville, Tennessee; it seems he first learned the guitar from an uncle, going out to play parties and picnics in the Brownsville area. At one of these events he met another local bluesman, Sleepy John Estes, and the two of them began appearing as a team at outdoor events. Rachell by this time had swapped to mandolin, encouraged by another Brownsville player, Willie Newborn, with whom he also appeared from time to time. In 1929 Rachell and Estes took off for Memphis, playing on Beale Street with Jab Jones as the Three Js jug band. Estes landed a deal with Victor and he generally fit Rachell onto as many sessions as he could, that distinctive mandolin sound obviously proving an unusual talking point for listeners and other professionals alike. Victor also saw possibilities in Rachell, for

they recorded the two men using Yank's name as the front man in the same month as Sleepy John's debut for the label in September 1929. However, the Depression put paid to any long-term recording prospects for Rachell and Estes alike, both being dropped by Victor by late spring 1930. Estes moved north in search of new work while Rachell went back to Brownsville and farm work, occasionally playing with other bluesmen when they came through the area. In February 1934 he made a long series of dates for ARC, much of which went unissued, and in 1938 he was in Aurora and Chicago recording with Sonny Boy Williamson. But the times were against him and he did not take up blues work on a regular basis until his wife died in 1961.

He teamed up again with his old friend and colleague Sleepy John Estes in 1962, the year Estes was "rediscovered," and the pair of them performed and recorded extensively in the few years left to Estes, who died in 1977. During this period Rachell also occasionally made recordings under his name, although Estes was invariably present for the session. Rachell more or less retired with Estes's demise.

**SEE ALSO:** Sleepy John Estes, Sonny Boy Williamson

# Bobby Radcliff

fact file

**BORN** 1950

**MUSICAL SELECTION**
Dresses Too Short

Bobby Radcliff
has played the
blues from
the age of 12
and brings a
contemporary
sound to much
of his work

guitarist and shouter Radcliff was born in Bethesda, Maryland, discovering the blues during his teenage years by listening to late-night radio broadcasts of Elmore James records. This inspired him to take up guitar, and he taught himself the way around the blues licks of the day (the mid-1960s). A flop at school and a restless soul at sixteen, Radcliff decided that Chicago – which he believed to be the home of bluesman Magic Sam – was the place to be. In fact, Sam was laid up in Cook County Hospital, where Radcliff finally tracked him down. The hero and his protegé quickly became friends, and Magic Sam, once back on the Chicago beat, introduced Radcliff to the West Side scene.

As the 1970s began, Radcliff decided he could only crack the blues circuit if he traveled outside of Chicago. Following a little experimentation he landed in Washington, DC, where he gradually built up a loyal local following; his flashing, intense

guitar and his "scorched-earth" vocals created a tremendous impact in the clubs. After proving himself in Washington, Radcliff set out for New York at the end of the decade, a time when it seemed that interest in the blues was fading. Day jobs kept him alive while he scrambled for musical work, but he eventually caught on with the new audience that was gradually being built around the area's blues clubs throughout the 1980s. Radcliff also came to the attention of guitarist Ronnie Earl, who in the late 1980s recommended Bobby to Black Top records. The label heard a demo tape and signed him up, releasing his first album, *Dresses Too Short*, in 1988.

In the decade since, Bobby Radcliff has enjoyed a burgeoning reputation both in the States and worldwide, cutting a number of further albums for Black Top, as well as thrilling live audiences around the world with his fiercely committed blues playing, to the delight of blues fans everywhere.

**SEE ALSO:** Elmore James, Magic Sam, Ronnie Earl

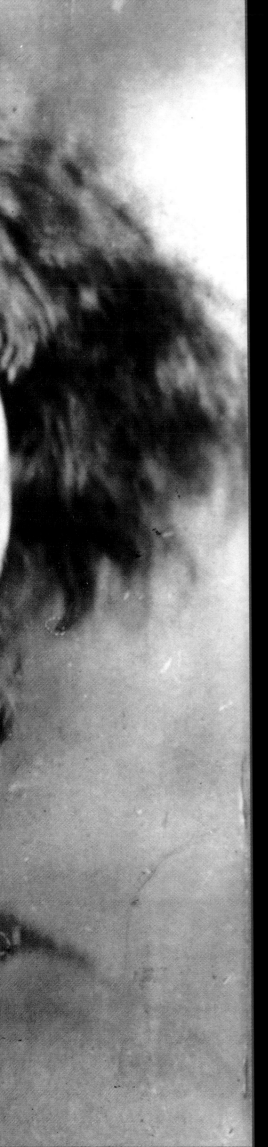

# Ma Rainey

born Gertrude Pridgett in Columbus, Georgia, Ma Rainey was to later become recognized as one of the two greatest female blue singers of the classic era, the other being Bessie Smith. She also had the title "mother of the blues" bestowed upon her. It was as accurate a description as any given to early black musicians. Gertrude had a head-start on most singers of her time in that she was born into a musical family, with both of her parents having spent time as minstrels and entertainers. Her vocal talents were spotted at an early age, and she appeared in a local talent show at Columbus Opera House in 1898, when she was just 12 years old. By the time she was 18 she had met and married the dancer, comedian and singer William 'Pa" Rainey, who was at the time associated with the Rabbit Foot Minstrels. Gertrude was quickly insinuated into Pa's act, at the age of 18 becoming "Ma."

The Raineys set out on their travels as minstrels, quickly building a new popularity based on their own routines together. They worked almost constantly through the next two decades, becoming top-drawing acts on the comedy, minstrel and tent show circuit. Ma Rainey claimed in an interview late in her life that she first came across the blues during her travels around the South about 1904-05. She heard another woman sing a plaintive piece unlike any she'd heard before, so struck by it that she incorporated it into her act. At the time, this type of piece had no name. Having been touched by the blues, Ma now began hearing it in various towns and districts they visited in the South; meanwhile her own set-piece became the highlight of her own act, guaranteeing a great response wherever the troupe went. Long before the end of that decade, this new type of music had acquired its name – the blues – and Ma had been recognized as one of its very first performers.

Ma lost Pa Rainey along the way but continued her touring, hitching up with the TOBA circuit during the 1920s and preserving the special balance of vaudeville and blues in her music. But no record companies approached her until 1923, three years after the first blues disc had been cut and two decades after her own debut on the professional stage. She was discovered in a down-at-heel revue at a decrepit Chicago theatre by record scout J. Mayo Williams, who was impressed by her voice and personality. Rainey made an immediate impact as a recording artist, her rough, expressive voice complemented by the first-rate musicians often brought in to accompany her – musicians such as Fletcher Henderson, Louis Armstrong, Charlie Green, Buster Bailey, Tampa Red, Coleman Hawkins and Don Redman. Her personality was strong enough to dominate any session she appeared on, and some of the songs she put her name to are still in the blues repertoire, including "See See Rider," "Ma Rainey's Black Bottom," "Stack O'Lee Blues" and "Jelly Bean Blues."

Rainey recorded consistently until 1928; by that time her popularity was on the wane, both on the stage and on records. Her last headlining tour, "Arkansas Swift Foot," took place in 1930. For three years after that she kept working, appearing in a string of shows run by other people. But times were hard and, well into middle-age, her heart was no longer in it. The deaths of both her sister and her mother in the same year, 1933, brought her to a decision-point. She left performing behind, settling in her hometown of Columbus; she passed away in 1939.

## fact file

**BORN** 1886

**DIED** 1939

**MUSICAL SELECTION**
"Ma Rainey's Black Bottom"
"Stack O'Lee Blues"
"Jelly Bean Blues"

The unstoppable Gertrude "Ma" Rainey, undisputed mother of the blues

**SEE ALSO:** Bessie Smith, Fletcher Henderson, Tampa Red

# Jimmy Reed

**fact file**

**BORN** 1925

**DIED** 1976

**MUSICAL SELECTION**
"Big Boss Man"
"Bright Lights Big City"
"Shame Shame Shame"

Jimmy Reed —
a virtual hit
machine during
the 1950s, his
success was
equalled only by
the trouble in
which he often
found himself

Jimmy Reed, one of the most commercially successful bluesmen of the entire postwar period, was also one of the most influential, bringing a new type of hybrid into fashion which combined the raw vocal passion of the South with the relaxed rhythms and slinkiness of rhythm & blues as developed by T-Bone Walker and others. Reed's steady-rolling style had as big an impact on the 1960s big-beat scene as it did on contemporary blues players.

Reed was born in Dunleith, Mississippi, and made a friend during boyhood who would be important to his subsequent career. Guitarist Eddie Taylor was a constant companion as he and Reed both reached manhood, Taylor showing Reed the rudiments of guitar technique. Reed also taught himself some basic harmonica licks, gradually developing a personalized style which was staccato and economical in approach, but which was to prove very effective as part of his later repertoire. Reed moved to Chicago in 1943 and was quickly inducted into the war effort, serving in the Navy. For a few years after his discharge Reed lived in Gary, Indiana, where he married Mary Lee Reed and once again

hooked up with Eddie Taylor, who had moved to Chicago after the war. By the early 1950s both men were in Chicago and beginning to play in the bars around the city. Even then their style concentrated on the pared-down, easy-rolling music which would soon bring Reed international fame. However, it took a while for Reed to land a recording contract, with Chess records actually turning him down before Albert King showed him the way to the Vee Jay label. His first single, "You Don't Have To Go," recorded in December 1953, began a long string of hits for the label and ushered in a new style of blues – an alternative to the harsh edge of Howlin' Wolf and Muddy Waters. In the next decade Reed was to enjoy a dozen such hits, including "Honest I Do," "Big Boss Man," "Bright Lights Big City," and "Shame Shame Shame." However, Reed had always been a heavy drinker, and though his career reached a peak in the 1960s, he was sliding into alcoholism. Vee Jay went under in the mid-1960s, and Reed moved to Bluesway, where he failed to land more heavyweight crossover hits. By the early 1970s he was no longer capable of sustaining a full-time career. Jimmy Reed died in 1976.

**SEE ALSO:** T-Bone Walker, Eddie Taylor, Howlin' Wolf, Muddy Waters

# Sonny Rhodes

**fact file**

**BORN** 1940

**MUSICAL SELECTION**
Just Blues
Disciple Of The Blues

Ever the eccentric, Sonny Rhodes wears a turban on stage in honour of Chuck Willis, an early influence

t exan Rhodes (he hails from Smithville) has spent most of his professional career on the West Coast, and his loose, relaxed, modern blues sounds are as distinctive as his ever-present turban and his lap steel guitar.

Rhodes took an early liking to fellow-Texan T-Bone Walker's music and became proficient as a guitarist before his stint in the Navy, which began in 1957. After discharge, Rhodes spent some time playing in the bands of Albert Collins and Freddie King, mostly playing bass, but Texas held little future for him and he relocated to Oakland, California. Once on the West Coast he met up with L.C. Robinson, who gave him a start on the lap steel guitar, and Percy Mayfield, whom he freely credits as being instrumental

in getting him to write good-quality songs and craft his own style.

A few singles for the Galaxy label made little impact but gave him something of a calling card in Europe. This was a double-edged sword, as the albums he made there at the end of the 1970s are ones he remains dissatisfied with. One of them included the Paris National Symphony Orchestra. In 1985 he made a self-financed album, *Just Blues* (recently reissued on Evidence), done on his own terms and with his own musicians, which shows him to have a fierce soul-tinged singing style and urgent yet melodic guitar technique, complemented nicely by a tight horn section. This got him attention and a second album in 1991, *Disciple Of The Blues* (Ichiban), but Rhodes remains underappreciated.

# Sherman Robertson

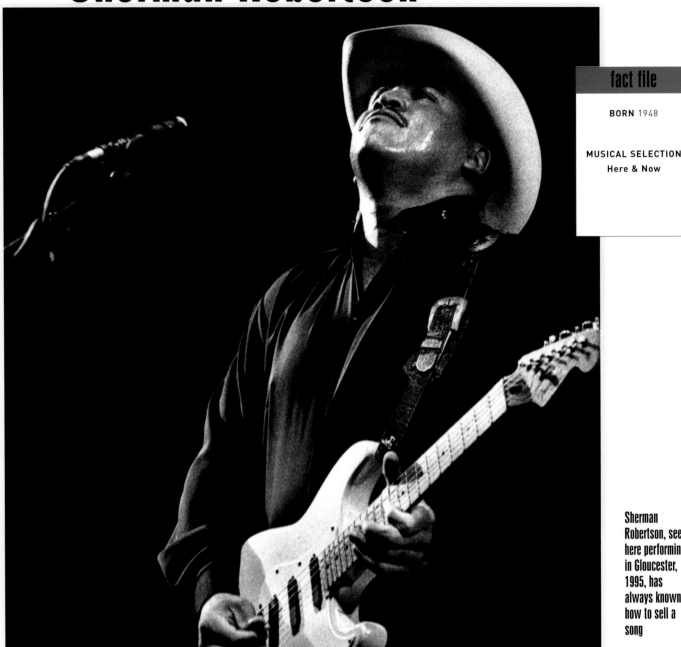

**fact file**

**BORN** 1948

**MUSICAL SELECTION**
Here & Now

Sherman Robertson, seen here performing in Gloucester, 1995, has always known how to sell a song

Louisiana native Robertson has shared his musical talents equally during his career between zydeco and swamp blues, building up a healthily cosmopolitan approach to his music in the process. Born in Breaux Bridge, Louisiana, Robertson first came to music through the country music he saw on television and heard on the radio. After being given a guitar as a boy by his father, Robertson began investigating the blues after his friend Floyd London introduced him to the music. As a teenager and immediately after, he ran a number of bands, including a forceful swamp-blues outfit, the Crosstown Blues Band. This established him as a local guitar slinger to the point that the great zydeco exponent Clifton Chenier, a friend of the family and on the lookout for a guitarist for his band, hired him. Robertson spent five years with Chenier

in the 1970s, touring extensively, including trips to Europe. This helped Robertson become known outside of the Louisiana circles he'd originally exclusively moved in, a process furthered by his joining the band of one of Chenier's principal zydeco rivals, Rockin' Dopsie. By now regarded as a quality guitar player in any number of contexts, he participated at the close of the 1980s in the sessions that led to Paul Simon's breakthrough *Gracelands* album and the renaissance of that artist's career in a world music context. Still working as a sideman in a number of contexts, Robertson was signed by the producer Mike Vernon to Indigo/Code Blue records in 1992. Since then he's been leaning decidedly to the blues side of his talents, his 1996 album, *Here & Now* showing his consummate studio skills as well as his way with a lyric and his sharp, unfussy guitar playing.

**SEE ALSO:** Burton Gaar

# Duke Robillard

**fact file**

**BORN** 1948

**MUSICAL SELECTION**
Turn It Around
Temptation

Co-founder of Roomful of Blues, Duke Robillard has earned a place in the blues pantheon as a powerful performer

robillard has been an important presence and influence on the post-1960s East Coast blues scene, co-forming Roomful of Blues and, later, treading an increasingly eclectic musical path which all through has been guided by the special excellence of his guitar playing and improvising.

Robillard was born in Roonsocket, Rhode Island, and early in life developed a wide-ranging enthusiasm for popular music in general and popular black music in particular, allied to a fascination for the guitar which reached its culmination when he began learning it while an adolescent. A blues addict by the mid-1960s, Robillard formed Roomful of Blues with the pianist Al Copley in 1967: the band toured all over the Boston and general New England area and by the early 1970s was breaking in New York and Washington as well. The band had recorded two albums by the time Robillard left, in 1979, to form his own band, Duke Robillard and the Pleasure Kings, in his quest to pursue a more diverse musical career. Robillard also worked for a while with other bands, including the Legendary Blues Band and Robert Gordon, but his focus now became the Pleasure Kings. They made a couple of albums for

Rounder during the 1980s which displayed Robillard's increasing certainty on guitar in a large variety of musical styles, both contemporary and old-time, from swing to jump to R&B, funk, and blues. His voice was also a developing asset. In 1987 Robillard recorded *Swing*, an album of tributes to early heroes of his in the jazz world – a choice of material which revealed Robillard to be as deeply affected by saxophonists as by guitarists, and a knowledgeable enthusiast for pre-bop jazz and R&B.

In 1990 Robillard became a member of the Fabulous Thunderbirds, a position that lasted for two years, though he kept up his own projects, such as *Turn It Around*, a 1991 Rounder album which featured his own group and the singer Susanne Forrest and took a considerably tougher, rock-oriented approach. This in some ways was a taster for what Robillard was to do next, once again striking out with his own band and taking a more aggressive stance to his music. Robillard has since moved to the Virgin/Pointblank label, his first for that company being *Temptation*, where once again his interest in past music, from soul to rock 'n' roll, is indulged.

**SEE ALSO:** Roomful of Blues

# Fenton Robinson

Fenton Robinson stands out among blues performers for his willingness to test other musical waters

## fact file

**BORN** 1935

**MUSICAL SELECTION**
"Somebody Loan
Me a Dime"

fenton Robinson pioneered an individual combination of blues, soul, and R&B roots-type approaches which made him a harbinger of the type of blues played by many young players today. He drew upon many sources for a sophisticated yet streamlined approach to the music. Yet Robinson has rarely been given exposure beyond blues circles and remains one of the idiom's best-kept secrets.

Born on a plantation near Greenwood, Mississippi, Robinson moved to Memphis at 18 and began recording in 1957. After leaving Memphis for Houston the following year and much traveling around the South, he finally hit Chicago in 1962. Since then the Windy City has been Robinson's base, although he has always traveled extensively and continues to do so. In Chicago he played with many headliners including Sonny Boy Williamson II, Junior Wells and Otis Rush.

Robinson cut a single of his own composition, "Somebody Loan Me a Dime," in 1967. It was covered two years later by Boz Scaggs with Duane Allman and became a classic; few people realized Robinson's prior claim on the song. He re-recorded the song in 1974 for Alligator (as the title tune of an album), and cut several more sides for the same label, his vocals revealing touches of vocalists as diverse as Sam Cooke and B.B. King. Fenton Robinson continues to perform and record in the same Memphis soul/blues style today, but has never managed to claim the success his originality deserves.

**SEE ALSO:** Sonny Boy Williamson II, Junior Wells, Otis Rush, B. B. King

# L C "Good Rockin'" Robinson

Louis Charles Robinson was "Good Rockin'" on both guitar and fiddle for decades and by all accounts enjoyed every minute

orn in Brenham, Texas – the nephew of Blind Willie Johnson – L.C. Robinson took the unorthodox career decision to play the blues on fiddle and bottleneck steel guitar, as well as on the usual six-string guitar. He and his brother A.C. played blues together in their early teens, traveling through Texas and taking work where they could find it. L.C.'s style came about through listening to people like his uncle and other great Texas originals. But he was also strongly swayed by a new style of music emerging from the region in the 1930s – Western Swing, especially that of Bob Wills and Milton Brown. During WWII, Robinson served in the Bay Area on the West Coast; after hostilities ended both he and his brother decided that San Francisco Bay was a better place

to live than Texas. Performing together as the Robinson Brothers around the Oakland area and beyond, they worked regularly through the 1950s until L.C. decided to switch over to gospel music. He didn't return to the blues until the mid-1960s, when he began playing as a guest with various bands visiting the Bay Area, including Muddy Waters. Still, very little in the way of recordings came along until, in 1971, he made a record for Arhoolie under the auspices of Muddy Waters and featuring many members of the Waters band of that time. This has since been released on CD with some extra tracks, five of which, cut four years later, feature L.C. with his brother A.C.

L.C. Robinson, a great entertainer and a performer full of energy and commitment, never made another album.

## fact file

**BORN** 1915

**DIED** 1976

**MUSICAL SELECTION**
Ups & Downs

SEE ALSO: Blind Willie Johnson, Muddy Waters

# Jimmy Rogers

**fact file**

**BORN** 1924

**MUSICAL SELECTION**
Gold Tailed Bird
Ludella

Newport 1995 –
Jimmy Rogers
plays with
feeling, as ever

r ogers, for years known principally as the second guitarist in the classic Muddy Waters band of the late 1940s and early 1950s, also led an independent career on records, mostly with the Chess label and its affiliates. But he has rarely been accorded the credit for his part in forming the sound and style that became so influential in Chicago and beyond.

Rogers was born in Ruleville, Mississippi, and moved to Atlanta with his family while still an infant. Soon after, he went with his grandmother to Memphis, where he spent his childhood and made his initial contact with the blues around him. While in Memphis he met Robert Jr Lockwood and other local musicians and began playing for change as a teenager, but by the late 1930s he was in St Louis for a while, meeting up with Sunnyland Slim, Walter Davis, and Roosevelt Sykes and playing some of the East St Louis clubs before finally hitting Chicago around 1941, shortly before America's involvement in World War II. After the war, Rogers began to circulate on the blues scene, appearing in clubs and on records with various players including Memphis Minnie and, in 1947, Little Walter. By the following year he had been introduced

by Sunnyland Slim to Muddy Waters, fresh from Mississippi, and Waters, Rogers, and Little Walter formed the nucleus of Muddy's first band. Rogers was making sessions as a leader for Chess by 1950, but produced nothing that sold in great quantities. He first appeared as part of Muddy's band on a Chess record in 1951, staying with the band until 1955, when he became disillusioned with the music business and, after disappointing sessions with Chess which stretched into 1958 and registered just one R&B hit, 1957's "Walkin' By Myself," opened a clothing store. That and a cab business kept him busy for the best part of the dozen years, the occasional sitting in with old friends and a guest spot on a Waters album from 1960 his only contact with music in this time. In 1971 Rogers came back to music full-time, making an album for Shelter, *Gold Tailed Bird*, in 1973 and becoming involved in the burgeoning European tour circuit. In 1977 he and Waters recorded together once more, for Blue Sky, on Waters' *I'm Ready*. Albums in France for Black & Blue during the 1980s and the fine *Ludella* on Antone's which kicked off the 1990s in style have kept Rogers in the public mind. He continues his career today.

**SEE ALSO:** Muddy Waters, Robert Jr Lockwood, Sunnyland Slim, Walter Davis, Roosevelt Sykes, Memphis Minnie

# Roy Rogers

Not the cowboy,
the blues
performer – Roy
Rogers enjoys
commercial
success without
sacrificing the
music

Californian slide guitarist Rogers has been one of the success stories of the last couple of decades, both with his own band the Delta Rhythm Kings and in his producing the latter-day recordings of John Lee Hooker, including the worldwide bestsellers *Mr Lucky* and *The Healer.*

Rogers was born in Redding, California, and grew up listening to and playing in various San Francisco-based blues and roots bands, his first being a high school band which he joined at the age of 13. His mature slide guitar playing, reflecting the influence of people such as Robert Nighthawk and Earl Hooker among others, nicely observed the traditions of the style, its easy fluidity allowing him to fit it into a variety of blues contexts. In the mid-1970s he joined up with the harpist David Bergin and cut a record as a duo, "A Foot In The Door," which did good business. In 1979

Rogers co-founded the Delta Rhythm Kings, a trio he continues to run, alongside his other projects. By 1982 he was part of John Lee Hooker's Coast to Coast Boogie Band, staying with the veteran four years until he released his own (self-financed) album, later released on Blind Pig, *Chops Not Chaps.* The follow-up album, *Slidewinder*, was also on Blind Pig and featured guest appearances from Hooker and the Crescent City piano star Allen Toussaint. All this activity led to Rogers producing the above two Hooker albums, both of which won a slew of awards on release and made Rogers an in-demand producer.

Rogers made two more albums for Blind Pig before moving on to the resuscitated Liberty label in 1993, producing albums for them which have an eye equally to the blues as well as the popular US markets.

**SEE ALSO:** Robert Nighthawk, Earl Hooker, John Lee Hooker

# Roomful of Blues

**fact file**

FORMED 1965

MUSICAL SELECTION
Roomful of Blues
Dressed Up To Get
Messed Up
Hot Little Mama

this blues group, with its on-going changes in personnel, was the brainchild of Duke Robillard and Al Copley, Roomful of Blues was formed in the late 1960s in Rhode Island and, over the subsequent 30 years, has given the start to a number of influential blues careers as well as providing plenty of good if unoriginal music of its own. Band members have included, apart from Robillard and Copley, Ronnie Earl, Greg Piccolo, Preston Hubbard, Doug James, Fran Christina, and Ron Levy.

Roomful of Blues was formed with the express intent of playing the music of the 1940s and 1950s live in clubs and bars around Rhode Island and neighboring areas, including Boston, and the stylistic brief was wide, incorporating blues, rockabilly, R&B, soul, and Stax-type funk, all done with a North-Eastern sensibility. By the mid-1970s the band was well enough known to begin

fulfilling live dates in the Midwest and Washington, DC, and in 1977 they recorded their debut LP, *Roomful of Blues*. During this and the next decade they appeared on the same stage as names like Count Basie and Lou Rawls, B.B. King, and Fats Domino, and also did double-headers with the Fabulous Thunderbirds. The Thunderbirds' vocalist, Kim Wilson, also appeared as guest singer on some of their gigs and albums, including *Dressed Up To Get Messed Up* (1986), on Varrick. By that time Robillard had left the band to start his own unit, his place taken by Robbie Earl, who was himself to leave in 1988 and lead The Broadcasters. Around the same time Copley took off on solo ventures and Hubbard swapped to the Thunderbirds. Such personnel changes, however, have not altered the basic R&B thrust of the band, who continue to record and play live all over the US, remaining one of the star attractions at concerts and festivals.

**SEE ALSO:** Duke Robillard, B. B. King

# Otis Rush

Otis Rush has always been an influence, becoming a guitarist's guitarist

ush was important, along with Magic Sam, Freddie King, and Buddy Guy, as one of the major spearheads of the West-Side sound in Chicago in the 1950s. A powerful vocalist with a taut, clipped guitar style and sound that conveyed the urgency of his message, Rush had much success on the Cobra label in the 1950s but stagnated at the time in the 1960s when other Chicago talents were making inroads on the new white blues audience.

Born in Philadelphia, Mississippi, Rush learned harmonica and guitar in his youth, incidentally landing himself with the same technique as Albert King, playing a right-handed guitar left-handed and upside down. He arrived in Chicago in 1948, gradually working his way up the pecking order until, in 1956, Willie Dixon helped clinch a deal with the small Cobra label. He had an early hit with one of Dixon's songs, "I Can't Quit You Baby," and had further success with songs later to be covered many times by others. These included "All Your Love," "Three Times a Fool," and "Keep On Loving Me Baby." After the demise of Cobra in 1958 Rush swapped labels a couple of times, but between 1958 and 1965 managed just two released singles, neither of which sold. However, in that year he cut five tracks for the acclaimed Samuel Charters collection on Vanguard, *Chicago/The Blues/Today!* and was introduced to a young audience previously unaware of his existence. This allowed him to join the rock 'n' roll support circuit which established artists like Albert and B.B. King, among others, with this new market, but his luck on the record company side remained unchanged: after a storming 1969 record for Cotillon, *Mourning For The Morning*, proved a sales failure, a disc made for Capitol in 1971, *Right Place, Wrong Time*, went unreleased. Two mid-1970s live albums from Delmark remained all that was new from Rush until 1977, when he made *Lost In The Blues* in Stockholm. Again, poor sales and a general lack of interest derailed Rush's prospects, and at one point in the 1980s he retired from music. He has since made a comeback, playing around Chicago, but has yet to make a new record.

## fact file

**BORN** 1934

**MUSICAL SELECTION**
Right Place,
Wrong Time
Lost In The Blues

**SEE ALSO:** Magic Sam, Freddie King, Buddy Guy, Albert King, Willie Dixon

# Jimmy Rushing

the career of blues shouter Rushing demonstrates just how close the links were between classic and swing jazz and the contemporary blues idiom. Rushing joined up with Walter Page's Blue Devils in Kansas City in the late 1920s and later sang with Bennie Moten's band in the same city. When Moten died and his replacement Count Basie gradually forged an international reputation, Rushing was the band's star male vocalist – singing undiluted blues phrases and melodies across shouting brass and swinging reeds, allied to the smoothest rhythm section in the business. Rushing's direct, ebullient blues phrases earned "Mr. Five-by-Five" a place in the early development of a style in which all big-band blues singers would be molded.

Rushing was born into a musical family in Oklahoma City, Oklahoma, and learned violin and piano as a boy. Enjoying an unusually thorough musical education, he studied theory as well as singing in the local church and amateur opera group. His teenage years proved decisive, however, as he was influenced by the exotic music – and even more exotic lifestyle – of an uncle who played piano in a local whorehouse; it was from him that Rushing learned the blues. Jimmy hit the West Coast in 1921, making his professional debut there as a pianist, but he returned to Oklahoma in 1926 and worked in his father's café. Music wouldn't leave him alone, however, and soon he became a member of Walter Page's Blue Devils, an influential band featuring many players who would later be in Basie's band, including Basie himself. A spell with Bennie Moten evolved into membership in the Count Basie band after Moten's death in 1935. Rushing was from the first an important part of Basie's initial success, as can be seen from the number of sides his vocals are featured on between 1936 and the breakup of the band in 1950. It was during his long partnership with Basie that Rushing's repertoire was decided for keeps, with songs such as "Evenin'," "Sent For You Yesterday," "Good Morning Blues," "Going To Chicago" and many others quickly attaining the status of classics, to be imitated by generations of blues shouters.

Rushing's career after Basie remained very much based on the swing genre, as his 1955 recordings for Vanguard or his 1957 reunion with Basie at that year's Newport Jazz Festival testifies. A contract with Columbia attempted to vary this formula, putting him in both big-band and small-group formats on standards such as "Russian Lullaby" and "My Melancholy Baby," but in concert Rushing stuck with his normal fare. He continued a highly successful career all over the world until 1971, when the effects of cancer took a deep hold. His last record, made in his late sixties for RCA in spring 1971, found him in a small-group swing setting, singing songs from the 1930s; it is one of his greatest performances. Jimmy Rushing died just over a year later.

## fact file

**BORN** 1903

**DIED** 1972

**MUSICAL SELECTION**
"Russian Lullaby"
"My Melancholy Baby"

The not-quite little Little Jimmy Rushing, an outstanding blues singer

SEE ALSO: Helen Humes, Julia Lee, Memphis Slim, Jimmy Witherspoon

# Saffire

**fact file**

**FORMED** 1984

**MUSICAL SELECTION**
Old, New,
Borrowed & Blue
Hot Flash

Saffire, "the Uppity Blues Women," features Gaye Adegbalola (r.), Earline Lewis (l.) and Ann Rabson (c.)

**S**affire, the "Uppity Blues Women" is a group made up of Gaye Adegbalola (Pitchford) (b. 1944), Earlene Lewis (b. 1945), and Ann Rabson (b. 1945), which came together in 1984 when Adegbalola and Rabson formed a duo for part-time work utilizing a wide variety of repertoire, spoken as well as played. That same year, Lewis joined on bass and the group began making an impact at a variety of women's festivals, clubs, and blues festivals. Their act included both originals and their own arrangements of classic material from the World War I and 1920s period, often happily mixing sexual metaphors with lyrics about work and observations of everyday situations. This freewheeling approach has been a major factor in their quick popularity.

All three women had been involved in music at an early age: Adegbalola concentrated on guitar and harmonica after moving from her birth state of Virginia to New York in the 1970s; Rabson, from New York City but raised in the Midwest, began on guitar before picking up piano in her thirties; Lewis made her start on

guitar as well, picking up a wide range of interests, from bluegrass to blues, during an early life spent between her birth state of California and Oklahoma, where her family had a little farm. She made the swap to double bass in her thirties, playing part-time in bluegrass groups. All three women relocated to Fredericksburg, Virginia, in the 1970s, keeping up demanding day-job careers and, after Saffire was formed, taking on the increasing workload of night-time performances. Something had to give and, in 1988, the group went full-time, finding quite quickly that there was certainly sufficient demand from the public for their special mix of classic blues and rag styles. In 1990 the group made their eponymous debut album for Alligator, a record that quickly became a blues bestseller, and a regular supply of new discs have kept the group's profile high. One of their latest, *Old, New, Borrowed, & Blue* (1994), keeps the mix much as before, though the stylistic net is cast somewhat wider as each member of the group continues to explore her individual heritage.

**SEE ALSO:** Angela Strehli

# Magic Sam

fact file

**BORN** 1937

**DIED** 1969

**MUSICAL SELECTION**
West Side Soul

Magic Sam,
nephew of
Shakey Jake,
found his feet
after a few
awkward steps,
only to die
unexpectedly
young

agic Sam, along with Otis Rush, Buddy Guy, and Freddie King, was the originator of the important West Side Chicago blues sound of the late 1950s – that second wave of Chicago-based musicians who helped bridge the gap between the older styles of blues and the disciplined, soul-influenced genre which attracted so many younger fans to the music in the next decade.

Sam Maghett was born on a sharecropper's farm near Grenada, Mississippi, putting him close to many other bluesmen in the Mississippi Delta region. He showed an interest in the blues from a very early age, making his first guitar himself, and when his family relocated to Chicago in 1950, Sam quickly reached a level of proficiency which allowed him to sit in with bands at local bars and joints. He was befriended by older players such as Shakey Jake and Homesick James, and by the mid-1950s was running his own band in the West Side venues. By 1957 he had attracted sufficient attention to be signed by Cobra, for whom he recorded a series of fiery singles, including "All Your Love" and "Easy Baby." An unwanted call to the Army in 1959 arrested his

career in more ways than one – he deserted, making a session for Chief records before being caught and landing a military jail sentence. A dishonorable discharge in 1961 allowed him to resume his career, becoming one of the major Chicago blues attractions through the 1960s. His move to Delmark in 1964 also heralded a move to LPs rather than singles, and the Chicago label debuted him with a live set at Club Alex.

His classic studio album, *West Side Soul*, was cut in 1967 and confirmed his place as one of Chicago's premier singer/guitarists, his flowing style of playing complementing his soul-influenced vocals to perfection. Following rave reviews from magazines and endorsements from blues-loving rock stars, Sam's fan base spread beyond the clubs of Chicago; he appeared at rock venues such as Fillmore West and at the 1969 Ann Arbour Blues Festival, where it is generally agreed he was the hit of the festival. This led to a call to appear at London's Albert Hall in October of that year. Unfortunately, Magic Sam had no chance to follow up on the explosion of interest in him; he died of a heart attack in December 1969.

**SEE ALSO:** Otis Rush, Buddy Guy, Freddie King, Shakey Jake, Homesick James

# Frank "Son" Seals

**S**eals, born in Osceola, Arkansas, long ago established himself as a premier guitarist on the Chicago scene after packing them in at the Chez Paris club in Little Rock, Arkansas. His slashing guitar sounds and his fiercely energetic, gruff vocals have made him a favorite of the crowds in clubs and at festivals across the US, though his reputation has never been as big in Europe as those of some of his contemporaries.

Seals came into contact with music virtually from day one of his life. He was the son of a juke joint owner, and the family lived on the premises. Watching the blues greats perform (and bumming the occasional lesson from the more generous ones, like Albert King), Seals formed his own band in the late 1950s and became a Little Rock favorite before going out on the road with Earl Hooker in the late 1960s, also doing some time behind the drum kit with Albert King. By 1971 he'd decided to move to Chicago, where he joined up with Hound Dog Taylor and jammed with big names such as Junior Wells and James Cotton. He also landed a regular spot at the Expressway Lounge, on the south side. From there he progressed to Queen Bee's and signed a deal with Alligator records, releasing his first LP, *The Son Seals band*, in 1973. His second for the label, *Midnight Son*, brought him a broader-based audience and established him as one of the outstanding blues guitarists of the time: it also put him on the road, playing many one-nighters as well as holding down his Chicago residencies. Seals has continued to promote his career assiduously, continuing to record up to the present day, his *Living In The Danger Zone* from 1991 showing the fires to be burning as bright as ever.

**fact file**

**BORN** 1942

**MUSICAL SELECTION**
The Son Seals Band
Midnight Son

As one of 13 children, it is no great surprise that Son Seals had to teach himself guitar

**SEE ALSO:** Albert King, Earl Hooker, Albert King, Junior Wells, James Cotton

# Alec Seward

**Alec Seward was fortunate enough to bring himself to New York in the 1920s, where he met Sonny Terry and Brownie McGhee**

## fact file

**BORN** 1902

**DIED** 1972

**MUSICAL SELECTION**
Creepin' Blues

S eward's story is that of many other country blues singers and guitarists. Known to the greater blues community as a fine performer and an honest, well-intentioned man, Seward played for many years in a great many circumstances, rarely for money and mostly so that people in his immediate community could have some fun.

Born in Virginia and raised in farming country, Seward worked in his youth in a succession of day jobs and played guitar for his own amusement. Developing a style very much indebted to the Delta tradition, Seward picked up a repertoire using much of the classic material of his youth, including songs such as "See See Rider," "Piney Woods," and "Trouble In Mind." He also evolved his own songs referring to his own experience. Unnoticed by the recording community, he moved to New York in the

postwar period and became friendly with the group of blues and folk musicians loosely based around Sonny Terry – indeed, Terry became a lifelong friend. Seward went unrecorded and making a living outside music all his career, but did cut one album, *Creepin' Blues* in 1962, for Prestige/Bluesville. It featured his strong guitar playing and vocals and the Terry-influenced harmonica playing of Larry Johnson. Four years later an apartment session with Terry, Brownie McGhee, and others was taped by friends: decades later it was released on Blues Alliance and demonstrates a typical evening session among Seward and his friends, reflecting the informal atmosphere preferred by Seward and in which McGhee and Terry were rarely recorded. Seward remained outside of the music business but often performed acts of kindness for friends, including Terry, to whom he was an occasional informal chauffeur.

**SEE ALSO:** Sonny Terry, Brownie McGhee

# Shakey Jake

"Shake 'em Jake!" — from the gambler's cry to the bluesman's moniker, the one and only Shakey Jake

armonica man Shakey Jake had as colorful a career as any of his contemporaries, combining like many others the professions of musician, cardsharp, gambler, and conman. Born in Earle, Arkansas, he moved as a small boy to Chicago in 1928, from then on spending much time on the road between his former home of Earle and other points south. Early on in life he decided to enjoy music rather than rely on it for a living, and concentrated most of his professional efforts on gambling – hence the nickname, a corruption of the cry at a crap game of "shake 'em, Jake."

Jake moved easily in the blues circles of postwar Chicago, forming his own band in 1952 and playing the West Side, eventually giving his nephew, Sam Maghett (later Magic Sam), his first steady work as a musician. Willie Dixon got him recorded in 1958 by the tiny Artistic

label and "Call Me (If You Need Me)" became a classic West-Side cut. The single featured Freddie King and Magic Sam, among others. However, Jake was a realist and, by the early 1960s and after a couple of disappointing records for Bluesville, he was prepared to put his music career on the back burner in order to manage Magic Sam. This he did adroitly for the rest of Sam's life, as well as making two albums in the mid-1960s for World Pacific which featured Sunnyland Slim and John Mayall, among others. By this time he had long been established on the West Coast, making LA his base and nurturing the embryonic careers of West Coasters like Hollywood Fats, Smokey Wilson and Rod Piazza. He even started his own record label, Good Times, which lasted a decade until ill-health and lethargy killed it off. In 1989 he left LA, dying of cancer in Arkansas, in March 1990.

## fact file

**BORN** 1921

**DIED** 1990

**MUSICAL SELECTION**
"Call Me (If You Need Me)"

**SEE ALSO:** Magic Sam, Willie Dixon, Freddie King, Sunnyland Slim, John Mayall

# Eddie Shaw

fact file

BORN 1937

MUSICAL SELECTION
Have Blues, Will Travel
In the Land of the
Crossroads

Working with
Muddy Waters,
Howlin' Wolf,
and Ike Turner,
Eddie Shaw's
fondness for
the blues is
understandable

In a postwar blues scene that has been largely dominated by the guitar and harmonica, Eddie Shaw is one of the few saxophone-playing bluesmen to make a significant impact. He's achieved this largely through his work as a sideman with such blues giants as Howlin' Wolf, Muddy Waters, and Magic Sam.

Born in Stringtown, in Bolivar County, Mississippi, the infant Shaw and his family moved to Greenville, where Eddie eventually learned a number of wind instruments – including the saxophone – at Coleman High School. After school he played at a number of joints and small venues with different local musicians, finally sitting in with Muddy Waters during the latter's visit to Itta Bena in 1957. Waters, impressed with Shaw's blues prowess, took him back to Chicago with him. Shaw did not become a permanent Waters fixture, however, and moved among a range of top

Chicago blues outfits, including those of Otis Rush and, most consistently, Howlin' Wolf. Shaw became increasingly part of Wolf's permanent working group, finally leading the Wolf Gang from 1972 until his boss's death in 1976. In the meantime he had taken over an old Chicago club and refurbished it, calling it Eddie's Place. After Wolf's death he cut an album with his old band, entitled *Have Blues, Will Travel*. Shaw's tours with Wolf had given him a strong following in Europe, especially in France, and he made a number of albums while there on tour over the next decade.

Still among the most influential saxmen playing the blues, Eddie Shaw continues to tour, record, and work with other leaders, mostly around Chicago or in Europe. His most recent album, *In the Land of the Crossroads*, was released by Rooster Blues in 1996.

**SEE ALSO:** Howlin' Wolf, Muddy Waters, Magic Sam, Otis Rush

# Bumble Bee Slim

## fact file

**BORN** 1905

**DIED** 1968

**MUSICAL SELECTION**
"B and O Blues"
"New B and O Blues"

Bumble Bee Slim (c.) sang songs for entertainment, not confessions or lamentation

S lim, aka Amos Easton, was part of the popular 1930s Chicago blues style whereby a stark personalized confession of anguish and loss such as often concerned the country-blues recording artist of the 1920s was replaced by a desire to make the audience forget their own circumstances for the three minutes' duration of the 78rpm record. As such he proved successful, for he was one of the most prolific and popular blues recording artists of the 1930s.

Easton was born in Brunswick, Georgia, and learned to sing and play guitar while a youth. He was never much as a guitarist, as his own records show, where his own work, if present at all, is usually inaudible behind that of his partner on any given recording date. Easton traveled extensively as a young man over an eight-year period, finally landing in Indianapolis at the back end of the 1920s.

He played the usual house-rent parties and other social occasions for what money he could drum up, then finally pushed on to Chicago at the onset of the Depression. By October 1931 he was recording for Paramount, moving the following year to

Vocalion, but did not hit his recording stride until 1934, when he recorded for no fewer than four different record companies – Vocalion, Bluebird, Decca, and ARC. By this time his "B and O Blues" of 1932 had been a substantial hit and he was even making "New B and O Blues" for the same label. His accompaniment changed from date to date, and included Thomas A. Dorsey, Big Bill Broonzy, Charlie Jackson, Washboard Sam, and Scrapper Blackwell. In 1935 alone he recorded over 60 titles. Activity was just as intense in 1936, but by 1937 the flow was arrested: just 20 tunes were cut, of which eight went unissued, including the whole of his last prewar session, in June 1937.

Easton, now universally known as Bumble Bee Slim, left Chicago and returned south, resurfacing in 1951 in LA on a session for Speciality featuring a number of jazz and R&B musicians. His last released session featured him, in 1962, recording with, variously, Les McCann, Leroy Vinnegar, and Teddy Edwards for Pacific Jazz, a session couched in Charles Brown's sophisticated blues patterns and somewhat at odds with the rest of his career. He died in Los Angeles six years later.

**SEE ALSO:** Thomas A. Dorsey, Big Bill Broonzy, Charlie Jackson, Washboard Sam, Scrapper Blackwell

# Johnny Shines

born just outside Memphis, Tennessee, Shines was of the same generation as Robert Johnson, and indeed spent time travelling through the northern US and, on one occasion, Canada with Johnson in the 1930s. This one fact tended to monopolize the interest of fans and historians when Shines was interviewed and he became increasingly reluctant to repeat the same Johnson anecdotes as time went on. Shines' style during the 1930s was a direct extension of the Johnson Delta tradition and like most of his peers he made his living playing jukes and clubs. In his case, the Memphis area was his base until 1941, when he cut out for Chicago in the hope of upgrading his career a few notches. About this time he had entertained thoughts of packing up and going to Africa, but Chicago proved the greater attraction and the more attainable goal. During his years in the South Shines met a string of young bluesmen who he would see again later in Chicago – including Howlin' Wolf (on whose guitar he learned to play in open tuning) and Walter Horton, a man who was often his partner in Memphis and was to be a lifelong friend.

Shines established himself on the Chicago scene during the war years, making his debut on Okeh in 1946 with Big Bill Broonzy helping out, although the sides weren't released until the LP era. A 1950 single for Chess featured Little Walter and Jimmy Rogers, but neither this nor a 1953 session for JOB – which features a track, "Ramblin," performed in a style almost exactly like Johnson's – sold well enough for Shines to be secure in his career at a time when the electrified urban blues style was dominant. After a number of years during which he had quit professional music altogether, Shines did not enter a recording studio again until 1965. He then appeared with his band featuring Walter Horton on the famous Vanguard series *Chicago/The Blues/Today!* The impact of this re-emergence gave him the impetus to record for a string of labels during the late 1960s, and to begin appearing at blues and folk festivals. He took the opportunity to leave Chicago and move to Arkansas, but most of his time was spent on the road in the US and abroad. A stroke in 1980 forced Shines to slow down, and he used the spare time to take courses in furniture refurbishing and car bodywork, among other pursuits. But music remained a key part of his life, and although he lost some manual dexterity as his condition worsened, Johnny Shines continued working and recording up to his death.

## fact file

**BORN** 1915

**DIED** 1992

**MUSICAL SELECTION**
Chicago/The
Blues/Today!

Johnny Shines was considered an articulate, intelligent man who recognized his own importance in the blues pantheon

SEE ALSO: Robert Johnson, Howlin' Wolf, Walter Horton

# Magic Slim

**fact file**

**BORN** 1937

**MUSICAL SELECTION**
Raw Magic
Son of a Gun

While living in Chicago during the 1950s, Magic Slim had the pleasure of working with Magic Sam

S lim was born in Grenada, Mississippi, and originally learned the piano. Switching to guitar and deciding to try his luck as a full-time musician, he moved to Chicago at the age of eighteen, in 1955. On his arrival he found the competitive Chicago scene hard to crack, for a while playing bass with Magic Sam, who bestowed upon him the nickname he plays under to this day. However, Slim felt he still had a way to go in his chosen field, and after a period with Robert Perkins' band, he returned to Mississippi, where he put together his own outfit, using people he could trust and whom he was certain respected his playing.

By 1965 Slim felt ready to try Chicago again, this time with his own band, The Teardrops in tow, he landed a residency at the 1125 Club. Slim by this time had created a guitar style which, although recognizably an amalgam of many noted Chicago players including Magic Sam, Muddy Waters and Otis Rush, was hard-driving and exciting enough for live audiences to begin rewarding him with a following. By the time of Magic Sam's death in 1969, Slim was established in the city; in the 1970s, when Slim had Junior Pettis in his band, his reputation began to take on wider foundations. Small independent labels began to make albums with his band, and Slim's loyal following kept him constantly in work and selling records throughout the 1980s and on. Today, Slim continues to play Chicago and beyond with his band, the Teardrops, and make new albums on labels like Blind Pig and Alligator.

**SEE ALSO:** Robert Perkins, Magic Sam, Muddy Waters, Otis Rush

# Memphis Slim

**fact file**

**BORN** 1915

**DIED** 1988

**MUSICAL SELECTION**
"Every Day I Have The
Blues"
"Kansas City"
"Memphis Boogie"

"Every Day I
Have The Blues"
made Memphis
Slim a household
name among both
jazz and blues
fans alike

memphis Slim was an influential and important blues piano stylist who was also a gifted singer and songwriter. Born in Memphis, Tennessee, he was one of the major inheritors of the barrelhouse and boogie tradition of piano playing, other exponents of which included Speckled Red, Cow Cow Davenport, and Jimmy Yancey. Slim's importance came in how he updated this tradition – originally learning the trade through imitating people such as the above and Roosevelt Sykes, and later through developing his own expansive, relaxed style, and combining it with an increasingly smooth, cultivated, but often spicily knowing vocal style. This again evolved from an initial copying of shouters such as Jimmy Rushing, relying on his own innate rhythmic sophistication.

Slim taught himself piano while hanging out in various clubs and bars on Beale Street in Memphis. Then around 1931 he began the life of an itinerant musician throughout the South before winding up in Chicago in 1939, where he soon entered into an association with Big Bill Broonzy; by 1940 he was Big Bill's accompanist, learning a great deal from seeing the great man entertain his audiences night after night. By the time he left Broonzy in 1946, Slim had developed his mature piano and vocal style, and was ready to lead his own band. This was Memphis Slim and his House Rockers, a variable aggregation which could one night be a trio, the next a sextet with sax and guitars. Mainstays of this band included saxophonist Edward Cotton and drummer Leon Hooper, both Memphis men. It was this band that recorded Slim's greatest single success, "Every Day I Have The Blues," although it was Joe Williams and Count Basie who would have the worldwide hit with it a handful of years later. Slim continued to run the House Rockers in various guises and with shifting personnel through most of the 1950s (though the name was dropped in 1951), regularly recording with rocking barrelhouse-type bands of his own. The 1958-59 Vee Jay sessions, heavily featuring both guitar and sax, are typical of this type of output.

Things shifted as the decade ended, however, for Slim became aware of the burgeoning folk-blues movement. A period as a duo with Willie Dixon, which included a long European tour in 1960 and a whole series of albums for various labels in 1959-60, convinced him that the change that was in the air could be profitable for him. Apart from two visits to New York in 1961, Slim spent most of the next couple of years exploring Europe and becoming established there as a major blues star. In 1962 he made the move permanent, Paris being his city of choice.

**SEE ALSO:** Speckled Red, Roosevelt Sykes, Jimmy Rushing, Big Bill Broonzy, Joe Williams, Willie Dixon

# Sunnyland Slim

**fact file**

**BORN** 1907

**DIED** 1995

**MUSICAL SELECTION**
"Johnson Machine Gun"

Sunnyland Slim brought the Delta with him to Chicago making him instrumental in helping establish the city's blues sound

P ianist Sunnyland Slim's long career has seen him playing the blues professionally for close on 70 years, performing all over the world and recording hundreds of sides for scores of labels. For most of his career Slim worked in the bands of or in the company of other blues greats, from Tampa Red to J.B. Hutto and Johnny Shines, and he has actively fostered the preservation of blues traditions through his passing on of his knowledge to younger musicians and his fostering of a multitude of blues careers.

Slim was born in Vance, Mississippi, and came to the piano early, learning the rough-hewn country-blues piano style from early and obscure Delta stylists. Playing in jukes and elsewhere, he also became a powerful vocalist and by the time he moved to Memphis in the mid-1920s he was also writing his own blues pieces. Moving to Chicago around 1942, Slim joined up with the crowd around Tampa Red, rehearsing at Red's house for the recording sessions Red was involved in for Victor and Columbia under the auspices of Lester Melrose. He also befriended Muddy Waters when he first arrived in Chicago, appearing on Waters' 1947 single for Aristocrat (later Chess), "Johnson Machine Gun."

While Slim was making waves with Waters at Chess, his hanging out with Tampa Red and Melrose gave rise to Melrose commissioning him to record eight sides for Victor in 1947 with Big Bill Broonzy and Blind John Davis under the pseudonym "Doctor Clayton's Buddy." These and his classic sides with Waters, which included "I Can't Be Satisfied," made Slim an in-demand musician for the duration of the 1950s and 1960s, and many great blues sides were cut for a plethora of labels and with a wide range of musicians, including Snooky Pryor, Robert Jr Lockwood, Walter Horton, Jimmy Rogers, Willie Dixon, Little Brother Montgomery, King Curtis, and Homesick James. Sixties sessions of note include ones with Mike Bloomfield and (separately) Buddy Guy in 1964 and the famous mid-1960s sessions for Delmark with J.B. Hutto.

Slim sustained his career right through the 1970s, running his own record label and touring Europe on a regular basis as well as making regular tours of the US. He continued to nurture younger players right to the end of his career and became one of the most respected and honored of bluesmen by his own peers. He worked right up to his death, from old age, in 1995.

**SEE ALSO:** Tampa Red, J. B. Hutto, Johnny Shines, Lester Melrose, Muddy Waters, Snooky Pryor, Robert Jr Lockwood

# Byther Smith

**fact file**

**BORN** 1933

**MUSICAL SELECTION**
Tell Me How You
Like It
Housefire

Thoroughly
versed in the
Chicago blues
scene, Byther
Smith represents
the truly modern
blues musician

**S**omething of a late arrival on the scene, Smith, a cousin of J.B. Lenoir, spent close to a quarter-century in Chicago before gaining enough attention to land his first recording date as a leader. His style, rooted in the Southern blues surrounding him as he grew up, is typically laden with West-Side Chicago characteristics grafted on by years of work in and around that blues capital over the past 40 years.

Smith was born in Monticello, Mississippi, and was introduced to music, as so many were at that time, by the church. By the time he hit Chicago in 1958, Smith was already proficient on harmonica and could also make out on bass and drums as well as being a singer. He took private tuition from Lenoir and others, including Hubert Sumlin and Robert Jr Lockwood, and began playing in the Chicago clubs in the early 1960s, playing in many backing bands and at various sessions, 1961–62, for tiny Chicago

labels. Unable to make real headway, Smith quit professional music before the 1960s had ended, but returned around five years later to take up residence as the house guitarist at Teresa's Lounge. He seemed set for the life of a blues journeyman, making the occasional single and continuing to play support to others, until he made an LP for Grits, *Tell Me How You Like It*, in 1985. This revealed his full talents for the first time and gave Smith an instant international profile, allowing him to tour beyond the USA for the first time (he cut an album for JSP while on one of his tours).

Smith's second album, *Housefire*, was initially released in 1987 and reissued in 1991 by Rounder: this again made the blues world sit up and listen, both to his stirring vocals and his stinging guitar work. Smith continues to record and perform from his base in Chicago, to the delight of blues fans.

**SEE ALSO:** J. B. Lenior, Hubert Sumlin, Robert Jr Lockwood

# Bessie Smith

b essie Smith was without a doubt the greatest and most influential singer to emerge from the blues idiom of the 1920s. Her striking voice, charismatic personality and creative ability were unmatched; although she tended to favor a particularly slow pace for her vocal delivery, the nuances of her singing were so varied as to make each recording a treasure. She performed with many of the greatest jazz musicians of her age and has influenced every female blues and blues-related artist since. Her great career, however, was not immune to changes in economics and fashion, taking a severe downturn during the Depression, with her reputation suffering decades of neglect after her early death. However, since the advent of LPs in the 1950s and the trailblazing biography by Chris Albertson some fifteen years later, Bessie Smith's position has become unassailable, her reputation secure.

Smith was born in Chattanooga, Tennessee, part of a large family. Her parents died when Bessie was small and she was raised by her sisters. In 1912 she followed her brother Clarence into a traveling show run by Moses Stokes (the show featured Ma and Pa Rainey), principally as a dancer, and she gained enough experience there to progress to other shows touring the black vaudeville circuit. A stint in 1913 at the 81 Theater in Atlanta gave her the chance to display her vocal prowess, as well as develop a lifestyle – loose-living, passionate, fed by alcohol and the thrill of performing – which would change little over the next couple of decades. By the close of World War I, Smith was a major star on the TOBA (Theater Owners Booking Association) circuit, and around 1921 she moved to Philadelphia, then to the Paradise Gardens in New Jersey in 1922. By this time the blues craze had spread like wildfire after Mamie Smith's "Crazy Blues" had been released in 1920. Yet Bessie found it difficult to land a recording deal, being perceived as a singer whose style was too unsophisticated – not sufficiently "vaudeville" – for the supposed "race" market. At last she was signed by Okeh, debuting in 1923 with "Down Hearted Blues." This was an immediate and immense hit, selling over 780,000 copies in six months. Bessie married Jack Gee in June 1923, and the pattern of her successful years was set: hard work on the circuit, recording, and domestic fireworks.

Over the next seven years Smith made over 150 classic sides, many of them accompanied by jazz greats such as Fletcher Henderson. Louis Armstrong and Don Redman. She covered an unusually wide range of subject matter, from "Back Water Blues" (later recorded by Dinah Washington) and "Cemetery Blues" to "House Rent Blues," and standards like "Ain't Nobody's Business," "Alexander's Ragtime Band" and "Mean Old Bedbug Blues." Her sweeping, vibrant delivery would get to the essence of anyone s lyric, transforming it into a personal testimony. In 1929 she was the star of a short feature film, *St Louis Blues*, which climaxes with her singing W.C. Handy's song accompanied by jazz band and chorus. Not long before the stock market crash, in 1929, Smith recorded one of her greatest classics, "Nobody Knows You When You're Down and Out." That title was to be prophetic, for in the face of falling sales and the economic crises brought on by the Depression, Smith was dropped from the Columbia roster in 1931, her last session for the label producing "Need A Little Sugar In My Bowl."

## fact file

**BORN** 1894

**DIED** 1937

**MUSICAL SELECTION**
"Nobody Knows You When You're Down and Out"

Bessie Smith picked up the blues torch from Ma Rainey to become one of the music's most impressive blues performers

SEE ALSO: Ma Rainey, Mamie Smith, Fletcher Henderson, W. C. Handy

# Clara Smith

Clara Smith, of the Clara Smith Theatrical Club, crossed the boundaries of both jazz and blues while performing in Harlem

## fact file

BORN 1894

DIED 1935

MUSICAL SELECTION
"Every Woman's Blues"
"So Long Jim"

Clara Smith is not to be confused with Laura or Bessie or Trixie, all of whom began their blues career on records within two years of each other, or Mamie, who made the first so-called "blues" record in January 1920 but who was much more a vaudeville singer who occasionally paid lip service to the blues fashion. Clara Smith made her debut in New York for Columbia just months after Bessie Smith and even shared the microphone with Bessie for Columbia on occasion. Her slow-drag, despondent blues numbers, usually accompanied by jazz musicians such as Fletcher Henderson, fit in with the general approach of the "classic" female blues singer of this time.

Smith was born in Spartanburg, South Carolina, and went into the traveling shows, serving the usual apprenticeship on constant tours through the South. She came to New York at the beginning of the 1920s and became an established act at the Harlem clubs, to the point where she was able to open her own, the Clara Smith Theatrical Club, in 1924. By then she was a recording artist, having released her first sides on Columbia in summer 1923, "I've Got Everything A Woman Needs" and "Every Woman's Blues." Smith's specialty, apart from the dirges she made out of "Every Woman's Blues" and other such material, were risqué songs and her own idiosyncratic versions of the popular songs of the day. Smith recorded right through the 1920s and into the 1930s, managing to outlast Bessie Smith at Columbia by five months, into the spring of 1932: her last session featured her versions of "Fattenin' Frogs For Snakes" and "So Long Jim." During her days at Columbia she had recorded with musicians such as Louis Armstrong, Clarence Williams, Lonnie Johnson, Porter Grainger, Charlie Green, Coleman Hawkins, and Don Redman. Her record career over, Smith's live work continued, both in New York and on tour.

SEE ALSO: Laura Smith, Bessie Smith, Trixie Smith, Mamie Smith

# George "Harmonica" Smith

George Smith may have been nicknamed "Harmonica" but his impressive playing did not always earn him the praise he deserved

**S**mith managed to make a decisive impact in both Chicago and on the West Coast at different times in his career, his inspired blues harp providing the backing at various times for talents as large as Otis Rush, Big Mama Thornton, and Muddy Waters. Smith formed his style before arriving in Chicago, but he has since become identified with the players who followed in the wake of the great Little Walter.

Though born in Arkansas, Smith was raised by his musically-minded mother in Cairo, a river town in the southernmost corner of Illinois. With his mother's help he learned a range of instruments in boyhood, playing them on street corners before he was 13. During the rest of the 1930s he earned money on various Federal work projects, but by 1941 he had joined a full-time professional group. This lasted for two years before Smith joined the Jackson Jubilee Singers, moving with them to Mississippi. Once there he experimented with amplified harmonica playing,

and by the time he hit Chicago in 1951 he was ready to take on any challenge. The first came in the form of working with Otis Rush; later, it was a short stint with Muddy Waters (he was replaced by James Cotton). Finding himself in Kansas City in 1955, Smith became involved with the RPM label and cut his first singles. Response to these records was good in LA, and before long Smith moved to the West Coast.

For the next decade he split his time between Southern California and Chicago, making records and playing gigs in both places. A couple of excellent albums for World Pacific in 1968, featuring Muddy Waters and Otis Spann, present Smith at his best.

As the 1960s faded into the 1970s, he decided to stick in LA, often playing in Big Mama Thornton's band and also joining Rod Piazza's outfit, Bacon Fat. Harmonica Smith's career stayed relatively buoyant up to the time of his death in 1983.

## fact file

**BORN** 1924

**DIED** 1983

**MUSICAL SELECTION**
Blowin' In The Wind
Harmonica Ace

**SEE ALSO:** Otis Rush, Big Mama Thornton, Muddy Waters, James Cotton, Otis Spann, Rod Piazza

# Trixie Smith

## fact file

**BORN** 1895

**DIED** 1943

**MUSICAL SELECTION**
"Ride Jockey Ride"
"Everybody Loves
My Baby"

**Trixie Smith was erudite and a polished blues performer with a university education**

trixie Smith was a member of the first wave of classic blues-singing Smiths, first felt in the early 1920s, and though she faded from the recording scene in the mid-1920s, she re-appeared in 1938 to record a set of excellent blues numbers with some of the top classic jazzmen of the day, including Sidney Bechet, Charlie Shavers, and Sammy Price. Smith's voice was distinctive and quite different from her namesakes, being considerably higher and lighter in tone and timbre. This, plus her unquestionable powers of interpretation, made her recordings memorable. A thorough professional and a highly intelligent woman, her performances were a mixture of showbiz glitz and striking singing.

Smith was born in Atlanta, Georgia. Little is known of her early life, but it must have included disciplined study, as she attended Selma University before becoming involved in the music and theater business and taking off for New York in 1915. She joined the TOBA circuit around the close of the Great War and built up

a name for herself in theaters and clubs in and around New York. She was a logical choice for Black Swan in January 1922, the early days of blues recordings. Smith stayed with Black Swan until its demise the following year. Switching to Paramount, Smith embarked on some fine blues recordings with a selection of early jazz greats, including Fletcher Henderson, Miff Mole, Louis Armstrong, Charlie Green, Buster Bailey, Jimmy Blythe, and others. Her outstanding sides include "Ride Jockey Ride," "Everybody Loves My Baby" and "Railroad Blues," the latter featuring Armstrong, Henderson, and Green. The emphasis in Smith's career shifted after 1926 to cabaret and revue performances, and it was not until 1938 that she returned to the studios, to cut the sessions mentioned at the top of this entry, incorporating a more swing-oriented rhythmic approach. The following year she made a single title for Decca, accompanied by Henry "Red" Allen and Barney Bigard. Smith continued to perform until her early death in 1943.

**SEE ALSO:** Bessie Smith

# Otis Spann

**fact file**

**BORN** 1930

**DIED** 1970

**MUSICAL SELECTION**
Otis Spann Is The Blues

Otis Spann, one
of the blues
most well-
rounded and
prolifically
recorded artists

k nown internationally as the pianist in Muddy Waters' classic Chicago band, Spann also latterly enjoyed a reputation as a pianist and singer in his own right, combining a vigorous two-handed piano style reminiscent of men like Memphis Slim, Roosevelt Sykes, and Big Maceo with a surprisingly light, though rich, sensitive voice. Spann also exhibited a considerable talent for writing blues tunes.

Yet another bluesman from Jackson, Mississippi, Spann was born in to a musical family – his mother was a guitarist and his father a pianist in the blues styles of the day. Young Otis learned piano by ear and by watching his father play, teaching himself all he needed to know to make a start at the blues. A local pianist by the name of Cose Davis helped him with phrasing and certain blues licks. Soon Spann was playing wherever he could get an audience, and by the time he was 14 he was a member of a local blues band playing dances and other locations. At the age of 17 he moved to Chicago and began establishing himself with the blues community, playing in a variety of settings. The event that changed the course of his life took place in 1953, when he joined the headlining Muddy Waters and his band, becoming a fixture in the group, with the occasional sabbatical, until his death. His busy but always sympathetic accompanying gave the Waters band a new dimension and spurred Waters to greater heights.

Spann seemed destined to a life in the background until his appearance with the Muddy Waters Band at the 1960 Newport Jazz Festival, where he sang a blues with words by the poet Langston Hughes. This performance led to the sessions that resulted in the classic Candid album, *Otis Spann Is The Blues*, featuring duets with his old friend, the guitarist/singer Robert Jr Lockwood. This album, plus the increasing presence of the Waters entourage in Europe, alerted blues fans to Spann's individual singing and piano playing, and he became a star in his own right, leading a number of sessions (including one from 1964 featuring James Cotton and Muddy Waters, the latter billed as "Dirty Rivers") right through the 1960s. In 1969 he made an album in New York with Fleetwood Mac and was widely recognized as the premier living Chicago piano bluesman. In spring the following year he succumbed to cancer.

**SEE ALSO:** Muddy Waters, Memphis Slim, Roosevelt Sykes, Big Maceo, Robert Jr Lockwood

# Speckled Red

## fact file

**BORN** 1892

**DIED** 1973

**MUSICAL SELECTION**
"The Dirty Dozens"
"The Dirty Dozens
No. 2"

The tough,
raw style of
Speckled Red
endeared him to
fans worldwide

**b**orn in Monroe, Louisiana, Rufus Perryman was raised in Hampton, Georgia, where his family had moved during his boyhood; still later, the family relocated to Atlanta. By this time Rufus, a black albino, had learned basic keyboard techniques and was equally adept on the local church organ as he was on piano: his listening at this stage included his own father, who performed under the name Fishtail. When the family moved once more to Detroit around 1917–18, the teenaged Red began hanging out in joints and bars and hearing a lot of pianists, including James Hemingway and Paul Seminole, and his mature style contains as much Detroit boogie as it does Atlanta.

Red prospered on the juke and party circuit in Detroit, his energetic and straightforward piano style complemented by his pleasing blues voice; he left Detroit in 1929 to go wandering around the US, insured against the vagaries of the road by a tidy sum of money. While in Memphis he was introduced to Jim Jackson, the local Brunswick talent scout, and Red cut his first sides in September, including the classic "The Dirty Dozens," which became a fast-selling item. The following spring he made

"The Dirty Dozens No. 2" and even, at the same session, "The Dirty Dozens, No. 3," the latter remaining unissued as No. 2 failed to repeat the original's success. Red disappeared once more, resurfacing for a 1938 Bluebird date with Robert Lee McCoy, with Sonny Boy Williamson appearing on one track, but his star had faded: he returned to St Louis, where he combined laboring work with scuffling for low-paid jobs playing in bars and joints. He was rediscovered in 1954 by an amateur enthusiast, Charlie O'Brien, and was reintroduced to the music community, this time playing piano in traditional jazz groups. Delmark recorded him in St Louis in 1956, where he played and sang in his original style, but other recordings from the 1950s remain unissued: the next glimpse of him comes from England and Copenhagen in 1960, where he is once again solo, though he had appeared in Britain in 1959 with Chris Barber.

Speckled Red, being an old-style barrelhouse player, raised no great enthusiasm among the guitar-obsessed young blues fans of the 1960s, and he once again passed from view, dying in 1973 after a number of years in retirement.

**SEE ALSO:** Sonny Boy Williamson

# Victoria Spivey

fact file

**BORN** 1906

**DIED** 1976

**MUSICAL SELECTION**
Woman Blues!

"The Queen,"
Victoria Spivey
promoted and
pushed her career
actively, as well
as the careers of
those around her

S pivey was one of the greatest of the classic female blues singers who first came to the fore in the 1920s, and was unusual in being not only a spirited singer, but also useful pianist and a good businesswoman. There is little coincidence in the fact that her music career extended a long way past the prime years of the other classic blues singers.

Born in Houston, Texas, and a singer very much in the raw, hard-voiced tradition of that State, Spivey moved to St Louis, Missouri, in 1926 before her twentieth birthday to make her debut recording, the song "Black Snake Blues," which broke new ground in the blues industry owing to its infectious rhythm and witty lyrics. A hit, it helped change the direction of blues singing, moving it away from the slow-drag vaudeville approach to the medium-tempo gait of much country blues. Many records followed, a lot of them with her friend and colleague Lonnie Johnson. Spivey became a star, even making it to Hollywood in

1929, appearing in King Vidor's *Missy Rose.* Overcoming the privations of the Depression, Spivey went into club work in the early 1930s, working at Chicago's Grand Terrace for record stays. She married the dancer Billy Adams after the two of them had joined Olsen and Johnson's *Hellzapoppin' Revue* in 1938, which also ran for over four years in New York's Winter Garden Theater. A life on the road was terminated in 1952 when Spivey left show business and took up a new career in the church.

This vocation was interrupted in 1961 when she made a string of fine records for Bluesville with varying line-ups, including one album, *Woman Blues!,* with her old friend Lonnie Johnson. Spivey used her classic combination of sexual double entendre and laconic observation to make powerful records in the old style. This led to her being taken up by a new audience, and she was kept busy touring and recording (mostly for her own label, Spivey) until her death in 1976.

SEE ALSO: Lonnie Johnson

# Frank Stokes

Frank Stokes, one of the original Beale Street Sharks, played up the role of the rake to perfection

## fact file

**BORN** 1888

**DIED** 1955

**MUSICAL SELECTION**
"You Shall"
"Tain't Nobody's
Business"

guitarist/singer Stokes was one of the first Memphis blues musicians to make his mark, bringing to it his experience as a solo performer and a member of various traveling troupes, including string bands and medicine shows. Stokes had a powerful voice which he used effectively, avoiding coarseness while preferring direct expression rather than nuance. His guitar playing was complex, often using figures associated with ragtime, but he was capable of supplying a strong driving beat when required.

Stokes was born in Whitehaven, Mississippi, and worked as an agricultural laborer and blacksmith while learning his guitar technique. When he was proficient enough he took off with the tent shows and moved around the South, playing solo or with different-sized groups. By the early 1920s he was settled in Memphis, playing in the streets solo or in groups with Jack Kelly and Will Batts. During this time he met the guitarist Doug Sane and the pair formed a duo, the Beale Street Sheiks. This quickly became a top-rate duo, the pair matched perfectly for guitar styles and able to interweave and support each other at appropriate moments. The pair began recording in Memphis in late summer 1927 and from the start their repertoire showed a wide mixture of material, from pre-Civil War pieces such as "You Shall" to the rollicking good-fun "It's a Good Thing" to more carefully crafted pieces, such as "Jazzin' The Blues." Stokes also recorded solo, sticking closer to more familiar blues cadences. The Sheiks made an early version of "Tain't Nobody's Business" in 1928. The Sheiks made their last records in March 1929: Stokes lasted on record only to the following September. The Depression put Stokes and Sane back on the Memphis streets. He died in Memphis in 1955.

**SEE ALSO:** Furry Lewis, Sleepy John Estes

# Angela Strehli

Angela Strehli, a strong force on the Austin, Texas scene

**V**ocalist Strehli, born in Lubbock, Texas – famous as the hometown of Buddy Holly – was exposed to a range of different music as a child, from West Texan blues and gospel to the Tex-Mex rhythms which also influenced Holly himself. Strehli learned the rudiments of harmonica and bass, but early on realized that her special gift was singing. When she moved to San Francisco in the late 1960s, the band she joined needed a singer more than anything else, and her vocal talents pushed her into the spotlight.

Back in Texas in 1970, Strehli settled in Austin, just then at the beginning of a blues scene which would prove an important source of Texas talent over the next couple of decades. She worked in a number of local bands including the Fabulous Rockets, the Cobras and Southern Feeling, but in 1975 decided to put performing to one side and

concentrate on working at Antone's, the Austin club where most of these bands became known. By 1982 she felt ready to go back to live performance full-time, and formed the Angela Strehli Band, which gave her continuous exposure all over Austin.

When Antone's set up its own record label, it was a logical move for Strehli's band to be the first to record for it. *Stranger Blues* was the debut record, released in 1986. She has recorded regularly for the label ever since, and even spent 1988-90 actually running the business side of the label before relocating in the San Francisco area to concentrate once more on performing. Strehli continues to run her own career and lead her own band, playing both on the West Coast and in Texas on a regular basis. As with Lou Ann Barton and Marcia Ball, Angela Strehli is a forceful blues singer deserving of the praise she receives.

## fact file

**BORN** 1945

**MUSICAL SELECTION**
Stranger Blues

**SEE ALSO:** Sue Foley, Janis Joplin

# Sugar Blue

**fact file**

**BORN** 1955

**MUSICAL SELECTION**
Cross Roads

Sugar Blue
has enjoyed a
successful solo
career and had
the pleasure of
working with the
best, including
Willie Dixon

**a** blues harpist who combines the tough and driving Chicago tradition with the showmanship and free spirits of the older, more folk-derived traditions as represented by Sonny Terry and others, Sugar Blue was born and spent his first 20 or so years in New York City. He was attracted to music early on, listening to blues and related music on the radio and on records and picking up harmonica technique from such sources: by the late 1960s he was proficient enough to consider a career in music, and by the early 1970s, still in his teens, he was able to work in clubs and on recording dates as a sideman for established older artists such as Roosevelt Sykes. After experiencing Europe while on tour accompanying such acts, Sugar Blue decided to give Paris a go as his headquarters, and in 1976 he relocated there. Although at first he was little better off

than in New York, playing clubs and busking, he met members of the Rolling Stones and was invited to contribute some harp playing to their 1978 album, *Some Girls*, including the hit single, "Miss You." This led to further work with the band, touring and recording, and to his own debut album as the 1980s began, *Cross Roads*. This and a follow-up gave him blues visibility back home in the USA, and this prompted a move to Chicago in 1983, after which he worked regularly with Willie Dixon, traveling with the band to Montreux in 1984 for a set that, when released on record the following year, would win a Grammy award.

Blue has continued in his dual career: he remained with Dixon until the older man's death, he continued to play and record with the Rolling Stones. His high profile is a result of such activities, and he continues to pursue a busy career.

**SEE ALSO:** Sonny Terry, Roosevelt Sykes, Willie Dixon

# Hubert Sumlin

**fact file**

**BORN** 1931

**MUSICAL SELECTION**
Hubert Sumlin's
Blues Party

The sweet
smiling face of
Hubert Sumlin,
the strong silent
support behind
Howlin' Wolf's
sound

lthough Howlin' Wolf is rightly recognized as one of the great blues originals, the inspirational guitar playing of band member Hubert Sumlin laid the foundations of the Wolf's trail-blazing live gigs and recordings for more than 20 years. Not possessed of a memorable voice, Sumlin has struggled since Wolf's death to maintain his public stature, only occasionally being able to find the right circumstances to re-create the magic that flowed so easily during the years on the prowl with the Wolf.

Sumlin was born in Greenwood, Mississippi, but spent the majority of his youth in Arkansas. As a youngster he played in the local juke joints, joining up in West Memphis for a period with James Cotton. While still in the same area, Sumlin met Howlin' Wolf and, though the guitarist moved on to Chicago, when Wolf too moved north in 1953 Sumlin joined up with him, making his first sides, including "Evil," with the band in May

1954. He would go on to be the guitarist on such classics as "Smokestack Lightnin'," "The Red Rooster," "Sittin' On Top of the World," and "Moaning For My Baby." The time with Wolf was anything but settled: Sumlin had a major run-in with the leader early in 1956, leaving him to play with Muddy Waters, but he was enticed back to Wolf's band in late 1957 and stayed there, despite the ups and downs of working with the Wolf, until the older man's death in 1976, even taking over at the helm of Wolf's last band after his death in an attempt to keep the old repertoire together. This eventually came to an end and Sumlin launched a solo career, touring both in Europe and parts of the US and recording for the French Black & Blue label, but his qualities as a guitarist were not reflected so brightly as a leader, and he has been unable to command the profile as a solo that his talent deserves. A 1985 record for Black Top, *Hubert Sumlin's Blues Party*, demonstrated undimmed talent.

**SEE ALSO:** Howlin' Wolf, James Cotton, Muddy Waters

# Roosevelt Sykes

Performer, composer, and early talent scout, Roosevelt Sykes was able to move easily between piano styles

## fact file

**BORN** 1913

**DIED** 1984

**MUSICAL SELECTION**
"Night Time Is The Right Time"

Sykes, one of the key artists in the development of the piano blues, is often listed as having been born in Arkansas in 1906, but he himself claimed to have been born in St Louis in 1913. What is not in dispute is the importance of the style he helped invent, using rolling chords in both hands, tremolos, octave melodies, and rapid, repeated staccato figures. Elements of this approach have been the basis for every blues pianist of note ever since.

Sykes came from a family with a religious background, and his first experience of music was from gospel. Later, he became fascinated by the organ in his local church, but preferred the piano as an instrument that could be, in his words, "pounded ... not mashed." From the age of 12 he took his piano playing very seriously, taking some theory lessons in his early twenties. Meanwhile, he'd been discovered by Okeh in 1929, and from that time onward he was a constant visitor to recording studios, operating under a number of pseudonyms to record for a raft of companies, including Victor and Paramount. For Victor, his pseudonym was Willie Kelly.

A record made for Decca in February 1936 by Sykes under the name of the Honey Dripper and using the same title, became a massive hit, just as "Night Time Is The Right Time" did in the same year. The insistent rocking style of Sykes's Honey Dripper style became something of a craze and was a harbinger of the rhythm-and-blues beats to come in the 1940s, when others would return to Sykes's theme and have hits for themselves with it. Sykes moved to Chicago in 1941 and continued to work and record regularly, but when the Chicago blues scene changed, he moved to New Orleans, a city where the piano was always a welcome sound, and spent most of the 1950s there. By the time he was rediscovered in 1960 by Prestige Bluesville's Chris Albertson through a chance remark to Memphis Slim, who knew where the older man was living, Sykes was still playing regularly, but had adapted to changing tastes by playing requests for "standards" by his clientele. The relaunch led to a non-stop schedule of recordings, concerts, and festivals in Europe and America until his death in 1984.

**SEE ALSO:** Memphis Slim

# Taj Mahal

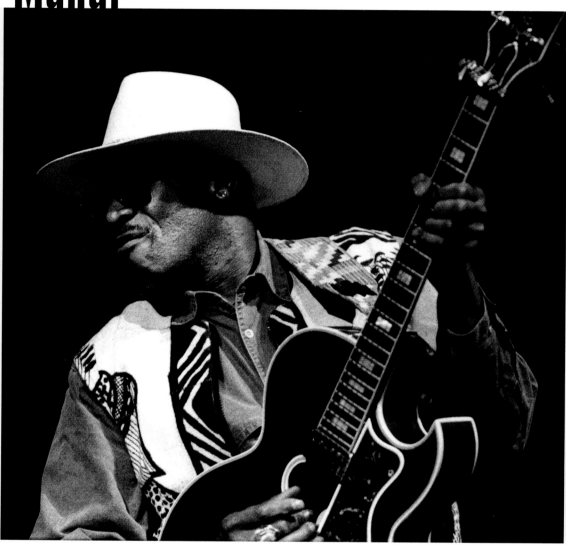

The inimitable Taj Mahal, bringing an appreciation for the world's music to the blues

born Henry St Claire Fredericks in New York City just six months after America had entered World War II, Taj Mahal was early on destined for a close involvement in music. He came from a musical family and one with roots in many cultural areas: his stepfather was Jamaican and he became interested very early on in both the music and culture of that country as well as the blues and other musics of America itself.

His family relocated to Massachusetts when he was still young, and he attended Massachusetts University, at the same time beginning to perform, accompanying himself on guitar, in the coffee houses and clubs around the campus.

During the early 1960s he became caught up in the rediscovery of those country blues greats who were still alive, such as Skip James, Sleepy John Estes, Son House, and Mississippi John Hurt. At the time the interest in this music stemmed overwhelmingly from the young white audience, so Taj was a distinct curiosity to these older men when he sought them out with a view to learning from them. This assiduousness paid dividends, however, as Taj Mahal began to develop his own synthesis of the many influences he had gathered together in his life. A 1965 move to Los Angeles brought him into contact with another of the great eclectics of folk and ethnic music, Ry Cooder, and the two of them formed a band, Rising Sons, which came to the attention of Columbia records, who signed them to a deal. An album was made but the band split before it was released.

Cooder went off in other directions, one of them being Captain Beefheart, but Columbia signed Taj Mahal to an exclusive solo deal. From the beginning, he recorded music which, although often centered on a great many traditional blues forms (songs by Sleepy John Estes and others appeared on his first album), drew also on disparate influences and styles, including reggae and other Caribbean genres.

Taj Mahal has continued to be a diligent student of and proselytizer for black music of all descriptions. He wrote the soundtrack for the 1973 film *Sounder* and has continued to record prolifically. His popularity with audiences of blues fans and music fans of all genres remains as strong as ever.

## fact file

**BORN** 1942

**MUSICAL SELECTION**
Sounder
Taj Mahal
Mo' Roots
Taj's Blues

**SEE ALSO:** Skip James, Sleepy John Estes, Son House, Mississippi John Hurt

# Tampa Red

Like many other blues performers, Tampa Red aka Hudson Whittaker came from an uncertain background and experienced a fragmented childhood. Born Hudson Woodbridge in Smithville, Georgia, he lost his parents early and was raised by his mother's family, the Whittakers, in Tampa, Florida. An accomplished guitarist by the time he reached Chicago in the mid-1920s, he was using his professional name Tampa Red on his arrival, becoming known as a street musician by that name. His smooth, effortless slide guitar technique brought him finally to the attention of record companies, and in the late fall of 1928 he was signed by Vocalion to record with the well-known singer, pianist, and songwriter Thomas A. Dorsey. Their first single was "It's Tight Like That," an immediate and major hit which the duo covered no fewer than three times, with varying personnel and pseudonyms, in the next three months.

This fast-paced and cheeky song launched the craze for the urban musical entertainment that became known as "hokum," although blacks had been making tongue-in-cheek and crazy records prior to this time (Jelly Roll Morton's "Billy Goat Stomp" from 1927, for example). The always impeccably dressed Red and the dignified Georgia Tom, though accomplished bluesmen, lost no time in cashing in on their own trend, recording under the name the Hokum Boys for the Paramount label. The winning team was broken up when Dorsey became disillusioned with the blues and turned increasingly to gospel, making the transition permanent after 1935. Tampa Red's predilection for risqué and bawdy lyrics must have exacerbated the situation, as the words to "Tight Like That" and the virtually pornographic "Uncle Bud" from 1929 can attest.

Undeterred by the breaking of the partnership, Red continued to record with pianists of his choice, including Big Maceo, with whom he made a series of first-class urban-blues records for Bluebird which stretched right up to 1946, when Maceo was forced to retire due to a stroke. A business relationship with Lester Melrose, an important man in the Chicago music industry of the day, kept Tampa Red in the mainstream of Chicago blues, and he recorded with most of the stars of the day, including Big Bill Broonzy, Memphis Slim, and Sonny Boy Williamson. He retained his popularity right up to the 1950s, having a hit in 1949 with "It Hurts Me Too," and was instrumental in getting the younger generation of Chicago blues musicians up and running. After this, his career faded as the new, harder rhythms of postwar music took over and his smooth good-time music faded from popularity. His wife died in 1954, leaving him desolate. He was one of the rediscoveries of the early 1960s, but his heart was no longer in the music, as the records made at this time demonstrate. He suffered a long physical decline and for years before his eventual death in 1981 was resident in a Chicago hospital, virtually forgotten by all but close friends.

## fact file

**BORN** 1900

**DIED** 1981

**MUSICAL SELECTION**
"Tight Like That"
"It Hurts Me Too"

"The Guitar Wizard" himself, the one and only Hudson Woodbridge, better known as Tampa Red

# Charles "Baby" Tate

**fact file**

**BORN** 1916

**DIED** 1972

**MUSICAL SELECTION**
**See What You Done**
"Truckin' Them Blues
Away"

Baby Tate,
named perhaps
for his baby-like
good looks or his
performances
with some of the
grand old men of
the blues,
including Pink
Anderson

born in Elberton, Georgia, Charles "Baby" Tate moved to South Carolina as a 9-year-old, and it was there that he became attracted to the blues. While still learning the ropes, he met Blind Boy Fuller (he even dated Fuller's sister for a while), and his own guitar style shows the marks of many evenings listening to Fuller play. On Fuller's death, Tate was offered a recording contract by Okeh to play under Fuller's name and in his style. World War II was about to break, however, and Tate went into the service instead. Okeh turned to Brownie McGhee to fill the void and "Baby" Tate's opportunity had passed. For the next twenty years, Tate worked as a bricklayer in Spartanburg, South Carolina. He continued playing parties and dances at night for pleasure rather than the money earned, but lost contact with the larger blues community altogether.

One of many older bluesmen rediscovered by Samuel Charters, Tate – then in his mid-forties – was finally introduced to the recording studio in 1961, where he made a fine session for Bluesville. The ripples of publicity from this record enabled him to appear more widely, but his second career stuttered just like the first. A long series of recordings took place in 1970 but only a handful were ever released; unfortunately, "Baby" Tate, one of the few remaining practitioners of the Carolina style of country blues, was largely passed over once again. He died in Columbia, South Carolina in 1977.

**SEE ALSO:** Blind Boy Fuller, Brownie McGhee

# Eddie Taylor

## fact file

**BORN** 1923

**DIED** 1985

**MUSICAL SELECTION**
My Heart Is Bleeding
Bad Boy

Eddie Taylor aka "Playboy" Taylor worked with his combo in Chicago with great success

eddie Taylor was one of Chicago's most valued guitarists during the postwar period. He appeared with many top bands, especially that of Jimmy Reed, contributing a distinctive, Delta-derived sound to nearly all of Reed's many hits.

Taylor was born in Benoit, Mississippi, and came into contact with the blues in infancy, having been nursed by his mother's friend from school days, Memphis Minnie. As a child Taylor absorbed Minnie's playing, along with that of Charlie Patton, Son House, and others, and claims it to have been a formative influence. He got his first guitar in 1936, practiced incessantly, and checked out every bluesman in sight or within earshot. By his late teens Taylor could imitate virtually any of the major bluesmen of the day, including Big Boy Crudup and Peetie Wheatstraw. Moving to Memphis in 1943, he worked for an army contractor and met locals like B.B. King and Johnny Shines. Six years later he was in Chicago, quickly working himself into the local scene through his use of electric guitar (which he'd picked up in 1947), and playing with many of that city's talent. He then hooked up with boyhood friend Jimmy Reed, and was instrumental in creating the Jimmy Reed sound. Still obliged to work day jobs at the time, Taylor started recording under his own name in the 1950s and followed up with his own albums at least once every decade. But he largely remained the quintessential sideman throughout his long career, adding his distinctive, punchy guitar work to sessions with such luminaries as Elmore James, John Lee Hooker, and Roosevelt Sykes. Eddie Taylor died in 1985.

**SEE ALSO:** Jimmy Reed, Memphis Minnie, Charlie Patton, Son House, Big Boy Crudup, Peetie Wheatstraw

# Eva Taylor

## fact file

**BORN** 1895

**DIED** 1977

**MUSICAL SELECTION**
"Hesitation Blues"
"Cake-Walking Babies
From Home"

Eve Taylor was on stage from the age of three, staying with the blues and performing in general throughout her lifetime

t aylor was one of the first of the classic female blues singers to be committed to disc, in 1922. From a vaudeville background – as were so many of her contemporaries – Taylor married a businessman and musician, Clarence Williams, and enjoyed a long and successful singing career. Her voice did not carry the weight or gravitas of some of her rivals such as Bessie Smith or Ma Rainey, but her combination of good-time humor, showmanship, and a handsome if not overwhelming timbre and range kept her popularity bubbling along throughout the 1920s and much of the 1930s.

Taylor was born in St Louis, Missouri, and was involved in showbiz from infancy, making a stage debut in a traveling show at the age of three. Immediately popular, she traveled widely with these shows, reaching Europe (1906), Australia (1900), and New Zealand (1914). In 1921 she came off the touring circuit and settled in New York, singing and dancing in clubs and cabarets. Before long she met Clarence Williams and they married. Williams lost no time in getting her on wax: she debuted on the ill-fated Black Swan label in 1922 before moving on to Okeh, a

label for which Williams acted as a talent scout. Her professional name of Eva Turner was adopted at the onset of her recording career. Turner recorded prolifically with Williams, using him as her accompanist but also singing with his Blue Five and other combinations, some of whose names were studio concoctions such as Carrot Cale and His Beat Roots or Clarence Williams' Morocco Five. Taylor also made a set of duets with the singer Sara Martin in 1923, including "Hesitation Blues." Her most famous performance of this period, however, was "Cake-Walking Babies From Home" (1925).

Taylor recorded over a hundred titles with Williams for various record companies between 1922 and 1940, but during the war her career path changed and by the end of the 1940s she had withdrawn from a full-time career. By the mid-1960s, when her husband Williams died, Taylor once again began performing, appearing at concerts and clubs on both sides of the Atlantic, playing to enthusiastic houses in London, Copenhagen, and elsewhere in Europe recognized as a true international star. She died in 1977.

**SEE ALSO:** Bessie Smith

# Hound Dog Taylor

**fact file**

BORN 1917

DIED 1975

MUSICAL SELECTION
Hound Dog Taylor &
The House Rockers
Beware of the Dog

Hound Dog Taylor,
pictured enjoying
a memorable
moment, was
another strong
blues player from
the Chicago
scene

t he career of Hound Dog Taylor is a perfect case of "better late than never": virtually unknown outside of Chicago before his first album in 1971, in the four years left to him Taylor cut an exciting swathe through blues fans with his rough-and-ready slide guitar playing and energetic vocals, backed by a take-no-prisoners band comfortable in any rhythmic environment, from fast stomps to slow drags.

Taylor was born in Natchez, Mississippi, and spent his early years on the farm. Discovering the guitar in his early twenties, he gained early experience in the time-honored way, playing parties and joints, before upping stake and moving to Chicago in 1942. By the late 1950s he was finally in a position to work full-time

as a musician but no records were made and he remained a purely local phenomenon until 1971, when he came to the attention of Alligator Records, then in the process of starting up. Taylor's first album for the label, *Hound Dog Taylor & The House Rockers*, proved a sensation among blues fans and gave him an instant profile as a no-holds-barred Elmore James-style guitarist, sometimes even outdoing the master in terms of emotional input and the manipulated distortion of his tone.

Taylor and his band quickly made a string of records for Alligator, the last being a live date, *Beware of the Dog* (recorded 1974), which was released posthumously. Taylor succumbed to cancer in December 1975.

# Koko Taylor

fact file

BORN 1935

MUSICAL SELECTION
Force of Nature
What It Takes
(The Chess Years)

Performances in such austere venues as Carnegie Hall reflect Koko Taylor's importance on the scene

aylor has long been recognized as the queen of the modern blues scene, presiding over the Chicago clubs and bars since the early 1970s. Her almost overpowering vocal talents, her outsize personality, and her absolute dedication to her chosen musical form have made her an inspiration to the musicians around her and a consistently popular performer with audiences and record-buyers over the past three decades.

Taylor was born onto a sharecropper's farm near Memphis, Tennessee, and, in classic fashion, first experienced music through church gospel singing. That gospel influence remains at the root of her vocal style. By 1953 she was 18 and already married (to Robert "Pops" Taylor) and ready for a music career beyond Memphis. She moved to Chicago, initially working menial day jobs while she and her husband looked for work in the blues clubs. Acceptance came slowly, Talyor sitting in with various bands and gradually becoming known for her powerful

style. She made her first singles for the USA label in 1963 (with J.B. Lenoir on guitar), but her first impact came with her hit recording of Willie Dixon's scurrilous "Wang Dang Doodle" for Chess/Checker in 1966. Taylor, now a name, continued with a singles-only policy for Checker, heading more for the burgeoning soul market than for the older blues audience, but by the end of 1969 she had left Checker and went on to join the emerging European tour circuit of the early 1970s. She became a major blues star in Europe, making a number of albums for Black & Blue in Paris and appearing at Montreux. She also appeared in a film documentary about Chicago and signed in 1974 for Alligator, starting a succession of records which would be top-selling blues albums and win a number of awards. One of her more recent albums, *Force of Nature* (1993), featured as guests Buddy Guy and Carey Bell. She is unchallenged in the female blues arena and even appeared in 1989 at the inauguration of President George Bush. Her career continues apace.

SEE ALSO: J. B. Lenoir, Willie Dixon, Buddy Guy, Carey Bell

# Melvin Taylor

**fact file**

**BORN** 1959

**MUSICAL SELECTION**
Blues On The Run
Melvin Taylor & The
Slack Band

Melvin Taylor, one of Alligator Records "New Bluebloods," has enjoyed working with greats including Carey Bell and the Legendary Blues Band

S till young in blues terms, Taylor is of the generation who came to maturity after the advent of the blues-rock brigade, including Hendrix, Winter, and Clapton as well as the high-powered blues guitar of Buddy Guy and Albert King. With this as his backdrop, Taylor has forged a dynamic blues guitar and vocal style from the whole range of options open to today's performers. In more recent years he has also studied the music of Wes Montgomery and Kenny Burrell.

Taylor was born in Jackson, Mississippi, but moved with his family to Chicago when still quite young. He grew up with blues in the house – his uncle, Floyd Vaughan, played local clubs and bars and played guitar around Melvin's house constantly. By the early 1970s he was competent enough on guitar to busk in the streets and at Maxwell Market, playing the blues, but his first band, the Transistors, played covers of current soul and R&B hits.

The experience stood him in good stead because, on its demise in the early 1980s, Taylor was asked by Pinetop Perkins to tour Europe as a member of the Legendary Blues Band, Muddy Waters' former backing band. This tour led to his being fêted in France (two records, *Blues On The Run* and *Plays The Blues For You*, were made for Black & Blue) to the point where he still regularly tours there.

Back in Chicago things were not easy and Taylor spent much of the 1980s as a backing musician in other people's bands, finally organizing his own group and establishing a residency at Rosa's Lounge with his own band which lasted over a decade. This has proved the launching pad of his recent career, one that has seen his modern style give him a profile in the US as well as Europe. His album for Evidence, *Melvin Taylor & The Slack Band* (1995), has been hailed as a modern blues classic.

**SEE ALSO:** Jimi Hendrix, Johnny Winter, Eric Clapton, Buddy Guy, Albert King, Pinetop Perkins, Muddy Waters

# Arthur "Montana" Taylor

**fact file**

**BORN** 1903

**MUSICAL SELECTION**
"Indiana Avenue Stomp"
"Detroit Rocks"

Arthur "Montana" Taylor earned his nickname the old fashioned way — he was born there

**t**aylor had a relatively brief career in the public eye, but he was a blues and boogie pianist of the highest caliber and deserves to be better known. Born in Butte, Montana, he moved to Indianapolis while still a boy and there taught himself piano, encouraged by his father. By the time his teens came to an end he was playing house-rent parties and clubs throughout the city. Looking for better opportunities, Taylor moved on to Chicago in the latter half of the 1920s. There he worked steadily and finally came to the attention of Vocalion, who in April 1929 released four sides by Taylor, two accompanied by the hokum-dispensing Jazoo Boys and two solo. These, especially "Indiana Avenue Stomp" and "Detroit Rocks," show Taylor to be a technically assured boogie pianist capable of ordering and shaping his material to create a unified performance. His style was to become widespread in the 1930s. Taylor, however, found the typical business practices of record companies distasteful in the extreme and he sought out no further recording opportunities. Moving to Cleveland for a while in the early 1930s, Taylor quietly made a living at the piano unnoticed by the wider world until he was located by some enthusiasts in 1946 and induced to record for the Circle label, a small record company specializing in "classic" jazz and boogie styles. Taylor cut a dozen or more sides in Chicago for Circle over two days in April 1946, all of which show his powers to be undimmed. At the same sessions he accompanied Chippie Hill on three sides. None of this increase in activity convinced Taylor that he needed to move back into the wider musical world, and he disappeared back into the obscurity from whence he came.

SEE ALSO: Chippie Hill

# Sonny Terry

**fact file**

**BORN** 1911

**DIED** 1986

**MUSICAL SELECTION**
Brownie McGhee &
Sonny Terry Sing
"Train Whistle Blues"
"Hootin' Blues"

The careers of
Sonny Terry and
Blind Boy Fuller
have intertwined
throughout their
lives as
performing
and recording
partners

Sonny Terry was not only one of the greatest harmonica players to come out of American folk and blues, but was one of the best-known musical figures in the world up until the time of his death. Terry's enthusiasm, oversaturated sound, whoops and filigrees behind his long-time partner Brownie McGhee, plus his use of a relatively small number of musical figures which were well loved by his audience, made him a hugely entertaining and reassuring musical presence.

A Piedmont man, Terry was born in Greensboro, North Carolina, but moved with his family soon afterwards to the town of Shelby. He was inspired to play music by his father, a harmonica man who stuck strictly to dance tunes and spirituals. Terry, however, was early attracted to the blues. Two separate accidents, one at the age of five, the other at 18, deprived him of his sight. By the time of the second accident his father was already dead and he was forced to work the streets with his harmonica in search of money – the only work option left to him. Terry, possessed of an unusually secure single-note technique among other things, soon attracted attention, and was appearing in traveling shows. During a trip to Wadesboro, North Carolina, he met up with Blind Boy Fuller who persuaded him to come to Durham to work with him. Fuller was by then an established

recording artist, and the following year, 1937, he brought Terry onto one of his sessions in New York City for Vocalion. Terry got noticed by John Hammond, who added him to his 1938 Spirituals To Swing concert at Carnegie Hall, and by 1940, although still with Fuller, he had begun making records under his own name.

Fuller died in 1941 and Terry began working occasionally with Brownie McGhee, whom he'd met in 1939 and who was now called Blind Boy Fuller 2 by his record company. By 1942 both men were in New York and running a loose working partnership which would gradually grow in popularity and cohesiveness until it had become a worldwide phenomenon. In the meantime the two occasionally recorded apart, and in 1946 Terry appeared in the Broadway production of *Finian's Rainbow*, an association that lasted for two years. Terry was also very active in the nascent New York folk music scene, appearing with many top acts. By the early 1950s he and McGhee had begun touring as a duo, and though the first half of that decade was a struggle against R&B and rock 'n' roll, the folk boom of the late 1950s, plus a stint from 1956–1958 in Tennessee Williams's *Cat On A Hot Tin Roof*, gave them a momentum they never again lost. During the 1960s they became a fixture of the student campuses and coffee houses, as well as at the festivals, all over the world.

**SEE ALSO:** Brownie McGhee, Blind Boy Fuller, John Hammond

# Henry "Ragtime" Thomas

Henry Thomas's "Texas Worried Blues" (pictured) on Yazoo Records was a popular release for this influential blues performer

homas, born in Big Sandy, Texas, and not recorded until he was in his fifties, was one of the elders of the generation of blues musicians who came out of the songster tradition. The songsters were blacks who traveled the South singing the songs and hollers of their people, and little of their music contained blues form or harmonic structure, often borrowing from ragtime, ballads, and other more primitive forms instead. Thomas's recordings are important as being some of the most vital representations of a tradition that was fast disappearing by the late 1920s.

Self-taught as a guitarist, Thomas was born into a family of freed slaves and went out on the road as a young man, traveling as a hobo on the Texan railroad network everywhere he could reach. A big-framed man with robust health, he relied on the railways to transport him from area to area for new sources of revenue: he would play for the railway employees as well as the local populace, paying his way in kind. Thomas's style, whether he was singing traditional pieces like "John Henry," "Jonah In The Wilderness," or "Chicken Rag," stressed the element of entertainment and storytelling that reflects the songster tradition. His blues performances on his 1927–29 Vocalion sides ("Red River Blues," "Texas Easy Street Blues") show a similar attitude to his material, with simple driving guitar and a vocal which is in no way introspective or personal, but is more concerned with providing a suitable background for his audience. Even on "Texas Worried Blues" his use of classic recycled blues phrases and lyrics suggests a construction to grab his listeners's attention rather than a heartfelt outburst. It is an entertainment, much as he was offering on the streets of Texas at the same time. Thomas died as a result of his hard-living life in 1930.

**SEE ALSO:** Albert Collins

# Henry Townsend

Henry Townsend was one of the blues most successful sidemen, working closely with Walter Davis during his career

**p**ianist/guitarist Townsend was a close associate of the pianist/singer Walter Davis (for whom he played guitar) and was a pivotal member of the St Louis blues scene of the 1920s and 1930s.

Townsend was born in Shelby, Mississippi, but was raised in Cairo, Illinois. He arrived in St Louis in his late teens, playing on the streets and forming working relationships with some of the other St Louis musicians. He was recruited by Columbia in November 1929 for four sides, recorded in Chicago. In the financial chaos after the Wall Street Crash, Townsend was overlooked until May 1931, when the ailing Paramount company made two sides with him, followed one month later by Victor, who again cut just two sides, "No Home Blues" and "Take A Chance." Roosevelt Sykes was the pianist on the date. After that Townsend again had to wait two years for a record date, cutting four sides for Bluebird in 1933. Bluebird repeated this practice in 1935 and 1937. Meanwhile, by 1935 Townsend was accompanying Walter Davis on his considerably more prolific and popular Bluebird recordings: he was on most of Davis's sessions for Bluebird until 1937, that year beginning an association on record with John Lee, Sonny Boy Williamson, and Robert Lee McCoy, again for Bluebird. Townsend remained in demand as a sideman but his own solo career came to a halt: he worked in St Louis with his regular partners until the early 1950s, when he dropped out of the scene. Brought back into the public eye by young enthusiasts, in 1961 he had a St Louis session for Bluesville accompanied by Tommy Bankhead. This led to intermittent public appearances (occasionally with his wife Vernell) and records through the 1970s and 1980s, including a 1979 album, *Mule*, which featured his piano playing. In 1984 he was featured in the documentary, *That's The Way I Do It*.

**fact file**

**BORN** 1909

**MUSICAL SELECTION**
Mule

**SEE ALSO:** Walter Davis, Roosevelt Sykes, Sonny Boy Williamson, Robert Lee McCoy

# Big Mama Thornton

t he big-voiced, exuberant blues shouter Willie Mae "Big Mama" Thornton suffered the fate of so many black performers, making definitive recordings of songs which would later become world-famous through later versions by white admirers. It was she who, through the auspices of Johnny Otis, made the original, rough-hewn version of Lieber and Stoller's "Hound Dog;" it was also she who wrote and originally recorded "Ball & Chain" in the early 1960s. Unfortunately, she assigned all rights to the record company, Baytone, and when Janis Joplin picked up on the piece at the close of the same decade, Thornton saw little reward.

Born in Montgomery, Alabama, Big Mama was not merely a vocalist; she was also an accomplished harmonica player and drummer, deploying both instruments from her earliest professional engagements around Alabama with the Hot Harlem Review. By the end of the 1940s she had settled in Houston, Texas – a fortuitous move which saw her accepted as a performer by such contemporaries as Clarence "Gatemouth" Brown, Lowell Fulson, and Junior Parker. At the beginning of the new decade she commenced her recording career, but frustration at her lack of progress led her to Los Angeles, where she linked up with R&B musician and impresario Johnny Otis. The two joined forces in 1952 to make "Hound Dog," a single which topped the R&B charts in 1953. This launched Thornton nationally on the R&B circuit and she led a profitable career up to the eclipse of the genre as the 1950s drew to a close. She returned to the West Coast, finally settling in the San Francisco area in the early 1960s, where she made fine blues records for Chris Strachwitz's Arhoolie label, among others. She also traveled to Europe with the American Folk Blues Festival of 1965.

The unlooked-for but provident intervention of San Francisco's Big Brother and the Holding Company in the late 1960s effectively re-launched Big Mama's career. For the next two decades she worked the international blues festival circuit and continued to make records for various small labels, often in conjunction with her traveling companions. In 1980 she appeared along with Sippie Wallace and Koko Taylor, among others, at the Kool Newport Jazz Festival's special concert, "Blues is a Woman." A much-loved figure, Big Mama Thornton finally succumbed to the rigors of a hard-led life during a visit to Los Angeles in 1984.

## fact file

**BORN** 1926

**DIED** 1984

**MUSICAL SELECTION**
"Hound Dog"
"Ball & Chain"
"Blues is a Woman"

Big Mama Thornton was big in girth and in heart – and she recorded the first version of "Hound Dog"

**SEE ALSO:** Johnny Otis, Janis Joplin, Clarence "Gatemouth" Brown

# Bessie Tucker

fact file

**BORN** ?

**DIED** ?

**MUSICAL SELECTION**
"Penitentiary"
"Whistling Woman
Blues"

**Bessie Turner was a driving force on the blues scene, with a singing, shouting style that earned her praise**

Little is known of Bessie Tucker's life: certainly her birth and death dates have gone unrecorded. She flourished in the 1920s and made all her known recordings for Victor between 1928 and 1929. She seems to have been based in Dallas, for that is where she traveled from to make her first recordings in Memphis in the late summer of 1928.

Most of her recorded repertoire relates to prison experiences, and the authenticity of the imagery and lyrics, plus her primitive, powerful Texas country-blues hollering, at least suggest that the songs come from personal experience. Unlike Ida Mae Mack, who made debut recordings for Victor in Memphis on the same day as Tucker but disappeared thereafter, Tucker's blues – "Penitentiary," "Fort Worth and Denver Blues," and "Got Cut To Pieces," for example – made sufficient public impression for Victor to record

her twice more. This occurred on field trips to Dallas, in August and October 1929, where she alternates between dark fatalism ("Whistling Woman Blues") and high spirits ("Better Boot That Thing"). The Wall Street Crash stopped any more recordings by Tucker, and she vanished from recorded blues history.

**SEE ALSO:** Bessie Smith

# Big Joe Turner

**fact file**

BORN 1911

DIED 1985

MUSICAL SELECTION
"Corinna, Corinna"
"Careless Love"
"Shake, Rattle
and Roll"

Big Joe Turner, mouth wide in enthusiastic song on stage, was part of the team that set the stage for boogie-woogie mania across the US

t he blues is a big church – and one of the reasons for that fact is the successful career of blues shouter Big Joe Turner, a man who, during the course of a long career, managed to combine jazz, swing, boogie, jump jazz, rhythm and blues and, finally, prototype rock 'n' roll. Yet he was probably at his best in the styles he started out with, either singing with Kansas City-style swing bands or with the type of boogie-woogie provided by his longtime partner, pianist Pete Johnson.

Turner was born in Kansas City learning to love music through his involvement with church music. As he grew into his teens, he began singing on street corners to earn some money, finally graduating at the age of 14 to the level of cook in Kansas City's club scene. The town was "wide open" in those days – even in the age of prohibition – and Turner soon graduated to being a barman and occasional entertainer, gaining the epithet "the singing barman." This led to occasional work with the top KC bands including Bennie Moten's and, later, Count Basie's, and to Turner's hooking up with boogie pianist Pete Johnson. The duo was invited by John Hammond to appear at the 1938 "Spirituals To Swing" Carnegie Hall concert and was one of the major hits of the show; Turner's exhortations to "Roll 'em, Pete!" even became a catch-phrase. This appearance was one of the major factors in the subsequent boogie-woogie craze. Turner and Johnson became resident performers at New York's Café Society and international stars after beginning their recording career in 1938.

With the shift in taste toward jump music and rhythm and blues, Turner moved into the R&B genre with ease, his big baritone and bluesy wail suiting the music perfectly. More standard parts of his repertoire were forged then, including "Corinna, Corinna" and "Careless Love." As the 1950s dawned, Turner continued to evolve his style, combining boogie shuffles with rhythm and blues electricity to pave the way for rock 'n' roll. His 1954 hit "Shake, Rattle and Roll" was neither the first nor last of such numbers, but had the most profound effect, becoming one of rock 'n' roll's earliest standards.

Turner stayed with the proto-rock 'n' roll style until sales fell off, then went back to his first love. Teaming up again with Pete Johnson and others, he spent the 1960s and 1970s traveling the world in various revivalist Kansas City troupes and combinations. Big Joe Turner died of a heart attack in 1985.

**SEE ALSO:** Pete Johnson, John Hammond

# Izear "Ike" Turner

## fact file

**BORN** 1931

**MUSICAL SELECTION**
"River Deep,
Mountain High"
"Rocket 88"
"Matchbox"

Known for years as Tina Turner's ex-husband, Ike Turner returned to the stage and the recording studio with the help of fellow musicians

**t**urner, born in Clarksdale, Mississippi, played a major role in the recording and promotion of a whole range of Memphis blues talents as well as producing his own series of fine blues and rhythm and blues records. As a bandleader and talent scout, he continually picked out top talents and knew how to inspire the best out of them, either as a backing musician or as a leader. He was a vital part of the move from blues and R&B to rock 'n' roll, being involved in the famous Jackie Brenston "Rocket 88" single of 1950 – which many observers now consider the first rock 'n' roll single, if such a thing can ever be identified.

Turner grew up in desperately poor conditions in Clarksdale. Always a highly-organized motivator, he formed his first band, a 14-piece unit called The Top Hatters, while still in high school, and ran a blues program on the local radio station while still in his mid teens. By 1950 the band had shrunk to small-group proportions, and Turner had adopted the name The Kings of Rhythm, with singer Jackie Brenston as vocalist. It was his name which appeared on the "Rocket 88" single of that year, much to

Turner's surprise and chagrin. Luckily, Modern records appointed Turner their Memphis talent scout and producer, and he helped churn out singles for them and a number of other labels until his relocation to St Louis in 1954. There he continued to lead his band and in 1956 hired young Anna Mae Bullock as lead singer. She eventually married the boss and changed her first name to Tina. By this time Turner had left Modern and was cutting a plethora of sides with varying personnel for many labels, including Cobra and Artistic, his band producing either pounding R&B or Coasters-style rock 'n' roll. By the early 1960s he had signed with Sue, picked up a set of sexy backing singers and stuck Tina out front in a revue-type show. They landed a number of hits for the company, culminating in the famous "River Deep, Mountain High" single produced by pop's Phil Spector – a massive hit everywhere but in the US. Following his break-up with Tina in 1974 – after which she went on to become a pop-music legend – Turner's own career largely went into eclipse. Only in the past handful of years has Ike Turner, now an elder statesman, made something of a comeback.

**SEE ALSO:** Robert Walker, Wynonie Harris, Earl Hooker, Howlin' Wolf

# Maurice John Vaughn

**fact file**

**BORN** 1952

**MUSICAL SELECTION**
Generic Blues Album
In the Shadow of
the City

While Vaughn's saxophone playing marks him as a unique voice in the blues, he is also proficient on piano, guitar and bass

**V**aughn is a fine representative of the current Chicago blues scene, combining a number of elements long associated with the city, from rolling, tumbling beats to soulful, tough vocals and razor-sharp horn lines arranged strategically around the guitar and voice at the center. Not a player to redefine a genre, Vaughn is more a thorough professional, giving top-class performances of mostly original material.

Vaughn was born and raised on Chicago's South Side, where he was fascinated from early youth by the music tumbling out of the clubs and bars he passed. This gave him the drive to become a musician himself while at high school he learned a panoply of instruments, including sax, clarinet, and drums. He made his first gigs as a sax player, but by the early 1970s had switched to guitar as the fashions in Chicago popular and blues music shifted. Vaughn worked with a large number of bluesmen, including Eddie Lusk and Phil Guy, and recorded with the saxophonist A .C. Reed. In 1984 he cut his first as a leader, a self-produced job called *Generic Blues Album*. Reissued by Alligator four years later, it spread his music far and wide and allowed Vaughn to progress from being a sideman to a leader of his own bands. His second album, *In the Shadow of the City*, was released in 1993 and demonstrated his commitment to powerful rhythmic grooves and tightly controlled group work, eschewing showmanship in pursuit of the overall enjoyment of the song.

**SEE ALSO:** Howlin' Wolf, Albert King, Elmore James

# Stevie Ray Vaughan

V aughan was something of a great white hope for the blues and blues-related rock during the 1980s when he became an ubiquitous figure on the American music scene, appearing as a guest on records by David Bowie and Bob Dylan and concerts by Eric Clapton. His driving, rock-fed rhythm and his elegant, clean-lined but intense guitar playing made him a standout in his field at the time of his rise to fame, paralleled perhaps only by Robert Cray, a man with similar drive, taste, and commercial sensibilities.

Vaughan was born in Dallas, Texas, and was part of a musical family – his elder brother Jimmie, who pursued his own career in the music, introduced his kid brother to rock and the blues via his record collection. In this way Stevie Ray Vaughan came to appreciate B.B. and Albert King, Jimi Hendrix, and Eric Clapton, as well as many other fine players, by listening to their records. The younger Vaughan learned guitar by borrowing his brother's instruments and followed Jimmie to Austin, Texas, in the early 1970s when his elder brother joined that town's Fabulous Thunderbirds. By 1975 Stevie Ray was a member of the Cobras, lasting with them two years before forming Triple Threat with a local singer, Lou Ann Barton, a band that gradually metamorphosed into Double Trouble (named after an Otis Rush song). With Barton leaving to run her own career, Double Trouble enjoyed a stable personnel and built itself into a formidably tight musical unit, capable of rough-house blues and more sophisticated rock-type ballads, with even the occasional use of synthesizers after the arrival of the keyboardist Reese Wynands. The band played the Montreux Festival in 1982, their set so enthusing David Bowie that he used Vaughan on *Let's Dance*.

The band went into the studio to record *Texas Flood* for Epic with John Hammond in 1983, an album that showed Vaughan's widening interests. After its release Vaughan and his band were the toast of the modern blues/rock scene. The album won a string of awards internationally and Vaughan was constantly in demand for prestige session work. A subsequent period of personal decline ended with Vaughan collapsing on stage in 1986 due to alcohol and drugs overindulgence. Three years later, after an intensive rehabilitation, Vaughan was back to top form on *In Step* (1989), an album evidencing awesome maturity and musicianship. Vaughan then recorded *Family Style* with his brother Jimmie (with Bob Dylan as a guest). Before the album's release Vaughan was killed in a private-helicopter crash in thick fog in Wisconsin after leaving a concert at which he'd appeared with Buddy Guy, Eric Clapton, and Robert Cray.

**fact file**

**BORN** 1954

**DIED** 1990

**MUSICAL SELECTION**
In Step
Family Style
Texas Flood

Stevie Ray Vaughan's shocking death in 1990 in a helicopter accident left the blues world stunned, but his recorded legacy lives on

SEE ALSO: Eric Clapton, Robert Cray, B. B. King, Albert King, Jimi Hendrix

# Eddie "Cleanhead" Vinson

Aside from having one of the cleanest heads in the business, blues saxophone star Eddie "Cleanhead" Vinson also possessed one of the strongest blues shouts

## fact file

**BORN** 1917

**DIED** 1988

**MUSICAL SELECTION**
"Kidney Stew"
"Cleanhead Blues"

Vinson was one of a handful of saxophonist/singers to successfully run bands in the postwar period that could comfortably play both bebop and rhythm and blues. His popularity was based largely on his fine blues singing, but his influence as a musician was felt widely, particularly in the world of modern jazz, where his intense, blues-driven alto and his ground-breaking songwriting were used as models by many who came after him.

Vinson was born in Houston, Texas, a fact that no doubt had an impact on the huge sound he developed on the alto sax. From a musical family, Vinson learned music while at high school, becoming proficient on the sax. Soon after leaving school he began his professional career and by 1935 he was playing alongside Arnett Cobb, Illinois Jacquet, and T-Bone Walker in the legendary Chester Boone band. The three men stayed with the band when Milt Larkin took it over, Vinson also developing his vocal prowess. By 1941, however, Larkin was no longer the leader and Vinson was ready to move on, first of all playing with blues artists such as Lil Green and Big Bill, then settling in New York and joining Cootie Williams's band in 1942. Vinson enjoyed a hit with Williams called "Cherry Red" in 1944, prompting him to go out as a leader. Setting up his own blues big band modeled closely on the Louis Jordan small-group approach, Vinson enjoyed a stream of hits during the 1940s, along the way acquiring his "Cleanhead" tag when deciding to go for the shaved look up top. His hits included "Kidney Stew" and "Cleanhead Blues." By the end of the 1940s he was running a small group along the same blues-based lines, but the 1950s were not kind to him and he returned to Texas, although he never abandoned music as a career. Switching to LA in the early 1960s, Vinson built a new fan base with the help of the veteran producer Johnny Otis, but had to wait until the 1970s to be rediscovered internationally.

**SEE ALSO:** T-Bone Walker, Lil Green, Big Bill Broonzy, Louis Jordan, Johnny Otis

# Joe Louis Walker

Joe Louis Walker — growing up in the midst of San Francisco's 1960s scene, he nonetheless developed a tie to the blues early in his musical life

g uitarist/singer Walker, born and raised in San Francisco, is one of the younger generation of blues musicians who effortlessly combine many different strands of popular blues-based music – including rock, R&B, soul, and different styles of blues itself – into a coherent and exciting brand of contemporary blues which, though its roots lie in postwar Chicago blues, has a sharper, more rock-based edge.

Walker began playing around San Francisco about the time that rock promoters in the city were experimenting with combining black and white acts on the same bill. As a result, Walker played in bands with many top blues talents, including Earl Hooker, and became a friend of Mike Bloomfield, who put him in contact with the larger Bay music scene and introduced him to many of the blues acts in whose bands he played at the Fillmore, among other venues. After a series of disappointments outside the Bay area he returned to San Francisco in the early 1970s,

for a time dropping out of the professional music scene, performing with a gospel quartet and studying while working a day job. By the mid-1980s Walker was ready for another try, picking up with the Mississippi Delta Band who toured Europe to great applause in 1985. A Japanese triumph with Earl King and Johnny Adams followed the next year, and Walker cut his first album as leader, *Cold Is The Night*, that year as well.

Two more albums were released before the end of the 1980s. While Walker remained based in the Bay area, his appeal to international audiences has taken him on many tours all around the world, playing festivals, clubs and the like. One of his most recent albums is *Blues Survivor* (1994) on Verve Gitanes which was received with both critical and popular acclaim.

Joe Louis Walker continues to satisfy his audiences on both sides of the Atlantic with his ever-popular, up-to-the-minute blues style.

## fact file

**BORN** 1949

**MUSICAL SELECTION**
Cold Is The Night
Blues Survivor

**SEE ALSO:** Earl Hooker, Mike Bloomfield, Earl King, Johnny Adams

# Phillip Walker

**fact file**

BORN 1937

MUSICAL SELECTION
The Bottom of the Top
Somedays You Have
These Blues

A modern bluesman, Phillip Walker brought his swamp sound from Louisiana to LA to record

**W**alker, born in Welsh, Louisiana, has proved a remarkably adept and adaptable guitarist during his career, swapping convincingly from swamp blues to zydeco to so-called "modern" blues sounds. This ability, however, has often gone unrecognized by the public, and Walker remains an underappreciated bluesman.

Walker grew up in Port Arthur, Texas, meeting up with and joining the zydeco specialist Clifton Chenier in 1955 at the age of 18. Walker stayed with Chenier for four years, touring and recording with him before branching out on his own in 1959. He moved in that year to Los Angeles and began to gather a reputation in the blues clubs, cutting two singles for the Elko label which made little public impact. He then joined Little Richard's touring outfit and spent a good part of the early 1960s on the road with him. Apart from this, Walker made a series of sessions during the 1960s with the producer Bruce Bromberg – the best of these were eventually released on Hugh Hefner's Playboy label in 1973, titled *The Bottom of the Top*. Though revealing an accomplished stylist, the sides were largely ignored. Further sessions with Bromberg resulted in a Joliet album in 1977, *Someday You Have These Blues*, but again this accomplished and versatile musician garnered little sales interest. Walker continues to work with a number of other players and to pursue his own rather low-key career.

SEE ALSO: Sam "Lightnin'" Hopkins

# Robert Walker

**fact file**

BORN 1937

MUSICAL SELECTION
Promised Land

Robert Walker in
full steam during
a heated
performance

born in Clarksdale, Mississippi, singer/guitarist Walker has spent the majority of his career working around the South and West, making various towns the base of his operations, from Bakersfield, California, to occasional forays into Chicago and constant returns to Mississippi. This has made it difficult for him to be more than a regional "name" and he has consequently spent much of his playing life working part-time in music, his day job being picking cotton, from Mississippi to Bakersfield. What is interesting about this approach to his career is that Walker has retained the earthy, unpolished approach of the South, which can add such raw excitement to what a band is doing.

Walker, a self-confessed Chuck Berry fan, taught himself piano, guitar, and drums and began playing piano in the jukes while still underage. As a teenager he preferred the guitar, playing it in his church group as well as practicing for the time when he could run his own band. Watching local stars like Ike Turner, Chuck Berry, and Raymond Hill play promotions and gigs, Walker gradually formed his own style, combining elements of rock 'n' roll, blues,

and gospel – he claimed to have got his rhythm from listening to Little Walter and Jimmy Reed. In the late 1950s Walker began as a solo artist on acoustic guitar, gradually moving to electric when the money was sufficient for him to get equipment, then adding personnel to his act until he had a regular blues band. Walker's flamboyant stage act won him as many fans as his natural rockin' blues. An affair with a female churchgoer in Chicago put him back into the gospel circuit for a while, but during the 1960s and 1970s he was a regular in Chicago, often traveling there from afar to appear at shows and clubs. Walker remained serious about his farm work, eventually getting his own cotton farm in California and employing laborers to do the work he used to do. He kept music as a highly enjoyable sideline rather than his only talent, capitalizing on every break he got and channeling his intensely competitive nature into creating a live show that would make people's jaws drop. Incredibly, considering how long he's been playing, Walker made his first album, *Promised Land*, in 1997, thus spreading his name internationally for the first time.

**SEE ALSO:** Ike Turner, Little Walter, Jimmy Reed

# Aaron "T-Bone" Walker

**W**alker's influence on the postwar development of the blues is so profound as to be almost incalculable. His most significant musical contribution was the virtual invention of the electric blues guitar style. Walker was also a noted composer of blues tunes, his single most famous title being "Stormy Monday," although "T-Bone Shuffle" and "I'm Still In Love With You" are also seminal recordings from the late 1940s. All of this talent was promoted by a dynamic stage presence, T-Bone being one of the first of the postwar artists to methodically employ a routine including doing the splits, duck-walking with his guitar, and playing it above his head. A sharp-dressing man, he was the epitome of new style blues and was the role model for all who meant to follow.

Walker was born in Linden, Texas, but moved when still in infancy with his family to Dallas. Coming from a family able to play an array of instruments, during his early teens he became a companion of Blind Lemon Jefferson, who was known to his family and a man used to having helpful acolytes around. This left something of a mark on Walker in the way he used classic Jefferson and Texan call-and-response patterns between his voice and guitar in his mature work. As he grew older, T-Bone joined traveling medicine shows, mostly playing banjo, developing his stage antics and showmanship: his repertoire was broad enough to include Cab Calloway covers. He attracted sufficient attention to cut his first record, as Oak Cliff T-Bone, for Columbia in December, 1929. With the onset of the Depression, Walker stayed at home and played different Dallas clubs and hotels, then in 1935 went out on the road with a vaudeville act: while on this tour he met Charlie Christian in Oklahoma City and was amazed by the jazz player's genius. Walker continued west, ending up in LA in 1936 and fitting into the very beginnings of small-group blues which gradually emerged from the jump-music scene of the close of the decade. By then Walker was a singer with the Les Hite band, a group freely combining boogie shuffles with big-band riffs and lots of vocals, and his "T-Bone Blues" was recorded in 1940, though he was not the guitar soloist. By now he'd been woodshedding with Gibson's electric guitar package long enough to unveil it to unsuspecting LA audiences late in 1940. Running his own small group, he quickly established a following during 1941 and eventually signed a recording deal with Capitol in 1942, cutting just one session before the Petrillo recording ban kept him out of the studios for another year. A move to Chicago, where he played to packed houses for an extended season at the Rhumboogie Club and recorded for the fledgling Rhumboogie label in 1945, saw the initial recording of "T-Bone Boogie," but by the fall of '46 he was back in LA and recording for the Black & White label. Within a year "Stormy Monday" had been released and become a massive hit. Of the millions who were powerfully influenced by the song's style, and T-Bone's playing and singing on it, was a young B.B. King. During the 1950s he kept very busy, touring America and abroad. One great album, *T-Bone Blues*, made for Atlantic, placed him with both blues and jazz groups and found him equally at ease in both contexts, but after the final sessions for Atlantic, he went unrecorded for five years.

By this time his relentless touring, fast lifestyle, and love of the bottle were wearing him down. His career on the back burner, he retired from performing in 1974 owing to health problems and died the next year.

## fact file

**BORN** 1910

**DIED** 1975

**MUSICAL SELECTION**
**T-Bone Blues**
"Stormy Monday"
"T-Bone Shuffle"

The mighty Aaron Thibeaux "T-Bone" Walker, blues guitarist extraordinaire, was immersed in the scene from a very early age, starting with Blind Lemon Jefferson

**SEE ALSO:** Blind Lemon Jefferson

# Sippie Wallace

**fact file**

**BORN** 1898

**DIED** 1986

**MUSICAL SELECTION**
Sippie

Sippie Wallace's career jumped up and down, but she always came back to the limelight whenever a "revival" hit the stage

S ippie Wallace first made an impression in the early 1920s, a period when the so-called "classic blues" singers were first making a phenomenal impact on the musical entertainment world. Many of the female singers came from an almost exclusively vaudevillian background but Wallace brought to her performances a deep understanding of the Texas blues style, as her rough, no-nonsense approach to lyrics and their sentiments makes clear, whichever jazz great was in the backing band.

Sippie Wallace was born Beulah Thomas in Houston, Texas, into a musical family. Her nickname was a family one, bestowed upon her due to her childhood lisp. She sang from an early age in church. Her move to Chicago came about when her brother, then in business with Clarence Williams, sent for her around 1923. Within months she was in the recording studios for Okeh and scored a hit with her first single, "Up The Country" b/w "Shorty George Blues," her strong, unsentimental approach instantly winning followers. Eddie Heywood was the piano accompanist. Shortly before this, Sippie had married one Matt Wallace, and it was his surname she used on her records. From

then until 1929, when she left Chicago for Detroit, Sippie Wallace had a string of successes, often from self-penned material: accompanists included Clarence Williams, Joe "King" Oliver, Rudy Jackson, Louis Armstrong, and Natty Dominique. The move to Detroit, coupled with the onset of the Depression, prematurely ended Sippie's blues career: she became increasingly involved in Baptist Church work and, after the death of her brother and husband around the mid-1930s, she abandoned blues altogether.

Along with so many other early blues artists, Wallace was tracked down by a young white enthusiast in the 1960s; in her case she was found, still in Detroit, in 1965. Albums followed in 1966 and in 1967, featuring her with giants such as Roosevelt Sykes, Little Brother Montgomery, and Otis Spann. She also appeared and recorded with white admirers such as Maria Muldaur and Bonnie Raitt, the latter meeting taking place at the 1972 Ann Arbour Blues & Jazz Festival. A stroke in 1970 failed to end her career. In 1982 she released a fine album, *Sippie*, which was Grammy-nominated that year, but by then she was becoming frail. She died in 1986.

**SEE ALSO:** Roosevelt Sykes, Little Brother Montgomery, Otis Spann

# Mercy Dee Walton

**fact file**

**BORN** 1915

**DIED** 1962

**MUSICAL SELECTION**
"One Room Country
Shack"

Mercy Dee
Walker's "One
Room Country
Shack" fast
became his
calling card

W alton's career followed a familiar pattern for those bluesmen born in Texas. From Waco, he made his living as a day laborer in the fields, yet by his first teenage years he was learning barrelhouse piano, picking up knowledge from a host of Texas-based players who never recorded and who have now mostly been forgotten or are at most just names in books. Walton decided to try his hand at a musician's life, playing to the cotton-pickers and other laborers at after-work gatherings and parties, but it was a grueling life and in 1938 Walton decided to try his luck on the West Coast, as so many other Texan blues musicians also did.

Walton, with his fine, rich baritone voice, his ability to write good, catchy blues songs and his rolling, fluid piano work, gradually established himself on the Los Angeles-to-Oakland scene, at first working by day as a laborer and playing by night,

then slowly becoming fully engaged as a musician. In 1949 he had attracted enough of a following for the Spire label to record four sides in Fresno, California.

These led to further sessions, with Imperial and Speciality in LA. A 1952 single, "One Room Country Shack," became a hit and his calling-card. During the 1950s he occasionally joined in on the West Coast version of the R&B market, playing with Big Jay McNeely and others and recording some rocking sides for Flair in 1955, but commercial recording activity dried up as rock took over. Walton's next appearance on record was for the roots-oriented record label, Arhoolie, and featured old-time musicians such as K.C. Douglas and Sidney Maiden. A very superior set of piano-based blues resulted, but it was too late to alter the course of Walton's career: he died tragically in 1962, the victim of a cerebral hemorrhage.

**SEE ALSO:** Muddy Waters, Sonny Boy Williamson II

# Little Walter

Little Walter aka Marion Walter Jacobs did more than any other harmonica player to establish the vital place of the blues harp at the center of the postwar Chicago blues scene, thereby ensuring its prime position in blues and blues-derived music the world over until the present day. Making his first records with Muddy Waters when still in his teens, he was quick to assume his place at the top of the Chicago harp hierarchy and never relinquished it, even to older players like Rice Miller, one of those from whom he had borrowed initially while he was creating his own terse, eloquent style, which involved deft and brilliant manipulation of microphone dynamics.

Walter was born into a poverty-stricken sharecropper family on the outskirts of Marksville, Louisiana. Interested in music while a boy, by the age of eight he had his first harmonica and quickly developed a consuming urge to conquer its intricacies. He imitated the music around him, including the Cajun songs and dances he heard from the French-speaking part of the local population. By the time he was 12 he had left home and was playing for change on the streets in New Orleans, but he decided to head north and by 1944 was living in Helena, Arkansas, where Sonny Boy Williamson II (Rice Miller) was based at the time. Williamson helped him get on his feet and within a year he was appearing briefly on his own radio show in competition with his erstwhile protector. Twelve months further on he'd progressed to Chicago and was quickly playing on Maxwell Street for change. He also sat in with various bands, but his quick temper didn't recommend himself to many. However, after a recommendation from Jimmie Rogers, Walter joined the fledgling Muddy Waters band in 1948, rehearsing hard with it to make it the formidably tight, powerful unit it was to become by the time Chess began recording it in 1950.

However, it was not until 1952 that Chess got around to recording Walter as leader, this time simply using him with the Waters band but labeling the resultant single, "Juke" b/w "Can't Hold Out Much Longer," as by Little Walter and His Night Cats. The classic instrumental, "Juke," quickly established Walter as Chicago's prime harp player and he left Muddy Waters, forming his own band, which began recording in 1953 as Little Walter and His Jukes. During the next five years he repeatedly reached the top echelons of the R&B charts with self-penned material, including the classic "My Babe" (1955). Other prime cuts included "Blues With A Feeling" (1953), "Mellow Down Easy" (1954), and "Blue and Lonesome" (1959). He toured constantly and held down top spots on the Chicago blues live scene, also establishing a burgeoning reputation in England. This he was to capitalize on during the early 1960s when he twice toured the country, the second time with the Rolling Stones. Walter continued to occasionally record and appear with Muddy Waters, but his always fiery and spontaneous nature continues to cause him trouble. This, allied to creeping alcoholism, made him an increasing risk to employ, and his career was on the wane as the blues boom of the 1960s picked up pace. A disdain for the young white kids, both as musicians and fans, who now looked up to him left him out on a limb and looking for a solid audience. By the mid-1960s he was something of a spent force artistically, unable to sing or play up to his old standards, equally incapable of running a stable private life. He died in 1968 from the effects of a pointless street fight with a bunch of drunks during which his head was repeatedly kicked.

**fact file**

**BORN** 1930
**DIED** 1968
**MUSICAL SELECTION**
"My Babe"
"Blues With A Feeling"
"Blue and Lonesome"

It took some time, but Little Walter's winning style eventually won him center stage

**SEE ALSO:** Muddy Waters, Sonny Boy Williamson II

# Baby Boy Warren

**fact file**

**BORN** 1919

**DIED** 1977

**MUSICAL SELECTION**
"Nervy Woman Blues"
"Please Don't Think I'm
Nosey."

The albums cut by Baby Boy Warren were memorable and distinct, allowing him to enjoy succes during the last decade of his life

**b**aby Boy Warren, although sparsely recorded during his long life, was a key presence on the postwar Detroit blues scene, having moved to the city in 1941 and developed the distinctive Detroit sound along with better-known figures such as John Lee Hooker and Eddie Kirkland.

Warren was born in Lake Providence, Louisiana, but raised in Memphis, the youngest of three children, a family position that gave rise to his nickname. He learned the guitar from other family members and began busking on Memphis streets and in parks for spare change, finally graduating to sitting in at clubs where he could find a way in (being still underage at the time). In this way he got to play with then Memphis-based musicians such as Howlin' Wolf, Robert Jr Lockwood, and Rice Miller. The prospect of regular work gave him the impetus to move to Detroit, where he got a day job on the car assembly line and pursued his blues career at other times. A fixture on the Detroit scene by the late 1940s with his powerful guitar and persuasive vocals, Warren made his recording debut in 1949 on the tiny Staff label, with Milt Hinton on bass, creating idiosyncratic classics with "Nervy Woman Blues" and "Please Don't Think I'm Nosey." Further recordings took place in 1950 and 1954, all for small local labels, one of the 1954 sessions featuring his friend and occasional colleague Rice Miller aka Sonny Boy Williamson II. These two continued to play together when Sonny Boy was in Detroit, but Warren, not prepared to take a chance on living off the blues, stayed working at cars in Detroit and his career gradually faded, though he managed appearances at Blues and Folk Festivals during the 1960s and 1970s when health and holidays from work permitted, even making it to Europe in 1972. He died in 1977 of a heart attack.

**SEE ALSO:** John lee hooker, Eddie Kirkland, Howlin' Wolf, Robert Jr Lockwood, Sonny Boy Williamson II

# Washboard Sam

### fact file

**BORN** 1910

**DIED** 1966

**MUSICAL SELECTION**
"Diggin' My Potatoes"

Washboard firmly in hand, Washboard Sam was one of the few blues artists to use the instrument to its full potential

he washboard was both the most basic of musical instruments and one of the most popular ways of propelling folk and blues music, whether country or city, during the 1930s and early 1940s, prior to the widespread use of drums. Washboard Sam was by far the most popular of the washboard men in the blues, recording many 78s and experiencing a major hit with "Diggin' My Potatoes" in 1939.

Sam was born Robert Brown in a small corner of Lawrence County, Arkansas, reportedly the illegitimate son of Frank Broonzy, former slave and Big Bill's father. He took his surname from his mother's family. Coming from a poor rural background, Robert accompanied his own singing from an early age on the washboard. Encouraged by his own progress, he ran off to Memphis, Tennessee, while still in his early teens, hoping to live as a musician. Like so many others, however, he ended up doing heavy manual labor throughout Arkansas and Mississippi to earn enough to survive. Fed up with that, in 1932 he went to Chicago and looked up his half-brother, Big Bill, who helped him out and occasionally used him at parties and on the streets. Two years

later he introduced Robert to a Victor talent scout, Lester Melrose, who quickly had him in to make some sides, with Broonzy as accompanist. Under the name Washboard Sam he became a consistent seller in the black communities, in the process helping bridge the gap between prewar and postwar blues by using progressively more percussive and hard-driving groups, featuring pianists like Memphis Slim and Roosevelt Sykes to back his vocals and washboard.

At his peak in the early 1940s, he was recording at least 20 sides a year and was one of the top blues artists in America. Yet during the war he changed careers, becoming a policeman, and apart from some quasi-R&B sides in 1947 and a link-up with Broonzy in 1953, he disappeared from music until 1963, when he retired from the Chicago police department.

Aware of the renewed interest in prewar bluesmen, he resumed singing and playing, making appearances at various festivals as far afield as Europe and recording again, but heart disease tragically took hold, and he died of heart failure in Chicago in 1966, a respected blue legend.

**SEE ALSO:** Big Bill Broonzy, Memphis Slim, Roosevelt Sykes

# Dinah Washington

**fact file**

**BORN** 1924

**DIED** 1963

**MUSICAL SELECTION**
Dinah Jams

Dinah Washington's popular style allowed her to incorporate the blues and R&B styles in her singing

d inah Washington (a name given her by her first employer, Lionel Hampton) was one of the few R&B stars of the 1940s who managed to not only survive the onslaught of rock 'n' roll in the 1950s but increase her popularity to the point that, on her death in 1963, she was an international star in both the pop and jazz worlds. Yet it is fair to say that her style changed very little over the 20 years of her career, and that blues remained at its very core. Her influence on other female singers was immense, her phrasing and emotionalism being imitated by scores of would-be crossover blues and R&B artists, but few had the quality of voice or sheer musicality Washington displayed in any musical context.

Born in Tuscaloosa, Alabama, she moved to Chicago with her family when an infant: by her eleventh birthday young Ruth Jones was appearing at St Luke's Baptist Church, both singing and playing the piano, and in 1938 she won an amateur talent contest at the Regal Theater by singing the blues. Her big break came when Lionel Hampton heard her singing while working as the washroom attendant at the Regal Hotel in 1943: he hired her on the spot and gave her the stage name that stuck with her for good. Her two years with Hampton gave her a wide following and

she picked up a contract with Apollo Records immediately on her leaving Hampton in late 1945. Her sessions for Apollo set the tone for many of her later records, concentrating on the slower blues but kept company by modern jazzmen of high quality. Joining the young Mercury label in 1948, she settled into a relationship that lasted until 1962, when she joined Roulette Records. Her years at Mercury put her in a vast array of musical situations, backed by trios, jump bands, big bands, orchestras, and more. She even presided over jam sessions (*Dinah Jams*, 1954) and dates with string orchestras. Her hits often crossed over to white audiences, the biggest perhaps coming with "What A Diff'rence a Day Makes" (1959) along with her duets with Brook Benton, but her blues roots were always in evidence: she even made a complete album of tributes to Bessie Smith, albeit in her own fashion. Her performance of Smith's "Back Water Blues" at the 1958 Newport Jazz Festival was a career highlight.

Explosive in temperament but a charismatic stage character, Washington led an increasingly hectic and chaotic professional and private life. In 1963 she went on a crash diet which weakened her constitution to the point where she died of an overdose of diet pills mixed with alcohol. She was just 39.

**SEE ALSO:** Bessie Smith

# Curley James Weaver

**fact file**

**BORN** 1906

**DIED** 1962

**MUSICAL SELECTION**
"Sweet Petunia"
"No No Blues"

Curley Weaver's reputation keeps him in the forefront of most blues fans's eyes

**W**eaver was an important member of the blues fraternity in Atlanta, Georgia, forming a string of partnerships with musicians such as Barbecue Bob, Buddy Moss, Blind Willie McTell, and the little-known Jonas Brown. Weaver was as adept at playing unaccompanied as with playing with others, and was a popular, easy-going personality who fit into the Atlanta scene through to the early 1950s.

Weaver was born in Covington, Georgia, and grew up on a farm outside of Porterdale. He developed a love of music from his mother's involvement in gospel: she was a pianist and guitarist, teaching Curley guitar during his boyhood. A friend, Robert Hicks (later nicknamed Barbecue Bob), also learned from his mother, and the two became fast friends. They, along with Bob's brother, Charlie Hicks, moved to Atlanta in 1925 looking for work as musicians, and in 1928 Weaver eventually landed a recording deal with Columbia through the good services of Bob, who was already recording for the label. In October 1928 Weaver debuted for Columbia as a solo act, cutting "Sweet Petunia" and "No No Blues," a disc that sold well enough for Weaver to record for QRS and Okeh in the next three years as well as appear as a fine accompanist for his Atlantan friends and colleagues. During the 1930s Weaver was more often an accompanist than leader, forming outstanding relationships with McTell and the Georgia Browns, in particular, while his own occasional sessions featured Fred McMullen and Buddy Moss, men he spent much time traveling and playing with, along with the Georgia Cotton Pickers. During and after World War II Weaver played mostly on Atlanta streets but also occasionally in clubs, most often with McTell; his prewar recordings ceased in 1935, but he had one more shot, for Fred Mendelsohn's Regal label, in 1949. McTell was present on three of the tracks recorded under Weaver's name while the majority of the sessions – over 20 tracks – found Weaver accompanying McTell. Weaver also cut four solo sides. Ill health and the gradual deaths of his colleagues blighted the 1950s for Weaver: by the time of his own death, in 1962, he had sight in only one eye.

**SEE ALSO:** Barbeceu Bob, Buddy Moss, Blind Willie McTell

# Muddy Waters

muddy Waters aka McKinley Morganfield was the dominant figure of the postwar Chicago electric-blues scene and a man who, more than any, defined the sound and style of that scene – rough, earthy, honest, full of ironic humor, with plenty of punch both vocally and rhythmically. He became the Chicago blues scene's most important member; no blues generation since has bypassed him.

Waters was born into the family of a Delta sharecropper: his father died while he was in infancy and he was raised by a grandmother on Stovall's plantation, not far from Clarksdale, Mississippi. He was singing and playing harp by his thirteenth birthday, moving to guitar by the time he was 17. His style was deep Delta, with bottleneck slide guitar and a crackling vocal delivery drawn from the repertoire of the great Eddie "Son" House, whom Muddy (his own name was a childhood nickname from his love of playing in muddy ditches) saw play many times. Waters set up a juke joint and profitted from gambling sidelines as well, and after he had married he seemed set for life in the South. His wider ambitions were perhaps awakened by the field recordings he made for Alan Lomax in 1941 and 1942. The records were not for commercial release, but Muddy knew they were good. A year later he moved to Chicago, starting from scratch and lodging with a sister. Realizing that his form of acoustic blues was unfashionable, Waters managed to avail himself of an electric guitar and after a while began playing with people such as Sunnyland Slim and Jimmy Rogers. This led to some sessions for Columbia in 1946 which went unreleased at the time, and it wasn't until the fall of 1947 that he recorded again, as part of a Sunnyland Slim session which imitated the more urbane Chicago style or the day. In early 1948 Waters lucked out when the Chess brothers heard him warming up with some electrified bottleneck during a session and asked him to cut a side in that style with just slap-bass accompaniment. "I Can't Be Satisfied" was the result, and it was an immediate hit in Chicago. Muddy's career was finally in top gear, although it would be two years before Chess allowed him to record with his full working band, which by this time included Little Walter on harmonica.

Waters was the figurehead for the Chicago scene throughout the 1950s with an unbroken line of, written either by himself or remarkable Willie Dixon. Such songs include "Mean Red Spider," "Rollin' and Tumblin'," "Rollin' Stone," "Stuff You Gotta Watch," "I'm Your Hoochie Coochie Man," "I Just Want to Make Love To You," "Mannish Boy," "Got My Mojo Working," "Evil," "Tiger In Your Tank," "I'm Ready," and "One More Mile." By the latter part of the decade Waters was a big enough name to travel overseas, reaching Britain in 1958 and shocking audiences who had never heard electric blues before. Although he proved his Delta roots by the acoustic album he recorded soon after, the electrifying performance by his band at the riot-marred 1960 Newport Jazz Festival broadened his appeal still more. Yet Waters had a hit-and-miss 1960s on record. The latter part of the 1960s found Muddy's band continuing to deliver pounding live performances while Chess records pursued an ever more erratic recording policy in their desperation for hits. The early 1970s continued this pattern until with a new manager and a new record company, Blue Sky, in 1976 (with Johnny Winter as producer), Muddy made a series of quality blues albums, epitomized by *Hard Again* (1977). At his death in 1983 he was the most influential Chicago bluesman of the postwar period.

## fact file

**BORN** 1915

**DIED** 1983

**MUSICAL SELECTION**
**Hard Again**
"I Can't Be Satisfied"
"Rollin' And Tumblin'"
"I'm Ready"
"Hoochie Coochie Man"

**Muddy Waters: not enough can be said about Muddy to celebrate his contribution to the art of the blues**

# Sylvester Weaver

fact file

**BORN** 1897

**DIED** 1960

**MUSICAL SELECTION**
"Guitar Blues"
"Guitar Rag"

Sylvester Weaver was said to have been the first blues artist recorded, though little is known of his background or musical influences

**W**eaver is important if for no other reason than he was the first country-blues musician to be recorded. Born in Louisville, Kentucky, 26-year-old Weaver made it into the New York City studios of Okeh in November 1923 to cut two solo instrumental sides, "Guitar Blues" and "Guitar Rag," a month after he had accompanied Sara Martin, already a year into her recording career, on two sides for the same company.

Weaver was an accomplished guitarist in the intricate rag and folk tradition who could also accommodate a variety of vocalists from different backgrounds. Weaver's style has similarities with that of Georgian guitarists such as Ed Andrews and George White,

but he spent most of his life in Louisville. Having moved to New York at the beginning of the classic blues era, Weaver for a short time was at the center of activity as a talent scout for Okeh. He also continued to cut the occasional record for the company, in various contexts, including a set of duets in 1927 with Walter Beasley. Those same session gave rise to nine tracks with the teenage Helen Humes. After this Weaver dropped from sight, returning to Louisville, but his instrumental legacy was felt in white country circles, where his clean and attractive guitar patterns and crisp rhythmic propulsion were widely admired and imitated. Weaver withdrew from the music scene, dying of cancer in 1960.

**SEE ALSO:** George White, Helen Humes

# Katie Webster

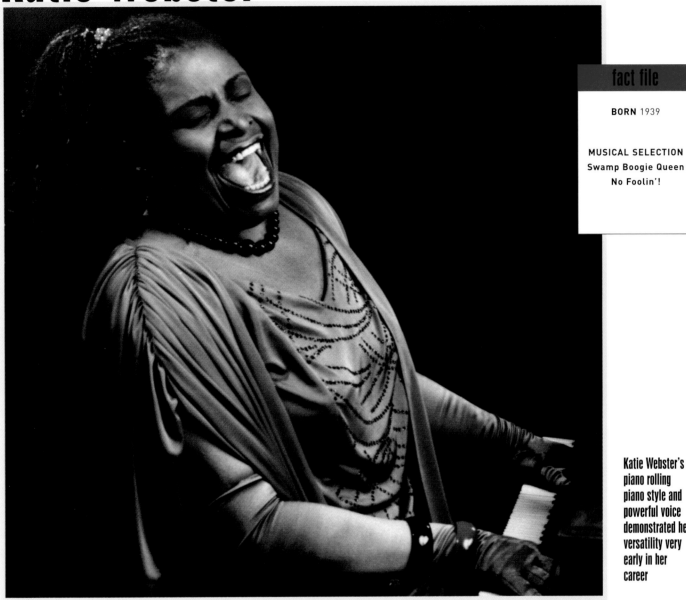

fact file

**BORN** 1939

MUSICAL SELECTION
Swamp Boogie Queen
No Foolin'!

Katie Webster's piano rolling piano style and powerful voice demonstrated her versatility very early in her career

**W**ebster was nearly 50 and had spent over 30 years in session and accompanist blues work before she became internationally known through a series of albums for the Alligator label. A blues pianist and vocalist with touches of zydeco and swamp blues, boogie, and R&B mixed in with her more orthodox piano techniques, Webster is a convincing and energetic entertainer live whose bigger-than-life personality comes across intact on records.

Webster was born in Houston, Texas, but moved to Louisiana with her family when young. Her parents encouraged her to learn piano, studying hymns and other religious music, but her ear was caught by the piano playing of Fats Domino and other rockin' boogie exponents she heard on the radio in the 1950s. By the end of that decade she had developed a formidable left hand of her own and was in demand in recording studios, especially for Jay Miller's Excello label, in Crowley, Louisiana. She laid down piano on over a hundred sides for some of the best bluesmen associated

with swamp blues, and in 1962, while living in Lake Charles, Louisiana, she came to the attention of Otis Redding, who was just embarking on his remarkable international career. She played in his band for the next five years until his death in a private-plane crash in 1967, soon after their Monterey triumph. Webster took a decade off from music, moving to California and returning to playing in 1979. During the early 1980s she made a number of albums for small Californian labels but the general US public remained ignorant of her talents, although her appearances in Europe on tour packages created something of a stir and a ready market for her imported albums. Her first record for Alligator, *Swamp Boogie Queen* (1988), affirmed the growing level of interest in her, and she has gone on to make a series of happy and entertaining records covering the wide range of her musical interests, of which *No Foolin'!* (1991) is as good an example as any, finding her even singing Otis Redding-type soul ballads. She continues to pursue her career.

SEE ALSO: Lonnie Brooks

# Valerie Wellington

**fact file**

BORN 1959

DIED 1993

MUSICAL SELECTION
Million Dollar Secret

Valerie
Wellington
continues to
make waves as
a blues singer of
great power and
subtlety

O ne of the best of the female blues belters based in Chicago, Wellington was a technically accomplished singer and musician who seemed destined for a high-profile career in the blues, her touring in Europe bringing her a considerable fan base. Her early death robbed the blues world of a talent of great potential.

Wellington was born in Chicago and was given a solid musical training starting at the age of five when her piano lessons began. By mid-teens she was singing in various soul aggregations in and around Chicago, and in 1978 she began a three-year course at the American Conservatory of Music in Chicago. During this time she performed in a huge variety of settings, from opera to rock to blues and jazz, and she also developed a taste for the theater (she played Ma Rainey in a Chicago production based on the life of Bessie Smith). Hanging out with a number of bluesmen, including Magic Slim, Albert Collins, and Walter Horton, she became intent on forging a blues reputation, recording her debut album in 1983, *Million Dollar Secret*, a record that combined her with Magic Slim and the Teardrops, Sunnyland Slim, and others, and showed her singing in a style that could be described as updated Bessie Smith. For the rest of her short life she spread her talents across a number of careers and perhaps did not make the progress in any of them her talent deserved. She died of a brain aneurysm in Loyola Medical Center, Maywood, in the first days of 1993.

**SEE ALSO:** Ma Rainey, Bessie Smith, Magic Slim, Albert Collins, Walter Horton, Sunnyland Slim

# Peetie Wheatstraw

fact file

BORN 1902

DIED 1941

MUSICAL SELECTION
Peetie Wheatstraw &
Kokomo Arnold

Peetie Wheatstraw, also known as "the Devil's Son-In-Law"

Wheatstraw was a product of the dark-hued St Louis "school" of blues. Along with people such as Walter Davis and St Louis Jimmy Oden, Wheatstraw produced a cooler, more world-weary attitude in his vocalizations than the contemporary Delta singers did. Enjoying associations on record with the guitarists Charlie Jordan, Kokomo Arnold, and Lonnie Johnson in the 1930s, pianist/singer Wheatstraw became one of the most prolifically recorded and popular of 1930s blues artists. Today, he is not perceived as having left a particularly memorable recorded legacy, although his singing and piano playing were copied by less commercially successful performers.

William Bunch was born in Ripley, Tennessee, and spent the majority of his adult life in East St Louis, Illinois, reaching that city in his late twenties. Basing himself in the roughest area of a notably rough place, the "Valley" district, he adopted his performing name in an attempt to give himself a colorful professional character – "Peetie Wheatstraw, the Devil's son-in-law." It clearly worked, for by late 1930 he had begun recording for Vocalion (who used his full pseudonym on their record labels) in Chicago and kept up a prolific recording schedule until a month before his death in an auto accident, colliding with a train in December 1941. His subject matter was mostly lowlife, and he was one of the first bluesmen to concentrate on the fate of hoboes and unemployed people in his lyrics, earning himself a loyal audience of people who had known similar hard times. He also sang about the supernatural, cashing in on his name and its associations, plus the usual smattering of songs with salacious double entendres.

SEE ALSO: Walter Davis, St Louis Jimmy Oden, Charlie Jordan, Kokomo Arnold, Lonnie Johnson

# Junior Wells

**W**ells aka Amos Blackmore has proven himself to be one of the most remarkable and enduring of all the great postwar Chicago bluesmen. On the scene at the same time as Little Walter and Sonny Boy Williamson II (Rice Miller), he further evolved the role of the harmonica in electric blues, firstly when he took over from Little Walter in Muddy Waters' band, latterly while teamed with his regular professional partner, Buddy Guy. The duo did much to widen the popular base of the hard-core blues that they propagated, allowing both Guy and Wells to assume the role of elder statesmen in the music in the present day.

Born in Memphis, Tennessee, to Arkansas farmer parents, Junior heard a great deal of blues and other types of music being played around Memphis as a youth, taking informal lessons from the singer Junior Parker. He went with his mother to Chicago in 1946 already convinced that music was to be his career, and two years later he purchased his first harmonica. Shortly after this he tried his luck, still underage, in a club, and managed to impress old pros like Tampa Red and Sunnyland Slim enough to be invited back. Getting to know people like Muddy Waters and the Myers brothers, Wells formed a group, the Aces, with the Myerses, which got regular work around the South Side until 1952, when Little Walter hijacked the band for his own and renamed it the Jukes, after his big hit. Wells took Walter's place in the Waters band but soon after had to do his national service – a stint that included desertion and eventual discharge in 1955. After a short spell back with Waters, Wells began recording under his own name for the Chief and Profile labels through the recommendation of Willie Dixon, re-forming a new version of the Aces (featuring Earl Hooker on many tracks) with which to record. By 1958 Wells was appearing occasionally with Buddy Guy, initiating a working relationship which would endure until 1980, but no recordings of the pair were made until 1963. Meanwhile Wells continued to work mainly in Chicago. In 1965 the classic *Hoodoo Man Blues* album was cut for Delmark, the label claiming this as possibly the first-ever custom-made Chicago blues LP, rather than a compilation of singles tracks. The success of this prime slice of Chicago electricity occasioned a swap to the Vanguard label, where the partnership continued to prosper. For the first time, Wells was in the forefront of the modern blues scene along with Guy, and by 1970 the pair began to travel together, appearing in Europe and elsewhere, and making the legendary *Buddy Guy & Junior Wells Play The Blues* session for Atlantic under the direction of Eric Clapton. Regular overseas tours during the 1970s proved their enduring drawing power, but the two men went their own ways in the 1980s, Wells running his own band and recording for Alligator and Blind Pig, among others. In the late 1990s Wells made a series of acclaimed albums for the Telarc label, including *Live at Buddy Guy's Legends* (1997). Wells died in January 1998 – his death is a great loss to the blues community.

## fact file

**BORN** 1934

**DIED** 1998

**MUSICAL SELECTION**
Hoodoo Man Blues
Buddy Guy & Junior
Wells Play The Blues

When Junior Wells passed away in 1998, he left behind a legacy of some of the greatest blues works recorded

**SEE ALSO:** Little Walter, Sonny Boy Williamson II, Little Walter

# Bukka White

**fact file**

**BORN** 1909

**DIED** 1977

**MUSICAL SELECTION**
"Shake 'Em On Down"

Bukka White, born Booker T. Washington White, enjoyed a variety of jobs as a youth, including boxer and baseball player

ississippi-born White was cut from the same cloth as Charlie Patton and Tommy Johnson, and created some of the most powerful and deeply-etched recordings of the early Delta blues style. But he had to wait a good deal longer for fame than did Patton and Johnson.

Hailing from the Delta town of Houston, Mississippi, Bukka White learned guitar from his railroad-man father – who also taught him to ride the trains, first to St. Louis and later up to Chicago and Memphis. White met Charlie Patton during the 1920s, and made his first recordings of gospel music in 1930, under the name Washington White. These failed to sell, and White was reduced to hobo status during the early years of the Depression, before supporting himself by playing professional baseball and boxing as the 1930s wore on. By then based in Chicago, White began making contacts with such important performers as Tampa Red and Big Bill. This led to the inevitable contract with "agent" Lester Melrose, for whom White cut two sides in 1937 – one of which would be his only hit, "Shake 'Em On Down." By the time the records were released, White was serving a jail sentence in

Parchman Farm for shooting a man in Mississippi.

Once out of jail, White hooked up with Melrose again, in 1940 recording a dozen original songs which are consistent in mood and intensity, and upon which his initial reputation was based. This collection of pieces include some of the starkest, most harrowing blues ever captured on disc. Unfortunately none of them sold and White was dropped from Melrose's roster. He subsequently disappeared and moved back down South, where he eventually married and began working in a defense manufacturing plant, a job he still held when "rediscovered" in 1963 by guitarist John Fahey. More than 30 years after his first session, White was quickly introduced to the recording studios once again. This time, his second career proved more successful than his first; his "sky songs" – so-called because he believed the inspiration came to him from the sky, and some of which he played for upwards of 15 minutes – became very popular among the folk-blues set of the 1960s. This new wave of interest in Bukka White's highly original creativity sustained his second career until his death in 1977.

**SEE ALSO:** Charlie Patton, Tommy Johnson, Tampa Red, Big Bill Broonzy

# Georgia White

### fact file

**BORN** 1903

**MUSICAL SELECTION**
Georgia White Sings and
Plays the Blues

The stunning
Georgia White's
talent was never
in doubt, though
her whereabouts
are a mystery

W hite was born in Sandersville, Georgia: little else is known about her early life, her place of birth being given by her colleague Big Bill Broonzy, although even he failed to give a proper forename to a woman who was a popular blues vocalist in 1930s Chicago. White arrived in Chicago at some point in the late 1920s and became accepted on the house-rent and speakeasy scene to the point that, by 1930, she was picked up by Vocalion and given Jimmie Noone's Apex Club Orchestra as backing band for her first date, in May of that year. The Depression kept her out of recording studios until 1935, when she reappeared on the Decca label, accompanied by just piano and guitar. Her smooth and effortless blues style, her voice capable of great dynamic fluctuations and a wide range, hit just

the right note with the audiences of the day and she recorded intensively between 1935 and 1941 as well as enjoying a long run of success on the nightclub scene in Chicago. Her accompanists included Richard M. Jones, Lonnie Johnson, Blind John Davis, Jonah Jones, and Sammy Price. A capable pianist in her own right, she often provided her own accompaniment. White began to fade from fashion at the advent of World War II. She remained resourceful and energetic, even at one point in the late 1940s forming an all-girl band (following a postwar musical fashion). But she continued to drop down the entertainment ladder in Chicago, finally relegated to appearing with second-string piano trios and variety acts to make a living. The date and place of her death remain unknown.

**SEE ALSO:** Big Bill Broonzy, Lonnie Johnson, Blind John Davis

# Josh White

**fact file**

**BORN** 1908

**DIED** 1969

**MUSICAL SELECTION**
The World Of
Josh White
The Blues and Josh
White

Josh White
enjoyed a long
career, always
including an
eclectic mixture
of songs and
styles

White in many ways took up the mantle of Leadbelly as a prodigiously gifted folk singer with a working knowledge of many facets of country blues, who reached out beyond his own race for an audience and found it among the young enthusiasts of many lands. Talented, articulate and charismatic, White was a natural spokesman for a musical movement, appearing on radio and television many times as the apostle of a new folk movement affiliated with the left-wing politics of the day – registering a major impact, and one which went far beyond the quite traditional repertoire and approach he adopted.

White was born in Greenville, South Carolina, and was brought up in a religious family surrounded by gospel music. Like many others he discovered the blues out on the streets around him at an early age; he then became a helper to a succession of blind street musicians, including Blind Willie Johnson, Blind Blake, and Blind Boy Arnold. He traveled with a number of players, reaching Chicago with Blind Joe Taggart in 1928 and cutting four sides with him for Paramount. By 1932 he was ready to cut his first solo sides (as Joshua White) in New York, though within weeks he'd adopted the name Pinewood Tom for all his blues releases.

He subsequently became Joshua White (The Singing Christian) for a long series of gospel sides, only dropping his various titles at the end of the decade when, as plain Josh White, he'd become such a popular artist that his name alone would sell any repertoire. Forming the Josh White Singers in 1939 and playing at Café Society, he also worked on stage with the likes of Paul Robeson, and in films with music themes.

White became further renowned in the 1940s, even performing for President Roosevelt, although by this stage his repertoire was so wide as to only partially include the blues. He recorded prolifically throughout the 1940s and 1950s. In Britain, especially, he became a star, appearing on television regularly with a range of musicians, including traditional jazz players and folk singers. White became one of the most well-known and best-loved folk-style performers in the world. His career only went into partial eclipse in the 1960s, when a new generation of folk and blues fans and performers grew up looking for what they felt to be a more authentic, less sophisticated approach to folk and roots music. Since his death in 1969, Josh White's reputation has never really recaptured its former levels.

**SEE ALSO:** Leadbelly, Blind Willie Johnson, Blind Blake, Blind Boy Arnold

# Robert Wilkins

fact file

**BORN** 1896

**DIED** 1987

**MUSICAL SELECTION**
The Original
Rolling Stone
Remember Me
"That's No Way To
Get Along"

The reverend
Robert Wilkins
came from the
Beale Street
school of the
blues and he
learned his les-
sons very
well indeed

b orn in Mississippi just a few miles outside Memphis, Wilkins is one of the most distinctive and accomplished of prewar blues musicians. Like many of his peers, Wilkins recorded very little, committing four titles to wax in September 1928 (only three being released), four in September 1929, and a further four in February 1930. By then the Depression had forced blues recording to virtually cease. Five years later a last five songs were cut, this time for Vocalion.

Wilkins had first come to music in his pre-teens and was writing his own songs prior to his induction into the US military for the duration of America's involvement in World War I. On his demobilization, he returned to Memphis and became a professional musician. His reliability as an employee (he remained a teetotaler during the whole of his long life) guaranteed him continuous employment during the blues boom of the 1920s, and though he never progressed from local entertainments to the TOBA traveling shows, he made it to Chicago in 1933 for the World's Fair there, though he was not part of the official entertainment.

Wilkins suffered the dilemma of many blues performers from this period, making a living from lowlife music when he aspired to grace through Christianity and the gospel. A particularly savage fight at a house-party where he was providing the entertainment gave him the impetus he needed to withdraw from his accustomed lifestyle and switch to plying his trade as a minister and as a purveyor of quack medicines. This change occurred in 1937, and in time Wilkins became an accredited minister of the Church of God in Christ. His rediscovery in the 1960s led only to gospel recordings and appearances. In 1968 the Rolling Stones recorded an updated version of his "That's No Way to Get Along," retitling it "Prodigal Son."

Wilkins's subjects were mostly conventional, but his approach to both form and content was highly idiosyncratic, using elements of rag and buck-dance traditions as well as constant variants from the classic blues chord progression. His lyrics range from the bucolic ("Police Sergeant Blues") to the tragic ("I Do Blues"), in which his admission of sexual and personal inadequacy achieves a rare pathos.

**SEE ALSO:** Jim Jackson, Blind Lemon Jefferson

# Big Joe Williams

J oe Williams was undoubtedly one of the greats of both his generation and of the country blues in general. As was typical of the musicians of his youth, Williams obeyed few rules when it came to playing the blues, preferring to make the music fit the emotional needs of the moment. This gave his playing and singing – already rough-hewn and stark – an urgent and almost brutally primitive quality at times. But it also amplifies the grandeur of his conception.

Williams was born in the Piney Woods country near Crawford, Mississippi, the first of sixteen children. While still young he left the farm to work as a laborer in various industries, on the levee, and in railroad and lumber camps, but he also began playing guitar on a homemade instrument using a cigar box. When proficient, he began playing and singing at the hastily assembled entertainment joints – honky-tonks – on the worksites throughout his area. More than once he ran into trouble with the law after brawls at one of these places. In the 1920s he travelled with the Rabbit's Foot Minstrels Revue, playing with the Birmingham Jug Band; this outfit made a few sides for Okeh in 1930. During the 1930s Williams settled in St. Louis, living with Bessie Mae Smith ("St. Louis Bessie") and hanging out with Walter Davis and Henry Townsend, among others. When Davis went to Chicago in 1935 to record for Victor, he took Williams with him through the invitation of Victor's agent, Lester Melrose. Before the year was out Williams had landed a major "race" hit with his own composition, "Baby, Please Don't Go," today one of the most-covered songs in the blues repertoire. Although not exactly prolific in his output, Williams continued to record for Bluebird for ten years, racking up more classics including his own "Crawlin' King Snake" from 1941, and "Highway 49" from the same year, with John Lee "Sonny Boy" Williamson. He and Sonny Boy did a fine remake of "Baby, Please Don't Go" in 1947. This and other performances of this time show just how close Williams's style was to the electrified music of the "new" Chicago blues as played by people like Muddy Waters and Little Walter. That same deep Delta resonance and stark simplicity is plainly evident in Williams's work of the period.

The 1950s were not a particularly good time for Williams, but he did keep recording and performing, and his St. Louis sessions for Bob Koester in 1958 marked a turning-point in the movement of the new young and serious audience toward the earlier blues and folk forms. Williams became one of the most-recorded artists of the country revival, his brutal, impassioned music making a direct, uncompromised impact on his new fans. He travelled widely across Europe and all around the USA, appeared at many of the blues and folk festivals, and made an album in London in 1968, his raw unaccompanied electric guitar sounds creating even more nervous energy than usual. His new fan base now in place, the pattern for the rest of Williams's life was set and he continued on the world tour circuit until his death in 1982, even reaching Japan in 1974. His records retained their power and simplicity right up to the end, with Williams relying on his innate ability to continually renew the old patterns in his own unique way every time he stepped in front of a microphone to perform. In the last decade of his life, Big Joe Williams was filmed on more than one occasion, his unique performing style thus captured for posterity.

## fact file

**BORN** 1903

**DIED** 1982

**MUSICAL SELECTION**
"Baby, Please
Don't Go"
"Crawlin' King Snake"

Big Joe Williams's life could have been a template for the "typical" traditional blues artist

**SEE ALSO:** Bessie Smith, Walter Davis, Sonny Boy Williamson, Muddy Waters

# Joe Williams

**fact file**

**BORN** 1918

**MUSICAL SELECTION**
Ballads and Blues
Master

Joe Williams
wide singing
style gave him
a distinctive and
appealing sound

t he rich baritone of Joe Williams (aka Joe Goreed) has been justly celebrated since his initial 1952 R&B hit for Checker, Memphis Slim's old number, "Everyday I Have The Blues," recorded with the King Kolax band. Already working with Count Basie, Williams was to re-record this number with Basie's band and deliver an international hit which would fix his singing style for the rest of his career.

Williams may have been born in Cordele, Georgia, but he moved with his family to Chicago when just four years old. His first singing experiences were in the church where his parents worshipped, but by the mid-1930s he had decided on a career in jazz. Working around Chicago, he sang for a while with New Orleans clarinettist Jimmie Noone, then progressed through the ranks of many bands, including Les Hite, Albert Ammons, and Lionel Hampton, without being recorded or making a larger impact. A fan of Billy Eckstine, Williams had a comparable voice

but avoided copying his hero, looking for a looser style. Yet the breaks failed to come his way until he began his long on-and-off association with Basie; in 1954, he cemented an occasional liaison which he'd begun by sitting in with the Basie Sextet in 1950. Within a year Williams and the band had registered their massive hit together. Joe stayed with the Basie band and scored more hits in the blues and rhythm and blues genre until 1961, performing a progressively wider pattern of material and moving closer to pop – a step that became more positive after he went solo.

Today, after enjoying a consistently successful multi-media career in every part of the world, Joe Williams continues to perform his own personal mixture of blues, standards, and jazz material. Although his contact with the blues scene is no more than sporadic, his credentials remain impeccable, as demonstrated on Verve's *Ballads and Blues Master*, which was released in 1992.

**SEE ALSO:** Memphis Slim, Albert Ammons

# Lucinda Williams

**fact file**

**BORN** 1953

**MUSICAL SELECTION**
Ramblin'
Happy Woman Blues

Lucinda Williams
has fast become
one of the blues's
best and most
active
songwriters

born in the same town as Joe and Nellie Lutcher – Lake Charles, Louisiana – Williams is the daughter of a Professor of English and spent much of her formative years moving around from one university town to another, at one time even reaching Santiago, Chile. When she was around 18, her family settled in Fayetteville, Arkansas, and there she began to explore an interest in blues and folk music.

By 1974 she had moved to Austin and become part of that town's energetic music scene before moving on to Houston and becoming fixed on a folk/blues career. In 1979 she recorded *Ramblin'*, a fine album of re-interpretations of blues classics, which immediately earned her stature as a refreshing and incisive blues and folk performer. Her follow-up album, *Happy Woman Blues* (1980), already gave clear signs of where she was going, balancing the repertoire more closely between blues and other folk material, although all the songs were self-written. These were Williams's last efforts in the blues idiom and remain a high-water mark in the modern acoustic tradition.

She has since moved squarely into the modern country genre, using her Louisiana roots to create a richly complex music, her own compositions now being recorded by many other artists of equal stature. Lucinda Williams now lives on the West Coast and continues to pursue a very active career, her fan-base stretching across North America and into Europe.

**SEE ALSO:** Angela Strehli, Robert Johnson

# Robert Pete Williams

Robert Pete Williams has Harry Orster to thank for his first recordings as a blues artist

## fact file

**BORN** 1914

**DIED** 1980

**MUSICAL SELECTION**
I'm Blues As A Man
Can Be

obert Pete Williams was born in Zachary, Louisiana, and developed his own extraordinary approach to blues singing and guitar playing. Williams, illiterate and almost completely unschooled, came from a desperately poor background, working as a farm-hand in his youth before moving to Scotlandville, where he worked in lumber yards and in other hard manual jobs. In 1934 he was sufficiently interested in making music to fashion his own crude guitar from a cigar box; his next instrument was one he bought for $4.50. He began playing parties, juke joints, and any other venues that would take him, but never managed to make music pay his way in life. This was doubly so after his marriage, and it seemed it would not change until, in 1956, he killed a man and was sent to Angola after being found guilty of murder. While there he was recorded in 1959 by the folk researcher and archivist Harry Oster, who released a selection of Williams's highly original music on a couple of albums. Ranging from accompanied spoken monologues about prison life and the pains of being denied a pardon to fears of death and the cruelties of being separated from all loved ones, Williams made a major impact on all who heard him. Oster and his associate successfully pleaded for a reduction in Williams's sentence, and he was released on parole. After fulfilling very strict parole rules (basically working for next to nothing for a farmer near the prison) until 1964, Williams was free to take up some of the offers of musical work he had received since his albums had come out. One of his first appearances was at the 1964 Newport Folk Festival, where he made a major impact. He also appeared on the 1966 Folk and Blues tour of Europe, and became established as a regular on the circuit, although his intense style and lack of showmanship counted against him in the popularity stakes. He continued making records up to his death in 1980, and attained a modest level of financial and material comfort. He also turned increasingly to the consolations of religion, but his best and most deeply moving work remained that recorded in Angola Prison Farm, most of which is now available on Arhoolie CDs.

**SEE ALSO:** Kelly Joe Phelps

# Sonny Boy Williamson

The original Sonny Boy Williamson, whose stammer may have had much to do with his singing style, was a master of his style of harp playing

there may have been blues harmonica players before Sonny Boy Williamson, but there is no doubt that he virtually invented its blues vocabulary and established it as a popular blues instrument. Williamson was born in Jackson, Tennessee, and learned to play harmonica while still a boy. When still an adolescent he left home and moved to Memphis, where he began to earn himself a reputation and develop his style, playing parties and juke joints and meeting fellow bluesmen, including Sleepy John Estes, Yank Rachell, and the harpist Hammie Nixon. Nixon had cut records with Sleepy John in 1929 and his simple but expressive playing quite likely influenced Sonny Boy measurably.

In 1931 Williamson moved on to Yazoo City, later passing through Arkansas on his way back to Memphis in 1933, where he teamed up with Yank Rachell. In 1934 Williamson relocated to Chicago: Rachell followed him soon after, and the duo played many gigs, both in Chicago and on subsequent returns South. During a period spent in St Louis the pair met Walter Davis and Robert Lee McCoy,

who arranged for Williamson to make his debut on Bluebird in 1937, recording in Aurora, Illinois. He landed a direct hit with his very first cut, "Good Morning, Schoolgirl," one of the most-covered blues songs of all time. From then on Sonny Boy was a regular visitor to the studios, cutting hundreds of sides for Bluebird and landing plenty of hits: he quickly became one of the most popular and influential bluesmen of the pre- and postwar periods. He performed and recorded with most of the great musicians then under contract to Bluebird, including Big Maceo, Big Bill, Walter Davis, Charlie McCoy, Yank Rachell, Tampa Red, and Blind John Davis.

He moved to Chicago in 1939, settling there with his wife Lacey Belle, who occasionally wrote Sonny Boy's lyrics for him. Sonny Boy suffered no postwar dip in popularity, even appearing to acclaim in New York, and offering guidance to the young harp-slingers in Chicago. Tragically, Sonny Boy was robbed and murdered while walking back home after finishing for the night at the Plantation Club, SouthSide Chicago, June 1948.

## fact file

**BORN** 1914

**DIED** 1948

**MUSICAL SELECTION**
"Good Morning Schoolgirl"

---

**SEE ALSO:** Robert Jr Lockwood, Robert Johnson, Elmore James, Sonny Boy Williamson, Junior Wells, James Cotton

# Sonny Boy Williamson II

t he fact that Sonny Boy Williamson is not his name and blues historians can advance strong theories for a number of years between 1894 and 1910 (his gravestone gives the year 1908) as his date of birth seems a perfect summation of the legend the blues harpist Aleck Ford aka "Rice" Miller built up around him during his musical career.

There is now general agreement that Sonny Boy was born in Glendora, Mississippi, and that, though illegitimate, he was kindly treated by stepfather Jim and mother Millie Miller. Aleck had scant education and worked on his family's farm well past the first flush of youth: it is quite probable that he was in his thirties when, as the result of a family quarrel, he hit the road and took up playing harmonica on the streets of Southern towns. As the 1930s ground on, Sonny Boy became well known in blues circles around the Delta states, befriending people such as Robert Jr Lockwood, Robert Johnson, and Elmore James (Lockwood would later become a regular sideman in his ever-varying band line-ups).

Sonny's harp playing and singing finally won him a modicum of public recognition when in 1938 he made his first appearance on the Arkansas radio show sponsored by the Interstate Grocery Co. and called *King Biscuit Time*. This sponsorship was crucial to his subsequent fame, for it gave him a wider public, better pay on club and juke dates, and the name he would later confusingly insist was his own – Sonny Boy Williamson. There is little agreement on who bestowed this name on him – some suggest the radio station did – but there is no doubting the motives. John Lee "Sonny Boy" Williamson of Jackson, Tennessee, was easily the most famous and popular blues harpist of the prewar period and, with his classic 1937 hit "Good Morning, Schoolgirl," helped define a whole period of the blues. Any blues harpist following in his wake – even one as distinctive as Rice Miller – was automatically nicknamed "Sonny Boy," and the adoption of the surname instantly broadened Aleck's appeal.

Sonny continued to be a frequent performer on *King Biscuit Time* show right through much of the 1940s, as well as spending much of his time roaming from state to state looking for live work. He married in 1945, the pattern of his life unchanging until 1951, when, three years after the ice-pick murder of John Lee "Sonny Boy" Williamson, he cut his first sides, for the tiny Trumpet label of Jackson, Mississippi. For this label between 1951 and 1954 he made first versions of classic Williamson material like "Nine Below Zero," "Eyesight To The Blind," and the rollicking "Pontiac Blues." With the demise of Trumpet in 1955 Sonny Boy saw little point in staying down South, eyeing balefully the success of other North-bound bluesmen, and he relocated to Milwaukee when his Trumpet contract was eventually reassigned to Chicago's Chess label.

Sonny Boy cut close on 80 sides for Leonard Chess, among them such Chicago gems as "Fattening Frogs For Snakes," "Cool Disposition," and "Help Me," and became an international blues celebrity and a substantial blues draw in Europe in the first half of the 1960s, recording with, among others, the Yardbirds (at the old Crawdaddy Club) and Roland Kirk (in Copenhagen's Club Montmartre). He told anyone who would listen that he was "the original Sonny Boy Williamson," but by the time of his return from Europe in 1964 he was a sick man. He died back in Arkansas in May 1965, fêted worldwide in the manner few bluesmen achieve.

## fact file

**BORN** 1909

**DIED** 1965

**MUSICAL SELECTION**
"Nine Below Zero"
"Eyesight To The Blind"
"Cool Disposition"

The infamous Aleck Ford aka "Rice" Miller aka Sonny Boy Williamson II, had an influence on an endless array of blues performers in his day and since

**SEE ALSO:** Sleepy John Estes, Yank Rachell, Walter Davis, Big Maceo

# Smokey Wilson

## fact file

**BORN** 1936

**MUSICAL SELECTION**
Smoke 'n' Fire

Smokey Wilson, like many blues performers, was playing guitar by the time he was eight years old

Wilson has a burning down-home guitar style in the Albert and Freddie King vein, but has not gone entirely ignorant of the impact of 1960s rock guitarists His gruff, no-nonsense vocals, allied to his hard-edged guitar sound and the boogie feels he is partial to, make him a highly enjoyable and authentic player and entertainer on today's West Coast scene. Wilson was born in Greenville, Mississippi, and started learning guitar when he was eight.

His father had presented him with an acoustic model after watching him trying to get sounds out of a broom handle with some wire attached. During the 1950s he listened to most of the blues musicians playing around the Greenville area and joined a number of bands, getting valuable experience with Junior and his Soul Searchers and Booba Barnes, and working day jobs driving trucks and doing other such manual work to keep himself

together. When he was 35, in 1970, Wilson moved out to Los Angeles and set himself up in South Central, playing the clubs and building his own band. He was part-owner of the Casino Club for a while, a center for much of the young white blues talent then just surfacing in the city, including Rod Piazza and William Clarke. During his tenure, many of the leading blues artists also appeared there. Wilson made a number of albums in the 1970s, mostly for Big Town and Vivid Sound, but remained a local phenomenon on the Californian coast, although in the 1980s he made it to Australia and other Pacific Rim countries.

His best and most representative album to date has been *Smoke 'n' Fire* (1993), on the Bullseye Blues label and featuring William Clarke's band with Ron Levy on keyboards. He continues to play and record in California and tours internationally, his popularity showing no sign of slowing.

**SEE ALSO:** Rod Piazza

# Jimmy Witherspoon

**fact file**

**BORN** 1923

**MUSICAL SELECTION**
"Ain't Nobody's
Business"
"In The Evenin' When
The Sun Goes Down"

Jimmy
Witherspoon did
not limit himself
to the blues but
always returned
to the style for
which his voice
was arguably
best suited

Witherspoon came to the attention of blues followers through his blazing, plaintive vocals with the Jay McShann band between 1944 and 1947, initially as the replacement for Walter Brown. He went on to become a major star, at home with jazz players, rhythm & blues groups and postwar blues outfits alike, his McShann-derived Kansas City musical heritage serving him well. His trademark powerful tenor, with its sustained notes, ever-present melancholy and typical fast vibrato "shake" to each held note, became a fixture on the US scene in the 1950s and 1960s, making him an in-demand vocalist around the world.

Witherspoon was born in Gordon, Arkansas, and sang as a child in his local Baptist church choir. Between 1941 and 1943 he served in the Merchant Marine, even performing in Calcutta for a time with a big band led by Teddy Weatherford. The McShann gig originated in California, where Witherspoon had based himself on his return to the US. The profile the singer enjoyed with this band, recording for Mercury and constantly touring, allowed him to go out as a solo at the end of 1947; he then recorded a major hit, the

old Bessie Smith song "Ain't Nobody's Business," which quickly became Witherspoon's trademark number. He followed this with "In The Evenin' When The Sun Goes Down," an old Leroy Carr hit, and continued to work the R&B side of the blues until the mid-1950s when, even though recording for Chess, he was unable to compete with rock 'n' roll's decisive impact. This caused him to switch to a more jazz-based audience, closer to his McShann roots, and led to his legendary set at the 1959 Monterey Jazz Festival (featuring Roy Eldridge, Coleman Hawkins and Ben Webster, among others, and available on CD) where he stopped the show.

Witherspoon subsequently became a reliable stand-by vocalist for the mainstream small-group jazz scene whenever a blues-tinged vocalist was called for, much in the way Jimmy Rushing became a fixture in a similar setting with the big bands. In this role, he has appeared on stages and in front of TV cameras the world over for three decades. A successful battle with throat cancer in the early 1980s led to a welcome reprieve; since then, Jimmy Witherspoon has returned to his best in both recorded and live contexts, and his career continues today.

**SEE ALSO:** Walter Brown, Bessie Smith, Leroy Carr, Jimmy Rushing

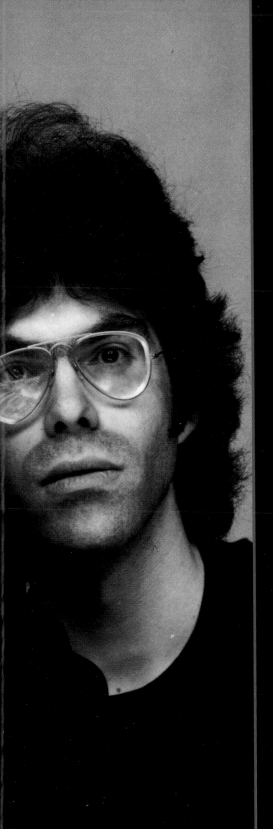

# Johnny Winter

**W**inter arrived on the scene at a time when young white America had discovered amplified blues in a big way through the guitar playing of a planeload of British and British-based guitarists in famous rock groups. The Texan albino was quickly groomed as America's answer to this invasion, his combination of rock and blues guitar techniques, from Muddy Waters and Magic Sam to Jimi Hendrix, instantly appealing on his debut album, made in late 1968, to a massive audience hungry for such sounds. Winter has seen his share of career ups and downs, and for periods has been content to stick with rock at the expense of blues, but his roots have in recent years called more strongly than any other force and he has carved a notable niche for himself in today's blues scene.

Winter and his brother, Edgar, were born in Beaumont, Texas, and before he was a teenager Johnny had discovered his love of stringed instruments, starting out on ukulele but swapping to guitar and copying blues artists he heard on the radio. So enthusiastic was he that he spent some time in 1963 in Chicago trying to crack the blues scene there, but his first success arrived via his own band, formed back in Texas and locally popular as a group capable of good blues and pop songs. In 1968 he threw the pop out and concentrated on the blues, getting noticed around the same time by prestigious media outlets. A move to New York and a contract with Columbia led to the much-hyped first album, *Johnny Winter*, in which his blues roots were laid bare for all to hear, his searing guitar lines plucked straight from the Chicago version of the Delta and brought to white heat by rock amplification and extended renditions. Winter quickly became an international star in both rock and blues fraternities, making a successful second album and appearing at Woodstock, but by 1972, exhausted and with a major drug problem, Winter took himself off the scene. On his return, amid the advent of disco and a waning interest in the blues, Winter took the rock road, to no particular acclaim. His next work of note was as a producer (and occasional participant) on Blue Sky records for Muddy Waters, a move that produced four outstanding albums in the last years of Waters' life.

Winter's own career was in neutral until his connection with Alligator records in the mid-1980s, a move that put him back in the blues camp to which he remains wedded today. He plays with a ferocity equal to that of his past efforts on Columbia, his slide guitar and his Hendrix-inspired picking as powerful as 20 years or more earlier. Both live and on record he remains an intense and exciting player and singer, able to switch at will between blues and rock 'n' roll repertoire.

### fact file

**BORN** 1944

**MUSICAL SELECTION**
Johnny Winter

Johnny Winter brought an electrified blues and rock style together, bringing both to a greater audience

SEE ALSO: Muddy Waters, Magic Slim, Jimi Hendrix

# Johnny Young

**fact file**

**BORN** 1917

**DIED** 1974

**MUSICAL SELECTION**
Chicago Blues

Johnny Young, another in a small club of blues mandolin players, had the opportunity to play with blues greats James Cotton and Snooky Pryor

ohnny Young was one of the tough, uncompromising guitarist/singers on the post war Chicago scene that helped give it such an up-front, vital edge. Leading his own band, he was a regular around Chicago, often using a virtually unique angle – playing blues mandolin on some songs to vary the accompaniment of his vocals.

Young was born in Vicksburg, Mississippi, on the first day of 1917, and like so many rural Southern blacks of the time, received only the most basic education. Moving with his family further south, he became interested in playing the blues during his early teens. By the age of 15 he was playing at parties and dances; after a sojourn in Vicksburg, he moved to Chicago in 1940, determined to make a living out of music. During his first years there he was a member of the pool of recently-arrived

Southerners, including Muddy Waters, Howlin' Wolf and others, who were making their way in Chicago and playing in various bands; he and Waters played with Sonny Boy Williamson. Times were hard and Young worked day-jobs to keep going, but in 1947 he finally got on wax, in Johnny Williams's band. The 1950s were also a lean time, but he made a regular living in the clubs on the South Side.

In 1964-65, as blues became hip again, Young made classic albums for both Testament and Arhoolie, the latter, *Chicago Blues*, featuring James Cotton and Otis Spann. Two years later he made a further album with Walter Horton, and for the rest of the 1960s it seemed as if his reputation was about take off. He was a regular with the Bob Riedy Band and continued to record, but in 1974 Johnny Young succumbed to a heart attack.

**SEE ALSO:** Muddy Waters, Howlin' Wolf, Sonny Boy Williamson, James Cotton, Otis Spann

# Mighty Joe Young

**fact file**

**BORN** 1927

**MUSICAL SELECTION**
Mighty Joe Young

Building up his career as a session musician, Mighty Joe Young did his first recording as a leader during the 1970s

Young's guitar playing is respected but not of the front rank, being an interesting amalgamation of many Chicago-based players and a style that suits perfectly his preferred role of accompanist to others. Young has played and recorded with a whole host of postwar greats, including Otis Rush and Howlin' Wolf, and it is in his contribution to their achievements that his best work is usually found.

Young was born in Shreveport, Louisiana and taught himself guitar while living there, but relocated to Milwaukee, Wisconsin, not a great distance from Chicago, while in his mid-1920s. He finally arrived in Chicago in 1956 and got down to proving himself on the club scene. After short periods with Howlin' Wolf

and Billy Boy Arnold, Young took the place of second guitar in Jimmy Rogers' band when he left the Muddy Waters Band in 1958. His own recording career began in 1959 on the Atomic label and continued in the early 1960s on, among others, the Webcor label. But his singles did little business and he remained essentially a sideman, doing solid service with Otis Rush between 1960 and 1963 and then becoming an in-demand blues session man for a number of labels, especially Delmark, who also cut an album under his name in 1970 with Jimmy Dawkins on second guitar. Young remained on the Chicago circuit until the early 1980s, when health problems forced him into convalescence until the end of the decade. He occasionally performs in Chicago.

**SEE ALSO:** Otis Rush, Howlin' Wolf, Billy Boy Arnold, Otis Rush, Jimmy Dawkins

# Index